CHILD CARE AND HEALTH

FOR NURSERY NURSES

Jean Brain and Molly D. Martin

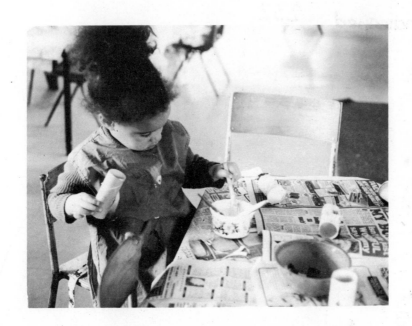

HULTON EDUCATIONAL PUBLICATIONS

First published in Great Britain 1980
by Hulton Educational Publications Ltd
Raans Road, Amersham, Bucks HP6 6JJ

Revised and reprinted 1981
Reprinted 1982

Text © Jean Brain and Molly D. Martin 1980, 1981
Illustrations © Hulton Educational Publications Ltd 1980

ISBN 0 7175 0824 2

Social & Emotional Deprivation   239-240

Abused Children 250

handicaped   232

Typeset at The Pitman Press, Bath

Printed in Great Britain by
Richard Clay (The Chaucer Press) Ltd, Bungay, Suffolk

Contents

Principal tables

Acknowledgements

We should like to express our thanks to all our friends and colleagues who have helped in the preparation of this book.

Mrs M. Alsford, Mrs D. Broadbent, Mrs B. Collins, Mr D. Godden, Mrs M. Fielden, Mrs E. Goss, Mr T. Hobbs, Miss C. Hodgson, Mrs D. Keeping, Miss E. Lloyd, Mr T. Newton Browne, Miss D. Taconis, Miss J. Spill, Mrs F. Watts, Mrs J. Watts.

and the staff and students at Bristol Nursery Nurses' College.

Lastly, we record our gratitude to our families for the tolerance and forbearance they have shown, and the support they have given.

Thanks are due to the following for allowing the use of copyright photographs: Mothercare, Wyeth Laboratories, The Daily Telegraph, The Mansell Collection and The Nursery World.

Foreword

Increasingly, responsibility for the care and education appropriate to the development and needs of young children is being shared between the parents and people trained in this specialised field. The nursery nurse is one of these people. Her skill is appreciated and applicable to many aspects of work with young children, and she can find employment in a wide variety of posts – in education, in day-care services, in residential social work, in the hospital services and in private families. Statutory and local authorities recognise her skill and training, as do voluntary agencies, and she can be found working both in this country and overseas.

To prepare for this skilled and rewarding work, training for the Certificate of The National Nursery Examination Board must be taken. During the lifetime of the N.N.E.B., a vast number of nursery nurses have benefited from this imaginative course, which has helped them to grow in confidence, as well as enlarging their knowledge, thus preparing them to work happily and successfully with young children, who have derived great benefit from contact with them.

It is appropriate, therefore, that Jean Brain and Molly Martin with, respectively, teaching and health-visiting backgrounds, who have tutored N.N.E.B. students over a long period, should find time to collect together their unified thoughts, knowledge and experience to make these available to students other than those they teach.

Bessie Wright
Chairman: National Nursery Examination Board

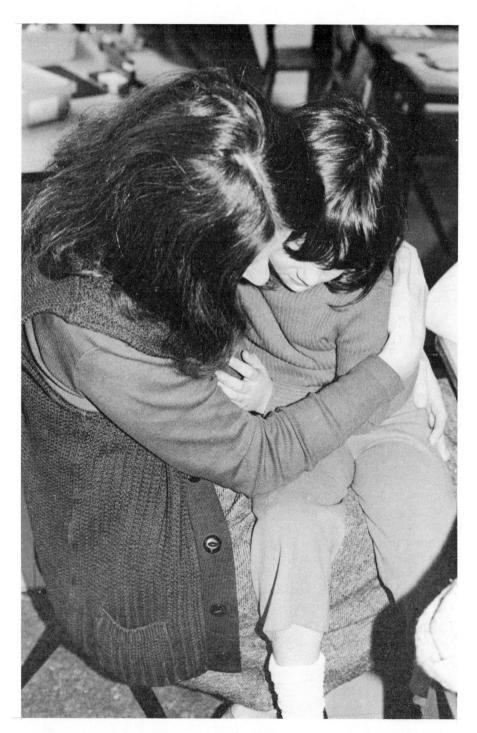

Introduction

So you want to care for children? Perhaps you have always cherished this ambition, or, perhaps it is an idea that has dawned recently, through your contacts with children in various situations.

It is sensible to find out what you are letting yourself in for. Caring for children is hard physical work which can also be mentally exhausting.

However, the rewards are infinite. To aid a helpless infant grow into a healthy well-adjusted child brings great joy. The value to society cannot be computed, but it must be very great.

Only comparatively recently has it been fully appreciated how vitally important are the years up to seven. Character, abilities, attitudes are all being formed during this period. Yet child-rearing is still under-valued. Anyone can become a parent, with no preparation or training. Although instinct will help a mother to do the right thing for her own child, instinct alone is certainly not sufficient when caring for other people's children.

Personal qualities in a nursery nurse

What qualities does an intending nursery nurse need? First, she needs to be a warm person who cares deeply about children in a way that is free from sentimentality or possessiveness. She must enjoy children's company and let this show through her dealings with them. She needs to be physically strong and healthy, and of wholesome and attractive appearance for the children. A sense of humour and a sense of proportion, patience and tolerance will be vital.

She must be able to get on with people, to accept them as they are without making hasty judgements. Resilience and self-control will be called for; so will ability to accept criticism, and a flexible outlook. Yet sensitivity, to adults as well as children, should underlie and characterise all she says and does.

The kind of person she is herself will determine the quality of the care she dispenses.

The National Nursery Examination Board

The Board was formed in 1945, conferring a nationally recognised qualification (N.N.E.B. Certificate) to fit women to work with young children up to the age of five. This was later extended to seven.

From the start, it was an imaginative and enlightened scheme, designed to continue the girls' education as well as train them for their chosen career.

Most courses are conducted within Colleges of Further Education, although one is housed separately. There are also a very few independent Colleges, the majority forming part of the state education system.

Students usually train for two years, at the end of which time they will take a national examination. Students must be sixteen or over when they embark on the course. The N.N.E.B. does not dictate academic entry qualifications, but competence in written English is an advantage and, for some courses, several O-Level equivalents will be required. In recent years, the emergence of boy students has made a valuable contribution to this predominantly female world.

Training varies with the centres, but the N.N.E.B. lays down a minimum number of days (at present 105) which must be spent in college-based study, and similarly a minimum number (at present 70) which must be spent in approved practical training establishments. Depending on areas and opportunities, practical training will take place in day nurseries, nursery centres, nursery schools, nursery classes, infant schools, hospitals, homes for handicapped children, or with private families.

Theoretical training in vocational subjects covers the development and care of the child from birth to seven and follows the outline syllabus of the N.N.E.B. Our book is an attempt to cover this syllabus according to our own interpretation.

JB
MDM

Chapter 1
The family and the child

The family is the fundamental social unit in the western world. Members of a family are related by blood or marriage, and think of themselves as a separate group in society. From very early times people have lived in groups, partly for protection and partly for the mating relationship. Human offspring, unlike those of animals, needed quite a long period of protection and training in subsistence skills – hunting, self-defence, crop-growing, etc. With the development of lethal weapons, the men began acting co-operatively in hunting common enemies and getting food. Rivalry for mating partners became less important and so the man/woman relationship became more permanent and the family unit slowly evolved. It also took on the task of looking after the old and the weak.

The family unit has undergone immense change through the centuries. An illuminating and entertaining account of changes in family life, and in particular the place of children, can be found in *The History of Childhood*, edited by Lloyd de Mause, Souvenir Press. Unfortunately, we cannot here begin to do justice to this fascinating subject.

But, to appreciate the impact of more recent influences on the family and family life today, let us look at families a hundred years ago in Britain.

The nineteenth century saw the emergence of a new social phenomenon – the British middle class, a direct reflection of Britain's prosperity and influence in the world, built on industrialisation, trade and colonisation. The middle class imitated the ways of the rich and aristocratic, and this affected many aspects of family life.

Family life in the nineteenth century

1. The middle-class family of Victorian times. The Victorian middle-class family consisted of father, mother and usually five or more children; quite possibly, one or two further children would have died at birth or in infancy.

The father was often an autocratic, remote figure whose word was law. He was the provider, and the mother had no need to work. Mother would preside over several servants, including a governess who would be employed to care for and teach the children while young.

The girls probably did not go to school and their education at home would

1

include accomplishments such as drawing, embroidery and playing musical instruments. They were expected to make a 'good' – meaning a financially satisfactory – marriage at an early age, to a suitable man of similar or higher social position. If still single at twenty-five, they were considered 'old maids', and had to find worthy occupations to fill their lives. Financial provision would probably be made by father or brothers.

Women were much the inferior of their husbands, with no property, legal, voting or other rights. Even if divorce had not been scandalous and unthinkable it would have brought great economic problems to women.

Religion affected many aspects of family life. For example, church and Sunday school attendance were compulsory for family and servants. Sunday was a family day and any activities regarded as flippant or over-industrious would be forbidden.

The church taught that children were conceived and born in sin. Baptism began the process of redeeming them, and was urgently sought for delicate babies who might pass into the next world in their sinful state.

Children were expected to be 'seen and not heard' and to obey their 'elders and betters' implicitly. Spontaneity and individuality were not encouraged. Mother/baby and mother/child relationships, however, were characterised by much sentimentality, as can be seen in paintings and writings.

Displays of affection, or passion, between adults were taboo, and excessive modesty about dress and conduct was prevalent. In extreme cases, even the piano legs had to be covered! The sex act was held, by women at least, to be an unavoidable necessity in the procreation of children; prostitution records in large cities indicate that many Victorian men maintained an outward respectability, while indulging their sexual desires away from home.

Without easy travel and communication, people's lives tended to be narrow, both geographically and mentally. They would work near their homes, and not move far from their families when they married. Consequently grandparents, aunts, uncles and cousins – the extended family – were influential in family life.

2. The lower-class family. For the very poor family having relatives close at hand was vital for its old, ill, bereaved or unemployed members. Often the shared experience of a hard life, made slightly easier by family help and support, forged bonds of loyalty and affection between members. The husband was the chief breadwinner, but if money was short wives too would work, in light industry, domestic service, or laundrywork either in their own homes or outside. To 'take in washing' was often a humiliation for the respectable poor.

The working day, week and year were long and hard. A woman might be allowed a few *hours* off to have a baby when working at a cotton mill. In country districts a newborn baby might be carried to work in the fields, tied in its mother's shawl, while her many other children came along too. Bank holidays were great events, and a day out at the nearest seaside resort – probably Southend for Londoners, Blackpool for many northerners – would be looked forward to, saved for and talked about afterwards for the best part of the year by working people fortunate enough to afford it. Otherwise, families had little leisure time to spend together or apart; all their time and energy went on eking out a mere subsistence. For those undeterred by warnings about hellfire and damnation, there were the escapes of gin and ale.

Traditional remedies were used to treat the sick because doctors' fees were out of the question. Epidemics of typhoid fever and other diseases raged in towns from time to time, accelerated by insanitary housing conditions. Whole families might be crowded into one or two small rooms and beds; incest was common-place.

After 1880 free education was compulsory and free for all. But the children of the poor left school at the earliest possible moment, by the age of thirteen, to begin work. In country districts, or areas with seasonal work, many children would be kept away from school to earn a few more coppers for the family budget at, for instance, potato harvesting or hop-picking. Apprenticeship in a trade was virtually the only further training available; college and university education was financially and socially out of reach for the children of the poor.

Family life in the twentieth century

In the second part of the last century, and the whole of this, far-reaching social and economic changes profoundly affected the family unit, and the quality of family life. Most were clearly of benefit, but others created problems and pressures.

A series of political reforms ended sweated labour of women and children and placed a greater economic responsibility on the male. In more recent times, working hours were steadily reduced, creating leisure for the masses.

The repeated raising of the school-leaving age reflected the enhanced status of the child in society, but also increased the dependency years. Life in a complex, technological age has made higher education and specialised training necessary for large numbers of young people, which has further lengthened the period of dependency.

Health and life expectancy improved dramatically and continuously with the development of medicine and science, drugs, preventive measures and knowledge of the factors that produce a healthy life-style. Infant mortality, although still not as low in Britain as we should like, is vastly reduced. Death is no longer an everyday occurrence and each individual life, from the ante-natal period onwards, is more precious, and the focus of high hopes and responsibilities for the parents. Paradoxically, now that death, suffering and acute illnesses, such as fevers which used to work up to a 'crisis', have almost passed out of our lives, with them has gone much drama. Some students of social behaviour believe that present-day problems such as depression or boredom leading to vandalism stem largely from this lack of real-life drama.

Because we live longer, marriages are undertaken for the best part of a life-time. As older people remain active, the popular image of white-haired granny knitting for and 'spoiling' her grandchildren may be replaced by a youthful fifty-plus-year-old who still does a full-time job.

Women were given the vote in 1928, mainly as a result of their contribution to the First World War effort in 1914–18. Subsequently, aided by legislation such as the recent Sex Discrimination Act, they have secured equal rights and opportunities, although there is still room for improvement. Today's marriages are voluntary commitments of equal partners to one another.

On the subject of representation in government, we should remember that at the beginning of this century even adult male suffrage ('one *man* one vote') had not long applied in Britain. The twentieth century has seen a steady increase in direct participation government by the people, and also an influence from the trade union movement and other bodies. Family considerations have been important in wooing the support of voters.

With a secure position in society, a good education and often career training too, many married women now choose to return to a former job, or take up a new career, after spending comparatively few years on child-rearing. In a later chapter, we shall look at how well society provides for the young children of such women. When the mother is working the father has to help with the household chores. Few modern families can afford servants. In any case, the idea of working as another person's servant is often distasteful, with its feudal echoes. Some marriages adopt a complete reversal of roles. The father stays at home to look after the house and children while the mother goes out to work. This makes sense if the mother can earn a higher salary, and both partners are happy with the arrangement. A woman can take maternity leave, knowing her job must be held open for six months. Many fathers are happy to be involved with the upbringing of their children, from birth onwards. There is no longer a taboo on male tenderness and in some countries fathers can claim paternity leave.

Women's equal rights to a social life have also been recognised, and whole families tend to enjoy leisure pursuits together, where once mother and children would have been left at home while father enjoyed his chosen hobby. We have to recognise also that marriage is no longer the one and only role for women. Many now *choose* to remain single. The term 'spinster' with its forbidding overtones has practically disappeared.

The general standard of living has improved greatly in the last fifty or so years. There is far less contrast between the lives of the so-called middle and working classes. Job and promotion opportunities have raised people's expectations of a comfortable, happy life. There is very little grinding poverty. But, when expectations are high, those who fail – for whatever reasons – stand out more painfully. Television programmes and many forms of advertising have encouraged a new materialism and acquisitiveness which can trivialise accepted values and are damaging to society.

Family planning methods and legalised abortion have enabled parents to limit their families to a chosen number – in recent years, one or two. Contraception has resulted in a sharp decline in the birth rate during the last decade, as economic pressures, inflation and the desire for a high standard of living have made married women plan for an eventual return to work. It remains to be seen whether economic or other factors will result in an upswing during the latter part of this century. Every child should and could be a wanted child. With such a power of choice, some parents find the responsibility too onerous. Newly-married wives may find the 'sensible' decision – to keep their job and defer motherhood for a while – hard to accept, when nature has designed their bodies for childbearing in the early twenties. Another power of choice, in this context, is the services of a fertility clinic for a couple who, two generations ago, would have remained childless.

Enlightened attitudes toward the study of man and the human body, and the development of psychology as a science, have freed sexual behaviour from the traditional sinful interpretation of the church. Sexual problems within marriage can be openly talked about and receive skilled and sympathetic help, so that sexual behaviour can be rightly and fully enjoyed by both partners.

Child psychology shows that positive promotion of all aspects of children's development is far better than repression. With the spread of such knowledge, through the press, radio and television, parents are now expected to keep abreast of the latest ideas on child-rearing and personal relationships, including careers guidance.

Easier divorce procedures are often blamed for the rising divorce rate and the resulting suffering of children. Undoubtedly, thousands of children do suffer every year through broken marriages; some are used as pawns in the preceding conflict; some are 'bought' and vied for with money and material possessions, some grow up with a distorted view of the absent parent, or his or her sex in general. Many have feelings of divided loyalty, loneliness, rejection, even guilt that somehow they were responsible for the break-up. But many others survive apparently unscathed. Large numbers also quickly adapt to a new parent and ready-made brothers and sisters. Most experienced people agree that for a child to live within a loveless marriage where partners stay together 'for the sake of the children' is infinitely worse.

However, the million or so children living in a one-parent family form a large part of the nation's statistics on poverty. Particularly vulnerable are unsupported young mothers, and children born illegitimately. (In children born outside marriage, there is still a distressingly high incidence of stillbirth, handicap and infant mortality.) Poverty, inadequate housing and social disadvantage commonly experienced by such families are more damaging than any trauma experienced during a breakdown, or the single-parent status. The fact that children of widows or widowers and, to a lesser extent, divorced parents, appear to suffer less in all respects, seems to indicate that even a short time living within a maturely-based family, with both marriage partners present, affords a child some safeguard against damage if a breakdown occurs.

Housing and sanitary conditions have become steadily better this century, thereby improving standards of health and mental well-being. Each new family *expects* to have its own home, and although local authorities cannot keep pace with demand, this is the goal towards which they strive. Unfortunately, after the Second World War, during a period of rising birth rate and diminishing availability of building land, many authorities built high-rise flats which have since been proved unsuitable and are frequently sources of discontent, depression, isolation and vandalism. They are particularly harmful to young mothers and children. In the private sector, there has been a great increase in the number of families who succeed in buying their own homes and achieve high standards of comfort and amenities. The high cost of labour for maintenance has meant that householders carry out most home improvements themselves. The sharing of labour by husband and wife increases their pride and joy in the home. Television has provided entertainment in the home, and is often a means of drawing family members together.

Geographic, occupational and social mobility has greatly increased. Two world wars extended the horizons of whole generations; improved education strengthened their desire for better jobs and housing, and governments strove to satisfy them. Motorised vehicles for a large section of the population made travel, for work and leisure, a practical possibility. This greater mobility and changing outlook also led to the growth of suburbs. As grown-up children moved away from their roots, however, family networks broke up, and the typical family today is a 'nuclear' family; that is, it consists of parents and child or children only. Contact between the nuclear family and other relatives now is often a matter of choice, and concern for relatives' well-being. Formerly, living in an extended family meant that contact was unavoidable. Today greater independence and more privacy in the personal lives and child-rearing patterns of the young mother and father are ensured. But children can be denied valuable contact with grandparents, peer cousins and other relatives who might enhance the sense of belonging to a distinctive, strong unit. For the parents, particularly young mothers, they can lead to a sense of isolation, lack of support and depression.

Economic independence – thanks to the welfare state – is welcomed by the older generation, but they, too, can feel lonely, abandoned, and deprived of the rejuvenating company of their grandchildren. The fact that people live to a greater age now also means that their years of retirement, which in many cases *can* mean years without a useful role, accentuate this sense of isolation. To offset this, improved health and freedom from poverty *can* make retirement a period of contented pursuit of interests and pleasures.

The welfare state has provided a 'safety net' for cases of hardship, unemployment, disability, child neglect, old age and so on. Critics claim that many of the traditional functions of the family have been taken over by the state, thus undermining the responsibility of the family.

Other less perceptible changes in society have had repercussions on family life. The historical influence of the church and the practice of church-going have diminished considerably. This fact is sometimes linked with a general 'moral decline' in family life and elsewhere. Yet however atheistic or secular a family appears to be, all our inheritance of ethics and moral code has descended from Christian teaching. Inner convictions and guiding principles in conduct are still passed on from one generation to the next.

Another subtle change has taken place in the status of the father in the family. Today, his job (probably industrial) is often simply a time-filling paid occupation, and affords him little satisfaction or self-respect. His position is very different from that of his craftsman or farming forebears. He plays only a minor part in a complex process. This lack of personal involvement may affect his personal and family life and even demean his standing in the family. Children educated to question past assumptions may not *automatically* revere him because he is their father. He is not necessarily the sole breadwinner, and must share the household tasks. Sources of dissatisfaction may multiply, and his view of his role in life may be hazy or tinged with disenchantment.

Let us take a closer look at the invisible forces at work *within* families, especially those which most affect the child. His position in relation to other family members is of great significance.

The small family and only child are common in society today. The traditional view that the only child must be a spoiled child may be partly true, for he will be the sole focus of the parents' love and attention, which may include material over-indulgence. On the other hand, many parents of only children, aware of this danger, may even be over-strict. They usually make special efforts to secure companionship for the child. He will probably develop social skills early in life, because he has no ready-made companions, he must win and keep them. He may become, of necessity, self-sufficient and prefer his own company to that of others. He may well be more than advanced in conversation, through adult company. His parents' expectations will probably be high, and they may over-protect or 'cling' to him, when he should be allowed increasing independence. He will miss the hurly burly of family life with brothers and sisters – teasing, rivalries, shared jokes, 'ganging-up' against parent or each other and the deep – often well-hidden – affection expressed at Christmas, birthdays and times of stress. Sharing, taking turns, waiting with other children are not quite the same if they only happen at school.

Large families are comparatively rare today. Traditionally they are happy loving groups in which to grow up, and indeed many undoubtedly are. Many others, however, are found in the poverty and 'problem' statistics. Sometimes the large number of children is the result of ignorance and carelessness rather than choice. If the parents are not reasonably well off and good 'copers', each new baby will increase their difficulties. Undoubtedly, such children learn to share, give and take, at an early age. Older children gain valuable experience in helping with younger ones. But the youngest may go short of adult attention and language stimulation. Material benefits have to be spread thinly. 'Hand-me-down' clothes and toys may be the lot of the youngest. There will be little privacy. Many people who have grown up in such a family feel that these disadvantages are, however, far outweighed by the experience of family solidarity, the development of resourcefulness, and the choice of particular closeness with one or more sibling, all of which may continue and afford great joy well into adult life.

The middle child out of three or five is often thought to be in an unenviable position; not for him the privileges and status of being the eldest, nor the babying and special treatment of the youngest. He may resent this, and resort to jealous or spiteful behaviour.

Twins often have to fight for their individuality to be recognised. Parents and teachers sometimes reinforce the image of 'the pair' by dressing them alike, referring to them as 'the twins' and so on. At times they may enjoy and even encourage this attention, but at others they long to make their mark as individuals. Often their early language development is slow, for they evolve their own private means of communication. Later, enforced closeness can accentuate differences in academic attainment, social success, etc. and lead to rivalry and resentment.

The child born to older (late thirties to fifties) parents is a common feature of family life today, now that wives' careers and second marriages are so prevalent. Such parents may be wiser and more patient, owing to greater maturity and life experience, but less physically energetic, and more aware of dangers and pitfalls, and therefore over-cautious and protective. They may not be familiar with contemporary child-rearing practices or, later, the fashions and freedom common to most teenagers today. This can be a particularly 'fraught' time for the child, who may be aware that his parents are different from those of his friends, and resent this.

The child born after an interval of years may experience some of the same effects, possibly coupled with those of being an only child. On the other hand, he may receive fond treatment from older brothers and sisters, and enjoy the company of contemporary nephews and nieces.

Readers can doubtless call to mind many other instances of how positions and relationships within families affect both their own functioning and the developing personality of the children.

The future of the family

There are pressures within and outside today's small family units. It is not easy to be a good mother, father, son, daughter – good in everyone else's eyes as well as one's own. In such a small and self-contained setting, each family member's role is constantly in the limelight. It is almost impossible to have an 'off' day, or disappear temporarily from the scene, without others noticing, and being materially and psychologically affected. This situation can lead to stress and discontent.

We have already seen how some of the traditional functions of the family –

protecting the very young, or the old and weak members, for instance – have been, at least in part, taken over by the welfare state.

New attitudes to sexual freedom mean that we no longer *need* to get married in order to enjoy sex. Contraception has effectively separated marriage from the idea of having children. When a marriage contract can be so easily broken, does it have any validity in the first place?

Marriage in our society still has an aura of romance, however. But in other societies it does not. The Asians, for instance, appear to manage very well by tackling it as a practical, economic arrangement. Should we not then, in western countries, look seriously for alternative approaches to family life, or even change the whole concept of marriage, and the family as society's basic unit?

While young people and others search in communes and kibbutzim for an alternative, superior unit, marriage becomes more and more popular. Despite increased life expectancy, people marry earlier. Most divorced people remarry within a few years. Clearly then, the high divorce rate does not reflect a rejection of the institution of marriage. In the USSR, which has undergone revolution, civil war and a great sweeping away of traditional values, and where the state wields far more power over the individual than in Britain, marriage and family life still thrive, despite assumptions that they would fade out. We know from irrefutable evidence that the family is infinitely preferable as a setting for the child's development to the impersonal, multi-staffed institution.

Surely these facts strongly suggest that marriage and the family still fulfil the deep-felt needs of human beings.

In conclusion

As human beings, we need to care, and be cared for by others. To do this we need a few – comparatively speaking – close, lasting relationships, rather than many superficial ones.

We need to matter to others, and how much we matter largely depends on how much we contribute to their well-being. We need a degree of stability in our environment. We need to create surroundings of our choice, and unless there is some guarantee of the future of those surroundings, all our efforts are wasted. We want our lives to be more than a mere speck in the universe, a chance interval of time. We like to feel a sense of continuity – handing on the baton in life's relay race, rather than merely sprinting the hundred metres.

In a world where our daily work may be frustrating or uninspiring, we can derive deep satisfaction from life within a family. In a world of changing values, we feel we belong to one safe, steadfast unit. Helped by this inner security, most parents do their utmost to fulfil their family roles.

In many ways more, rather than less, is asked of parents today. They are expected to decide how many children to have, and at what intervals, depending on economic and other circumstances. They are expected to keep informed about all the institutions – clinics, schools, government agencies and so on – which will affect their children's development and education so as to derive as much benefit as possible from these. Catering for their children's physical, social, emotional and intellectual needs, parents must equip their children for a society which is itself constantly changing. A family which succeeds in this task contributes immensely to the community and is rewarded with status, prestige, reinforcement of its solidarity, and recognition of its identity.

We now have to consider in more specific terms how a good family life can benefit a child. In the first place, intimate knowledge of and interaction with loving parents who also love one another, gives the child a secure emotional base, where he *knows* he is loved and valued. He has no need to resort to attention-seeking behaviour, then or later. Building on shared experiences and memories, and emerging tastes, talents and characteristics, he gradually forms a clear picture of himself as an individual and feels at ease with that self. Text books call this 'self-image' or 'concept of self'. He will model his future conduct on that he sees in the home. He grows up with a clear idea of male and female roles in marriage, family and society. In moments of stress, he seeks refuge, comfort, reassurance from the family, and good moments are crowned by shared pleasure and pride.

As the years pass, he uses the family as a sounding board, punchbag, haven, anchor, cushion, and springboard. He learns to cope with failure and success, conflict, frustration, his own strengths and weaknesses and those of others. He learns loyalty to a group, and the safe feeling and confidence of belonging. He learns how to give as well as accept support. He contributes to the strength of the family and in doing so becomes stronger himself. Having received love, he can give it, wholeheartedly and wisely, without restraint, resentment or hopes of reward. In short, he can play his part in creating the next generation of good families.

Exercise 1

Multiple-choice questions

1. What is meant by a nuclear family?
(a) a family living in this, the nuclear age;
(b) a family consisting of mother, father and child or children;
(c) a family where the father works in a nuclear power-station;
(d) a family consisting of three generations and other relatives;
(e) a family with one child.

2. Which of the following innovations has most profoundly affected women's position in society today?
(a) easier divorce;
(b) opportunities for work outside the home;
(c) television;
(d) Women's Liberation Movement;
(e) the 'pill'.

Essay questions

3. How have parental roles within the family changed during the past fifty years?

4. What might be some of the difficulties facing a one-parent family today?

Discussion topic

5. How might a child be affected and influenced by the proximity of grand-parents throughout his early years?

Project

6. Find out all you can about childhood in other cultures.

Suggestions for further reading

D. W. Winnicott, *The Child and the Family*, Tavistock Publications Ltd
David Kennedy, *Children*, B. T. Batsford Ltd
Edward Shorter, *The Making of the Modern Family*, Fontana
Eleanor Allen, *Victorian Children*, A. & C. Black Ltd
Russell Ash, *Talking about the Family*, Wayland Publishers Ltd
Eileen Bostock, *Talking about Women*, Wayland Publishers Ltd
Jean Collin, *Never had it so Good*, Victor Gollancz

Chapter 2
Marriage

Preparation for marriage

Western marriage today is a voluntary commitment to share one's life with a chosen partner. Young people are often 'prepared' for marriage in a semi-formal way in the upper half of secondary schools, in youth clubs, church classes for engaged couples, and elsewhere. The group leader may be a teacher, doctor, marriage guidance counsellor, family planning adviser, or health visitor. Precise information on sex and contraception may be given – as a responsible way of preventing unwanted births and abortions. However, this narrow interpretation of growing up has recently been broadened, and the whole subject is seen as education for personal relationships, of which marriage, naturally, is an important part. The group leader gives the young people a chance to air their views, and poses hypothetical situations, to stimulate deeper thought and discussion.

Is it possible to prepare people effectively for marriage? Probably not. Each marriage is a unique combination of two unique individuals. Therefore there can be no one formula for a happy marriage. We have all seen apparently ideal marriages flounder, and the most unlikely marriages flourish and last. Each evolves its own way of working to the satisfaction of the two partners within it. Those that do not either drift into sterile misery, or break up. Why then do we still provide education for marriage when success cannot be demonstrated?

The answer is partly that young people need to know that adults are trying to help and guide them, and are concerned for their well-being. Besides, this exchanging of opinions helps young people broaden their understanding and tolerance of others and helps them to examine their own attitudes towards the sex roles, the function of marriage and what may be expected of them in marriage. It is a modifying (perhaps only very slightly) influence in the heat of a moment's emotions.

Whether or not young people attend such classes, they all have preconceived ideas about marriage. They derive these:

1. most importantly from their own families;
2. from the marriages and homes of others;
3. from the television, films, advertising, the press, radio.

1. One's own experience of family life, and the marriage at the centre of it implant such deep feelings and attitudes that they are difficult to analyse – even recognise. Sometimes, in our own marriage we seek something as far removed as possible from what we know. In other cases we seek something similar.

2. Seeing other kinds of marriage – for instance where a wife is the chief breadwinner, or where there is a large, loving family – can be enormously broadening and beneficial.

3. Popular ideas on marriage are often unrealistic and glamorised. Young people should understand that a gleaming kitchen, with every latest appliance and refinement is not essential to a good marriage. Nor are the sex and family roles in real life stereotyped, as they often appear in the media. It is not unmanly to change nappies or take a turn with the saucepans, and it is not unwomanly to find home-making not wholly fulfilling. And the stereotype mother-in-law, fierce and formidable, is often far from the truth.

Inside or outside formal sessions, young people can be helped to see the many reasons why people marry, and why they choose the partners they do. Physical attraction is an overwhelming, yet superficial, part of it. Practicalities like loneliness, unhappiness at home, proximity and availability can all play a part, as can social pressures and a wish to conform. Complex emotional factors are also involved. Many people seek in their partners a quality they feel themselves to be lacking. This may work – if both partners are not seeking the same quality, or if the quality was not perceived from too slight an acquaintance. A good marriage can transform the personal development and emotional well-being of both partners. Gaps and wounds remaining from former less happy relationships can be filled in, or healed. But as personalities grow, needs and expectations change. The good marriage, allowing for this, grows and changes accordingly.

Such a close relationship, must produce ambivalent feelings and conflict. It is often only with the person with whom we feel most safe that we are confident enough to be aggressive and reveal our innermost selves, not all of which is lovable. The value of communication cannot be overstressed. If this breaks down, the marriage is doomed. Where there is genuine affection and – very important – a sense of commitment, communication resolves most difficulties and problems of adjustment.

These are a few of the deeper implications of marriage. But marriage should not be presented in too sober or depressing a light. Although it involves surrendering a certain amount of personal freedom, the partners should ideally exchange this narrow freedom for a deeper one within which each can grow.

Preparation for parenthood

Many schools offer instruction and discussion in parentcraft. Opinions vary about how and when this should be done. Sadly, often only the less academic pupils are given this opportunity, and sometimes only the girls. Statistics shows that young parents are most likely to come from this group but *all* prospective parents could undoubtedly benefit from learning how to handle a baby. The utter dependency of the newborn can thus be understood. The parents' role in ministering to his needs can be shown, with practical demonstrations in bathing, nappy changing, making up feeds, etc. Most young people respond well to such sessions, and on this physical level education in parentcraft is probably most effective at this stage.

Later, when baby is on the way, ante-natal classes can offer a more detailed preparation. Besides instruction on reproduction and the birth process, advice on how the mother can prepare her body by exercises and correct breathing can be given to *both* parents. Handling routines can be learned or re-learned.

At this stage, committed to parenthood, the young couple are usually receptive to advice on a deeper level. They can be made aware how, by performing these tasks for the baby, they will also fulfil other needs – for close contact and emotional security. Foundations will be laid for relationships and the means of communication. The need for mental stimulus can also be stressed, and again, both partners shown the importance of suitable equipment, play materials, making an environment safe and introducing stories and books at an early stage. Such topics will provide the themes for meetings of Mother and Toddler Clubs later on in the child's development. In recent years there have been several excellent television series about this stage in a family's life.

Preparation for parenthood is not, of course, confined to formal sessions. An awareness of all the many reasons *why* people have babies is important; it is not always to crown a happy marriage – a joint adventure in 'person making'. Some girls deliberately get pregnant to escape from an unhappy home life, lack of success at school or socially. Some 'trap' a man reluctantly into marriage. Some single women choose to be unmarried mothers for personal fulfilment. Sometimes pregnancy is a desperate bid to save an ailing marriage. Sometimes, even with contraception widely available and accepted, it is a half-deliberate 'mistake' because a couple, or more probably a wife, feels that planning babies is too cold-blooded. Contraception, after all, is not a natural phenomenon. Biologically, women are designed to produce babies in their early twenties.

In matters of timing, the head must often rule the heart. Most people believe that a baby is entitled to a start in life of economic and financial security – otherwise he will be affected physically. Emotionally too, he will suffer if, for instance, parents are harassed by money worries, or his arrival has curtailed either parent's training or career, or ended hopes of paying off a mortgage. Timing also involves awareness of the couple's adjustment to each other, and their emotional stability. It often takes a little while for a couple's sexual relationship to settle down satisfactorily, or gradually change from being their main preoccupation. Parenthood is bound to cause a little disruption here, so it is important that a mutually satisfactory and balanced approach has been achieved.

The fact must be faced that a baby will bring some restrictions. Money will almost certainly be shorter and have to stretch further. This will affect social life, hobbies, holidays, and many of the small pleasures of our too-materialistic society. Sleep and privacy may be affected. Many demands will be made on parents, but especially on the mother. Although today there is a much more relaxed approach than formerly about babies happily fitting into parents' lives, it is still true to say that expectations of a pink, cuddly bundle who will bring only light, joy and love into his parents' lives may be quickly followed by disillusionment and resentment. An expectant mother may not immediately experience a great surge of maternal feelings towards her baby. Apparent 'failure' here can bring reactions of guilt and anxiety. The attitudes of her mother and mother-in-law and the advice they give her during this waiting period may be critically influential – for good or bad – as she will be extra sensitive, and very anxious to do the right thing. As parents, the husband and wife will be the targets of much conflicting advice; even the 'experts' differ. Skill at picking one's way through such advice takes time, tact and maturity.

Parentcraft is not something that is learned once and for all. Parents go on learning all their lives, until the role merges into that of grandparent.

In the early days, many different individuals and agencies will play a part – the midwife, doctor, health visitor, baby clinic and above all, the young parents' own families. Besides information, advice and expertise, all these people should give reassurance and support, dispel alarm, discourage comparison with other babies, and help the parents to enjoy the whole procedure, grow in self-confidence and reap the maximum rewards.

Reproduction

All animals and plants reproduce in order to continue their species, and pass on characteristics to the next generation. Human beings are mammals and their reproduction is sexual; one male and one female together can produce offspring by each contributing one cell – a spermatozoon from the male and an ovum from the female.

Although the reproductive system is complete at birth, it is not mature, and boys and girls only become capable of producing babies at puberty which takes place some time between the ages of nine and eighteen years. The changes from girl to woman and boy to man are very gradual processes; the time taken varies with each individual. The physical changes needed to mature the reproductive system are determined by the pituitary gland which lies at the base of the brain in both sexes. At puberty the pituitary produces secretions known as hormones which travel through the bloodstream to all parts of the body, causing the production of sperm in boys and ova or eggs in girls, and changes known as secondary sexual characteristics in both sexes. These physical changes are usually completed before a person becomes mentally or emotionally mature. This can lead to problems. For example, a baby can be produced by juvenile parents who lack the maturity to devote the necessary amount of time and energy to his upbringing.

The male reproductive system

Secondary sexual characteristics which develop at puberty
(a) broadening of shoulders and development of muscles;
(b) growth of hair in the pubic region, on the chest and under the arms;
(c) change of voice from a high pitch to a low pitch due to growth and development of vocal chords;
(d) production of sweat which has a characteristic odour (intended to attract the opposite sex) by the opocrine glands in the skin;
(e) increase in size of penis;
(f) production of semen (fluid containing spermatozoa) which may be emitted.

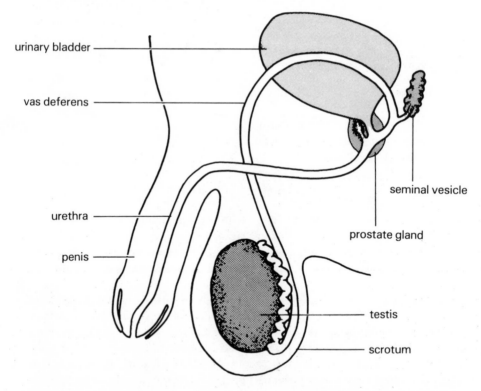

(A) *Scrotum* – a loose bag or sac of skin outside the body containing the testes. The sac is retracted towards the body when cold and away from the body when hot to enable the sperm to stay at the optimum temperature, which is slightly below normal body temperature.

(B) *Two testes* – produce spermatozoa.

(C) *Vas deferens* – a duct or tube, leading from each teste upwards to loop under the bladder and join up with the urethra, which carry spermatozoa.

(D) *The urethra* – a tube leading from the bladder through the penis to the outside of the body.

(E) *The seminal vesicles* – these produce fluid which joins the spermatozoa in the vas deferens.

(F) *The prostate gland* – also produces fluid which joins the spermatozoa in the urethra.

The fluid containing spermatozoa is known as semen and it collects in the top part of the urethra and vas deferens ready to be released during sexual intercourse or masturbation. The penis is made of erectile tissue which means that during sexual stimulation the tissue is suffused with blood which enables it to become firm and erect and therefore capable of entering the female vagina. During the climax of the act semen containing millions of spermatozoa is ejected and deposited in the vagina. The spermatozoa are shaped like minute tadpoles, with a head and a long flexible tail which enables them to move rapidly into the female uterus and up into the fallopian tube to meet the ova.

The female reproductive system

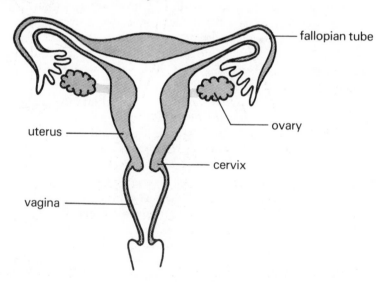

Unlike that of the male, the female reproductive system is inside the body and is completely separate from the urinary system. The organs lie between the bowel and the bladder and urethra, and consist of:

(A) *The vagina* – a narrow corrugated passage which leads from the exterior of the body to the uterus.

(B) *The uterus* (or womb) – a hollow pear-shaped organ, size 7.5 cm × 5 cm × 2.5 cm (3 in × 2 in × 1 in) and which protrudes into the vagina at the lower end, forming a cervix or neck.

(C) *The fallopian tubes* – two narrow tubes which lead from the upper two corners of the uterus.

(D) *The ovaries* – two small almond-sized glands which contain ova, or eggs. Approximately every twenty-eight days during a woman's reproductive life, one of the ova 'ripens' and is released into the fallopian tube.

Secondary sexual characteristics which develop at puberty
(a) rounding of hips;
(b) enlargement of breasts;
(c) growth of hair in the pubic region and under the arms;
(d) production of sweat, which has a characteristic odour, by the opocrine glands in the skin;
(e) beginning of menstruation.

The menstrual cycle is the name used to describe the regular preparation of the uterus to receive a fertilised egg (ovum), and the subsequent discarding of the uterine lining if the egg is not fertilised. For most women this occurs during a period of twenty-eight days but it may vary between twenty-five to thirty days.

The cycle is controlled by hormones produced by the pituitary gland, which, in turn, stimulate the ovary to produce further hormones called oestrogen and progesterone. At the beginning of the cycle oestrogen produced by the ovary causes the lining of the uterus to thicken. This continues for about ten days until the ovum is released from the ovary and is wafted into the fallopian tube. With the liberation of the ovum the ovary begins to produce progesterone as well, which causes the uterine lining to become even thicker and more ready to receive the fertilised ovum. This continues for another fourteen days but then, if the ovum is not fertilised, progesterone ceases to be produced. This 'cut-off' of progesterone causes the lining of the uterus to deteriorate and to be shed for three to five days. This is known as the menstrual period, and is facetiously referred to by obstetricians as 'the weeping of a disappointed uterus'.

Two days after the period is completed, the entire cycle begins again. However, if the ovum is fertilised, about six days after its release it becomes implanted in the uterine lining. The fertilised ovum produces another hormone which causes the ovary to continue producing progesterone. This prevents the uterine lining from being shed, therefore there is no menstrual period.

Incidentally, the hormone produced by a fertilised ovum is called chorionic gonadotrophin and this hormone is excreted in the urine, where it can be detected and used as confirmation of pregnancy a week after fertilisation has taken place.

Contraception

For thousands of years people have sought ways of controlling their own fertility, but it is only in the past twenty years that this has been universally possible with any degree of certainty.

Several methods of contraception are now available and many general practitioners give advice on family planning. Family planning clinics exist in the majority of health centres and most of the contraceptive devices can be obtained on prescription. The following are used in Great Britain:

1. The sperm can be killed by the use of *spermicides* in the form of foams, creams, pessaries or jellies. These are inserted into the vagina just before intercourse. Although fairly efficient, it is recommended that this method is used with a mechanical barrier as well.

2. A temporary or permanent *barrier* can be placed between the egg and the sperm to prevent them meeting:
(a) a rubber diaphragm cap which is inserted into the vagina and prevents sperm entering the cervix. When used with spermicidal cream this is very effective;
(b) a condom; this is a rubber sheath which encloses the penis, after erection, but before penetration, so preventing sperm entering the vagina. When used with spermicidal cream it is very effective;
(c) *female sterilisation* (this is permanent). The fallopian tubes are cut and the cut ends are tied so that the egg cannot travel to the uterus;
(d) *male sterilisation* (this is permanent). Both vas deferens are cut and the cut ends are tied so that sperm cannot travel through the tubes. This is called a vasectomy.

3. The egg can be prevented from being released. If a woman is given 'the pill', which is usually a mixture of the female hormones oestrogen and progesterone, or progesterone alone, ovulation does not occur. This is the most effective method at present.

4. The conditions inside the uterus can be made unsuitable for implantation of a fertilised egg. This is caused by inserting an intra-uterine device consisting of a loop or coil of plastic wire into the uterus.

5. Use of the safe period. Since ovulation occurs only at monthly intervals, then it is possible for a woman to work out when this happens and avoid intercourse within two to three days of this date. If a woman has a regular cycle of menstruation, it is a simple matter, because ovulation occurs fourteen days before the next menstrual cycle. To be certain of the date of ovulation, the temperature can be taken daily, because at ovulation time there is a slight drop of about half a degree (F) followed by a rise of about one degree (F). This method takes time and self-control but many parents manage to plan their families this way and it is the only method allowed to Catholics.

Pregnancy

Conception takes place when a spermatozoon reaches the ovum in the fallopian tube and penetrates it. This is when pregnancy begins and it continues until the birth of the baby. Immediately after the sperm and the ovum unite, they begin dividing, first into two, then into four, then into eight cells, and so on. These cells will eventually become the baby and the placenta (or afterbirth).

At the same time as this cell division is taking place the fertilised egg (or morula, as it is called at this stage) is being wafted down the fallopian tube into the uterine cavity. Then, at about the sixth day after conception, the morula will embed itself into the lining of the uterus (or womb).

The development of the fertilised egg is very rapid. Soon the morula will separate into two halves that will become the foetus and the placenta and, by about the twelfth week, the foetus will be recognisable as a baby.

The foetus obtains nourishment and oxygen from its mother via the placenta, which is attached to the wall of the uterus. Between the placenta and the foetus is the umbilical cord which acts as a lifeline carrying food and oxygen to the foetus and removing waste products. Food, oxygen and the waste products are exchanged through the walls of the placenta and uterus and the mother's bloodstream.

The foetus is surrounded by a bag of membranes which contain fluid in which the baby floats. The fluid acts as a cushion, protecting the baby from any blow. It also enables the baby to have free movement and exercise which aids its physical development. Most of the baby's development occurs during the first three months of pregnancy; during the remaining six months the baby will grow and mature until he is ready to cope with the outside world. Because of the rapid development, the foetus is very vulnerable to any damage in the early weeks of pregnancy. At one time it was thought that the placenta acted as an impenetrable barrier to anything which could harm the developing foetus but we now know that certain viruses can get through to the baby, and some drugs too. Smoking can also be harmful to the baby's development. The degree of damage suffered by the foetus will largely depend on what stage it has reached. For example, if the mother has German measles (rubella) at the time the baby's ears are developing, then the baby will probably be born deaf. On the other hand, if the damage occurs very early in pregnancy, there may be such a distortion of development that the foetus is unable to survive and the pregnancy will end in abortion.

Heredity

The hereditary factors passed to a baby by its parents are contained in the twenty-three chromosomes present in both the ovum and the spermatozoon. When the ovum and the spermatozoon combine to form a single cell, each of the twenty-three chromosomes from the ovum unites with a matching chromosome from the spermatozoon and twenty-three distinctly different pairs are produced. These forty-six chromosomes form the blueprint for the new individual and, as the cell divides and sub-divides, each new cell will contain an identical set of chromosomes.

At the moment of conception the sex of the baby is decided in the following way. One particular pair of chromosomes are known as the 'sex chromosomes', and the sex chromosome from the ovum is always an 'X' one. But the spermatozoon may contain either an 'X' or a 'Y' chromosome. If the sperm contains an 'X' chromosome then the baby will have 'XX' chromosomes, and will be female. If the sperm contains a 'Y' chromosome then the baby will have 'XY' chromosomes, and will be male. This means that the sex of a baby is always determined by the father's sperm. It is probably a matter of random chance whether a sperm containing an 'X' chromosome or one containing a 'Y' chromosome reaches the ovum first. But, nevertheless, more boys are conceived than girls. The ratio is fairly constant at 106 boys to every 100 girls. However, boys are more vulnerable to injury and disease and this causes the ratio eventually to even out.

Each chromosome carries thousands of genes and each gene contributes to the general make-up of the child. For example, a gene from one chromosome determines eye-colour, another will determine the shape of the eye, and so on.

Because the chromosomes are in matched pairs, it follows that every individual has two genes for each characteristic, one from each parent. Although genes look alike, they can carry different instructions. For instance, a person could have a gene from his mother containing instructions for a round chin, and a corresponding gene from his father containing instructions for a pointed chin. He may be born with the round chin but, because he also carried the gene for a pointed chin, he could pass the pointed chin characteristic on to his future children.

In many cases it is not known why one gene of a pair is used in preference to the other; indeed it may be accidental. But in some cases a gene can be 'dominant' or 'recessive'. Dominant genes always take precedence over other genes so that if one parent contributes this type of gene then the child will always inherit that particular characteristic. Recessive genes, on the other hand, always allow other genes to take precedence. A good example of this is with genes that determine eye-colour, because the genes controlling dark colours are dominant. If a child has a blue-eyed mother who has passed on her blue-eyed characteristic, and a brown-eyed father who has passed on his brown-eyed characteristic, then the child will have brown eyes. However, the child will also carry the gene for blue eyes inherited from his mother, so that when he becomes a father he could pass either the blue gene or the brown one. In some families it is possible to see certain characteristics carried down through each generation in this way, for example, a cleft chin.

As each chromosome carries about 15 000 genes, it can readily be seen that the possible combinations of genes are endless, even when children have the same parents – hence every child is a different individual, apart from identical twins, which are formed when the fertilised ovum divides into two, and so have the same chromosomes and genes. But differences in people can also occur because of environmental effects, so that even identical twins may show some variation in characteristic and development if they are brought up separately.

B = gene for BROWN EYES

b = gene for blue eyes

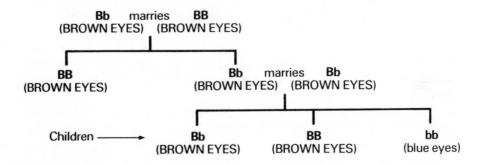

Exercise 2

Multiple-choice questions

1. If two brown-eyed parents produce a blue-eyed child, then:
(a) both parents must have had a blue-eyed parent;
(b) both parents must carry a blue-eyed gene;
(c) both parents must have had two brown-eyed parents;
(d) both parents must have had two blue-eyed parents;
(e) one parent must carry a blue-eyed gene.

2. The purpose of the placenta is to
(a) protect the baby from any foreign body;
(b) act as a cushion;
(c) digest food for the baby;
(d) enable the exchange of food, oxygen and waste products between mother and baby;
(e) make extra blood for the baby.

3. The most effective method of family-planning is:
(a) the 'pill';
(b) the rhythm method;
(c) the sheath;
(d) the inter-uterine device;
(e) withdrawal.

Essay questions

4. 'Every baby should be a wanted baby.' Elaborate this statement, and explain how this is possible in today's world.

5. Explain what factors a couple should bear in mind when planning a family.

Discussion topic

6. Is marriage really necessary? What are the advantages and disadvantages?

Suggestions for further reading

Geraldine Lux Flanagan, *The First Nine Months of Life*, Heinemann Ltd
Eric Trimmer, *Having a Baby*, Heinemann Ltd
Dennis Fox, *Facts for Life*, Macdonald Educational Ltd Granada Television
Kenneth Rudge, *Relationships*, Macmillan Education Ltd
Jacky Gillott, *Connexions – For Better for Worse*, Penguin Books Ltd
Joy Groombridge, *Connexions – His and Hers*, Penguin Books Ltd
Ellen Peck, *The Baby Trap*, Heinrich Hanam Publications
Diagram Group, *Mothers (One hundred mothers of the famous and infamous)*, Paddington
    Press Ltd

Chapter 3
Preparation for baby

Signs and symptoms of pregnancy

1. menstruation ceases – there is no period;

2. early morning sickness – may vary between slight nausea and actual vomiting;

3. lassitude and tiredness;

4. frequency in passing urine and/or constipation – this is due to alterations in muscle tone caused by the hormonal changes;

5. chemical test of urine for pregnancy is positive by about the fifth day after conception.

Ante-natal care and advice

Most women wait until they have missed their second period before consulting a doctor for confirmation of a pregnancy and the beginning of ante-natal care. However, some authorities feel that the mother should be examined earlier than this, perhaps even before pregnancy begins. This is because a healthy mother will have fewer problems during her pregnancy and has the best prospect of producing a healthy baby. Also, as the foetus is at its most vulnerable during the first twelve weeks of pregnancy, the mother, if seen early, could be warned of the possible dangers to the baby of smoking, drug-taking or exposure to any infectious disease.

Ante-natal care is mainly preventive medicine – detecting potential problems and either stopping them developing, or minimising their effects on the mother or baby. The aim of good ante-natal care is a fit mother and a fit baby at the end of pregnancy. It is of little use to deliver a healthy baby if the mother is not in a fit state to take proper care of him.

Usually the mother-to-be will first visit her own family doctor (general practitioner). Some doctors do not undertake ante-natal care, and if this is the case they will refer the mother to another doctor in the same health centre or to a maternity hospital.

On the first visit, a full examination is made of the mother's general health, as well as confirming that she is pregnant. The date of delivery is calculated by adding nine calendar months and seven days to the date on which the last menstrual period began. This last date is used because it is the one which is easily remembered. It is not usually possible to ascertain when conception actually took place, as there are no visible signs. Taking an average of thousands of pregnancies, it was found that the commonest length of pregnancy varied between thirty-eight and forty-two weeks, so that the average was forty weeks from the first day of the last menstrual period. The date of birth given to the mother is referred to as the estimated date of delivery, or EDD. The doctor will ask the mother for details of any family illness or past personal illness which may affect her pregnancy. A full examination is carried out to determine the present state of her health. This will include the following:

1. The mother's heart function is tested, because pregnancy can be a burden to a woman with a defective heart.

2. The blood pressure is measured because an abnormal blood pressure is an indication that disease is present; investigations and treatment at this stage may prevent future problems. Also the blood pressure may rise during pregnancy because of 'toxaemia of pregnancy', so it is necessary to know the mother's normal blood pressure for purposes of comparison.

3. The urine is tested for the presence of abnormalities:
(a) sugar – which may mean the mother is a diabetic needing treatment;
(b) albumen – which usually means that the kidneys are not working as efficiently as they should;
(c) pus – which indicates an infection is present in the urinary tract.

4. The blood is also tested:
(a) to determine the blood group, which is recorded so that if the mother should need a blood transfusion the correct blood can be given quickly;
(b) to determine the rhesus factor, because if the mother is rhesus negative she could produce antibodies which could affect her baby's blood, causing him to need an exchange blood-transfusion at birth. This condition more commonly affects second or subsequent babies but, if a mother is found to be rhesus negative early in her first pregnacy, it is possible to protect her future babies by giving her an injection within forty-eight hours of the birth, which will prevent her forming any antibodies;
(c) for anaemia – this can affect both mother and baby if not treated early in pregnancy;
(d) to check whether the mother is suffering from syphilis, because the baby will be affected unless treatment is started early in pregnancy.

5. A check is made for varicose veins, as these tend to become worse during pregnancy.

6. Teeth are examined and the mother is advised to go to the dentist for a check-up.

7. The size of the pelvis is checked and any abnormalities noted.

8. The mother is weighed and measured.

Arrangements for the confinement are discussed at this early visit. At present about 99 per cent of births take place in hospital although, if all is normal and her doctor agrees, the mother can choose to have her baby at home with a community midwife in attendance. Some mothers may choose to go into hospital for the delivery only and come home within forty-eight hours of the birth, provided the doctor agrees and all is well with the mother and baby. In this case, in many areas, the community midwife and doctor will go into the hospital to attend to the delivery and then the same midwife will visit the mother daily at home until the baby is fourteen days old. The choice of home delivery or a shortened hospital stay will obviously depend on there being adequate domestic help in the house, as the mother should not be doing housework.

Other mothers will go into hospital when labour begins and will stay for about six to ten days after the birth. The decision about the place of birth depends not only on the mother's choice, but also on various medical factors, because certain groups of mothers have a slightly higher risk of complications at the delivery. These mothers should be in hospital where there are facilities to deal with any problem promptly. Examples of women 'at risk' include women over thirty years of age having their first baby and diabetic mothers. In other cases, warning signs of complications such as a raised blood pressure, may occur during pregnancy, indicating that this mother would be best to have her baby in hospital.

The mother-to-be usually attends the ante-natal clinic monthly until the sixth month of her pregnancy and then more frequently for the last three months. At each visit checks are made on the mother's health. She is weighed, her blood pressure is taken and her urine is tested. Any abnormality in one or more of these tests can indicate problems needing further investigation. One of the hazards of pregnancy is the development of pre-eclamptic toxaemia which, if left untreated, can lead to fits in the mother and death of the foetus. Although a lot of research has been and still is being carried out on this condition, little is known of the cause. However if a mother shows any of the signs of the disease – raised blood pressure, albumen in the urine and excess weight gain due to water retention – rest in bed and the use of sedatives can prevent her condition deteriorating.

As the baby grows in the uterus the doctor or midwife can, by palpating the mother's abdomen, determine the position of the baby and listen to his heart with a foetal stethoscope. His size and rate of growth can also be monitored. If there is any cause for concern, an ultrasonic scanning machine can be used to check the position of the baby in the uterus and gauge its size. It will also show the position of the placenta and whether there is more than one baby.

Nearer to the estimated delivery date the midwife will check that the baby is in a good head-down position ready for birth and the head is 'engaged'. This means that the head has passed through the bony pelvis. If this is so, then the baby can be born normally, as the head is the largest part of the body at this stage in life.

All expectant parents may attend and participate in parentcraft classes held in health centres and maternity hospitals. These classes explain the process of pregnancy and birth, advise parents on the care needed during pregnancy and how to look after the baby. They usually take the form of weekly discussion groups over periods of ten to twelve weeks. Each week a different subject is discussed and this is followed by a demonstration and practice of various exercises and methods of relaxation which will help the mother to co-operate in the birth of her baby. The birth is described in detail and films are shown, so that both parents know what to expect. This is very important, and helps lessen the fear of the unknown which can cause tension, leading to increased pain in labour and birth.

During classes and at ante-natal examinations, mother is advised about the care of her health. Some topics discussed during the ante-natal period are:

1. Diet (see Chapter 6 on food). The mother must eat a good mixed diet containing protein, calcium iron and vitamins. She should not increase her consumption of carbohydrates, because this is unnecessary for the baby and will make the mother put on weight. During pregnancy the mother should not put on more than 20 lbs (9 kilos) in weight, otherwise there may be problems at the birth and the mother may have difficulty in regaining her figure afterwards. On the whole the baby will take the nutrients he needs at the expense of his mother, so if her diet is poor her health will be affected first. Iron is especially important, because in the last two months of pregnancy the baby stores enough iron to last him until he is about six months old. Consequently if the mother is already anaemic, she will become more so at this time. If, on top of this, she loses more blood than usual at the birth, she will be in a poor state of health to care for her baby. Because of this, iron tablets are usually prescribed to boost the mother's diet. Vitamin A, D and C tablets are also advised as a supplement to her diet.

2. Clothing. Clothing should be loose and comfortable, preferably hanging from the shoulders rather than the waist, which usually disappears early in pregnancy. Breasts should be supported by a well-fitting brassière, which should be checked for size at intervals because the breasts enlarge as pregnancy advances. Shoes should have medium heels and be comfortable so that the mother stands up straight.

3. Exercise and rest. Exercise is necessary and will not harm the baby, provided it is regular and the mother does not get over-tired. Cycling, horse-riding and walking are all beneficial in moderation. Rest is also important – a rest during the day with the feet up and a regular reasonable bedtime all help to keep the mother-to-be healthy and happy.

4. Care of teeth. Dental care is free for all pregnant women and they should make full use of this facility. During pregnancy the baby takes calcium for his bones and teeth. This may leave the mother short, so affecting her dental health.

5. Smoking. This should be avoided if possible because strong evidence suggests that smoking affects the baby's rate of growth. Babies born to mothers who smoke are often smaller than the average. If the mother is a chain-smoker and finds it very difficult to give up, she is persuaded to try to reduce the number of cigarettes she smokes to under ten daily.

6. Drugs. No drugs of any description should be taken by a pregnant woman, unless they are prescribed for her by a doctor who is aware of the pregnancy.

7. Maternity benefits and services are available to all pregnant women. They are as follows:
(a) free ante-natal care;
(b) free hospital care;
(c) free services of doctor, midwife, obstetrician, paediatrician and health visitor;
(d) free prescriptions until the baby is one year old;
(e) free dental care until the baby is one year old;
(f) home help services for a small charge;
(g) free milk and vitamin tablets if the family is on a low income or if there are two or more children under five years of age;
(h) Maternity Grant – this is a lump sum (at present £25) paid to the mother to help with the expenses of the birth. If twins are born, the grant is doubled;
(i) Maternity Allowance – this is a weekly sum payable for approximately eighteen weeks to expectant mothers who have been in full employment until they are twenty-six weeks pregnant. It is paid from twenty-eight weeks pregnancy until six weeks after the birth of the baby;
(j) safeguard of employment – the mother is entitled to have her job back within six months, provided she has been employed by the same firm for more than six months.

8. The layette and equipment. Planning and preparing the baby's room and buying clothing and equipment can be an enjoyable part of pregnancy which both parents can share. Shopping is best carried out during the middle months of pregnancy before it becomes too tiring for the mother. Many shops catering for babies' needs will send catalogues on request and these can be a great help. Books on baby care usually list suggested clothing and equipment. Generally it is best to buy only the minimum and then add more when the size of the baby is known. New babies are often given presents of clothing, which may duplicate clothes already bought. Babies grow very rapidly in their first few months, so that most clothing is usually outgrown rather than outworn.

There are several points to remember when buying clothing for a baby. Firstly, the materials used for the clothing should have the following qualities for comfort and safety:

(a) warmth;
(b) softness;
(c) lightness of weight;
(d) absorbency;
(e) ease of washing;
(f) non-irritating to baby's sensitive skin;
(g) non-flammable.

Natural fibres such as cotton and wool are usually found to be the most comfortable fabrics to wear because of their absorbent qualities, but cotton is not very warm and wool needs very careful washing. Some babies' skins may be sensitive to wool and find it irritating. A wool/cotton mixture, such as Viyella or Clydella, combines the good qualities of both fibres and is ideal for comfort. Man-made (synthetic) fabrics, such as nylon, terylene, acrilan, courtelle and orlon, have become very popular in recent years because of their cheapness compared with natural fibres. They have many advantages, being hard-wearing, warm, soft and light. They are also easily washed, and quickly dried, and need little or no ironing. However, their big disadvantage is that they do not absorb moisture and this makes the clothing uncomfortable, especially in hot weather. They should not be worn next to the skin because of the discomfort and also because some children develop an allergic rash from contact with synthetic fibres. But fabrics which contain a mixture of synthetic and natural fibres, such as wool and cotton, overcome many of these disadvantages. The material is absorbent and easily washed and dried, requiring little or no ironing.

Clothing for a baby should have the following qualities:

(a) It should be of simple design, so that it is easy to put on and take off.
(b) It should have easy fastenings – no fiddly ties.
(c) It should be easy to wash and iron.
(d) It should allow free movement.
(e) Seams should be flat, so there are no uncomfortable ridges.
(f) It should be suitable to the climate.

A basic list of clothing and equipment

24–36 nappies
3 pairs plastic pants
4 nappy pins (safety type)
3 vests
3 day dresses, rompers
   or all-over suits
3 nightdresses or all-over suits
3 cardigans or jumpers
3 bonnets
3 pairs mittens

3 pairs bootees
2 pram suits or sleeping bags
3 bibs or feeders
tray, bag, basket or box for toilet
   requirements
cotton-wool balls in plastic container
   with lid
soap
talcum powder
baby shampoo

2 flannels (if used)
brush and comb
nail scissors
simple baby cream, such as Vaseline
  or zinc and castor oil
3 towels
apron for mother, plastic/towelling
pail with lid for soiled nappies
bath and stand
low chair without arms
crib and mattress, sheets and blankets
  (if wanted)
cot
cot mattress with waterproof cover

6 cot sheets
4 cot blankets
1 cot spread
pram
pram mattress with waterproof cover
4 sheets (but the same sheets and
  blankets could be used for cot and
  pram)
3 blankets
1 pram cover
sun shade (canopy)
cat net
safety harness

Nappies

100% per cent cotton terry towelling. These consist of a large square which can be folded into a triangular or kite shape and pinned on the baby like a pair of pants. An alternative version now on sale is the padded triangular shape, which fits better but is more difficult to wash and takes longer to dry than a flat square. Cotton terry towelling is ideal for nappies because it absorbs a large quantity of fluid. It also washes easily and can be sterilised by boiling. Recently it has been possible to buy terry towelling nappies made of terylene, or of 50 per cent cotton and 50 per cent viscose. These are not suitable because of their poor absorbent qualities, although they wash and dry easily. When the baby passes urine, it is not absorbed into the fabric, but remains on the skin causing the nappy to rub, and results in a sore bottom.

The baby will need at least six clean nappies every day, so if they can be washed daily then twenty-four will be enough. However, if the mother's washing and drying facilities are poor, more will be required.

Muslin nappies. These are made of squares of muslin which can be folded in the same way as terry towelling nappies. They are very soft and light and can be washed and dried easily and quickly. Muslin nappies are useful for the very tiny baby, the baby with a very sensitive skin and the baby who lives in a hot climate. But they are not very absorbent because they are so thin, so they are mostly used as nappy liners for terry towelling nappies.

Disposable nappies. These are made of a pad of absorbent material which can be flushed down the lavatory after use. Some are made with a plastic outer covering which does away with the need for pants. Others are worn with a pair of plastic pants which may have a pocket to hold the pad. Disposable nappies are satisfactory in use, provided the manufacturers' instructions for disposal are carefully followed. They are invaluable when travelling or on holiday because of the time saved by not having to wash, dry and fold nappies. They are also hygienic because there is no need to carry soiled nappies home to wash. They may seem expensive, but if the cost is compared with the cost of conventional nappies, washing powder and electricity for washing machine and dryer, it will be found that there is very little difference. Moreover, if the time saved is spent with the baby, then the baby will derive considerable benefit.

Nappy liners. There are several types of liner available:
(a) Disposable tissues may be put inside the terry towelling nappy, to prevent it being badly soiled. The tissue and excreta can be shaken down the lavatory and flushed away, leaving only a wet nappy to wash.
(b) One-way liners may be washable or disposable. They allow urine to soak through to the outer nappy, whilst remaining dry themselves, so that the baby has a dry surface next to his skin. They are very useful at night because when the baby stops his night feed, he will sleep through and not be disturbed by a wet nappy. They are also useful if the baby has a sore bottom owing to his concentrated urine affecting his skin.

Plastic pants

If conventional nappies are used, plastic pants will be needed, otherwise clothing and bedding become saturated every time the nappy is wet. They should be chosen with care, making sure that the leg holes are loose enough to allow some ventilation. The more expensive ones with adjustable side fastenings are best, not only for comfort, but also because the better-quality plastics are softer and can be washed many times without deteriorating.

Vests

As vests are worn next to the skin, they should be made of cotton or a wool/cotton mixture for comfort. The easiest ones to put on are those with an envelope-shaped neck which goes over the head.

Dresses, rompers, nightdresses

These can be obtained in various fabrics, and choice depends on time of the year and climate. Cotton, wool/cotton mixture or cotton/synthetic mixture are all suitable. The clothes should be easy to put on and do up. Sleeves should be wide-fitting, preferably raglan, and seams should be flat to avoid rubbing the skin.

All-over suits

These are very popular with mothers and have the advantage of being all in one. However if they are used there are three important points to consider:

(a) They must be big enough. The 'stretch' should only be used to allow a reasonable fit, because the baby will not be able to stretch the fabric himself – instead he will be restricted by the elasticity in the suit. If he cannot move freely he will lack exercise and can become very cold. He will also feel very frustrated. A baby's bones are very soft and a too-tight garment could cause deformed feet in the same way as badly fitting shoes or socks.

(b) They should be made from cotton or a cotton/nylon mixture for warmth and absorbency. All-nylon suits are not at all comfortable.

(c) They should not be used day and night, as the skin needs ventilation. So if they are worn during the night then a dress should be worn during the day, or vice versa.

Cardigans or jumpers

These may be hand-knitted or bought. Again, a wool/nylon mixture is better than an all-synthetic material. They should be knitted into a firm, close fabric rather than too much openwork, as the baby's fingers can get caught in the wool. Raglan style sleeves are easier to put on.

Sleeping bag/dressing gown

These are very useful garments, as they can be put on like a coat and closed like a bag at the bottom. They can be used in the pram and at night so that it does not matter if blankets are kicked off – the baby will remain covered and warm. They are usually made of a brushed synthetic material and are satisfactory when worn over natural fabrics.

Bonnets, mittens and bootees

These can be hand-knitted or bought and should be made from wool or wool/nylon mixture.

Bibs and feeders

These are best made from cotton terry towelling. Plastic is not suitable because a plastic bib can easily flap up over the face and form a seal, causing suffocation.

Toiletries

These should be as plain as possible. There are many bath-time products on the market and mothers and nurses may find all the advertising claims confusing. As a general rule, a baby needs nothing other than a good baby soap for his skin, and this should be used sparingly and always well rinsed off. Baby shampoo is useful for hair washing, but again should be very well rinsed. Baby powder may be used for a light dusting after the bath. If the baby develops a dry skin, sore bottom or any other skin problem, medical advice should be sought before buying any of the preparations in the chemist's shop. A baby has very sensitive skin and can easily develop an allergy to an ingredient in a new product. Once an allergy develops, it may cause problems for the rest of his life. Some lotions, oils and creams even though promoted as being good for baby's skin, may contain complicated ingredients about which little is known of their effect on the human skin.

Cribs and cots

A crib is a small cot which may be used for the first two months of a baby's life. It is not essential and nowadays many babies go straight into a big cot. Some mothers use a carrycot placed inside the big cot for the first few weeks to make the baby feel secure.

Cots are covered by the British Standards Institution BS 1753 and there are several points which must be observed if the cot is to carry the 'kite' mark of the Institution.

(a) Spacing of bars – these should be not less than 7 cm ($2\frac{3}{4}$ in) and not more than 7.6 cm (3 in) apart to prevent a child jamming his head between them.
(b) Cot sides should be 50 cm (20 in) high measured from the top of the mattress.
(c) Dropside fastening should be safe, so that the child cannot undo it.
(d) Paintwork should be lead-free.
(e) Mattress should be firm, so that the baby cannot bury his head.

A mattress with a waterproof covering is a good buy, as it saves having to use waterproof sheets. The sheets can be of cotton/polyester in summer and cotton flannelette in winter. Fitted cot sheets which fit over the mattress are very convenient and easy to use, so worth the extra cost.

Blankets can be of wool or a wool/synthetic mixture. Cellular blankets are good because they are light in weight and warm. The warmth is due to the fact that the tiny holes trap air which acts as an insulator.

The pram

The pram chosen depends on the use made of it. There are many types on the market from very large to very small. If the pram is to be used for long shopping expeditions and walking out, then a large one, which is well sprung, would be the best choice. On the other hand, if the mother drives and wants to take the baby in the car, the type of pram which divides into a carrycot and folding wheels would be the better choice.

Again the British Standards Institution has various regulations about prams:

(a) Material used should be physically and chemically free from substances harmful to the child.

(b) Materials used should be resistant to normal weather conditions and use.

(c) Materials should be reasonably non-flammable.

(d) Brakes should be on at least two wheels and should be out of reach of the child.

(e) Wheels should be strong and well attached.

(f) Provision should be made for fitting a safety harness.

(g) Padding should be firm to prevent suffocation.

(h) Hood should be positioned to deflect rain.

(i) Inside depth should be at least 19 cm ($7\frac{1}{2}$ in) above the mattress.

(j) Design of the pram should ensure maximum stability.

(k) Soft-body prams should have fittings which are safe and will not become detached from the chassis or allow the body to fold up during use.

In addition, a shopping tray which fits under the pram, across the axles, is safer than one fixed to the handlebars, as the weight is distributed more evenly. A cat net is necessary to prevent a cat getting into the pram to sleep and so smother the baby. In summer a fitted canopy will protect the baby from direct sunshine.

The pram mattress should be firm and waterproof. Sheets and blankets are necessary, the same as those needed for the cot. As a general rule three covers are needed over the baby, as well as a sheet, so that two pram blankets and a coverlet are sufficient. In the early days a baby does not need a pillow at all, but from about four months will like to be propped up when awake to see what is going on in the world. A special 'safety' pillow can be used for this. He will need a safety harness from about eight weeks of age, because of his increasing mobility.

The baby's room

When planning the room, allowance should be made for the baby's growing interests and future activity. If possible, it should be a bright, sunny room with adequate space for play.

Walls – bright and colourful; washable; area for pictures, including child's own paintings later; area at child level can be painted with blackboard paint when baby is old enough to use chalk.

Ceiling – white will reflect light; a hanging mobile within child's field of vision.

Floor – cork tiles, plastic or linoleum are all easy to clean and provide a good surface when child is learning to walk; colourful, washable rug.

Windows – large, providing adequate ventilation; guarded by bars for safety; curtains in light, washable material, lined to keep out light when baby sleeps.

Heating – if possible a steady background heat is best. Safety factors are important here. In order of choice

(a) central heating radiators;

(b) oil-filled electric radiators;

(c) fan heater;
(d) open coal fire with an adequate safety guard.

Lighting – a central light; a bedside lamp for reading.

Furniture – this should be both sturdy and washable, as the child will pull himself to his feet by holding on to it. In addition to the cot, bath on stand and low chair: a chest of drawers for baby's clothes; a hanging cupboard; a low cupboard for the baby's toys; a low table and chairs will be useful later; a screen can protect the baby from draughts – this can be improvised by covering a two-winged clothes airer with material.

Exercise 3

Multiple-choice questions

1. The most reliable indication of pregnancy is:
(a) morning sickness;   (d) missed period;
(b) a feeling of lassitude;   (e) frequency of passing urine.
(c) fainting;

2. A routine blood-test is carried out in early pregnancy to:
(a) check blood-pressure;   (d) confirm pregnancy;
(b) see if there is any infection;   (e) check whether mother is anaemic.
(c) discover the baby's blood group;

3. When a woman is pregnant she is advised to:
(a) rest as much as possible;   (c) take up strenuous exercise;
(b) carry on normal life,   (d) refrain from intercourse;
    taking care not to get too tired;   (e) eat for two.

4. It is best to use a fabric containing natural fibres for a baby's clothes because:
(a) it washes easily;   (d) it looks pretty;
(b) it is absorbent;   (e) it comes in a variety of colours.
(c) it does not need ironing;

5. Two thin layers of clothing are better than one thick layer because:
(a) they look nicer;   (d) they are more absorbent;
(b) they are warmer;   (e) they are easier to wash and dry.
(c) thin clothes are cheaper;

Essay questions

6. What is the aim of ante-natal care, and how is this achieved? List the statutory services available to pregnant women in Britain.

7. Plan a room suitable as a nursery for a new-born baby. How could it 'grow' with the baby?

Project

8. Visit the local shops and choose a suitable layette. Give reasons for your choice of each item, including the material it is made from and the cost. Compare the cost of using conventional nappies and laundering with the estimated cost of disposable nappies.

Chapter 4
Parenthood

The birth of a baby

By the time an unborn baby has reached the thirty-eighth week he is usually in the head-down position ready for birth and the mother will have already experienced minor contractions and relaxations of the muscles of the uterus. Like all muscle fibres, the uterine ones shorten (contract) and lengthen (relax) in use, but in labour these fibres gradually shorten altogether because when they relax they do not lengthen as much as before. The process of birth consists of the gradual shortening of the muscle fibres which cause the cervix to 'thin' out and slowly open to enable the baby to pass through. At the same time the baby's head is being pushed down into the vagina by the pressure of the contractions and later in labour by active pushing by the mother. The birth of a baby is a long, slow process, and may be painful for the mother, although the amount of pain varies. The birth of a first baby takes on average fourteen hours and for a second and subsequent child it could take about eight hours.

Labour is described as being in three stages:

1. first stage – this is the longest part and lasts until the cervix is open;

2. second stage – the baby is pushed out;

3. third stage – the placenta or afterbirth is expelled.

1. First stage. There are three possible ways in which labour begins and a mother is advised to contact her doctor/midwife or hospital when any of these things happen:

(a) the onset of contractions occurring at regular intervals and gradually becoming more frequent;
(b) a 'show' – a small plug or blood-stained mucus which blocks the cervix comes away as the cervix opens (this is not always noticed);
(c) the membranes rupture ('breaking of the waters') and some of the fluid surrounding the baby gushes out of the vagina.

During this stage the mother will experience some discomfort as the contractions become more frequent. At first it helps if the mother moves around, but towards the end of this stage she will probably prefer to be lying down.

Discomfort varies from mild cramp to real pain, and various drugs can be given for relief, including gas and air administered by the mother herself. Relaxation exercises will also help to relieve some of the pain.

2. Second stage. At the end of the first stage when the cervix is fully-dilated (open) the mother usually experiences a great urge to push down with her abdominal muscles when each contraction occurs. The vagina gradually stretches as the baby's head is pushed down the canal and outside the mother's body. After the head is born, there is a pause and then with another contraction and push from mother the rest of the baby is born. This second stage may take about twenty minutes. The baby usually cries immediately. The midwife will clean his eyes and mouth with swabs and separate him from the placenta by tying the umbilical cord in two places with catgut (or synthetic material) and cutting between the ties, or she may use a clip. He is very quickly examined, wrapped in a wrapper and given to his mother to hold.

3. Third stage. There is a slightly longer pause and then the mother feels another contraction and the placenta is pushed out of the vagina. Sometimes the midwife or doctor will help this by pulling gently on the umbilical cord. There may be some bleeding at this stage from the raw area in the wall of the uterus left by the placenta. The uterus rapidly contracts, which prevents further bleeding. Sometimes a drug is administered to the mother to accelerate this contraction.

After the birth is completed the baby is weighed and measured and examined for any defects. He is labelled with a bracelet which gives his name, sex, date and time of birth. A label is also prepared for his cot which will be ready and waiting for him. His mother is encouraged to cuddle him and check for herself that the label is correct and that he is a normal, healthy baby. This is very important for 'bonding' to begin. Not only does a baby need to 'know' his mother, but she needs to get to know her baby. Father is usually present at this time even if he chose not to be there at the birth.

Other methods of birth

1. Induction. Birth can be induced by rupturing the membranes around baby, or by giving the mother an artificial hormone which stimulates contractions of the uterus. This is done mainly for one of three reasons:
(a) The baby is overdue – about a week after the EDD.
(b) The mother has toxaemia so the birth is induced early (from 3–8 weeks) to avoid complications.
(c) The placenta is beginning to fail

2. Episiotomy. A small cut, called an episiotomy, may be made in the mother's vagina to ease the birth and prevent tearing. It has to be stitched under local anaesthetic after the birth.

3. Forceps delivery. If progress is slow in the second stage of labour, or if either baby or mother is showing signs of distress, the doctor may decide to use forceps, a pair of large blades which can be put around the baby's head. The doctor can then guide the head and ease it out of the vagina. This is usually performed under a local anaesthetic and an episiotomy is needed before inserting the forceps.

4. Caesarean section. If, for some reason, the baby cannot be born through the vagina, then under an anaesthetic an incision is made through the mother's abdomen and the wall of her uterus and the baby is extracted. The placenta is also removed and then the incision is stitched up. The mother is usually in hospital some days longer and the baby may need special care for a short time, but usually both recover reasonably rapidly. Reasons for caesarean births vary, but the most common reason is that the mother's bony pelvis is too small for the baby's head to pass through. Another reason is that the placenta may be positioned in the lower part of the uterus, preventing the baby's head from advancing.

5. Breech birth. Sometimes a baby does not settle in the head-down position, but instead 'sits upright' in the uterus so that his bottom is ready to be born first. Usually this can be diagnosed in the middle months of pregnancy and the baby can be turned by pushing him through the mother's abdomen. If the mother goes into labour with a breech baby, there may be complications because when the body is born the baby may take a breath before his head is out of the vagina. Other complications, such as early separation of the placenta or compression of the umbilical cord, may cause brain damage by starving the baby of his oxygen supply.

The post-natal period

Although most mothers appear exhausted at the time of birth, because it is a period of hard work, the majority recover almost immediately. They see their baby – and it has all been worth while! However, a period of rest is necessary and usually the baby is placed in a warm cot whilst his mother is given a blanket bath and then a cup of tea. She is left then to rest and if she is too excited to sleep a sedative may be given.

The following day she can begin to care for her baby, whilst she herself is being cared for by the midwife. During the next six to ten days the mother and baby get to know one another. The mother's uterus gradually contracts to its original size and the raw area of the placental site heals up. There is a small vaginal loss which gradually ceases. A watch is kept for any fresh bleeding which indicates that the healing process is not taking place. A check is also kept on the mother's temperature, as a rise could indicate infection entering the raw area in the uterus. Strict hygiene measures are practised to prevent such infection which can have serious consequences for a mother.

The mother is encouraged to practise post-natal exercises to 'tone up' her muscles and help her regain her figure. Breast-feeding begins with the help and supervision of the midwife. The baby is weighed at regular intervals and, after a small initial loss, should begin to gain about 28g (1oz) a day if feeding is adequate.

Also during this period, mothers are shown how to care for their babies. Bathing, changing and topping and tailing, sterilising bottles and making up feeds are all demonstrated. As soon as the mother is able and confident, she is encouraged to change her baby and look after him. The baby's umbilical cord gradually shrivels up and usually falls off between the fifth and seventh day. In the meantime it must be kept dry to prevent infection so a special powder is used, and, in some hospitals, the baby is not bathed until the cord is off.

Before being discharged from hospital or care of the midwife, the baby is given a complete examination to ensure that there are no defects, because many of these can be put right at this early stage. The mother is also examined and given an appointment for a post-natal examination six weeks after the birth.

Any creative process is hard work. Not only has the mother created a new baby who has brought awesome responsibilities, but her body has undergone a tremendous change.

Following the long period of expectation, it is understandable if she should now experience a sense of anti-climax. The hormonal changes, as her body goes back to normal, cause mood swings which may make her suffer from depression. Both she and her husband may fail to understand the physical origin of these feelings, especially as the common belief is that her prevailing mood should be one of elation. Relatives and visitors tend to concentrate on the lovely baby and seldom ask the mother how she is.

Few married couples realise what is in store for them. The physical demands of the baby can be exhausting. He will need four-hourly feeds round the clock at first, and as each feed takes at least half an hour, this is a large proportion of the day. There are the additional household duties – washing, ironing, etc. – besides the usual cleaning and meal preparation. Some mothers feel overwhelmed at first by the amount of work involved. There is little energy left for the mother to treat her husband as she did before. It requires a mature man to accept this and realise that it is a temporary state of affairs. Satisfactory sexual relationships may not be resumed as soon as the husband would like, which could cause rifts. Again, the man needs to exercise tolerance and understanding.

He may have to overcome jealousy and resentment at this small creature taking over the home. Some men are unable to adapt, and react by abdicating their responsibility as a parent and resuming their former social pastimes. The mother, at this stage, is wary of baby-sitting arrangements, and in any case, lacks the energy to join her husband. This can lead to further tensions.

Fortunately most parents do adapt. The pleasure from having created a family more than counteracts the problems. If the marriage was good to begin with, the child will cement the relationship.

In the past twenty years there has been a blurring of mother and father roles, and therefore a revolution in the position of the father. Now it is accepted that he should be involved in all aspects of the ante-natal preparation, birth and ensuing care of the baby. Fathers involved in this way are found to have a much closer bond with both wife and child, leading to a close family relationship. It is important that the mother does not become so wrapped up in the baby that she excludes the father from these activities. The mother of the family is the pivot around which the family revolves, and from now on her attitudes will chart the family's future.

Her physical health is of prime importance. If at all possible, help should be provided for her during the first weeks of the baby's life. Often there is a relative able and willing to help at this time. Failing this, the social services department of the local authority can provide a home help on a doctor's recommendation. Payment is according to family income. This help relieves the mother of some of the household duties so that she can concentrate on the baby, and both she and her husband can enjoy him to the full.

The health visitor will visit after the tenth day to give advice on the care and health of mother and baby. She is a trained nurse with midwifery experience and special training in the care and development of children and the promotion of good health. She is usually attached to the practice of the mother's family doctor and visits all babies and children on his list. By law all births must be notified to the local authority which informs the health visitor responsible, so that she can visit the mother as soon as possible after her return from hospital. In many cases she will already be known to the mother because she has paid ante-natal visits or been involved in parentcraft classes. When she calls the health visitor will invite the mother to attend the local child health clinic to have the baby's development assessed. During the next five years she can, if needed, be a great source of support to the family.

Six weeks after the birth, the mother should attend a post-natal clinic where she is given a physical examination to ensure that her body has returned to its pre-pregnant state. Her doctor may check for anaemia, which is often the cause of tiredness after childbirth. This is an ideal time for the mother to be given family planning advice so that she can space her family.

Most doctors recommend a two-year gap between babies, but of course this is largely a matter of personal preference, and the mother's ability to cope. Other factors affecting parents' decisions here include the economic circumstances of the family, whether the mother is planning to return to her former career, the ages of the parents, and the ultimate size of the family they hope to have.

The growing family

Another period of adaptation for the family occurs when the second baby is born. Wisely and sensitively handled, this can be a happy and rewarding time for all concerned. It must be remembered, however, that for the first child it could be traumatic. From being the focus of all the parents' love and attention, he has to adjust to being one of a pair.

With the young child (under five) lengthy explanations about the coming baby are unnecessary. Once the pregnancy has been established at about three months, casual references to babies can be brought into conversation with both parents. There are many children's books dealing with the subject, but they should be carefully chosen to suit the child's age and understanding. Opportunities to admire babies seen on shopping expeditions, outings to the park, etc., can be used. The wise mother will not mention the new baby as though he will be a ready-made playmate. This can lead to deep disappointment. The child can be involved in practical preparations for the baby. If any equipment used for the child is to be passed on, the transfer should be done well in advance – for example, the change from cot to bed. Any other major changes in the child's future life – for instance, starting playgroup or nursery school – should also be planned in advance so as not to coincide with the actual birth. Arrangements for the care of the child during the mother's confinement should be carefully considered, especially if the child is to leave his home. The inevitable separation from mother can be made easier by accustoming him to short periods in other homes without her.

The ideal arrangement for the birth is that the baby is born at home and the older child can remain in his own home with a familiar adult. However, most doctors prefer the baby to be born in hospital, even if the mother comes home within forty-eight hours. In any case, for the child it is best to stay in his own home. If this is not possible, then the home he goes to should be one he knows.

As soon as possible after the birth of the baby, he should see his mother. Nowadays hospitals are aware of the bond between mother and child and allow unrestricted visiting. The reunion of mother and child is most important to establish the relationship; time together is needed before the introduction of the baby. Some parents like to present the child with a special gift at this time. A doll can be particularly useful in preparing the child for sharing later in the care of the real baby.

Many children find it hard to cope with their feelings when they see the closeness between mother and baby, particularly during breast-feeding and bathing. This may lead to difficult behaviour and is commonly seen in children under stress. A reversion to baby ways, such as wetting, soiling, refusing food and bedtime mutiny, may occur. This is known as regressive behaviour and can be exceedingly trying, both to the harassed mother and staff at the nursery, who frequently see children undergoing this stress in the family. The child strives by any means to gain extra love and attention. Understanding adults will realise that this is a normal and transitory stage. The child should be helped to overcome his feelings, not by punishment or projecting guilt feelings on to him, but by making time to give him complete individual attention. In the home, the father can help a great deal by showing the child the delights of being the older one. With care and forethought, the baby can to a large extent be fitted into the existing routine of the family, thus minimising disturbance to the older child. Visitors to the family can assist by showing attention to the child before going to the baby and by refraining from comments and criticisms of the child's behaviour. Great tolerance, self-control and understanding are required of all concerned adults at this time. When the child makes himself most unlovable that is when he most needs love. Physical contact, cuddles and spoken assurances of love will go a long way to counter his temporary insecurity. So will a retained 'special' bedtime routine with stories, etc., difficult though it may be to keep going. Play materials which lend themselves to expressed aggression and anger, such as dough, woodwork, sand, earth, hammer toys and so forth are also beneficial as they healthily channel the hate and resentment away from baby. Even so, it is not wise to trust the child alone with the baby. Mothers often deceive themselves that *their* child feels only love towards the new baby; even if this is so, the young child has no idea of how to express that love safely. Violent rocking, and embracing which is more akin to throttling are common; so is the 'sharing' of wildly unsuitable play materials. Fortunately babies are tough creatures and, happily, survive much rough handling, but it is sensible to avoid situations which could give rise to anxiety and tension on the mother's part, and guilt and feelings of rejection on the child's.

A nursery nurse seeking a position as nanny will often be taken on by a family at this very time. She would do well to remember that the child is being expected to accept another new face at this critical stage, and moreover will be 'forced' into her company for long periods, when he would probably much rather be with Mummy or Daddy. She may also have to cope with expectations of grandparents, and possible tension between adults in the family. She must remember the need for consistent handling of the child and must realise how badly he needs frequent contact with his mother, and assurances of what a valued member of the family he is. The baby will not suffer from a little 'neglect' at this stage; her prime concern should be the well-being of the older child. Extra trouble taken and understanding shown now will pay dividends in terms of adjustment and happiness of the whole family in the months to come.

Exercise 4

Multiple-choice questions

1. How long after the birth should the mother undergo a post-natal examination?
(a) two weeks;
(b) two months;
(c) six weeks;
(d) not at all, as long as she feels fit;
(e) six months.

2. A two-year-old exhibits regressive behaviour after the birth of his sister. To deal with him you, as mother or nanny should:
(a) smack him when he behaves 'badly';
(b) explain carefully to him why such behaviour is not acceptable;
(c) tell him he is a big boy now;
(d) ensure individual time and attention for him when the baby is asleep;
(e) find a relative or friend to take him out of the way as much as possible.

3. Who is the most appropriate person from whom to seek advice about a two-week-old baby with feeding problems?
(a) district nurse;
(b) midwife;
(c) hospital;
(d) grandmother;
(e) health visitor.

Essay questions

4. What factors would influence parents planning the timing of their second baby?

5. How should a mother prepare a child of two for the birth of a brother or sister?

Project

6. Follow the developments, in a family you know well, during and after the arrival of a second child. Note especially the domestic arrangements at the time of the birth and the older child's reaction. Study the parts played by all adults in contact with the family to help them at this period.

Suggestion for further reading

Claire Rayner, *Family Feelings*, Arrow Books Ltd

Chapter 5
Care of the young baby

Attending to a baby's needs

A newborn baby's needs are simple, but urgent and of vital importance. They appear to be mainly physical but, in keeping him clean, fed and comfortable, we are fulfilling other basic needs as well.

To achieve and maintain physical and mental health, all human beings, whatever their ages, have certain basic needs:

Physical
1. food
2. cleanliness
3. rest
4. exercise
5. fresh air
6. warmth
7. medical care
8. protection from infection and injury

Mental and emotional
9. security
10. affection
11. stimulation
12. social contacts
13. independence

Obviously, these will sometimes overlap, and during babyhood and childhood the emphasis may move from one aspect to another, but the basic needs will remain the same throughout life. So, when we plan the daily care of a baby, we must ensure that all his needs are covered. This planning is especially important in busy nurseries where a 'good' baby could easily be overlooked.

In practice it is difficult to separate the physical care from the mental and emotional needs but, for the sake of clarity, each will be dealt with separately, remembering that they all contribute to the proper care of the baby.

1. Food (See Chapter 6 for greater detail). Most normal babies will want to be fed approximately every four hours, and any routine planned would have to be arranged around the feeding schedule. Usually babies are settled into a routine before leaving hospital or the care of the midwife. Commonly this means that feeds are given at 6.00 a.m., 10.00 a.m., 2.00 p.m., 6.00 p.m. and 10.00 p.m. (and 2.00 a.m. also, if necessary). There is no need to be rigid about these times, but obviously the baby must fit in with the mother's (nursery nurse's) routine and she has other duties as well as the care of her baby.

As a general rule, if the baby wakes and cries more than three hours since his last feed, it is better to feed him early rather than let him cry until feed-time. If it is less than three hours since the last feed, then he is probably thirsty, or may need attention. He should be offered cool, boiled water, and be picked up and comforted. Should early waking and crying occur often, then it would be wise to add an extra 25 mls (1 oz) of milk to his bottle if he is bottle-fed. The breast-fed baby may need some extra milk, too. On the other hand, if the baby sleeps for more than five hours after a feed (except in the middle of the night) then he should be woken and offered his feed, because sleeping for such a long period may be an indication that he is ill.

As the baby grows older, he will establish his own pattern of feeding and sleeping, and his mother (nursery nurse) should adapt to this and become more flexible. Breast-feeding enables a mother to be more flexible over the feeding routine, but she still needs a framework so that she has time for her other duties.

2. Cleanliness. Cleanliness is very important to the health of a small baby because he is vulnerable to infection. He has not had time to build up his own resistance to infection, and the resistance inherited from his mother is by no means complete. Therefore, he needs to be protected from as many germs as possible. Germs live on our skin and all around us, especially in dirt, so cleanliness of the baby and his surroundings will help to reduce the risk of infection. The skin also needs to be kept clean to enable it to carry out its function to excrete waste products.

A high standard of personal hygiene is necessary in a person caring for a young baby, as germs can easily be passed on by dirty hands and dirty habits. It is even more important when babies are in nurseries, because infection can also be spread from one baby to another by the hands of the nurse. Handwashing by mother (nursery nurse) before handling the baby, before preparing his feed, and after changing his nappy is essential and should become an automatic action.

The baby's surroundings should be kept clean:

(a) His room should be cleaned daily and well ventilated because sunlight kills germs and fresh air will dilute their numbers.

(b) His cot and pram should be cleaned regularly, and the bedding changed frequently.

(c) Clothes need to be changed morning and evening.

(d) His nappy should be changed whenever necessary, and at least every four hours.

(e) Clothing and nappies should be washed daily and rinsed well and, if possible, dried in the open air.

(f) Nappies need to be boiled or treated with a sanitising preparation to kill germs.

(g) Special care is needed with feeding equipment which must be cleaned and sterilised after each use.

(h) Cleanliness for the baby should be incorporated in his daily routine.

Bathing baby

He will need a bath or all-over wash at one end of the day, and a 'top and tail' at the other end. This can be fitted in with the mother's (nursery nurse's) preference. Some mothers prefer to bath their babies in the morning before the 10.00 a.m. feed. Other mothers prefer the evening because Dad wants to be involved and he is often only available at this time of day. If the baby is restless and miserable in the evening, a bath may soothe him and can be a good preliminary to bedtime. When the baby gets older and begins to crawl, the evening is probably the best time for his bath, because he can get so dirty playing on the floor that this is the best way to clean him. Whenever the bath is given it is best to choose a time just before a feed, rather than after, because he needs peace and sleep following the feed to enable digestion to take place.

Bath time has other values as well as cleanliness. It is a time of contact between mother and baby when affection is shown and there is much shared enjoyment. It is also an opportunity for exercise as the baby is able to kick and splash the water with great enjoyment.

There are many variations in methods of bathing a baby, and most young mothers are shown at least one way. Some adults prefer to stand up to bath a baby, so the bath is placed on a table and a changing-pad is used beside the bath to undress the baby. Another method is for the mother (nursery nurse) to sit in a low chair with the bath on a stand in front of her. The baby is undressed on his mother's lap. This latter method gives the close contact that the baby needs and is more natural. However, many new mothers feel very unsure of their ability to hold the baby on their knees and, if this is the case, they may feel safer in using the table method.

Sitting method:
(1) Ensure room is warm – close windows and check the temperature. It should be about 21°C (70°F).
(2) Collect all the equipment needed:

low chair	soap
bath on stand	cotton-wool swabs in
bucket with lid for soiled nappy	covered container
container for other washing	paper bag for used swabs
set of clean clothes, including	shampoo
nappy	talcum powder (if wanted)
mother's apron	brush and comb
towel	nail scissors.

(3) Have baby's feed ready, if bottle-fed.
(4) Wash hands.
(5) Put some cold water in the bath.
(6) Add hot water to make the bath water the correct temperature. Either use a thermometer 38°–40°C (100°–105°F), or test with bare elbow when water should feel pleasantly warm.

(7) Put on apron.

(8) Pick up baby and undress to nappy.

(9) Wrap baby in towel, keeping his arms inside.

(10) Using first a swab dampened with bath water, then a dry one, wipe each eye separately from the nose outwards. Discard each swab after one wipe.

(11) Wash face with a damp swab. Wipe around nose and ears but do not probe into them.

(12) Dry face with corner of towel.

(13) Hold the baby under the neck and shoulders with one hand, and tuck his legs under your arms so that you can hold his head over the bath. Using your other hand, scoop up bath water to wet his hair. Add a small amount of shampoo, then wash head thoroughly by rubbing this in. Then rinse well.

(14) Move baby back on to your lap and dry his hair with the corner of the towel. NB: The shampoo should only be used once or twice a week because it tends to dry the scalp.

(15) Unwrap towel around baby and remove nappy.

(16) Place nappy in bucket with lid.

(17) If nappy is soiled, clean baby's bottom with swabs.

(18) Soap both hands and massage all over the baby's body, making sure the lather reaches all the creases – neck, under-arms, groin and between fingers and toes.

(19) Grasping the baby securely by putting one wrist and hand under his neck and shoulders and holding the arm furthest away, use the other hand to hold his legs. Lift him into the bath, releasing his legs when he is fully in the bath so that he is in a half-sitting position.

(20) The free hand can then be used to splash and rinse off all the soapy lather.

(21) If the baby is happy in the bath, let him kick and splash for a few minutes – this time should be increased as he gets older.

(22) Lift him out on to your lap and wrap loosely in the towel.

(23) Pat, rather than rub, him dry, making sure that he is dry in the creases.

(24) Discard damp towel.

(25) Smooth on a little talcum powder.

(26) Put nappy on first.

(27) Dress him and give him his bottle.

Method of 'top and tail':

(1) Collect equipment:

bowl of warm water	towel
cotton-wool swabs	clean clothes
paper bag for discarded swabs	low chair and table
soap	nappy bucket with lid
talcum	container for soiled clothes.

(2) Wash hands.

(3) Spread towel on lap and undress baby to nappy.

(4) Clean face with damp cotton-wool swabs, and dry.
(5) Clean hands of baby with swabs.
(6) Put on clean vest.
(7) Remove nappy and place in bucket with lid.
(8) If soiled, clean bottom with cotton-wool swabs.
(9) Rub soap on one hand and use this to wash nappy area thoroughly.
(10) Rinse with swabs, or a flannel may be used.
(11) Dry with towel.
(12) Smooth on a little talcum.
(13) Put on clean nappy.
(14) Complete dressing.

3. Rest – sleep. Many 'experts' claim that a young baby will sleep twenty hours a day. However, close observation of babies reveals that they vary considerably in the amount of sleep needed. A newborn baby invariably falls asleep after a feed, and should be allowed to sleep in reasonably quiet surroundings as long as he will. Many babies 'cat-nap' during the day, and when awake are content to lie watching any movement or activity around them and then fall asleep again. Crying is usually because of boredom. Therefore it is important to provide visual stimulus in the baby's surroundings to interest him when awake. His room should be colourful, with hanging mobiles moving in the air. When he is outside in his pram, put it where he can see something interesting, such as branches of a tree.

As he gets older, his periods of wakefulness become longer, and he is best put to sleep near mother or nurse during the day so that she can talk to him when he is awake. Normal household noises should not disturb him and this is better than leaving him isolated in his room. If he has enough stimulation and contact with others during the day, he should sleep well at night. It is wise to begin a regular bedtime routine because this establishes the habit of sleep. A bath or 'top and tail' can be followed by feeding and winding, and then he can be put into his cot in his own room, with a cuddle and perhaps a lullaby from nurse/mother. This will all suggest to him that it is time to go to sleep. He should then be left alone, someone should be within hearing distance. If nurse/mother hovers over him to see if he will sleep, he soon begins to realise that it is easy to get attention. Many babies have a 'sleep' cry, so if he does not settle at once it is worth waiting five minutes before going to him. Of course, he should not be allowed to get too distressed and if he is still crying after five minutes, check that he is not uncomfortable. Staying with him for a while may be necessary but he should not be taken to wherever he spends his daytime hours, or he will come to want this every night.

In the early weeks the baby may wake at four-hourly intervals for a feed but, surprisingly quickly, will adapt to night-time sleeping as soon as he is able to take enough food during the day.

4. Exercise. All babies need exercise because this encourages good circulation which, in turn, improves muscle-tone, and aids development of muscles.

All movement, including crying, is exercise, and opportunity must be given for this. The baby's clothes should be loose enough to allow free movement, especially of arms and legs. Bed clothes should not be tucked in so tightly that movement is hampered.

In the past, babies were 'swaddled' most of the day and night. They were wrapped up very tightly in a shawl, or even sewn into their clothes. It was thought that this would make a baby feel more secure. Certainly, some babies will sleep better when wrapped up, but it is no coincidence that since the practice of swaddling was abandoned, babies have shown earlier motor development. When a baby is learning to move and control his body, he needs plenty of opportunity to practise. Therefore, at some time during the day, he should be placed on a rug on the floor, without his nappy, so that he can kick and move freely. In summertime this can be done outdoors. When the baby is in his bath, time should be allowed for him to kick and splash.

As the baby gets older, and stays awake for longer periods, more of his time should be spent on the floor. A play-pen can be used for short periods, but it is better to remove valuable or dangerous objects from the room and give the child freedom to explore, roll over and pull himself up on the furniture rather than imprison him in a small area.

5. Fresh air. We all need fresh air to provide oxygen. When air is trapped in a house it becomes stale. After it has been breathed out it contains more water vapour, more carbon-dioxide and it is much warmer. There is still a good proportion of oxygen, so the effects of poor ventilation are mainly due to increased warmth and moisture which cause an unpleasant humidity. As humidity increases, human beings become distressed and, if left in these conditions for long, can become ill and eventually die. The humidity supplies micro-organisms with ideal conditions to multiply rapidly. This is why infection can spread so easily in poorly-ventilated rooms. It is especially important for the nursery nurse to be aware of this in a nursery where several babies are together in the same room.

Babies' rooms should be aired thoroughly at least once during the day by opening windows and doors to create a strong draught. There should always be a window or ventilator open, except in very cold weather. The baby should be protected from draughts by a screen.

The baby should be taken out into the fresh air every day except in extremely cold or foggy weather. In the summer he can sleep in his pram in the garden during the day.

Sunlight is very beneficial to all human beings, but care should be taken when exposing a baby to the sun. His skin must become accustomed to sunlight gradually, to avoid sunburn, so he should be protected from very hot sunshine by a sun-shade on his pram, and a hat. Starting with five minutes exposure one can increase the length of time by five minutes every day as appropriate.

6. Warmth. The new baby, emerging from the constantly controlled warmth of the uterus, has little ability to maintain that temperature for himself. His temperature-regulating mechanism is very immature and will not become fully effective for many months. In addition, he has a relatively large skin area in proportion to his weight and so can rapidly lose body heat by evaporation from the skin when exposed to cold air. As small babies do not move a lot, they will not generate much heat from exercise, either. It is important to realise that a baby who is cold can rapidly become colder. Unfortunately, the cold baby does not look cold and does not usually protest. In fact, he appears to be contented and has a healthy pink colour. It is possible for his condition to be overlooked so that he develops hypothermia, which can lead to death if undetected.

The baby should, therefore, be kept in warm surroundings, especially in the early weeks. His room should be at a temperature of 21°C (70°F) for the first two weeks of life, then it can be reduced to 18°C (65°F). A check should be kept on the temperature, especially during the night, to ensure that it does not drop below 16°C (60°F). The ideal form of warmth is central heating, but a guarded nursery fire or fan-heater would be suitable. With constant heating the room must not be allowed to become too dry – a bowl of water placed near the heat source will prevent this.

The baby's pram should be sturdy and weatherproof, and his clothing should be loose and thin to prevent restriction of movement. Natural fibres such as wool and cotton are warmer than man-made fibres such as nylon, courtelle, polyester and acrilan. Two thin layers are better than one thick one, because air trapped between the layers acts as insulation. The baby should be warm when his clothes are put on, or the clothes will only serve to keep him cold. The cot or pram can be pre-warmed in cold weather by a hot water bottle which is removed before the baby is put in. When bathing or exercising a baby, make sure the room is warm and after the bath dry him and dress him quickly. The clothes can be warmed before use on a radiator or in front of the fire. The baby should wear a bonnet when outdoors in cooler weather, as he can lose a lot of heat from his bare head. A sleeping-bag/dressing gown is useful at night, so that if the baby kicks off his blankets, he is still covered. He should not be put outdoors in very cold or foggy weather because breathing cold air will chill him rapidly, even if he is warmly clad.

To test whether a baby is warm enough, it is best to put a hand under the covers and feel his abdomen and chest which should be pleasantly warm to touch. Babies' hands and feet often feel cold, so are not a good indication of internal temperatures. If the baby is very cold, the best way to warm him up is to cuddle him, meanwhile raising the temperature in the room. Do not wrap him in more blankets, as these will only keep him cold. If he is very cold and unresponsive, then medical aid should be summoned as fast as possible.

7. Medical supervision. A baby is usually given a thorough examination after birth to ensure, as far as possible, that he is healthy and has no defects. Although it is rare to find anything wrong, it is worth examining all babies for the sake of the few who may have a defect which can probably be put right at this early stage. Even if the defect cannot be put right, it may be possible to prevent it getting worse, or to lessen the effects.

Most doctors like to examine a baby at intervals throughout the first five years, to ensure that he is developing in the normal way. Usually such examinations take place at these stages: six weeks, nine months, eighteen months and then at two years, three years and four years. Various tests can be given at different stages. For example, between six and eight months a hearing test can be carried out to ascertain whether the child has any defect of hearing. If there is such a defect, then he can be fitted with a hearing-aid, and, even if the aid does not wholly overcome the baby's deafness, it will still be immensely valuable if it lets him hear some sounds. A baby who has never heard any sounds at all will have great difficulty with language development.

Soon after birth the health visitor will call to see the mother and baby. At the first visit she will check that the mother and baby are well, and advise on the care of the baby, if the mother needs any help. Her aim is to be a friend of the family and, by giving the mother help and advice, make sure that the baby grows and develops into a healthy individual.

A health visitor is a state registered nurse who has had extra training and experience in child development and family welfare. Besides visiting the mothers at intervals, she also runs the local Well Baby Clinics and invites mothers to attend there with their babies. At the clinic the babies can be weighed and progress is checked, while mothers can meet and compare notes. This can give reassurance to a mother and help to make friends for herself and her child.

Signs of good health

clear firm skin
good colour
bright eyes
shiny hair
firm muscles
taking feeds well

sleeping well
a slow, steady weight gain
alert
interested
contented
normal development for age

Illness is rare, but there can be minor problems which may worry the inexperienced mother or nursery nurse. If there are doubts, then a health visitor or doctor should be consulted.

Hiccups

These are common in young babies and can be safely ignored.

Excessive crying

Babies vary considerably in temperament – some are placid and contented, others are active and some will cry and demand attention. If a baby is crying, go to him and pick him up and comfort him. Try to discover and correct the cause, which may be any of the following: hunger, thirst, coldness, over-heating, wet nappy, pain due to teething or colic, boredom, or it may be just that he wants his mother. This last reason may be difficult to deal with, and there are times when the only solution is to carry the baby around with you for part of the day. It is worth asking the doctor to check that the baby is well and that there is no other reason for the crying.

Colic (three-month colic)

This usually occurs in the first three months of life (hence the name) and can be very distressing. A typical case is a healthy normal baby who is contented most of the time except after the 6 p.m. feed, when he appears to be in extreme pain. He screams and draws up his knees. Picking him up and cuddling him may soothe him for a short while, as will rubbing his tummy or back or giving him a drink of cool boiled water. But, whatever you do, the screaming continues on and off all the evening. Then at 10 p.m. he takes his feed and settles down and sleeps all night. There is little anyone can do in the way of treatment, apart from nursing the baby, but the doctor can prescribe medicine which *may* help. Whatever treatment is given, this evening colic will usually last for about eight weeks, so that often by three months the problem disappears. The condition is not yet fully understood, but babies do not seem to suffer any harmful effects from it.

Teething

Teething should not cause illness but it may cause a lot of discomfort which can lower a baby's resistance to infection. Teething usually begins at about six months, and this is the stage when the antibodies the baby obtained from his mother are diminishing and he has not produced enough of his own to give him protection from all infections. Therefore it is important not to assume that any illness is 'only teething', because a serious infection could possibly be overlooked until it is too late.

Signs and symptoms of teething:
(a) dribbling (salivation);
(b) red patches on cheeks;
(c) sore chin and chest from dribbling;
(d) child bites on anything available – his fist, mother's chin and jaw, edge of cot, etc.;
(e) reluctance to suck because of pain (but not sufficient to stop him eating);
(f) sore bottom – this is due to loss of fluid by dribbling which leads to

concentrated urine causing soreness;
(g) fretfulness and misery.

Treatment:
(a) Give extra fluids to drink – cool boiled water.
(b) Give him something to bite, e.g. hard rusk, bone ring or teething rattle.
(c) Comfort him.
(d) Try one of the proprietary brands of teething jelly.

Consult the doctor if:
(a) He pulls his ears.
(b) He has diarrhoea and/or vomiting.
(c) He becomes chesty.
(d) He becomes very distressed.

8. Protection. There are two important areas of risk where a baby is especially vulnerable and will need protection:
(a) *Infection* (see Chapter 8 on Infection). The newborn baby has little resistance to the germs he will meet, so he needs to be protected as far as possible until he has developed some defences.
   (i) The best protection a baby can be given is to be breast-fed, because breast milk is uncontaminated and contains antibodies which help fight infection.
   (ii) The need for cleanliness has already been mentioned, especially the sterilisation of bottles.
   (iii) All water and milk should be boiled.
   (iv) If the baby has all his needs fulfilled, he should have good general health which will help him resist infection.
   (v) He can be immunised against specific infectious diseases, such as tuberculosis, whooping cough, diphtheria, poliomyelitis, tetanus and measles.
(b) *Accidents* (see Chapter 17 on Accidents and First Aid). Accidents are one of the chief causes of death for children under five. This is because children have little sense of danger and are often in the charge of careless adults.

As baby grows up and becomes more mobile, his natural instinct is to explore and experiment, so a safe environment must be provided to enable him to do this. Adults caring for a child must always be aware of potential dangers and should guard against them, without being too negative or frightening the child.

9. Security. A newborn human baby is among the most vulnerable and helpless of all animals, and to survive he must be cared for and protected. He is probably aware of this in a limited way, because he has an innate fear of falling, and if held insecurely will cry. This makes it difficult for the inexperienced mother or nursery nurse because the crying can make the adult even more nervous. The baby senses this and reacts by more crying. Therefore he needs to be handled in a firm, confident way to make him feel secure.

The establishment of a regular routine helps the mother/nursery nurse to be confident and sure, and as the baby learns to expect certain actions to follow others he begins to develop a trust that his needs will be satisfied. He learns to anticipate, and to recognise various signs. For example, the sound of water running and bath preparations tell him that it is nearly bathtime. Anticipation and regular fulfilment of his needs build up his feeling of security. This is especially true of feeding. Sucking milk gives a baby intense satisfaction because his hunger is satisfied and sucking is a comfort to him.

Having a stable, loving mother and frequent physical contact with her is very important to a child's inner security. His mother's pleasure in him will convey itself at a very early age and make him feel a worthwhile and important person in the home.

10. Affection. A small baby needs one person's consistent care so that he develops a deep relationship. Once this relationship is formed, he can branch out and make others and gradually widen his contacts. The quality of that first relationship is very important, because it can colour all future expectations and feelings about whether people are 'good' or 'bad'. If he is treated with love and tenderness, and all his needs are met by this person, then he will grow up with friendly feelings towards others and confidently expect that people will be kind to him.

It does not seem to make a difference to the child's well-being and development whether this first relationship is with his own mother or a substitute – such as a nursery nurse – provided this one person cares for him consistently for the first few months of his life.

From about four weeks, the baby recognises his 'mother' and will smile and begin to make noises when she leans over him. This brings a response from his mother and leads to a two-way communication. This is part of the process known as 'bonding', and we know from recent research that this is just as important for the mother as for the baby. It is seen also in the animal kingdom where, if the baby is separated from its mother for a period of time, the mother may completely reject it.

Among humans lack of bonding can sometimes be seen in cases of concealed parental violence (baby battering). Investigations shows that the children who suffer in this way were often born prematurely and received special medical care which caused an unnatural separation from their mothers in the early weeks of life when bonding should take place.

Fortunately, most parents find it easy to love and show their love to their baby. But if there should be a feeding problem, excessive wakefulness or constant crying, then it is important to seek help and advice. If not dealt with, these problems can lead to feelings of failure and fatigue which may end in the mother's rejecting her child.

The growth of love between mother and child is encouraged by close physical contact, which happens naturally as she looks after the child's physical needs. But there should be time, too, for face-to-face contact, talking and singing to the baby, and the enjoyment of playing together. It is not a question of 'spoiling', but of giving the baby the emotional necessities of life. Of course, he should be fed and allowed to sleep, but when awake he needs the company of his mother and family so that he knows where he belongs. He should not be left alone to cry for hours 'so that he will learn to amuse himself'.

Finally, lack of affection and stimulation can affect growth and development. Children in institutions, who are looked after by a variety of people, are often small for their age and backward in many aspects of development, especially walking and speech. Some of these babies, who have never been mothered, later develop severe personality disorders. But, now that the effects of lack of affection are understood, people are realising that institutions should be smaller and more like a normal home. The children are placed into 'family groups', and each group has a 'mother' to look after them. Students in day and residential nurseries will be conversant with family grouping and realise the importance of the 'mother figure'. By caring for her children over a period of time, she can create an invaluable mother/child relationship and this makes all the difference between looking after their physical needs and really 'caring' for them.

11. Stimulation (play). All human beings need stimulation in order to learn about the world around them, and young babies are no exception. In the very early days of his life, a baby will appear just to sleep and feed, and not need stimulation, apart from that caused by hunger. However, even a newborn baby is awake for short periods so from the beginning ways should be found to make his environment stimulating and interesting.

Stimulation of a baby's senses should start as early as possible. By seeing, hearing, touching, tasting and smelling he experiences many objects, events and sensations. At first they make little sense, but gradually he is able to sort them out and use the information to form ideas about the world.

Sight

A baby can tell the difference between light and dark at birth and can see, but barely follow, a moving object. From about two weeks, the baby will gaze at his mother's face when she talks or attends to him. By six weeks he recognises her and smiles at her.

At birth a baby's eyes tend to work separately but, from six weeks, he is gradually able to use them efficiently together. By the time he is three months old, he can focus on an object and follow its movements quite well. So, from early days, as we have mentioned, the baby should have some visual stimulation – colours to look at, a hanging mobile, which will move gently in any current of air, and toys such as strings of beads strung across the pram. When his pram is out of doors it should be placed so that he can see something interesting, such as trees and people, when he awakes.

His mother, or nursery nurse, should spend time talking to him, allowing him to gaze at her face. Later, as he becomes more active, brightly coloured, well-designed toys should be provided for play on the floor.

Hearing

Hearing sounds, and responding to them with his own noises, are the beginnings of a baby's speech.

At birth he can only hear high-pitched sounds but, by ten days, he can hear all sounds audible to the human ear. From about three months he begins to turn his head, trying to see where sounds come from; he can also make all the sounds necessary for speech. By six to seven months he can locate sounds fairly accurately.

To stimulate speech development, babies should be talked to and placed where they can hear voices around them. A baby enjoys the sounds of family activity and will respond when someone talks to him, by making his own noises in reply. As he grows older, he begins to experiment and 'play' with his own voice. There is no need for absolute quiet when a baby is asleep; he can sleep undisturbed through all normal domestic noises in the same way that people living near a railway line are able to sleep with trains thundering past.

One of a baby's first playthings is a rattle, and he will react to the sound of it by first stiffening, 'quieting' and, later, by kicking and using his voice. Musical boxes and bells also stimulate a baby with their familiar, enjoyable sounds. Attractive musical sounds appeal to babies and, from early days, they can be soothed or settled to sleep by mother or the nursery nurse singing a lullaby.

Touch

A baby's skin is sensitive to touch, and very early in life he responds with pleasure to stroking and patting and the feel of bath water. Later, he enjoys being tickled and curls up in anticipation. His lips are especially sensitive, and this, combined with *taste*, makes him enjoy sucking, especially at the breast.

Sucking is necessary to a baby, not only for satisfaction and comfort, but also for finding out more about things than his senses of sight and hearing can tell him. A baby uses his sense of touch to find out more about himself by sucking his hands and, when he can manage it, his feet. As soon as he can hold an object he attempts to get it to his mouth and feel it with his lips and tongue. Touch teaches the baby the difference between a soft, woolly blanket and a smooth, cold rattle. Therefore toys with different textures should be provided for him to explore in this way.

Smell

A baby's sense of smell reinforces his visual and aural impressions. He learns to associate people, and things, with their particular odours. The smell of his mother's body becomes as familiar to him as the sight of her face or the sound of her voice.

The stimulus that adults give stirs up curiosity and enthusiasm in a baby and helps him become mentally alert. A baby should be given the chance to use all his senses. He needs freedom of movement and space to move around in, a familiar adult to talk to, and a selection of toys suitable for his age and ability.

Playthings for a baby should be chosen carefully, bearing in mind the following:

(a) colour – bright, primary colours attract the eye;
(b) safety – no sharp edges or loose pieces, no dangerous wires, eyes securely attached in cuddly toys, lead-free and colour-fast paint, shatterproof;
(c) hygiene – washable or easily cleaned;
(d) size and weight – not too large or too heavy for a baby to handle, not too tiny or it may be swallowed;
(e) shape – interesting and varied, suitable for a baby to hold;
(f) texture – interesting varieties;
(g) quantity – not too many toys should be provided at the same time, as this can be confusing.

Suggestions for play materials

(a) *0–3 months:* mother's voice, own voice, mobiles and lightweight rattles (to be hung where they can be seen), strings of beads across the pram, musical box, music;
(b) *3–6 months* (during this period the baby learns to grip and relax, and can hold toys): bath becomes enjoyable – kicking and splashing, bath toys, plastic cups, rattles – manufactured or home-made, bell-on-a-stick, coloured beads on a string, teething rings, teddy bear;
(c) *6–9 months* (during this period the baby can sit up and may crawl): finger-plays and games – e.g. 'This little pig went to market', saucepans with lids, wooden spoons, bricks and blocks, ball, drums, cotton-reels, musical toys, more bath toys including colander, measuring jug, sponges and flannel;
(d) *9–12 months* (during this period the baby becomes mobile – crawls, creeps or even walks): baskets of oddments of different textures, push-and-pull toys, push-along baby walker, strong books, small toy cars, rag doll, old handbag.

12. Social contacts. At first, the newborn baby needs only his mother or mother substitute. But as he grows older his interests widen to include his father, and then his brothers and sisters. Later, familiar adults such as grandparents, aunts and neighbours are greeted with smiles and gurgles. His mother remains his anchor and, during his first year, he always turns to her for reassurance and approval. He should be given opportunities to meet other people, and watch children playing – for example, in shops and supermarkets and parks, and in other people's houses.

13. Independence. A young baby is wholly dependent on his mother or mother-substitute, but gradually he becomes less helpless and, over the years of childhood, steadily develops the ability to take care of himself.

Part of the skill of being a parent is to let a child develop naturally as an independent being, whilst protecting him from any adverse consequences. Letting the child learn new skills when he is ready to do so, taking over when he is tired or 'just not in the mood', takes skilful observation, understanding and knowledge of a child's character. But it is of great importance, because we now know that if a child is not allowed to practise a skill when he is ready, it will take him far longer to learn.

Exploration is an important biological drive and begins very early in life, so that the baby should be allowed the freedom of the floor to kick and roll over, crawl and walk. Practice is necessary for normal physical development, and freedom to experience things first-hand is essential for emotional and intellectual development.

Planning a routine

All these various needs have to be considered when planning a baby's routine. We must also remember that mothers and nursery nurses have their own needs and should have time to pursue them. A mother is a wife as well, and will need time for her husband. She also has housework, cleaning, washing, shopping and cooking, all to be done during the day.

Most babies are settled into a feeding routine by the time they leave hospital, so that it is a question of fitting the other needs into a daily programme.

Suggested daily routine for a baby of under six months

6 a.m. (or when baby wakes): change nappy; feed; sleep.

9.30 a.m.: top and tail, to be followed by:

10.00 a.m.: feed; sleep – outside in pram if possible.

11.00 a.m.: baby can be taken out shopping, or to the park in his pram.

2.00 p.m.: change nappy; feed; sleep; when he wakes, place him on the floor and allow him to kick. Talk to him.

5.15 p.m.: prepare bath and bath baby, allowing time for playing in the bath.

6.00 p.m.: feed; sleep.

10.00 p.m.: change; feed; sleep.

Exercise 5

Multiple-choice questions

1. A baby is teething when suffering from the following signs and symptoms:
(a) raised temperature, and misery;
(b) dribbling and rubbing his gums;
(c) crying most of the night and pulling his ears;
(d) diarrhoea and vomiting;
(e) a 'chesty' cold.

2. Young babies sleep:
(a) twenty out of the twenty-four hours;
(b) five minutes at a time;
(c) twelve hours at night;
(d) according to their individual needs;
(e) best in very quiet surroundings.

3. Which of the following statements is correct?
(a) A baby should be put outside every day, regardless of the weather.
(b) A baby should be put outside every day, except in very cold or foggy weather.
(c) A baby should never be put outside.
(d) A baby should never be put outside in winter.
(e) A baby should be taken out for a walk every day.

4. A baby of under three months would be attracted to a plaything because:
(a) it is safe;
(b) it is expensive;
(c) it is improvised;
(d) it is colourful;
(e) it is washable.

5. A mother should talk to her baby:
(a) when he can understand language;
(b) when he begins to respond to her;
(c) from birth;
(d) not for at least six months – it's a waste of time;
(e) when he says his first word.

Essay questions

6. What are the basic needs of a young baby of under six months? How can these be met in the day nursery?

7. How does a mother show affection to her baby? What could be the effects of lack of care?

Suggestions for further reading

Ronald and Cynthia Illingworth, *Babies & Young Children*, Churchill Livingstone
Mary and Richard Gordon, *A Baby in the House*, William Heinemann Ltd
Hugh Jolly, *Commonsense about Babies*, Times Newspapers Ltd
Penelope Leach, *Baby and Child Care*, Michael Joseph Ltd

Chapter 6
Food

To understand the principles of planning the feeding of babies and young children, the student must know the component parts of foods and how they are digested and used in the body.

Food is found in many forms and must be broken down so that the body can absorb it and then reform it into a state that it can use. For example, carbohydrate is converted into simple sugars, which can easily be absorbed and then used for energy.

We need food for various reasons:
1. to form new body cells for general growth; ✷
2. to repair any damaged body cells;
3. to provide us with energy:
(a) to maintain body temperature;
(b) for all muscle movements.

Digestion

Food enters the body and travels through the alimentary tract (digestive system), a long hollow tube stretching from the mouth to the anus. Different parts of the tube perform different functions and may differ in shape. Food travels along the tube by peristalsis, a muscular churning action which pushes the food onward.

There are two types of digestion.

1. Mechanical. The breaking down of food by teeth and peristaltic action which grinds it into a soup-like consistency.

2. Chemical. At various stages in the alimentary tract fluids called enzymes mix with the food and cause chemical reactions which split complex food into simple forms (see diagram).

Once food is broken down it can be absorbed through the walls of the small intestine and blood vessels into the bloodstream. From there it is taken to the liver where it is re-formed into substances which the body can use and distributed by means of the bloodstream to wherever it is needed. The parts of food which cannot be digested, for example, roughage, collect in the lower part of the large intestine (rectum) and when sufficient in amount are excreted through the anus as faeces. This usually occurs every twenty-four to forty-eight hours. All the time

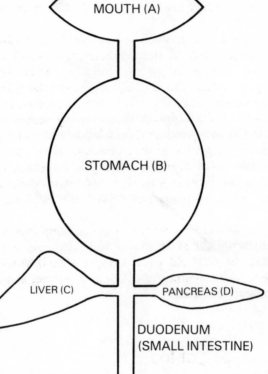

(A) *Mouth:*
(a) teeth – break down food;
(b) tongue – rolls food into ball;
(c) saliva – starts digestion of carbohydrates.

(B) *Stomach* – churns food:
(a) hydrochloric acid – renders food acid; kills some germs;
(b) rennin – clots milk; starts digestion of milk;
(c) pepsin – starts protein digestion.

(C) *Liver* – bile sent to duodenum; digests fats

(D) *Pancreas* – enzymes to digest carbohydrates and fats.

(E) *Small intestine:*
(a) enzymes to complete digestion of starch and protein;
(b) absorption of broken-down food

(F) *Large intestine:*
(a) absorption of water;
(b) excretion of waste products

MOUTH (A)

STOMACH (B)

LIVER (C)

PANCREAS (D)

DUODENUM
(SMALL INTESTINE)

SMALL INTESTINE (E)
approximately 7.3m (24ft)

LARGE INTESTINE (F)

RECTUM

ANUS

that the residue of food remains in the large intestine water is being absorbed from it, so if there is a delay in emptying the rectum the waste products become firmer and harder and, when eventually evacuated, painful. This is known as constipation.

Digestion takes place all the time and the whole process is delicately balanced and synchronised. We feel hunger when the stomach is empty – usually about four hours after a meal. This gives us an appetite for food. When food is anticipated by the sound of preparations, the smell of cooking and the sight of a meal, saliva is produced in the mouth, ready to start the digestive process, and the stomach, too, produces its enzymes. An increased blood supply is needed by the stomach to give it the extra energy to cope with the meal. If the body is involved in other strenuous activities when digestion in the stomach is taking place, the extra blood supply is not available and indigestion may follow. For example, if a child is jigging up and down in his chair, or if he is seriously worried about his ability to eat his 'nice' dinner, any extra energy will be used up in these activities instead.

It is, therefore, best to eat at regular intervals, approximately four to six hourly. A quiet period before a meal to relax and anticipate, and a calm, unhurried atmosphere during the meal aid good digestion. Meals should be attractive and well presented, with a contrast of colour and texture, and meal times should be enjoyable, social occasions.

Types of food

There are many different types of food or nutrients and the student must know the classification of foods and what each type does in the body. The charts on the following pages provide a summary.

This may look a formidable list, but a study of the main sources of the nutrients will show that most people eat most of the foods mentioned. There are many fads and customs about diet, but nutritionists and dietitians generally agree that mixed diets are best. When religion forbids the eating of certain foods then alternative sources of the nutrient are usually found, so that the diet is balanced. If children are offered a wide variety of foods, they will instinctively choose a diet which is best for them, provided they have not been given an excess of sugar early in life and so developed a craving for sweetness.

It is possible to measure the *energy content* of food and this is expressed in kilojoules or the more familiar calories. We can estimate the amount of energy needed by a person, taking age, sex and occupation into account. Again, this can be expressed in kilojoules. To balance the diet the two figures must match.

You will see from the charts that the main energy-giving foods are fats and carbohydrates. It is possible to use protein as an energy source as well, but this is very wasteful of an expensive resource. We know from research that a certain

Name	Some main sources	Function	Effect of too little	Notes
Proteins			if early in life when brain is developing rapidly, may prevent child reaching his intellectual potential.	Made up of any combination of 22 amino-acids, 8 of which are essential to man. Excess protein is used as energy source or excreted in urine.
(a) Animal proteins	meat fish eggs cheese milk	1. to build new body cells for growth; 2. to repair wear and tear in body cells.	1. poor growth and development; 2. poor healing powers. *Extreme* kwashiorkor – death	Contain all 8 essential amino-acids.
(b) Vegetable proteins	soya bean peas beans lentils nuts			Contain only some of the 8 essential amino-acids so good variety must be eaten.
Carbohydrates	sugar flour	to provide energy and heat.	1. lack of energy; 2. thinness; 3. feel cold.	Excess is stored as body fat.
Fat	lard olive oil butter cheese nuts meat fat	1. to provide energy and heat; 2. to carry fat-soluble vitamins; 3. to form padding in body, for example around kidney; 4. to make food more palatable.	1. lack of energy; 2. feel cold; 3. thinness; 4. vitamin A and D deficiency.	

Anaemia

Rickets & Dental Caries

Minerals				
Iron	liver eggs chocolate meat	forms haemoglobin in red blood cells which carry oxygen around body.	anaemia: pallor; breathlessness; lack of energy.	
Calcium	milk cheese butter bread flour	1. to build strong bones and teeth; 2. aids clotting of blood when injured; 3. to aid normal working of muscles.	1. rickets (bones fail to harden); 2. dental caries; 3. delayed blood clotting; 4. cramp in muscles.	Works together with vitamin D and phosphorus.
Phosphorus	milk cheese fish oatmeal	1. to helps build strong bones and teeth; 2. needed for the formation of body enzymes and all body tissue.		Deficiency rarely occurs alone because calcium will also be deficient.
Iodine	sea foods water supply vegetables may be added to salt	working of the thyroid gland which regulates use of food in body.	*Adult* goitre – enlarged thyroid gland. *Baby* – cretin.	
Sodium chloride (salt)	added to food kippers bacon	to maintain concentration of blood.	cramp in muscles.	too much: thirst; dehydration.
Potassium	cereals	needed for growth.		

Name	Some main sources	Function	Effect of too little	Notes
Fluorine	water supply may be present naturally or added artificially	to combine with calcium in teeth so making enamel more resistant to decay.	dental caries.	
Vitamins				
A, fat soluble	milk butter cheese cod liver oil margarine	1. to promote growth; 2. aid to healthy skin; 3. prevention of poor night vision.	1. retarded growth; 2. poor resistance to infection especially skin infections; 3. poor night vision.	Animals can make vitamin A from carotene.
Carotene (red and yellow vegetables and fruit)	carrots tomatoes apricots			
B (group) water soluble	yeast marmite wheatgerm milk meat green vegetables	1. to aid healthy working of muscles and nerves; 2. to aid conversion of carbohydrate to energy and iron to haemoglobin.	1. wasting of muscles; 2. loss of appetite; 3. digestive disturbances; 4. anaemia etc.	There are at least 9 'B' vitamins.

C water soluble	oranges lemons blackcurrants green vegetables	1. to act as 'cement' for bone, skin and blood; 2. to aid resistance to infection.	1. scurvy (bleeding under skin, gums); 2. poor resistance to infection.	Easily destroyed by heat.
D fat soluble	milk butter cream egg yolk margarine cod liver oil sunlight	to combine with calcium for bone and teeth formulation.	1. rickets – bones fail to harden; 2. dental decay.	vitamin D can be made in skin by the action of sunlight on substance in skin
Roughage	cell walls of vegetables (cellulose) apples celery bran	help digestion by adding bulk to food which stimulates peristalsis.	constipation; diverticulitis; ? bowel cancer.	
Water	present in all foods	makes up 70 per cent body tissue. necessary for all the workings of the body and to help eliminate waste products.	thirst; constipation; dehydration; death.	

amount of protein is necessary, varying according to a person's age. For example, a young baby will need a high proportion of protein in his diet because he is growing rapidly and needs material for new body cells. On the other hand a person in middle age will need only enough protein for repair of wear and tear.

So diets are planned by first calculating a person's protein requirements in kilojoules, and then making up the rest of kilojoules by adding fruit and vegetables, fats and carbohydrates, making sure that enough roughage, vitamins and minerals are included.

However, if a person eats enough food to feel satisfied, and remains healthy with a static weight, then he must be having a satisfactory diet.

Nursery nurses are not expected to be experts but they do need to know how to plan a suitable diet. The following is a useful guide to the daily needs of adults and children. We begin with a basic amount of protein for the average adult, add fruit and vegetables and then make up the energy requirements, as needed, with carbohydrate and fats. Obviously a manual-worker will need more energy-giving foods than a female clerk but both will have the same basic protein requirements. Pregnant women, adolescent children and children under seven need extra protein because of their growth requirements. A child under seven in fact needs more protein than his father.

DAILY FOOD NEEDS OF NORMAL ADULT

Protein
285 ml (½ pint) milk
1 egg
28 g (1 oz) cheese
56–84 g (2–3 oz) fish
serving of nuts
peas, beans or lentils
50–100g (2–4 oz) meat
570 ml (1 pint) water

any 3 items of protein (3 of one kind or one each of 3); any 3 servings of fruit and vegetables

Fruit and vegetables
orange
grapefruit
apple
potato
swede, carrot, cabbage

Sugar and preserves – enough to make food palatable. Other carbohydrates (flour, bread, cake, etc.) – variable according to energy needs and appetite. Fats – enough to make food palatable.

1. Pregnant women. They will need extra protein, calcium, iron and vitamins. Therefore add to normal adult diet: 570 ml (1 pint) milk, 1 egg, 1 orange, vitamin A and D tablets, iron tablets (if prescribed by a doctor).

2. Lactating women. They will need extra fluids, protein, calcium and vitamins.
Therefore add to normal adult diet: 570 ml (1 pint) milk, vitamin A and D tablets.

3. Children one to five years. They will need extra protein for growth, extra calcium for bones and teeth.
Therefore add to adult diet: 285 ml ($\frac{1}{2}$ pint) milk, vitamins A, D and C in the form of drops.

4. Infants from birth to one year. The very rapid rate of growth during the first year of life means that small babies need a large amount of protein in their diet. They also need some carbohydrate and fat for energy, some calcium and all the vitamins.

Breast-feeding

All a baby's nutritional requirements can most easily be provided during the first four to six months by breast milk with the addition of vitamin A, D and C drops. From four months onwards the baby also needs iron, which can be provided by the addition of other foods such as egg yolk, liver and meat during the weaning period.

Breast milk is ideal for babies; not only does it contain almost all the nutrients they need, but the protein contains all the essential amino-acids in the correct proportion for the human body. Breast milk is therefore easily absorbed, needing very little digestion. There are many other advantages to breast-feeding, which can be listed as follows:

(a) The carbohydrate in breast milk is in the form of lactose, which is not sweet to taste, so avoids the danger of the baby developing a craving for sugar.
(b) The milk is unlikely to be contaminated, as it comes straight from mother to baby.
(c) Breast milk is at the correct temperature.
(d) It is economical.
(e) Very little preparation is required.
(f) Breast milk contains protective antibodies and vitamins which help protect the baby from infection.
(g) There is evidence to suggest that a breast-fed baby is protected from developing an allergy.
(h) Breast feeding gives the ideal mother and baby contact which aids 'bonding' and therefore the baby's emotional development.
(i) The baby must suck vigorously in order to obtain milk and this helps good jaw development.
(j) Breast-feeding helps the mother's figure to return to normal by causing the uterus to contract more rapidly.
(k) Breast-fed babies very rarely develop obesity.

The majority of mothers could breast-feed their babies if they wished. However there may be problems in the beginning and the mother will need encouragement and help to establish good breast-feeding. During the ante-natal period it is important for the positive aspects of breast-feeding to be emphasised, so that the mother has an optimistic approach to the subject. Most normal babies will turn instinctively to the breast and suck and, if the mother is relaxed all she need do is guide her baby to her nipple. Problems arise if the mother becomes tense and anxious, because this will be communicated to her baby.

Occasionally the baby may be sleepy and uninterested during the first few days. Problems may then arise because the flow of milk is stimulated by vigorous sucking. Other problems which can occur include poor nipple formation, sore nipples and a temporary excess or shortage of milk. Although the baby is put to the breast soon after birth, the milk does not appear immediately. At first a fluid called colostrum is produced. This is very valuable to the baby as it contains many antibodies. About the second or third day the mother may experience discomfort as the milk 'comes in'. Expert help is usually given in maternity units and most problems can be overcome.

By the time the mother and baby leave the care of the midwife, breast-feeding should be well established. The baby is usually being fed every four hours and is sucking for ten minutes on each breast at every feed-time, although a small baby may be fed three-hourly at first. The baby is fed during the night as well as the day, but this is usually discontinued by the baby himself at about four to six weeks of age when he can take enough milk during the day to last all night.

Requirements for breast-feeding
(a) low, comfortable chair;
(b) a drink for mother;
(c) a clock in sight;
(d) a tray containing bowl of water, swabs in jar with lid, container for soiled swabs, soft towel.

Method
(1) Baby should be changed and made comfortable.
(2) Mother should wash her hands and then clean her nipples with swabs and water, drying them carefully.
(3) She should sit comfortably with baby on her knee, leaning slightly forward and guiding the baby to her breast – a pillow on her knee under the baby may help to get baby in the right position.
(4) The baby will 'fix' by opening his mouth wide and taking the nipple far back into his mouth. Sucking is a 'munching' action with the lips behind the nipple.
(5) The baby's nose should be kept free to enable him to breathe.
(6) The baby should be offered alternate breasts at each feed. Ten minutes sucking at each breast will be sufficient. A pause is needed after the first ten minutes, and when feeding is complete, in order to bring up any air (wind) swallowed with the food. To bring up baby's wind:
    (i) Support him sitting on your knee by placing one hand on his tummy. Use the other hand to rub his back gently until he 'burps'; OR
    (ii) Put the baby over your shoulder and gently rub his back.

Signs of adequate feeding. Most mothers worry about whether the baby is getting enough milk, but there are several pointers which indicate that he is satisfied:
(a) He will be contented and will sleep most of the time between feeds.
(b) He will gain weight steadily at the rate of 115 to 225 g (4 to 8 oz) a week.
(c) His stools (faeces) will be soft, yellow and inoffensive, and may be infrequent. (This is because there is very little residue from breast milk.)

Signs of underfeeding
(a) Misery – the baby may cry a lot and will probably wake one to two hours after a feed.
(b) The baby will look anxious and worried.
(c) The weight gain will be small – under 56 g (2 oz) a week.
(d) His stools will be small and dry and may be green.
(e) He may become too lethargic to cry.

Test weighing. If there is any doubt about the adequacy of feeds then the amount of each feed can be measured by test weighing. The baby is weighed just before his feed and then immediately after, without changing clothes or nappy. Subtract the first weight from the second and this will give you the amount of milk taken. To be accurate this should be recorded over twenty-four hours and averaged out.

Average requirements. For estimating a baby's food requirements, we use the following formula:

$2\frac{1}{2}$ fl oz milk per pound body weight over 24 hours;
or 150 ml milk per kilogram body weight over 24 hours.

For example:
A 4.5 kg (10 lb) baby requires:
       700 ml (25 fl oz) milk per 10 lb body weight over 24 hours.
       The 700 ml is divided into 5 feeds for the 24 hours
       = 140 ml (5 fl oz) feed.

Some babies will require up to 25 ml (1 fl oz) more in each feed to satisfy them.

Insufficient milk. If the baby is not getting enough breast milk, then the first thing to do is to reassure the mother that this often happens for a temporary period and that it is possible to increase the milk supply by various measures:

(a) Ensure that the mother is getting plenty of rest and not too many visitors. Provide household help.
(b) Encourage mother to drink more: Milk, milky drinks, 'Complan', beer, etc.
(c) The baby should be offered extra milk (of the proprietary kind sold for bottle feeding) to make up the correct amount after each feed. He should still be put to the breast to suck for ten minutes each side, as sucking stimulates the

breast to produce more milk. Extra milk should be given immediately afterwards, either by spoon or in a bottle. This is known as complementary feeding and can be continued for one to two weeks. In most cases it will be enough to encourage extra milk production, so that the baby will in time refuse the complementary feed.

However, if these measures do not succeed then it may be necessary to change to bottle-feeding. If a change from breast-feeding to bottle-feeding is decided upon, then it should be achieved gradually by substituting one bottle for one breast-feed each day until the baby is having all feeds by bottle. The mother's breast milk will then dry up naturally as the baby ceases sucking.

Artificial or bottle feeding

Some mothers are unable to produce enough milk for their babies, especially in the case of twins; other mothers do not wish to breast-feed at all, so that a substitute has to be found. The word 'substitute' is used deliberately, because even in this modern age, we cannot make a perfect copy of breast milk.

Most artificial feeds are based on cow's milk because this is readily available. If we compare the composition of cow's milk with breast milk we notice several differences. The percentages are approximate.

		Breast milk %	Cow's milk %
Protein {	Casein	1	3.4
	Lactalbumin	1	0.5
Sugar		7	4.0
Fat		3.5	3.5
Mineral salts		0.2	0.7
Water		87.3	87.9

The main differences are in the protein, sugar and mineral salt content. The protein is not only increased in amount in cow's milk but there is a change in proportions. Instead of equal small amounts of casein and lactalbumin there is three times the amount of casein and the lactalbumin is reduced by half. As casein is a difficult protein to digest, this amount may cause problems to a baby.

For many years babies were fed on cow's milk modified in the following way:

Water was added to dilute the protein, the milk mixture was boiled to make the casein more digestible and sterilise the milk, and finally cane sugar was added to make the sugar content similar to that of breast milk. The mineral salt content was ignored, as it was thought that the baby could excrete any excess. When dried milk was introduced, the milk was modified in a similar way before being dried – the drying process helped to break up the casein and rendered it germ-free so that it could be kept for a much longer period. Some dried milk had some of the fat content removed and was known as 'half cream' milk, which was suitable for very small babies. Evaporated milk was also used, with similar modifications.

The next development in baby feeding was the introduction of 'humanised' milks, which were spray-dried instead of roller-dried as in the past. The result was more like breast milk, with a finer curd and therefore more easily digested. Being spray dried, the milk powder was much easier to mix with water. These milks had vitamins and iron added as well, but the natural mineral content remained the same as straight cow's milk.

However, the majority of babies thrived on ordinary dried milks, which for many years were thought to be satisfactory substitues for breast milk. But in the early 1970s research began to suggest that young babies' kidneys have only a limited ability to get rid of excess mineral salts. Furthermore, some have even less ability than others. If the kidneys cannot excrete excess mineral salts, the body gradually becomes overloaded and this imbalance can cause illness. In fact there was evidence to suggest a link with sudden 'cot deaths' which occasionally occur in bottle-fed babies under three months of age.

In older children and adults, excess mineral salts (which include common salt) can be excreted in the urine by the kidney, using water already present in the body cells and bloodstream. This leads to thirst, which can easily be satisfied by drinking water, so that the important water balance of the body is maintained.

If a young baby becomes thirsty he cannot ask for water. He can only cry. Most mothers assume the baby is crying because he is hungry and respond by giving more milk which he takes eagerly because of his thirst. But the milk only serves to increase the burden, because it contains more mineral salts. This situation can be exacerbated if the baby is losing fluids for any reason – for example diarrhoea or a runny nose due to a head cold. Inaccurate measuring or adding extra milk powder when making up milk feeds is another danger, for it will make the milk too concentrated.

To avoid these problems it was recommended in a government report in 1976 that all babies under six weeks of age should be fed on breast milk or milk with a low mineral salt content. Humanised milks were rapidly adapted so that the mineral salt content was the same as in breast milk. These milks include SMA (Gold Top), Osterfeed and Premium Cow and Gate and, in practice, most babies stay on these milks until they are fully weaned. A baby's feed can be made by the method below. But it is always most important to follow the manufacturers' instructions.

Requirements
(a) milk powder and scoop;
(b) a container of sterilising fluid in which is immersed:
    (i) wide-necked feeding bottle;
    (ii) screw collar and cap;
    (iii) 2 teats;
    (iv) 1 plastic spatula.

For cleaning bottle after use:
(c) a bottle brush;
(d) detergent;
(e) salt.

NB: Milk is an ideal medium for the growth of germs so cleanliness is essential to prevent infection. Dried milk should be kept in a covered container in a cool place. All equipment must be cleaned and sterilised to kill germs, and hands must be washed before making up the feed.

Preparation
(1) Fill kettle and boil.
(2) Read instructions on packet (for amounts see page 77).
(3) Remove bottle from sterilising unit.
(4) Pour correct amount of boiled water into the bottle.
(5) Cover with lid and screw top.
(6) Cool to body temperature by holding under running cold water.
(7) Measure and add correct number of scoops of powder to bottle – make sure all measures are levelled off with the spatula. The powder should not be packed down in the scoop.
(8) Replace lid and screw top on bottle.
(9) Shake gently until powder and water are mixed.

The milk made in this way should be at the correct temperature for the baby. Put the teat on the bottle, then check temperature by allowing a few drops of milk to fall on your wrist. It should feel pleasantly warm. If cold, the feed can be warmed up by standing the bottle in a bowl of hot water; if too hot, then cooled in a bowl of cold water. If need be, enough bottles can be made up to last twenty-four hours. They should be stored in a refrigerator and can be warmed up when required, as described above.

Immediately after the feed is given, the bottle and other utensil should be cleaned and sterilised by the following method:

(a) *Cleaning*
(1) Pour away any remaining milk.
(2) Rinse bottle and teat, outside and inside, under cold-water tap.
(3) Wash all utensils in hot detergent solution using a bottle brush for the bottle.
(4) Clean teat by turning inside-out and rubbing with salt (removes milk film).
(5) Rinse all utensils again in cold water.

(b) *Sterilising*
(6) Immerse all utensils in a solution of one part sodium hypochlorite to eighty parts of water.
(7) Make sure all equipment, including teats, is immersed in the fluid.
(8) Cover and leave for at least one and a half hours or until needed.
(9) The solution needs to be changed every twenty-four hours or it will lose its effectiveness.

(*NB:* Metal should not be sterilised in this way or it will rust.)

There are many brands of sterilising fluid containing sodium hypochlorite on the market and it may be obtained in liquid, crystal or tablet form. Follow the directions given on the packet for making up the correct solution. In an emergency, when a sterilised bottle is needed urgently, utensils can be sterilised by boiling. All utensils except the teat should be immersed in a saucepan of cold water, brought to the boil, and boiled for ten minutes. The teats should be added for the last minute of boiling. A lid should be used on the saucepan and the pan should remain covered until its contents are needed.

Method of giving a bottle feed. A spare sterile teat should be available in a covered container in case the one in use becomes blocked.
(1) Baby should be changed and made comfortable.
(2) Mother/nurse should wash hands.
(3) Mother/nurse should sit comfortably and cuddle the baby as if she were breast-feeding.
(4) Check temperature of milk and flow from teat.
(5) Introduce the teat into baby's mouth, holding the bottle up to ensure that the teat remains full of milk.
(6) If baby sucks the teat flat, then remove teat and allow air into bottle.
(7) Halfway through feed remove bottle and 'wind' baby as for breast-feeding and again at end of feed.
      The feed should take ten to fifteen minutes and it is usually given four-hourly, as in breast-feeding.

Problems which may occur
(a) Baby takes too long to feed or refuses to feed:
      (i) Teat hole may be too small – enlarge by using a sterilised darning needle.
      (ii) Baby's nose may be blocked – medical aid.
      (iii) Baby may be ill – medical aid.
(b) Baby wakes and cries after one or two hours:
      (i) Baby may be thirsty – offer boiled water.
      (ii) Baby may be hungry – offer boiled water and at next feed time increase milk by 25 ml (1 oz).

Vitamin supplement

All babies need extra vitamin A, D and C, usually given in the form of drops. Dosage depends on whether the baby is breast- or bottle-fed, and if bottle-fed, which brand of milk powder. Read instructions which come with drops.

Water

Extra cool boiled water should be offered between feeds, especially during hot weather.

Weaning

This means the gradual change over from milk to mixed diet, as in family meals. Fashions change and in the past have gone from one extreme to the other. Babies have been suddenly weaned at nine months, and gradually from two weeks. However, most babies are found to be ready for extra food around three to four months and they thrive best if there is a gradual transition from milk to mixed feeding. Between three and four months the baby will be waking early for feeds and if he is given extra milk it will not satisfy him. He should not, in any case, be given more than 230 ml (8 fl oz) – a bottleful – at each feed.

It is necessary to start weaning a breast-fed baby by four months because the baby's stock of iron, obtained from his mother before birth, is being used up and breast milk does not contain enough iron to make up for this. Bottle-fed babies do have the advantage of iron being added to humanised dried milk. By about five to six months the baby is beginning to chew, whether he has teeth or not, so, at that age, he should be given food to chew on.

Methods of weaning vary, but there are several important points to remember: (see also chart opposite)

(a) Start gradually by offering just one teaspoon of sieved food before one of the baby's feeds – 10 a.m., 2 p.m. or 6 p.m.

(b) If he refuses, try giving some of his milk first and then the 'taste'.

(c) Use a plastic spoon as this is softer to his gums.

(d) Preferably give savoury foods, rather than sweet, to encourage a liking for savoury flavours.

(e) Food containing iron should be introduced early, e.g. bone broth, egg yolk, chocolate, liver.

(f) Once he has accepted the 'taste' at one feed time, introduce another 'taste' at another feed time, and then a third taste, so that he is having solids at 10 a.m., 2 p.m. and 6 p.m.

(g) Then gradually increase and vary the solid food.

(h) If baby refuses, leave for three to four days and then start again.

(i) Do not introduce more than one new food at a time, so that if baby is upset, the cause will be obvious and the offending food can be avoided for a couple of weeks.

(j) As soon as baby begins making chewing movements (between five and six months) whether he has teeth or not, introduce more solid food to his diet – that is, mashed instead of sieved, and hard rusks to chew.

NB: Do not leave him alone with a rusk, as he may break off a piece and choke on it.

(k) As soon as he is willing and keen, give him a spoon and let him 'try to feed himself. Food should be in small pieces rather than mashed, so that he can use his fingers and/or spoon easily. He should also be introduced to a cup when ready.

Stages in weaning
Milk = milk from breast or bottle. Each stage may take from 3 days to 2 weeks.

Stage	6 a.m.	8 a.m.	10 a.m.	12 midday	2 p.m.	4 p.m.	6 p.m.	10 p.m.
	milk		milk vitamin drops		milk		milk	milk
1 (4 mth)	milk		milk vitamin drops		milk		1 teasp. dinner milk	milk
2	milk		1 teasp. breakfast milk vitamin drops		milk		1 teasp. dinner milk	milk
3	milk		1 teasp. breakfast milk vitamins		1 teasp dinner milk		1 tablesp. 'tea' milk	milk
4 (5 mth)	milk		1 tablesp. breakfast milk vitamins		dinner + fruit juice in cup		1 tablesp. 'tea' milk	milk
5 (6–7 mth)	fruit juice or water in cup	breakfast milk		dinner + fruit juice in cup		'tea' milk	milk at bedtime	
6 (9 mth)	fruit juice or water	breakfast milk in cup	fruit	dinner + juice in cup		'tea' milk in cup	milk at bedtime	

Suitable food for weaning

Note: In the menus listed below a CHOICE of suitable foods is given.

(a) *3–5½ months:* All home-cooked food should be put through a 'baby-mouli' or liquidiser to make it a smooth semi-liquid mixture. No extra salt should be added, as babies need very little salt and too much can cause problems. Tins or jars of strained baby food are useful (if expensive) but it must be remembered that eventually the baby will have to eat his mother's cooked food so the sooner he gets used to it the better.

> *Breakfast* (10 a.m. feed): baby cereal – milk (no added sugar), egg yolk (lightly boiled), mashed banana, fruit puree (apple/apricot/prune), tin or jar strained baby food;

Dinner (2 p.m. feed): bone and vegetable broth, scrapings of roast joint –
potato – gravy, steamed kidney, liver, white fish, braised steak, tin or jar
strained 'dinner';

'Tea' (6 p.m. feed): egg custard, milk pudding, cauliflower cheese, grated
cheese on cereal, fruit puree or egg yolk (not the same as breakfast).

(b) *5½–8 months* (from the time baby begins to chew): Stop making food into
puree – mash instead.

Breakfast: as above, or: scrambled egg, Weetabix, porridge, crisp bacon,
crisply fried bread, mashed sardines;

Dinner: as family: minced or chopped meat, chicken or bacon + vegetables,
steamed white fish + vegetables, 'junior' tin or jar dinner, followed by
fruit puree;

Tea: rusks, sandwiches – Marmite, egg, flesh of tomato, grated cheese, plain
sponge cake, jelly, bread, jelly jam, honey, any tin or jar 'junior' supper;

(c) *8 months onwards* – 'finger' food. Change to cow's milk.

Breakfast: as above; may need two courses, i.e. cereal + egg, whole boiled
egg with toast fingers;

Dinner: as above, + salad vegetables cut small;

Tea: as above, cheese on toast, wholemeal bread.

Under 1 year: Avoid food which is very salty, i.e. salt bacon, kippers. Avoid
highly-seasoned food such as curry. Avoid food containing pips.

From one year: The child's diet should be the same as the rest of the family.
Sample menus for the one year old are as follows:

Early morning	fresh orange juice	tomato juice	fresh orange juice
Breakfast	Weetabix + milk boiled egg toast fingers milk	porridge toast + jam milk	crisply grilled bacon fried bread toast milk
Mid-morning (if wanted)	milk	milk	milk
Dinner	minced beef and gravy mashed potato carrot apple water to drink	liver and bacon casserole potato chopped cabbage fruit jelly water to drink	chopped chicken roast potato cauliflower pineapple dessert water to drink

Tea	cauliflower cheese pieces of orange sponge cake milk or milky tea	sandwiches wholemeal bread grated cheese Madeira cake banana milk	salad with grated cheese carrot, chopped lettuce + tomato wholemeal bread and butter
Bedtime (if wanted)	milk or hot chocolate	milk	milk

Special diets

From time to time a nursery nurse will have in her care a child on a special diet. Sometimes the child will be unable to eat certain foods because of the family's beliefs, which must be respected. In other cases the child may be suffering from a disease which can be controlled by a special diet or by avoiding certain foods. Whatever the reason, it is important for the nursery nurse to know from his mother exactly what the child can or cannot eat. *All* staff at the nursery or school must be aware of this diet so that no mistakes are made.

A vegetarian diet. The term 'vegetarian' has various meanings so it is essential to find out what is meant when the parents of a child say they are vegetarian. In some cases, the family simply does not eat meat, but others are true 'vegans' and do not eat any animal products at all. In between are the Hindus, whose vegetarian diet is based on the doctrine of *Ahimsa* which says that it is wrong to kill any living animal or fish for food, but permits the eating of animal products which do not involve killing, for example eggs, milk, butter and cheese.

If a child must not eat meat, then meals provide few problems because meat protein can be replaced by using eggs, cheese and milk or a mixture of vegetable proteins. But, in the case of the true vegan with his restricted diet the biggest problem is to ensure that there is enough protein for growth and sufficient iron for the maintenance of good health. Children need more of these nutrients than adults because of the large amount of growth which takes place. In normal diets the easiest way to provide protein and iron is by including a mixture of meat and animal products in a child's meals. This is because proteins are made up from a selection of about twenty-two amino-acids, of which eight cannot be manufactured by the human body. These *eight essential* amino-acids are all found in meat, eggs, fish, milk and cheese. Iron is also present in meat and eggs.

Only human milk and eggs supply the essential amino-acids in the correct proportions for humans but, by giving a mixed diet containing meat and animal products, we can ensure a child gets sufficient protein for his needs. The protein which is present in vegetables, such as nuts, peas, beans and lentils is known as an incomplete protein because it only contains a selection of some of the essential amino-acids. This means that a child must eat a large amount and variety of vegetables to ensure that all the essential amino-acids are available. Iron is present in green vegetables, but it is in the form of iron oxide which is not readily absorbed by the human body. Fortunately iron is also present in bread, curry powder, cocoa, chocolate, baked beans and lentils. Most vegetarian diets provide adequate amounts of the vitamins and calcium.

By co-operating with his mother, it is possible to ensure that the vegetarian child has a balanced and varied diet every day.

Some religious beliefs specifically forbid the eating of certain foods and these must be respected. Examples of these are:

Jewish diet. Observant Jews do not eat pork in any form and this includes food cooked in pork fat, pork sausages and bacon. An orthodox Jew will only buy his meat from a 'kosher' butcher because he knows that the animal has been killed and the meat prepared in the accepted way, according to the 'Talmudic' ritual.

Hindu diet. Hindu people consider the cow to be a sacred animal and will not eat beef. They consider the pig to be unclean and uneatable. Some Hindus are also vegetarians.

Diet for the overweight child. A child who is overweight should be examined by a doctor who will prescribe a diet for him, usually a low carbohydrate one, so that his meals will consist mainly of protein and vegetables. He will not be allowed in-between snacks of sweets, biscuits, crisps or sweet drinks and the sugar, bread and cake content of his diet will be reduced. Chips are usually forbidden. This can cause him a great deal of misery at first, and a child on this sort of diet needs a good deal of support and encouragement. Meals should be colourful and interesting with plenty of varied vegetables to fill up his plate. Sometimes it helps to use a smaller plate – the meal looks bigger! He can have carrots, apples and celery in between meals and this may help to console him.

A child with an allergy. There are children who are found to be allergic to specific foods, for example, cow's milk or eggs. Usually the child has a reaction such as vomiting, an eczema-like rash, or 'wheezing', after he has eaten the offending food, or allergen. In these cases these particular foods must be avoided at all costs. If the allergen is cow's milk then a substitute such as goat's milk or a fluid made from soya bean can be substituted.

Eggs are more difficult to avoid because many cakes, biscuits and puddings are made with eggs and these must also be withheld.

A gluten-free diet. A child suffering from coeliac disease is invariably on this diet, because his bowel is unable to digest gluten, which is the protein in flour and many other cereals. Whenever he eats gluten he suffers from diarrhoea, sickness and loss of weight, so all foods containing gluten must be excluded from his diet. Cakes, bread and biscuits, etc., should be made from gluten-free flour. Manufactured foods which are gluten-free are now specially labelled with a symbol representing a crossed-out ear of wheat, so that they are easy to identify.

A diabetic diet. A child suffering from diabetes has difficulty in converting carbohydrate into energy because he does not produce enough insulin. To correct this deficiency, insulin is usually given daily by injection and the amount of carbohydrate in the diet is carefully balanced to the amount of insulin. The diet *must* be adhered to – both the timing of meals and the amount of food are important. The child must eat his meals at the time prescribed following his injection of insulin, and all food must be measured and weighed out exactly.

Diet for phenylketonuria. A child suffering from this defect is unable to make use of the amino-acid phenylalanine, which builds up in the brain, causing damage leading to mental retardation. If this condition is discovered early enough, and the child put on a diet low in phenylalanine whilst his brain is developing, then the damage is avoided. Unfortunately, most proteins contain phenylalanine, so that much of the child's food must be specially manufactured and is obtainable only on a doctor's prescription from a chemist.

Diet for galactosaemia. This is a similar condition to phenylketonuria, but in this case the affected child cannot use galactose, which is a type of sugar. Again specially manufactured foods, with a low galactose content, are necessary.

Diet for cystic fibrosis. This disease affects the chest and pancreas. Excessively sticky mucus is produced and causes problems in the lungs. Mucus also blocks the tube carrying enzymes from the pancreas, and this means that some digestion, especially that of fats, cannot take place. The child is usually given a low-fat diet and, in addition, may be prescribed pancreatin – an extract of pancreatic enzymes – to be given daily before meals.

Exercise 6

Multiple-choice questions

1. Which of the following foods is the best source of vitamin 'C'?
(a) steamed-sponge pudding;
(b) cooked cabbage;
(c) an orange;
(d) milk;
(e) sugar.

2. Lack of vitamin 'D' will cause which one of the following diseases?
(a) scurvy;
(b) rickets;
(c) influenza;
(d) anaemia;
(e) pellagra.

3. How is protein used in the body?
(a) to strengthen nerves;
(b) to make fat;
(c) to harden bone;
(d) to repair wear and tear;
(e) to make haemoglobin.

4. A child suffering from coeliac disease:
(a) must be given a special diet, from birth;
(b) must avoid eating meat;
(c) must avoid gluten in his diet;
(d) must have his meals at regular intervals;
(e) must have his food weighed out exactly;

5. Which of the following is the best source of iron?
(a) chocolate;
(b) milk;
(c) biscuit;
(d) potato;
(e) apple.

Essay questions
6. How would you prepare a bottle-feed for a normal baby of three months of age? Describe how you would give the feed to the baby.

7. Describe when and how you would wean a baby from milk to a mixed diet. How can you ensure that this child has a balanced diet and enjoys his meals?

Project

8. Plan all the meals for three days for the following family, making sure that each member has a diet suitable for his or her needs:
(a) mother, three months pregnant;
(b) father, manual-worker;
(c) son, aged five years;
(d) daughter, aged one and a half years.

Suggestions for further reading

Sylvia Close, *The Know-How of Breast-Feeding*, John Wright & Sons
Patty Fisher and Arnold Bender, *The Value of Food*, Oxford University Press
Elizabeth Norton, *Feeding Your Family*, Mills & Boon Ltd
Present Day Practice in Infant Feeding, HMSO

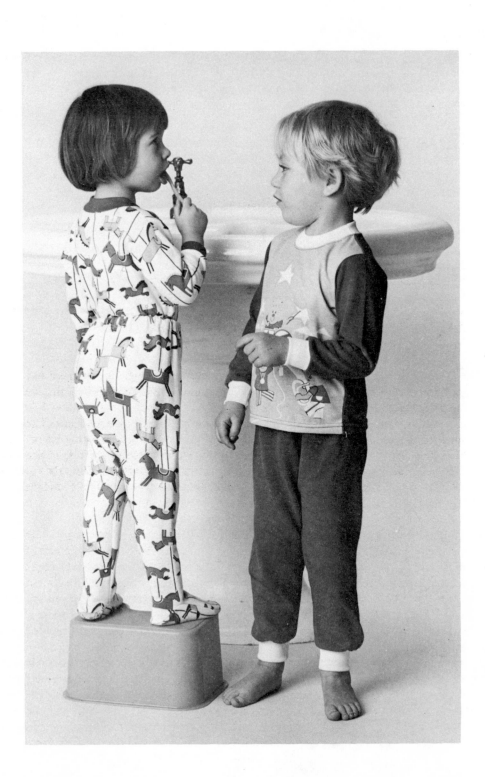

Chapter 7
Care of the child

Basic needs

1. food;
2. cleanliness
3. rest and sleep;
4. exercise;
5. fresh air and sunlight;
6. warmth;
7. good health;
8. protection from injury and infection;
9. security;
10. affection;
11. stimulation;
12. social contacts;
13. independence.

The needs of a child remain the same at any age, but changes in emphasis and in the pattern of his daily routine will occur naturally as he grows from a passive baby to an active child. As he becomes more mature and more able, more will be expected of him, so that he gradually moves towards ultimate independence. The small baby's routine is based on his four-hourly feeds, but once weaning begins his mealtimes gradually change to come into line with those of the rest of the family. He can then become an active participant in family life. All his needs will overlap, but in the following pages they will be dealt with separately, before planning a routine to encompass them all.

1. Food (see Chapter 6 on Food). A child needs a mixed diet containing a wide variety of nutrients at regular intervals during the day. He should have one pint of milk and extra vitamin A, D and C drops until he is five years old. He needs protein for growth and repair, calcium for bones and teeth, iron for his blood and some fats and carbohydrates for energy. However, he should not be given too much sugar, as this will affect his health adversely. If he is given snacks such as sweets or biscuits, or drinks such as lemonade or cola, between mealtimes, they can spoil his appetite for protein meals, cause his teeth to decay and make him grow too fat. If he should need something to chew between meals, then an apple or a carrot should be enough and if he is thirsty, water is the best thirst-quencher. Sweets are best given as a special treat after a meal.

From the time a baby is able to sit comfortably and steadily in a chair, he should be allowed to sit up to the table with the rest of the family. When he shows willingness, he should be given a spoon and allowed to try and feed himself. Help should be given, of course, and his food should be chopped into small pieces, rather than mashed, so that he can easily pick it up, either with his fingers or his spoon. He will make a mess at first, but gradually with practice becomes more proficient. Sitting with the rest of the family at the table will enable him to watch and to copy. A child learns by imitation and it is important to let him practise new skills when he is ready and willing, because that will be the right time for him to do so.

A baby of ten months will probably still be having a bottle-feed or a breast-feed last thing at night, and it is important that he continues this practice until he is ready to give it up. Not only is it a source of food but sucking brings comfort and satisfaction to a child. Most babies spontaneously give up this last feed some time between one year and eighteen months because they find other sources of comfort.

Until he is about a year old, a baby will eat almost all the food he is offered because he needs it for growth. But, from this age, his appetite will taper off for two reasons. First, he will no longer need as much for growth and secondly his interests will have widened, so that meals will not be as important to him as they once were. This reduction in appetite can cause much anguish in mothers, and nurses too, if they do not realise it is a normal occurrence. A child is quick to sense anxiety and may take advantage of this and refuse to eat in order to draw more attention to himself. Provided he is offered a good balanced diet at mealtimes and is not given sweets and other snacks in between, he will eat what he needs. It is unnecessary to entice a child to eat, or to force food into him. It does a child a disservice to make him eat food he does not need, bearing in mind that one of the biggest problems of malnutrition in Britain at the present time is obesity. Fat children are not fit children and fat children often become fat adults. Once the habit of over-eating is established, it can be very difficult to break.

Small, attractive helpings should be offered at family mealtimes. Food should look inviting with a contrast of colour and texture. The child should sit with the family and no comment should be made on his eating. After a certain length of time his plate should be removed, whether the child has eaten or not. The atmosphere at mealtimes should be that of an enjoyable social get-together which is conducive to good digestion. A period of outdoor play before a meal will often stimulate an appetite, but there should be a quiet ten minutes just before a meal with a regular routine of handwashing and general preparation.

If a child has an actual dislike of a particular foodstuff, then it is best to present it in a different way, or provide a substitute without comment. For instance, milk can be given in the form of milk puddings, milk shakes or hot chocolate. If soft boiled eggs are disliked, try hard-boiling them, or a raw egg can be added when mashing potato. Some children prefer to eat vegetables raw rather than cooked and there is no reason at all why they should not have them that way. Nothing is gained by forcing a child to eat a hated food; the child usually wins anyway. He may vomit it, or store it in his cheeks like a hamster. One of the authors' children resorted to filling his pockets with mashed potato because otherwise he would have been made to eat it by his nursery school teacher.

Children can become very conservative in their tastes and mostly prefer familiar foods, so it is important in the early days, when they will accept it, to give a wide variety of different foods. If they are presented at three or four years of age with an unknown food, many children will automatically say they dislike it. Sometimes the problem can be overcome by suggesting that the child helps himself to a very small sample to taste.

As the child becomes more mature he can be encouraged to join in the conversation at the table. Later he will want to be involved in preparations, such as laying the table and cooking the meal. This will all add to his enjoyment of mealtimes.

When a child starts nursery school or begins having school meals, there may be difficulties at first, such as refusal to eat because it is all so strange to him. He may never have seen a properly set table before, or used a knife and fork. Some children are still being spoon-fed at three years of age because their mothers dislike mess; others may be fed separately from their family, and some children sit watching television while they eat and are not used to sitting at a table. Therefore it is important for a nursery nurse to ensure that a new child is made familiar with the arrangements and the routine of mealtime in the nursery. If this is done in a kindly way, the other children will follow her example and will assist the newcomer to settle down. Most children eagerly conform if they are shown the way.

2. Cleanliness. From about eight months of age, a baby should be on the floor most of his waking time, which means that he will need his daily bath more than before. Once a baby has achieved a sitting position, he makes great efforts to become mobile. He progresses from 'swimming' on the floor, to rolling over and over, crawling and creeping and later on standing and walking. By the end of the day his knees and elbows will have become very grimy and a bath in the evening is a good idea, as it not only cleans the child but also acts as a good prelude to bedtime.

Somewhere between six and ten months of age he will have graduated to the 'big bath' and this will give him more space in which to play. After a wash all over he should be allowed time to enjoy this and be able to splash around for pleasure. Toys which float, and those which sink, plastic cups and containers for scooping up water and sponges for squeezing all add to the fun of bathtime. After the bath it is important to ensure that the child is dried thoroughly, especially in all the creases, such as those between his toes.

A child should have his own towels, flannel, toothbrush, hairbrush and comb. They can be marked with a symbol which he can begin to recognise as his own, or in a family each child could have his own colour.

On waking in the morning the baby will need a 'top and tail', but when he has finished using nappies, washing his face and hands only will be sufficient. He should have clean underclothes and socks daily. During the day, hands should be washed after using the lavatory or potty, and before meals. Nails should be kept clean and trimmed weekly. His hair should be brushed and combed daily and washed once a week, when a check should be made for the presence of nits and lice. His comb and brush should be washed at the same time as his hair.

Children often hate having their hair washed because they dislike water being splashed on their faces. The easiest way is probably to wash the hair while the child is having a bath. The head should be tipped back when rinsing, to avoid water on the face. A spray attachment is very useful for this. Use a baby shampoo because the solution will not sting if it should come in contact with the eyes.

Teeth cleaning, after meals and last thing at night, should begin as soon as a tooth appears. There is no need for toothpaste at this stage – a soft brush and tap water are sufficient.

All this starts to teach good habits, and as soon as a child is willing he should be encouraged to help with washing and dressing himself and cleaning his teeth. With practice he will gradually become more proficient, so that by about five years of age he should only need reminders and supervision.

Care of the teeth

Although the first teeth are only temporary, it is important to prevent them from decaying. There are several reasons for this:

(a) Care of the teeth forms a good habit which will continue throughout life.
(b) Decayed teeth cause pain.
(c) Painful teeth may prevent a child from eating properly.
(d) Painful teeth prevent a child chewing, which could adversely affect his jaw development.
(e) These first teeth act as 'spacers' for the permanent teeth; if a tooth has to be removed because of decay then the other teeth can close together, causing overcrowding when the second teeth come through.

Tooth decay (dental caries) is caused by plaque. Plaque is a jelly-like coating of carbohydrate debris which clings to the teeth. This coating forms an ideal medium for bacteria, because it provides food, warmth and moisure. Bacteria plus plaque produce acid, and it is the acid which attacks the tooth enamel. It gradually dissolves the hard enamel, eventually penetrating to the pulp or inner core of the tooth where the nerve endings are. There is no pain until the nerve endings are exposed. Once there is a hole, then bacteria can get into the pulp of the tooth and may cause an abscess. Usually the tooth has to be removed when it reaches this stage.

Prevention of dental caries can be tackled in several ways:

(a) by making the enamel of the tooth harder and so more resistant to decay by giving fluoride by mouth;

(b) by cutting down the amount of carbohydrate (especially sugar) consumed – don't let children chew sweets all day. If they must have sweets, then they should be given over a short period and the teeth cleaned afterwards;

(c) by cleaning off plaque as frequently as possible – clean teeth after meals, and especially before bedtime, with a good toothbrush, making sure that all surfaces are brushed;

(d) by giving hard foods such as carrot and apple to encourage chewing and to scour teeth;

(e) by visiting the dentist regularly so that any early cavities can be detected and filled before they become big and painful.

Toilet training

This usually begins at about ten months of age. The choice of this age is logical because the child:

(a) is capable of understanding what is wanted of him because he understands language;

(b) is physically able to sit steadily on a pot;

(c) is capable of some bowel control;

(d) may at this stage be showing definite signs when he is about to have his bowels open, for example, red face and a quiet, concentrated manner;

(e) he may at this stage be having his bowels open at a regular time each day (perhaps after breakfast).

A baby is very anxious to please his mother or nursery nurse and will try to co-operate with her, so it is possible to capitalise on this. Praising the child for effort will help to increase his co-operation. A calm, matter-of-fact attitude is best. Talk to him about what you want. Sit him on the pot for about five minutes after breakfast or at a time he usually has his bowels open. If he does perform, then praise him; if not, just dress him again. If he doesn't object, the child can be placed on the pot for about five minutes after every meal and this will then become part of his routine. Eventually he will get the message, but it does take time and patience. He will have some difficulty in 'letting go' at first, so that sometimes he will sit on the pot and do nothing and then when he stands up and relaxes, his bowels will open. This is not a deliberate action – he cannot help it. Gradually this problem is overcome as he becomes more mature.

Helpful hints

(a) Putting the child into pants may help because
　　(i) it makes him feel grown up;
　　(ii) it is difficult for him to accept that it is now wrong to wet his nappy, when it was all right before;

(iii) when he does wet, he is well aware of it, as there is no nappy to soak up the urine.

(b) If he rebels against the pot, it is best to leave it alone for a week or two and then start again.

(c) It is important to have the right size pot or lavatory for the child. He should be able to sit comfortably with his feet squarely on the floor.

   NB: If an adult-sized lavatory is used, then a small stool or box should be put in a position so that the child can rest his feet on it.

(d) Some children are frightened of the lavatory and the flush and these fears should be respected. Others prefer to sit on the lavatory, possibly with a special seat to make the hole smaller. Boys may prefer to stand up to pass urine.

(e) Clothes such as pants and trousers should be easily removed as the need to use the pot is often urgent.

Bowel control is usually attained before bladder control. By about eighteen months the child will indicate or give a vocal warning of a bowel action, sometimes after the event, but mostly before. By about two years he should have control and be able to indicate in time. In fact, he often has such control that he can refuse to have his bowels open if he thinks it will annoy his mother, or if he wants to demonstrate his own power to control his actions.

Bladder control comes a little later. By one year nine months a child will usually report when he wants to pass urine, but may be too late. By about two years he should have control during the day, but accidents may still occur. Between two and a half and three years of age, night control is possible, but this varies with different children. Girls usually attain control before boys. Once control is achieved then the next step is teaching the child to cope with his own toilet needs. Again, clothes should be easy for him to remove and he will need reminders and supervision. Regular visits to the lavatory should become part of his daily routine, especially after breakfast and before going to bed. Time must be allowed for this, so the morning and evening routines should not be rushed.

Toilet training should be straightforward, but problems can arise if too much is expected of a child too soon, or if the whole business is taken too seriously. A child cannot attain bowel and bladder control until his central nervous system has matured enough to let him control the muscles in his pelvic area. Just as there is a large variation in the age at which a baby can walk (nine months to two years) so there is also a variation of age at which a child controls his bowels and bladder. It is important for those in charge of children to be aware of these variations, so that they do not compare one child unfavourably with another, or expect too much from individual children.

Even after a child has control, there may be accidents or setbacks. For instance, losing control of his bowels or bladder is one way in which a toddler can get back his mother's attention from the new baby. It can also be a way of annoying his mother, or asserting himself. It should also be remembered that if a person is frightened, he tends to pass urine more frequently and may get diarrhoea (this is a side effect to the production of adrenalin which is produced when a person is frightened, to enable him to fight or run away), so this may explain why children 'in care' are often incontinent.

Most children gain complete control of their bowels and day control of their bladder fairly easily, but night time control of the bladder often take much longer. In fact about twenty to twenty-five per cent of children still wet their beds at five years of age. However, by ten years of age, the figure is about 0.05 per cent. As so many children do still wet their beds at five it should not be considered abnormal. Unfortunately many people regard bed-wetting at three years of age, as abnormal and can create problems by conveying to the child that this is 'dirty' and wrong. Children cannot make a distinction between what they do and what they are. So these children may begin to feel they are dirty and unworthy of love. The tension and worry created by these feelings can increase bed-wetting. Threats used to induce the child to be dry only increase his fear.

In the authors' experience 'treatment' for bed-wetting before the age of seven years often increases the problem. If a child is still wetting the bed at the age of five he should be seen by a doctor, so that his urine can be tested in case there is a physical reason for wetting, such as a urinary infection (this is very rare). Apart from this, the best attitude to the child with this problem is one of optimism. Protect the mattress by continuing to use a plastic sheet on the bed. From the age of four years stop using a nappy at night. Make sure there is a light on at night so that he can see his way to the toilet – or give him his own torch to keep under his pillow. Train him to pass urine just before bedtime. Some people find it helpful to 'lift' the child and take him to the lavatory in the late evening. If this is done, then the child must be woken up completely, otherwise he is being trained to pass urine in his sleep. This may cause sleeping problems, and if it does the practice should be stopped.

An optimistic attitude from the whole family, praise for a dry bed and very little comment when it is wet will help a child gain control. However, if bed-wetting continues after six years of age then the doctor should be consulted again. The medical name for bed-wetting is enuresis and it is one of the common problems which concern parents and nursery nurses in the early years.

Other problems include sucking – thumbs, fingers or blankets, nail-biting or picking, masturbation, etc., and they will be discussed in Chapter 14.

Soiling

It can be distressing and irritating to find that after a child has mastered bowel control he begins soiling his pants every day. It may be that he is unable to clean himself properly after having his bowels open, so this child needs some help. More commonly this problem arises because he delays having his bowels open and consequently becomes constipated. The faeces becomes dry and hard and create a blockage around which liquid faeces tend to seep, thus soiling his pants.

The reason why a child delays having his bowels open could be one of the following:

(a) He has much more interesting things to do, so he ignores the 'call'. After a while his rectum will stop signalling that it needs to be emptied.
(b) His morning routine may be so rushed that he may not have the time or opportunity to try to have his bowels open.
(c) He may have been constipated on a previous occasion and found it extremely painful when he did eventually pass the stool, so he tries to avoid this pain. *NB:* In some cases there may be a split in the anus caused by the passage of a very hard stool and this is extremely painful.
(d) He may be rebelling against his mother trying to show her that he is in control and will have his bowels open in his own good time.
(e) Extreme deprivation and other emotional reasons may result in soiling.

The best treatment for this problem is to give him a diet which contains extra fluids, and roughage (bran, porridge, prunes, vegetables and fruit) and to encourage the child to try and have his bowels open at the same time each day – usually after breakfast when the meal has caused peristalsis to increase. This can re-establish the habit of emptying his bowels at regular intervals.

If this does not work within two to three weeks or if the child appears to be in pain, then the family doctor should be consulted.

Another cause of soiling (and also smearing of faeces) may be threadworms in the child's intestine. These worms come out of the anus to lay their eggs around it and cause intense irritation. The child scratches in and around his anus and his fingers become contaminated with faeces which are wiped on his pants or anywhere else. Diagnosis is easy, as the worms can be seen in his faeces. They look like threads of cotton and when freshly passed will move around. Treatment is simple – a medicine prescribed by a doctor will kill the worms. The life cycle of these worms can be broken by ensuring that the child's hands and nails are scrubbed frequently to prevent him transferring the eggs to his mouth (see chapter on diseases).

3. Rest and sleep. As a baby grows he will need less sleep. By about a year he should be sleeping about thirteen hours a day, at least eleven of these hours being night time. His day-time naps will gradually become shorter but he should still be given the opportunity for rest periods, one during the morning and another after his midday meal. If he does not want to sleep, then a quiet period in his cot with some toys will serve as a restful time for the child and for his mother or nursery nurse. From about two years the child will enjoy a story read to him or a quiet sitting period watching a suitable programme on television.

Children vary a lot in the amount and character of sleep needed. Some children catnap for short periods at intervals during the day, others need one to two hours of unbroken sleep at one time during the day. The child's routine should be adapted to allow for his particular needs.

A regular routine at bedtime is essential if the good sleeping habits established during babyhood are to continue. It also helps to give a child a feeling of continuity and security. The child should be warned in good time that bedtime is approaching and should be given ten minutes to finish his game. He can then be encouraged to help tidy up his toys and get undressed. A bath at bedtime should be a 'winding down' period which is soothing and conducive to sleep. If a final bedtime drink is part of the routine, then the child's teeth should be cleaned afterwards. Then he should be tucked into bed affectionately. A story should be read to him and his bedtime 'ritual' with favourite toy or 'cuddly', light on or off, curtains pulled back or not, etc., should be observed. He should then be left to sleep.

If he has had an interesting day, with his needs satisfied and adequate physical and mental stimulation, he should sleep well. A good test of whether he has had enough sleep is to note whether he wakes naturally in the morning. If he does not, and has to be woken, then he needs more sleep.

Unhappiness should be avoided at bedtime – if a child has been in trouble during the day, all should be forgiven before he goes to bed. Meals, especially the last one of the day, should be adequate and easily digested. A child's room and bed should be comfortable and welcoming. Never use bed as a punishment because it can cause sleep problems if a child comes to associate bed with misery.

Crying when put to bed. This may be just a 'testing' time in which he tries to get his mother back, so wait at least five minutes before returning. Then comfort him, tuck him in and leave him to sleep.

Screaming when left in bed. This is very difficult to deal with. Probably the best cure is to sit with him until he goes to sleep. Do this in a matter-of-fact way. Tell him you will stay and read a book or do your knitting and do just that. It is unwise to pick him up and take him downstairs, for he will come to expect that every night.

Try to find out the cause of his problems and remedy it. Sleep problems can be caused by:
(a) a feeling of banishment from the rest of the family. This may be remedied by not rushing his bedtime preparations and by sitting with him for a while;
(b) jealousy – there may be a new baby, or an older child who is allowed to stay up later. Extra attention during the day may help to overcome this;
(c) insecurity – the worst kind of insecurity stems from having parents who are always in conflict with one another. The stability of the child's home is shattered each time they argue and he may be too frightened to go to bed in case one or other of his parents should leave while he is asleep. It is important for parents to avoid arguments in front of children. Small children respond more to the tones of voices raised in argument. What is only a small dispute to an adult can sound very frightening to a child, and keep him awake worrying. Similarly, other worries about events during the day can cause sleeping

problems. Look over the child's routine and see if he needs more attention or more demonstrated affection;

(d) fear of the dark – provide him with a light;

(e) other fears – try to find out what they are and help overcome them. For example, if he is frightened of a large dark cupboard then take him in with you during the day and explore it together.

Bad dreams; screaming in the night. This is fairly common and the child does not usually wake up. If he does, he cannot tell you what is wrong, so don't ask him. Just go to the child and cuddle and comfort him until he is calm and settled.

Falling out of cot. Once a toddler starts climbing and trying to get out of his cot he is likely to have a fall. The best remedy is to put him into a bed where, if he falls out, it will only be a small drop.

Waking in the night. If a child wakes at night and comes into his parents' room, the best thing is for one parent to take him quietly and firmly back to his own bed and stay with him until he settles down to sleep again. This can be a wearisome task in the middle of the night and the temptation to take the child into his parents' bed is very great. But the alternative to taking the child back is to have him expecting to come into his parents' bed every night.

Early waking. Place some toys at the bottom of his cot or bed so that when he wakes up there will be something for him to do.

4. Exercise. Exercise is essential for good growth and development. Muscles which are used become 'toned' up, which enables them to perform more tasks and to become more efficient. Active muscles need food and oxygen which is carried by the bloodstream. They also produce wastes (carbon dioxide and water) which are removed by the blood. Therefore active muscles increase and stimulate the circulation of blood. The presence of extra carbon dioxide in the blood stimulates respiration so that breathing deepens in order to expel it. Therefore, more oxygen is taken into the lungs and all the body benefits because increased oxygen supply leads to:

(a) increased activity, especially in sweat glands, liver and kidneys;

(b) improvement in appetite and digestion;

(c) stimulation of nervous system resulting in clearer mental processes.

Children are naturally active creatures but they do need space, opportunity and stimulation for exercise. If a child is kept strapped in his pram all day he will at first make strenuous efforts to move, but after a time will give up his efforts and become passive. A baby should be placed on the floor for increasingly long periods of time, so that his natural curiosity will give him the impetus to become mobile. Furniture should be stable so that he can safely pull himself to his feet. Push-along trolleys, push-and-pull toys and balls will all help to increase his mobility. Later, as he becomes more skilful, tricycles and go-carts, a climbing frame, paddling pool and sand-pit will all provide stimulation for different activities which will aid his growth and development. The day should consist of alternating periods of quiet, restful play and active, noisy play, especially outdoors so that the child can let off steam.

5. Fresh air and sunlight. Activity in the fresh air has a stimulating effect on the whole body and if possible all children should play outdoors for part of every day. Good ventilation in buildings is important, because it circulates fresh air and so replenishes oxygen. Well-ventilated rooms in nurseries and schools help to reduce the spread of infection between children, because germs prefer the conditions found in unventilated rooms – warmth and humidity.

Sunlight is necessary to all life. It warms the earth and gives us light. We all feel better when the sun shines. Sunlight on the skin enables the body to produce vitamin D. It also kills many germs. However, care should be taken when exposing young children to the sun, because of the danger of burning. Sun-hats should be worn and a suntan lotion used on the skin to prevent burning. This is especially important at the seaside because a fair skin can burn very quickly when sunlight is reflected off the sea. Exposure should be for gradually increasing periods each day.

6. Warmth. As a child matures, his body becomes better able to control its temperature. He will still need warm surroundings for comfort, but because he is more active will be able to keep warm more easily.

Clothing

Materials used for clothing should be as follows:
(a) capable of being easily washed;
(b) hard-wearing;
(c) absorbent;
(d) warm;
(e) safe – flameproof.

As already discussed in the section dealing with the layette, the most suitable materials are fabrics made from natural fibres or a mixture of natural and synthetic fibres. Synthetic fibres are uncomfortable next to the skin because they do not absorb moisture.

Clothes should have the following qualities:
(a) They should be easy to put on and take off and fastenings should be simple, so that a child can easily learn to become independent, for his toilet needs and for dressing and undressing himself.
(b) They should not restrict. Restrictive clothing can be unsafe and will frustrate an active child.
(c) They should be safe in design. For example, there should be no loose ends, as with wide flared trousers which could catch on projections.

(d) They should be suitable for the occasion – for example, not too dressy for nursery school or the child will worry about keeping them clean.

(e) The child should have some choice in colour and design. When buying clothes take the child with you and select two or three suitable articles and let him choose between them.

A suitable outfit for children

(a) underwear: cotton pants, cotton vest, cotton/nylon socks (summer), woollen socks (winter);

(b) boys: dungarees, or long or short trousers, shirt, jumper or cardigan and anorak or other jacket (for colder weather);

girls: pinafore skirt or trousers and blouse (or dress), jumper and anorak (for colder weather).

In addition children need pyjamas or nightdresses and a dressing gown. In very cold weather children also need a hat and gloves. In wet weather, wellington boots are useful to keep their feet dry. A child needs at least three sets of clothing, so that one can be worn whilst one is being washed, and the other is in the drawer ready for use.

Shoes. A baby will not need shoes until he has learned to walk properly. His bare feet will give him a better grip on the floor, and shoes at this stage would only hinder him. As the bones in children's feet are not fully calcified, they are soft and can easily be deformed by shoes or socks that are too tight. In China, girl babies' feet used, at one time, to be bound tightly so that the toes were doubled back, and this meant that the feet grew that way and the forming bones set in that position. This is an extreme example of deformity, but it does serve to illustrate how a child's feet can easily be pushed out of shape. Tight all-over suits, socks, shoes, bootees and even tightly tucked-in bedclothes can damage the feet. It is not painful to the child because at this stage his bones are flexible, and the effects are not usually seen until he is much older – perhaps in middle or old age when corns, bunions, hammer toes and other allied problems give rise to pain and lack of mobility.

Children's feet grow fairly rapidly, so socks and shoes should be carefully fitted and checked every three months for size. A stretch sock should be big enough to fit the foot, not to be stretched by it. When shoes are bought, both feet should be measured for length and width and the shoes fitted by a trained fitter. Some manufacturers of children's shoes have special courses where shoe-shop assistants are trained in the correct fitting of children's shoes. It is well worth seeking out a shop with trained assistants.

Slippers should also be carefully fitted. Where possible, children should be encouraged to run around without shoes and socks in the house, as the feet benefit from this freedom.

7. **Good health.** As already mentioned, children should be seen at regular

intervals by a doctor to ensure their development is progressing at a normal rate and that there are no defects.

Early visits to the dentist are important, too, so that the children will get used to him before any treatment is actually needed, and also to ensure that only minor future treatment will be necessary to prevent loss of teeth. Most dentists will begin regular inspections from about two and a half years of age. This is a good time to begin, because the twenty temporary teeth are usually complete by this age and a child is capable of co-operating. First visits are often just a 'ride' in the chair and a brief glimpse of the teeth but, gradually, as the surgery and dentist become more familiar, the child will allow a more thorough inspection. His mother or nursery nurse should accompany the child into the dental surgery.

Signs of good health	*Signs of subnormal health*
clear firm skin – good colour	pallor – skin looks doughy
bright eyes	dull eyes
firm, well-developed muscles	flabby muscles
breathing through nose – mouth closed	mouth breathing
eating well with good appetite	constantly runny nose
sleeping well	poor appetite
bowels normal	poor sleep
normal progress and development	constipation
weight and height within normal limits	poor progress and development
alertness	apathy
interest	miserable, whining disposition
contentment	dullness
ability to accept frustration of wishes	

If a child presents any signs of subnormal health one must check his daily routine and see if any changes can be made to imporve his health. In any case, the family doctor should be consulted about the child's general health. (Signs of acute illness are dealt with in the chapter on Nursing Care of the Sick Child.)

8. Protection. A child over one year of age still needs some protection from infection but has developed a certain amount of immunity to his family's germs. His drinking water or cow's milk (in Great Britain) need not be boiled after he is a year old. Provided his feeding bottle and teat are cleaned thoroughly with very hot water, they no longer need be sterilised. However, care should still be taken with handwashing, disposal of nappies, use of potty, etc. This is especially important in the day nursery and nursery school because a child takes longer to build up a resistance to the many different germs he will meet there.

The course of immunisation against whooping cough, diphtheria, tetanus and poliomyelitis is usually completed by the end of the first year. Measles immunisation may be given between one year and one year three months (this varies from area to area). A child should have a booster immunisation of whooping cough, diphtheria and tetanus vaccine at four and a half years of age and a booster for poliomyelitis so that he has protection when he starts school. In some areas a baby is also immunised against tuberculosis at one to two weeks of age.

Protection from accidents is especially necessary for the one to seven year old as they are a major cause of death. (See chapter on Safety.)

9. Security. A child's security is founded on his close relationship with his mother and, later, with all the other members of his family. He needs to be aware that he is part of a united family group. A regular and consistent routine will give structure to his life by forming a pattern so that he knows what to expect and what is expected of him. He needs a few simple rules which will maintain a simple standard of behaviour within his capability. Discipline is really a matter of control which will gradually become self-control, but until that happens we must help him, both by giving him rules to follow and showing him by example. He should be allowed to pursue his own interests provided there is reasonable consideration for others. If he is not given any rules at all and is allowed to do as he wishes, he will get the impression that nobody cares what he does.

A child likes to please his mother and this fact can be used to advantage. Praise for 'good' behaviour or efforts to help will enable a child to learn in a positive way what is acceptable. A child usually knows the meaning of the word 'No' from about nine months of age – he also responds to his mother's tone of voice. But 'No' should be used in moderation, or it ceases to have any meaning. A child under two and a half years is not amenable to logic, so it is better to be positive and direct his activities towards what you want than to keep using the negative. Constant criticism can destroy a child's security, but distraction from an activity you do not like is a useful alternative.

From about three years of age children love rules and regulations and will soon tell newcomers to the nursery that they are 'not allowed to do that', etc. Children enjoy belonging to an ordered society where things remain much the same, apart from certain events which are predictable – for example, birthday parties. They also like to feel that the adults in their life have similar attitudes and standards. This can be difficult in a nursery or school because standards do vary. It is very important for a nursery nurse to avoid innocently causing conflict in a child's mind by voicing criticisms or remarks which could apply to his mother. It is better to try to find out what is done at home and then resolve any differences in a tactful way. Mothers should be free to visit the nursery or nursery school at any time and see for themselves how activities are carried out and how well their child is settling down. It is to be hoped that both mother and nursery nurse can learn from one another for the ultimate good of the child's security and development.

A child's security also involves having his own possessions and a place to keep them – even if it is only a cardboard box. Ideally he needs a cot or a bed of his own, a cupboard and drawers for his own toys and clothes. This is especially important for the child in residential care or hospital, as keeping his own possessions and wearing his own clothes will continue to provide a link with home.

If a child during his first seven years grows up with a feeling of belonging and being a valued member of a family group, it gives him an inner security which should last all his life and which nothing is likely to destroy.

10. Affection. A child needs someone to love him unconditionally, despite his faults. This unconditional love is closely linked with security.

Love can, and should, be demonstrated by cuddles and hugs and other physical contact, but these are only the outward signs. To pick up a child and kiss him is an easy way to demonstrate love, and it can be done even when affection is absent. But to deal with a young child's dirty nappy cheerfully and wipe up his vomit needs a basis of real affection. The quality of care and concern brought to bear on all the duties and chores – especially the tiresome ones – of rearing a child show him just how deeply he is loved and wanted.

Mothers and nursery nurses should show their affection by talking and listening to a child and praising his efforts. They should let him see the pleasure they get from his company. A child needs to be reassured that he is 'a good boy' and given approval so that he feels a valued person. The worst thing that can happen to him is to lose his mother's or nursery nurse's approval, so it is necessary to let him know, when he is naughty, that it is the deed you dislike and not him. To threaten to withdraw love is a terrible punishment and should *never* be used.

The deepest kind of love must normally come from a child's natural mother. Other people can only do their honest best. Nursery nurses must possess an affectionate nature, because a child can detect differences between impersonal concern and truly affectionate care.

11. Stimulation (see chapter on Play). Much of a child's stimulation arises out of his natural curiosity which impels him to explore and discover. But curiosity needs satisfaction so that it can continue to help a child's development. Opportunity and space, as well as playthings suitable to his age and ability, must be provided to stimulate his five senses. Once he is mobile and on the floor, all kinds of things will interest him and many playthings can be improvised – saucepans and lids, wooden spoons, plastic beakers and cups and spoons, old handbags, paper bags, clothes pegs, etc. A child also needs to play with natural materials such as water, sand, clay and mud so that he can explore their qualities. Through play he learns about the world around him.

Stimulation also comes from his mother's pleasure in his efforts and achievements. She will share with him the triumph of being able to stand upright and walk and make sounds which gradually take on meaning. Talking, singing and reading to him, listening and responding to his noises, and interpreting those noises, will all help to encourage his all-round development as well as speech and language.

A child's surroundings should be bright and gay and his own attempts at drawing and painting should be displayed on the walls for all to see.

12. Social contacts. Until about two years of age a baby is very dependent upon his mother and the rest of the family and they, together with family friends and neighbours, provide all the social contacts a child needs. Between one and two years many children become shy of strangers and an enforced separation during this time (such as a hospital stay) can be harmful.

From about two years of age a child should gradually become more confident and ready for more contact with the outside world. The two-year-old child will like to play alongside other children and, towards the end of the year, the beginnings of co-operative play will be seen.

By three years of age most children are ready to join in group play, and this is the usual age for starting nursery school or play group. Provided a child has a secure background, he should settle into a group and enjoy the companionship of others, eventually being able to dispense with his mother's continual presence. Within a group he widens his outlook and learns the 'give and take' necessary in social life. From three years of age a child should be able to relate to other adults as he does to his mother and respond to a friendly approach. By the time he begins 'real' school, at five, he should be friendly, confident, able to make friends and play in harmony with others.

13. Independence. Gradually, a child must become less dependent on others, although his mother will remain his anchor. Until two years of age, he will want to be near her all the time. From about the age of two he begins to move away from this dependence on his mother, and this change should be encouraged. The first two years should be regarded as a preparation towards a child's independence. He must learn, gradually, the skills needed to care for himself so that he can eventually take over from his mother. Learning to feed himself, dress and undress himself, attend to his toilet needs, etc. cannot be achieved without opportunity to practise. When he shows he is ready to learn he must be encouraged to try and be praised for his efforts. Gradually from about two years of age he should take over these personal tasks so that by the time he is seven only reminders are needed.

Exercise 7

Multiple-choice questions

1. If a child of twenty months consistently refuses to eat boiled eggs, what would you do?
(a) force him to eat them;
(b) make him sit until he has eaten some;
(c) play games, e.g., 'aeroplanes', to coax him to eat some;
(d) serve egg in other forms, with no comment;
(e) remove eggs altogether from his diet.

2. A child of eighteen months refuses to sit on the pot. How would you deal with this problem?
(a) leave toilet-training for two weeks, then start again;
(b) force him to sit on the pot;
(c) punish him each time he soils himself;
(d) tell him you don't love him if he does not use the pot;
(e) shame him.

3. What preparation is most likely to lead to a good night's sleep for a young child?
(a) a good romp with his father;
(b) an hour in front of the television;
(c) a discussion of the day's events, including misdemeanours;
(d) a bath, a story and a cuddle;
(e) letting him stay up until he is really tired.

4. For which of the following diseases is there no immunisation to protect the child?
(a) measles;
(b) whooping cough;
(c) gastro-enteritis;
(d) diphtheria;
(e) poliomyelitis.

5. Which of the following would be the most suitable play material for a child of between one and two?
(a) a book of pictures for colouring;
(b) a rattle;
(c) a clockwork toy;
(d) small blocks in a pull-along truck;
(e) sewing cards.

Essay questions

6. Describe a satisfying day in the life of *either*
(a) a one-to-two year old *or*

(b) a four-to-five year old
fulfilling all their essential needs?

7. What might lead you to suspect that a young child in your care was less than completely happy and healthy, and how would you deal with it?

8. How does a mother, or a mother-substitute, show affection to her child, and why is this so important?

Project

9. Improvise a toy suitable for a one-to-two year old, and explain its value and relevance.

Observation

10. Observe a baby or a young child at bathtime.
Notice his anticipation, initial reaction to water, reaction to being washed, reaction to having his hair washed, removal from the water.
How does he play? How does he show his enjoyment of the water? Does the bathtime ritual affect his mood afterwards? How did the adult interact with the child to make it an enjoyable experience?

Suggestions for further reading

Gwendolene E. Chesters, *The Mothering of Young Children*, Faber & Faber Ltd
Lee Salk, *What Every Young Child Would Like His Mother to Know*, Fontana/Collins
M. L. Kelmer Pringle, *Caring for Children*, Longman Group Ltd

Chapter 8
Germs and disease

Infection

People who choose to work with babies and children must always be alert to the dangers of infection which can make a child seriously ill, and even cause death. A baby is born with little defence against germs and, as they are all around us, on our skin, in our noses and throats and in the air we breathe, the child is at risk all the time. Fortunately, as children grow older and encounter the many different germs, they gradually develop an ability to fight them.

We cannot keep a baby in a germ-free atmosphere, and it would not be a good idea if we could, because he would never develop any resistance to infection. But until he has developed resistance, we must protect him by ensuring that his environment does not contain an overwhelming number of disease-causing germs.

Germs are a category of micro-organism, so-called because they are so small that they can only be seen under a microscope; in fact you could fit about 80 000 on the head of a pin. They are mostly organisms consisting of only one cell, so they have a very simple make-up. Many of these micro-organisms are harmless; some are even essential to maintain life on earth, but others cause various diseases in man.

The many thousands of types of micro-organisms are divided, and subdivided, into groups. The two main groups are:

1. **Non-pathogenic** (harmless to man)
These include:
(a) the organisms which turn milk into cheese;
(b) The organisms which convert organic matter (leaves, faeces, urine, etc.) into fertiliser.

2. **Pathogenic** (causing disease in man)
There are many subdivisions but the most important ones include the following:

(a) *bacteria* divided into groups according to shape:
    (i) cocci (round shape); *examples:* streptococci, staphylococci;
    (ii) bacilli (rod shape); *examples:* tubercle bacilli, tetanus bacilli;
    (iii) vibrios (curved shape); *examples:* cholera.

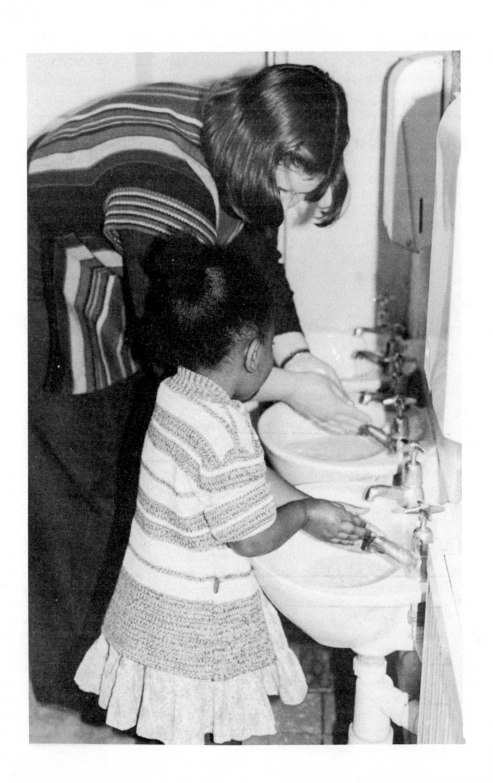

(b) _viruses_ – these are so small that they cannot be seen under an ordinary microscope; *examples:* measles virus, influenza virus.

In addition to bacteria and viruses there are some other more complicated living organisms which can cause disease in man. These are:

(a) *protozoa* – simple one-celled animals; *example:* amoebae which cause amoebic dysentry;

(b) *fungi* – *examples:* thrush, athletes foot, ringworm;

(c) _animal parasites_ – *examples:* lice, intestinal worm, itch mite (scabies).

Most of the micro-organisms are able to reproduce by simply splitting into two and, when conditions are favourable, will do this every twenty minutes. Consequently, one or two germs can become millions in a few days providing that their essential needs are supplied. These are:

(a) moisture;
(b) warmth – average human body temperature;
(c) food;
(d) time.

Some of the organisms need oxygen, but others do not. Some are tougher than others, and can survive longer in an inhospitable environment. For instance, some of the bacilli are able to form a tough outer covering and survive without food or moisture for a considerable time. This is known as a spore formation and spores can be found in dust and dirt. When conditions become favourable to spore, it will resume its old life-style.

So although micro-organisms surround us, they are more likely to be found in warm, moist places favourable to their survival. The areas on the human body providing ideal conditions for micro-organisms are warm parts where there is moisture and food (from perspiration or other body fluids). So, although we have the micro-organisms all over our skins, they are concentrated in the armpits and groin and any breaks in the skin surface. They also occur in large numbers in the body openings – mouth, throat and nose and anus and therefore will be found in used tissues, handkerchiefs, sheets and used dressings from wounds and on potties, lavatory seats and lavatories.

In the home and nursery most organisms are found in warm, moist places with poor ventilation – in the bathroom on damp, used face-flannels, sponges, toothbrushes, towels, bathmats and carpets; in the kitchen on damp tea-towels, dishcloths, floorcloths and mops, and on exposed food, utensils and crockery which has traces of left-over food. Micro-organisms also thrive in overcrowded, under-ventilated rooms, where the air breathed out is warmer and contains more water vapour.

Infection occurs when pathogenic organisms enter the body and develop and multiply, producing toxins (poisons) which cause symptoms such as raised temperature, headaches, loss of appetite and various aches and pains. An organism may also produce a specific reaction, such as a skin rash.

Some germs can cause only one particular disease. Diphtheria bacillus, for instance, only produce diphtheria in man. Others cause different diseases according to where they are in the body. For example streptococci will cause tonsillitis if lodged in the tonsils, but will cause nephritis (kidney infection) if lodged in the kidney.

Micro-organisms can enter the body in three different ways:

(a) *inhalation* – breathed in through nose and throat;

(b) *ingestion* – swallowed through the mouth (usually in food or drink);

(c) *inoculation* – penetrating through the skin, usually through a break.

A disease is said to be *infectious* when the organism causing it can easily be transmitted from one person to another, or to a live or inanimate host on which it lives until it infects another person. These are known as direct and indirect infections respectively.

A disease is said to be *contagious* when the organism causing it can only be transmitted by actual bodily contact.

Direct infection

Actual contact is not always necessary for direct infection but the person being infected must be within the range of the infecting organism.

1. Droplet infection. When we speak we constantly spray out mostly invisible droplets of moisture from our mouths and noses. These droplets contain any of the organisms present in a nose, mouth and throat and can be passed on to any person within the range of the droplets. If a person coughs or sneezes without covering his nose and mouth, the droplets will be propelled several yards and could be inhaled by all the occupants of the same room.

In a similar way droplets from urine and faeces can be sprayed around the lavatory area. These droplets can easily contaminate hands, with the result that the organisms may later be transferred to food and eaten.

2. Kissing. Organisms will be transferred directly from mouth to mouth.

3. Sexual contact. Again a direct transfer of organisms.

4. Touch. Touching an infected skin will result in a transfer of organisms.

Indirect infection

Objects which carry infective organisms must supply some of their needs as well, or the organisms would not be able to survive for long. So, although cups, plates, pens, books and so on are often blamed for the spread of infection, they are not such a likely cause as hands, which are warm and moist with sweat. The exceptions to this are the bacilli organisms, some of which can turn into spores and survive for long periods without food, moisture and warmth. However, the commonest diseases caused by spore-forming organisms are tuberculosis, tetanus and diphtheria and we can be protected from these by immunisation.

The commonest causes of indirect spread of infection are as follows:

1. Hands. As already stated, hands can become contaminated with pathogenic organisms, especially by airborne droplets. People can infect themselves by licking their fingers or eating food with contaminated hands. They can also infect other people if they prepare food and drink for them.

2. Flies. The common house-fly prefers to feed on excreta and garbage, which are ideal breeding sites for infective organisms. Flies carry these germs in their bodies and stomachs and distribute them wherever they land. As flies feed by regurgitating some of their stomach contents on to food before sucking it up, it is easy to see how the organisms can be transferred to exposed foodstuffs prepared for human consumption. Typhoid fever and food poisoning are two examples of diseases spread this way.

3. Mice, rats and cockroaches. These can all carry pathogenic organisms on their bodies and contaminate man's food supply.

4. Food and water. Both can be contaminated at source and so infect people.

5. Certain types of dust. Those which contain animal dung and street rubbish may contain pathogenic organisms which can contaminate uncovered food.

6. Carriers. Some people are carriers of pathogenic organisms, although they are not ill at all. They may have in the past suffered from the disease but are now fit. The organisms may be carried in large numbers in the nose and throat or bowel. The commonest organisms carried in this way are the streptococci in the throat and the food poisoning germ in the bowel.

Such people can be a menace if they are not careful of personal hygiene, especially if their work is the care of young children or the preparation of food for others. They can infect large numbers of people before being detected.

These people can be identified by taking throat swabs or specimens of faeces for bacteriological examination, as the pathogenic organisms can be detected. This is often done in maternity hospitals, nurseries and food factories when an epidemic occurs. It can also be performed before a person is engaged for an occupation where employing a carrier would be hazardous to other people, for example a cook or midwife.

Fortunately we do have certain natural defences against pathogenic organisms and sufficient knowledge to protect ourselves and those most vulnerable to infection.

Natural defences

1. **Good general health.** This will help a person fight infection.

2. **Natural specific protections – examples of these are:**
(a) Acid produced by the stomach will destroy some organisms.
(b) Tears contain an antiseptic which prevents organisms multiplying.
(c) An intact skin acts as a barrier to most organisms.

3. **The white blood cells.** These will devour pathogenic organisms. When infection begins, the white blood cells increase and, travelling via the lymphatic system, go to the site of the invasion and fight the organisms either on the site or in the nearest lymphatic glands.

4. **Immunity.** Antibodies present in the blood stream are able to neutralise specific pathogenic organisms. There are several types of immunity:

Natural immunity

Antibodies are passed on from mother to child before birth and after birth in breast milk. This will protect a baby to a certain extent, until he is able to produce his own antibodies.

Actively acquired immunity

(a) If a person has an attack of an infectious disease, the presence of the organism and its toxins stimulates his body to produce antibodies to neutralise them. Afterwards the body retains the ability to produce these antibodies should the organism be met again.
(b) A similar reaction will occur if the person is given a modified (weakened) organism or its toxins. The disease itself does not appear but the stimulus is sufficient to induce the body to produce antibodies. This is known as vaccination or immunisation.

Passively acquired immunity

Antibodies can be given to a child who has been in contact with a serious infectious disease. Serum (liquid part of blood) is taken from a person who is convalescent from the disease as it will contain antibodies. This protection does not last long, but protects the child long enough for him to make his own antibodies.

Other defences

We can also protect against infection in several other ways:
1. by building up resistance;
2. by reducing the number of pathogenic organisms;
3. by preventing the spread of the organisms.

1. Build up resistance
(a) Ensure that people are as fit as possible by supplying their physical and mental needs.
(b) Ensure that the skin is kept intact and thus prevent organisms entering the body in this way:
    (i) Avoid cuts and breaks.
    (ii) Use hand cream to prevent 'chapping'.
    (iii) Good nutrition aids good skin.
(c) Breast-feed babies so that they receive the maximum amount of antibodies from their mothers. Also breast-fed babies usually have good general health so can resist infection.
(e) Protect babies from specific infections with immunisation. Diseases which can be prevented by immunisation include measles, diphtheria, poliomyelitis, whooping cough, tetanus, rubella and tuberculosis. A doctor will advise on when immunisation should take place.

    Although there are slight risks attached to immunisation procedures, they are statistically very small compared with the risk of catching these diseases and developing complications leading to permanent disability or death.

2. Reduce the number of pathogenic organisms. There are several methods of doing this:
(a) Kill the organisms. It is impossible to kill all pathogenic organisms because any effective method would kill *all living organisms* indiscriminately. However, sometimes one has to kill organisms. Those which cause gastro-enteritis, for example, may be present in a baby's feeding bottle, and they can be destroyed by sterilisation. Pathogenic organisms can be killed by several methods:
    (i) application of a chemical solution such as sodium hypochlorite solution;
    (ii) exposure to heat by boiling and cooking;
    (iii) exposure to heat and pressure, as in pressure cooking;
    (iv) exposure to radiation;
    (v) exposure to sunlight.

(b) Prevent reproduction of the organisms. This can be achieved by depriving the organism of one or more of its conditions for survival. For example:
  (i) moisture – therefore we should dry articles; hang up towels and face flannels to dry;
  (ii) warmth – most pathogenic organisms need the same temperature as human beings, so we can either raise or reduce the temperature to prevent reproduction (as in pasteurisation of milk or the refrigeration or freezing of food);
  (iii) food – we should wash skin to remove perspiration;
  (iv) time – we should eat meals as soon as they are ready.
(c) Dilute the organisms. Good ventilation ensures circulation of air which dilutes the organisms. Washing the skin with soap dilutes the number of organisms on our skin.

3. Prevent the spread of pathogenic organisms by:
  (i) good personal hygiene;
  (ii) good hygiene in the home and nursery;
  (iii) public health measures.

Good personal hygiene
This is essential for anyone caring for children, because not only does it help to prevent the spread of infection but it teaches the child good habits. Children learn by imitation, and much of the teaching of good hygiene they absorb unconsciously. It is far easier to be clean if one has been trained since childhood, as it becomes automatic.

Good personal hygiene should include the following:
(a) a daily all-over wash or bath;
(b) handwashing and nail-scrubbing: before meals, before preparing food, before touching baby, after using a lavatory, after changing a napkin, after touching a pet, after using a handkerchief;
(c) use of handcream to prevent cracks in the skin;
(d) regular nail-trimming and filing;
(e) cleaning of teeth after meals and before going to bed;
(f) daily brushing and combing of hair and weekly washing; it should be trimmed regularly;
(g) covering of nose and mouth when coughing or sneezing;
(h) careful disposal of tissues and handkerchiefs – used handkerchiefs and tissues should be put in a covered container (a paper bag will do) until they can be dealt with – handkerchiefs must be washed and boiled; tissues should be burned or flushed down the lavatory;
(i) frequent changing and washing of clothing – underclothes and tights should be washed daily, and other clothing as necessary;
(j) isolation of sick adults and children – if an adult in contact with children

develops a cold, sore throat, diarrhoea or a skin infection, she should report sick and remain isolated from children until she is better.

Hygiene in the home and nursery

Home: General cleanliness and neatness in the home are necessary, to reduce the numbers of pathogenic organisms present and to help prevent accidents. It is better to rely on a good standard of cleanliness and good ventilation to prevent the spread of infection, rather than lavish use of disinfectant, which tends to give a false sense of security. In any case, if a disinfectant is powerful enough to kill all germs, it will also destroy our body cells, so is a very dangerous thing to have in the house. Most domestic disinfectants sold in the shops are really antiseptics, which means that in the correct solution they prevent germs multiplying. This can also be achieved by reducing the temperature or depriving the germs of food or moisture.

There should be a daily routine of tidying and cleaning. Floors should be cleaned regularly and furniture and ledges dusted with a clean, damp duster. Carpets, rugs and upholstery should be cleaned regularly with a vacuum cleaner to remove dust. Rooms should be well ventilated so that they get a change of air. Beds and bedding should be aired daily by turning the bedclothes back and opening the windows wide for about twenty minutes. Sheets, pillowcases and towels need to be changed weekly. In addition to these daily chores, regular washing and cleaning of walls, paintwork and windows is needed. The kitchen and the bathroom need extra care because both can provide ideal conditions in which germs can multiply.

Kitchen: Modern fittings and surfaces have made kitchens much easier to clean. All working surfaces and the floor should be washed daily with hot, soapy water and scrubbed once a week. However, repeated scrubbing may in some cases be rather drastic and not necessary for modern laminates and composition flooring, and here manufacturers' instructions should be followed. Cupboards should be kept tidy. The food cupboard or store-room should be well-ventilated. This cupboard and the refrigerator should be cleaned weekly. Perishable foods should be kept in a refrigerator. Cooked food should never be left exposed because of the danger of contamination, especially from flies. Flies can be kept out by fitting fly-screens over the windows and a plastic strip curtain over the doorway. If they do find their way into the kitchen, they can be killed by the careful use of fly-spray. However, if the kitchen is kept clean and all food is covered, they will not be tempted in. Food scraps, dirty plates, milk bottles and open rubbish bins all invite the presence of flies. So food scraps should be disposed of quickly, and the rubbish-bin should have a lid on at all times and should be emptied at least once a day. A waste-disposal unit under the sink is very useful and hygienic because it minces up all organic rubbish, which is then flushed down the drain.

Washing up should be done immediately after meals, and the sink and draining board wiped down after use. Sink cleaning with a suitable proprietary cleaner should be carried out after washing up the utensils from the main meal of the day. Mops, dishcloths and floorcloths should be well rinsed after use and hung out to dry. Once a week they should be sterilised by soaking in household bleach or boiling in water.

Washing up is best carried out by the following method, using a double sink:

(1) Remove food scraps.
(2) Rinse all food debris by holding the plates under a running water tap and using a mop or brush.
(3) Use very hot water and detergent to wash crockery and utensils – start with the cleanest glasses and crockery, leaving the dirtiest items and saucepans until last.
(4) Rinse in very hot water in the second sink.
(5) Place in a rack and allow to dry – if the rinsing water was hot enough, this will only take a few minutes.

Hand washing facilities should always be available in the kitchen so that hands can be washed before preparing food.

Bathroom: All members of the family should have their own flannel, towel, toothbrush, etc. There should be enough hooks, racks and rails for these items to be hung up to dry after use. Family members should be trained to rinse the washbasin and clean the bath after use and to hang up towels and flannels and the bath mat to dry. If this procedure is followed, then the bath and basin will only need a thorough cleaning once a week, using an appropriate cleanser.

The lavatory should be checked daily, the seat should be kept dry, and bleach or some other cleanser put down last thing at night. Once a week the seat and lavatory basin should be scrubbed with hot soapy water and rinsed and dried. The lavatory brush should be hung up to dry after use. The floor of the bathroom and lavatory should be washed weekly. Ventilation is important, so windows should be left open when practicable.

The nursery or nursery school: As in the normal home, a regular routine of tidying and cleaning must be carried out daily. In addition, extra care must be taken to prevent the spread of infection from child to child. Children can fairly easily build up a resistance to the germs present in their own homes, but take far longer to do so for the many and varied germs of all the other children. The younger the child, the longer it will take for him to build up such a resistance. It follows that in the day nursery where there are very young children a high standard of cleanliness is absolutely necessary. Many children are admitted to day nursery because of poor social conditions, which means they are often in a poor state of health because they live in substandard housing and eat an inadequate diet. Consequently they have even less resistance than the normal child. Another reason why infection can spread rapidly and easily in a nursery is that children have habits which encourage the spread of germs. For example, they pick their noses, lick their fingers and cough over other people unless they are watched every moment of the day.

Nurseries and schools usually have their own routines to ensure cleanliness and these will vary. Student nursery nurses will learn in their practical situations how to clean and care for the nursery as well as for the children. Although actual practices vary, the principles remain the same – cleanliness and good ventilation both help to reduce the number of pathogenic organisms.

In the children's rooms floors are usually cleaned daily by cleaners, but nursery nurses often carry out the damp dusting and general tidying necessary. Waste paper bins and bins containing used tissues must be emptied daily. Tables will need to be wiped down before and after use. All rooms should be thoroughly aired by opening all the windows for a while before the children arrive in the morning and again at mealtimes. A window should be left open during the day.

In the bathroom every child should have his own flannel, towel, toothbrush, brush and comb. These are usually marked with a symbol for each child so that he can recognise his own. There should be provision to hang these articles up separately so that they dry between uses. They should be washed weekly in hot, soapy water, and rinsed and dried in the open air.

Each child who needs one should have his own potty, which should be emptied and washed thoroughly in hot, soapy water after use.

Lavatories should be kept dry. Once a day the seats, lavatory pans and surrounds should be scrubbed with hot, soapy water and rinsed and dried. Household bleach can be left in the lavatory-pan overnight and flushed away in the morning before the children arrive. Children should be supervised at all times in the lavatory and bathroom so that puddles and spills can be wiped up immediately they occur. The children should be taught to pull the flush and to wash their hands after using the lavatory. The handbasins should be rinsed after use and cleaned thoroughly once a day with a cleaning powder.

Nappies – any excreta can be brushed off into a lavatory pan or sluice (this task is made easy by the use of disposable nappy liners). The nappy should then be rinsed thoroughly in cold water, wrung out and placed in a covered container. Methods of washing nappies depend on the facilities available. They can be soaked in a nappy cleansing solution (according to directions on the packet) or they can be washed in hot, soapy water and boiled. Whatever method is used, they must be rinsed thoroughly in plenty of water and dried in the open air if possible.

In the nursery kitchen, as in the home, all surfaces must be kept clean and flies and other pests must be kept out. Washing-up is often carried out in a washing-up machine which, because of the heat produced, will sterilise crockery and utensils. If there are babies under one year of age in a nursery, there should be a separate milk kitchen where feeds can be prepared and feeding equipment cleaned and sterilised. All babies should have their own feeding utensils marked with their name and kept separate from one another. The room should be cleaned daily – all surfaces should be washed and dried.

Cots for babies and beds for the older children should each be marked with the child's name and kept separate, not only from the point of view of hygiene but also so that the child has a place of his own. Bedding should be changed frequently and the cot or bed should be cleaned thoroughly after a child leaves the nursery, before using it for another child.

Any child suffering from a cold, sore throat, diarrhoea, vomiting or a skin infection should be isolated from other children until he has recovered. Similarly, any nurse suffering in this way should stay away from work until cured.

Public health measures. It was not until the early 1800s that it was recognised that the public authorities could take various sanitary measures which would help to prevent the spread of infection and improve health standards. The first Public Health Act was passed in 1848 and was followed by another in 1878 which laid the foundations for modern public health. These are based on the environmental needs of any community which are:

(a) a supply of pure water;
(b) the prevention of water and air pollution;
(c) the provision of adequate drainage;
(d) the removal and treatment of sewerage and refuse;
(e) a supply of clean, wholesome food;
(f) healthy dwelling houses;
(g) regulation of disease by notification and prevention of the spread of infectious diseases;
(h) provision for burial of the dead;
(i) registration of births and deaths.

The Public Health Acts are administered by Environmental Health Officers who work in the Public Health Departments of the Local Health Authority.

Exercise 8

Multiple-choice questions

1. Infectious diseases are mostly passed from person to person by means of:
(a) articles handled by an infected person;
(b) lavatory seats;   (d) droplets;
(c) registered post;   (e) personal contact.

2. Which house is the most hygienic?
(a) one where the floors are scrubbed with disinfectant;
(b) one whose drains are cleaned daily with disinfectant;
(c) one which is aired daily by opening all its windows;
(d) one which is centrally-heated;
(e) one in which all the occupants have a daily bath

3. Which of the following articles is most likely to harbour a large number of pathogenic organisms?
(a) a stale loaf of bread;
(b) an old book;
(c) a dish of warm rice-pudding left in the kitchen for some time;
(d) an unopened bottle of milk;
(e) a lavatory seat.

4. Which of these micro-organisms can turn into a spore when survival conditions are unfavourable?
(a) tetanus bacilli;
(b) influenza virus;   (d) *Spirochaeta pallida*;
(c) streptococci;   (e) fungus.

5. Which of the following diseases can be prevented by immunisation?
(a) the common cold;
(b) chicken-pox;   (d) mumps;
(c) measles;   (e) impetigo.

Essay questions

6. What do you understand by the term 'immunity'? Describe the different types of immunity, briefly. How do we use our knowledge of immunity to protect young children from various diseases?

7. What precautions should be taken in the 'baby-room' in a day nursery to prevent the spread of infection?

Suggestion for further reading

A. B. Christie, *Infectious Diseases*, Faber & Faber Ltd

Chapter 9
Common infectious diseases and the sick child

Infectious diseases which affect young children are becoming much less common since the advent of mass immunisation campaigns and public health measures to prevent the spread of infection. We are able to protect children from many diseases by means of immunisation. Unfortunately, as a generation grows up never having seen just how serious and damaging are these diseases, the number of children being immunised drops. This leads to another epidemic.

There are risks attached to being immunised, just as there are to any medical procedure, but many people fail to realise that the risk of an adverse reaction from immunisation is far lower than the risk of damage from the actual disease. In the past, thousands of children died from complications following diseases such as measles, whooping cough and diphtheria.

Most infectious diseases follow a similar pattern, although the organisms causing the disease and their manifestations are different. First the organism enters the body. Then follows a period of incubation during which the organism multiplies rapidly. This is when the child will be most infectious, but there will be no outward signs of the disease, although the child may be miserable and 'off colour' towards the end of this stage. The next stage is when the disease manifests itself and causes the child to become obviously ill. His temperature will be raised, causing him to shiver and be generally miserable with aches and pains, and a rash or some other specific sign will appear. After a period of illness, the signs and symptoms will subside and the child will either recover or will become more ill with complications.

Although the nursery nurse is not expected to diagnose a child's illness, she should be aware of the signs and symptoms and the progress of the common infectious diseases. It is important for her to know when medical aid is needed and to know what to expect if a child in her care has been in contact with an infection. In all cases of suspected infectious disease a doctor should be called and his instructions should be followed if the child is subsequently nursed at home. The following charts summarise the causes, symptoms and treatment of the commonest infectious diseases.

Caring for sick children at home

Many parents and nursery nurses are hesitant to call a doctor to a sick child because they fear it may prove to be something trivial which does not warrant a doctor's attention. However, it is better to be safe than sorry and as a child's condition can change from hour to hour he can become seriously ill very rapidly. If you are in doubt, telephone the child's doctor and ask advice, rather than wait until late at night and have to call him out. The following list of conditions indicate an urgent need for a doctor's advice:

1. severe pain;
2. suspected ear infection – pulling ears, banging head, etc.;
3. vomiting – for twenty-four hours if a baby under one year;
4. diarrhoea – for twenty-four hours if a baby under one year;
5. abnormal urine;
6. hoarseness or noisy breathing;
7. loss of interest in what is going on around him by baby under one year;
8. rash which causes irritation or is accompanied by illness;
9. convulsions or fits;
10. raised temperature:
    – a temperature of 38.3°C (101°F) or higher;
    – a temperature above 37.3°C (100°F) over a period of four hours.

Every nursery nurse should be able to take a child's temperature and read a thermometer. The normal temperature range for a child is 36.1°C to 37.2°C (97° to 99°F) and temperatures are usually slightly higher in the evening. Young children do not have an efficient temperature regulating mechanism, so their temperatures rise easily when they are excited or playing. Therefore a raised temperature must not be used as the only indication of illness.

1. To take a temperature. Always shake mercury column down to below 35° (95°F). For children under fourteen years of age temperatures should be taken in the axilla (armpit) or groin.
(1) Explain to the child what you are doing and show him the thermometer.
(2) Sit child on your lap.
(3) Dry axilla (or groin) with a towel.
(4) Place thermometer between two folds of skin.
(5) Hold limb and keep thermometer in position for *three minutes*.
(6) Remove thermometer, put child in cot.
(7) Read thermometer and record temperature.

Temperatures may also be taken in the rectum but only by a trained and experienced person. When quoting a temperature to a doctor, always say where temperature was obtained, as there is a slight difference in reading.

Care of thermometer

Wash well in luke-warm water after use. Shake mercury column down to below 35° (95°F).

Infectious diseases

Disease	Cause	Spread	Incubation period	Signs and symptoms	Rash or specific sign	Treatment	Complications
Diphtheria	diphtheria bacillus	direct contact	1–6 days	sore throat, slight temperature, prostration, pallor	grey membrane in throat	rest, fluids diphtheria antitoxin, antibiotics, diphtheria toxoid	paralysis of muscles, throat obstruction, heart involvement
Scarlet fever	haemolytic streptococcus	direct contact: droplets; indirect contact	2–5 days	sudden onset of fever, sore throat, vomiting, 'strawberry' tongue, flushed cheeks, pallor around mouth	*1st or 2nd day:* bright red rash with raised pinpoint spots behind ears, spreading to trunk, arms and legs; skin peels after 7 days	rest, fluids, observation for complications, antibiotics	middle ear infection, kidney infection, heart involvement
Tonsillitis	streptococcus or staphylococci	direct infection droplets		very sore throat, white patches (pus) on tonsils, swollen glands in neck, aches and pains in back and limbs	no rash	rest, fluids, medical aid – antibiotics	middle ear infection
Measles	virus	direct contact: especially droplets	10–15 days	misery, high temperature, heavy cold with discharging nose and eyes, *later* harsh cough, conjunctivitis	*2nd day:* Koplik's spots; white spots inside cheek *4th day:* dusky red, patchy rash; starts behind ears and along hairline, spreads to face, trunk and limbs	rest, fluids, sponging to reduce temperature, dark room if photophobia	eye infection, chest infection, middle ear infection, encephalitis

Disease	Cause	Spread	Incubation period	Signs and symptoms	Rash or specific sign	Treatment	Complications
Rubella (German measles)	virus	direct contact droplets	14–21 days	slight cold, sore throat, slight fever, enlarged glands behind ears, pains in small joints	1st day: rash-like sweat rash, bright pink; starts at roots of hair; may last 2–24 hours	rest if necessary (mild disease)	none unless patient pregnant woman; virus can seriously affect foetus in first 12 weeks of pregnancy
Chicken pox	virus	direct contact droplets	7–21 days 14–21 days	slight fever, irritating rash	1st day: red spots with white raised centre on trunk and limbs, mostly very irritating	rest, fluids, lactocalamine or solution of bicarb. of soda on spots	impetigo
Pertussis (whooping cough)	Haemophilus pertussis	direct contact droplets	10–14 days	heavy cold with fever followed by cough	2 weeks: spasmodic cough followed by characteristic cough and vomiting	rest, supporting during and coughing, feed after bout of coughing	bronchitis, broncho-pneumonia, haemorrhage, due to strain of coughing, prolapse of rectum, mouth ulcers, debility, encephalitis
Mumps	virus	direct contact	7–28 days	fever, headache, swelling of jaw in front of ears, difficulty opening mouth	no rash	rest, bland fluids through straw	orchitis (inflammation of testicles), meningitis encephalitis (rare)
Infective hepatitis ('jaundice')	virus	direct contact: especially droplet; indirect contact: food or water	23–35 days	gradual onset of headache, loss of appetite, nausea, urine dark, faeces pale putty colour	5th–7th day: yellow skin, itching, also yellow conjunctiva	fluids with glucose, fat-free diet, isolation	liver damage, meningitis

Disease	Cause	Spread	Incubation period	Signs and symptoms	Rash or specific sign	Treatment	Complications
Poliomyelitis	virus	direct contact: especially droplets indirect contact: food or water	5–14 days	sudden onset of headache, stiffness of neck and back followed by paralysis	no rash	rest, medical supervision	permanent paralysis
Gastro-enteritis	may be bacillus or virus	direct contact; indirect – infected food and drink	7–14 days ½ hour–36 hours	vomiting, diarrhoea, dehydration	no rash	fluids – water only, urgent medical aid	weight loss, debility, death
Dysentery	(1) bacilli (2) amoebic	flies	1–2 days 1–2–7 days	vomiting, diarrhoea – blood and mucus, abdominal pain	no rash	fluids and medical aid	dehydration
Food poisoning	Salmonella or Clostridium welchi	indirect: infected food or drink	½ hour – 36 hours	vomiting, diarrhoea, abdominal pain	no rash	fluids only 24 hours	dehydration
Typhoid and paratyphoid fever	Salmonella typhi	direct contact; indirect contact: especially food and drink	12–14 days	headache, malaise, diarrhoea/constipation, fever	7th day: red papules on abdomen	rest, hospital (medical aid)	intestinal haemorrhage, intestinal perforation

Casual use: Dry and replace in case.

Daily use: Place in a small jar of antiseptic solution. Cotton wool in base of jar will prevent damage. The thermometer will not need to be washed again before use.

2. To check the pulse. It is useful to be able to count a child's pulse rate as well as take his temperature, because the pulse can give information regarding the rate and force with which the heart is beating. It may be felt on the thumb side of the wrist where an artery passes over a bone. The first three fingers should be placed over the artery and the rate counted for a full minute. A child's pulse is usually about 120 beats a minute.

3. Routine for the sick child. When a child is ill he tends to regress and act as though younger than his true age. He may become very frightened so he needs a familiar person to care for him and to stay close to him. It is a good idea to keep as much as possible to his normal routine, whilst making adjustments for his illness, because this makes him feel secure. He still has the same needs for cleanliness, rest and food, etc. but the provision of these needs will have to be adapted to his condition.

The sick room should be warm, cheerful and uncluttered. It will need to be well-ventilated and easily cleaned without causing too much disturbance to the child. If possible there should be a water supply and washing facilities in the same room. A potty should be available for the child so that he doesn't have to be taken to the lavatory. The mattress should be protected by a mackintosh because even if he has achieved bladder control, he may regress during his illness. Whilst he is very ill a child will want to stay in bed, but once he is on the mend he should be allowed to get up and dress. He can lie on the top of the bed or a settee for rest periods. When he is in bed let him lie in the most comfortable position for him. For example, if he has a cough he will want to be propped in a sitting position. This can be done with pillows for the child over a year, but if it is a young baby then the head of his cot can be raised by propping the legs securely on blocks. In this case make sure the baby is lying on his side.

A child will still need his daily bath, but, if necessary, this can be in the form of an all-over wash in bed. His hair should be brushed and combed daily and his teeth should be cleaned after every meal to keep his mouth fresh. He will need to be encouraged to use the potty before and after meals, and his hands should be washed after the toilet and before he eats. His bed should be made night and morning, and sheets and pillowcases changed frequently.

A sick child will not feel like eating, so meals must be light and appetising and in small helpings. Suitable foods include egg custard, steamed fish, chicken, milk pudding and ice cream. If he does not wish to eat, offer plenty of fluids and make sure that he drinks them.

If you have to carry out any nursing procedure explain what you are going to do first, and then proceed. Medicines are best measured into a small glass or cup rather than a spoon, and the child can be offered a sweet afterwards. Tablets can be crushed and mixed with jam. Do not put medicines in baby's bottle or a child's food because unless all the milk or food is eaten the correct dose will not be taken. Medicine must be taken and most children will accept the fact if you are firm and honest with them.

4. Hygiene during sickness. A sick child becomes very vulnerable to any infection because his resistance is lowered by his illness. Therefore the nurse should be scrupulous in her personal hygiene to protect him from further illness (see page 116).

5. Prevention of infection. If a child is suffering from an infectious disease it may be necessary to isolate him from people who have not already had the disease. Some doctors believe that, as the most infectious time is during the incubation period, it could be too late to prevent infection spreading when the disease becomes obvious. However, the dangers of infection remain until the main signs and symptoms, such as a rash, have subsided; so if you do not want other children to be infected they should be kept away from the sufferer until this period is over. A child attending day nursery or nursery school will usually be excluded until his doctor says he is clear of infection.

6. Very high temperature and dehydration. These are two of the most dangerous conditions for a child and they often occur together, causing serious problems needing hospital treatment. As a child is unable to regulate his temperature as finely as an adult, it can rise rapidly, causing a convulsion or fit. This can be very frightening to the child and to the adult in charge and may even lead to brain damage. The best treatment is prevention. Even without a thermometer it is possible to tell that a child's temperature is rising. He looks limp and miserable. He shivers because the air feels cold to his hot skin and when you touch him his body feels very hot. The easiest way to bring down a child's temperature is to put him in a bath of tepid water for about ten to fifteen minutes. This can be repeated at intervals. In bed he should be lightly clad and be covered with only a sheet. Resist the temptation to wrap him up because he is shivering – this will only make his temperature go higher. If a bath is not practicable, then strip off his clothes, place a towel under him and sponge him down with very tepid water. Pat him dry with another towel. Like the bath, this can be repeated whilst waiting for the doctor to arrive.

Dehydration occurs with fever or if the illness causes a loss of fluid, such as vomiting, diarrhoea or a head cold. The mouth and tongue become dry and parched and cracks appear on the lips. The child's urine is sparse and very concentrated, which gives it a dark colour. Dehydration means that the body fluids are not balanced and as this balance is necessary for health the child can become very ill. The treatment is prevention, by giving a sick child frequent drinks of water or any other fluid. If it is a baby under a year, then the fluid should be cool, boiled water and if he is too weak to suck from a bottle, then he must be spoon-fed at frequent intervals. The older child can have a variety of fluids – freshly squeezed orange juice or ice lolly, tomato juice, lemon barley water, glucose drink, clear soup, beef broth, or beef extract. These must be offered at frequent intervals because he will not ask for them or help himself. A straw (especially a 'bendy' one) may be useful to persuade him to drink, or a special glass or a doll's cup and saucer.

7. Convalescence. Fortunately, because a child's condition can change so rapidly, he usually recovers very quickly. He will need a period of convalescence so that he can recover his strength and adjust back to normal life again. He will also need a nourishing diet high in protein to repair his damaged body cells and he should not be allowed to get over-tired.

Amusing a sick or convalescent child means planning ahead and good organisation. As the child will regress, activities suitable for a younger-aged child should be provided, remembering that a child has a very short attention span. If he is confined to bed, a large tray or bed table is useful for his games. He can have a variety of materials and toys and most of the activities carried on in nurseries can be adapted to play in bed. If he must rest, reading stories, letting him listen to records and singing to him will all help him to relax. See chapter on play.

Hospital

When a child has to be admitted to hospital, if at all possible time should be given to prepare him for this, so that he knows what to expect. Most hospitals have arrangements so that mothers can stay with their children all day and in some cases sleep in. This is very important because a child needs his mother most of the time, especially when he is ill or frightened.

Further charts on children's ailments

The following charts set out a further list of ailments, including skin diseases, which may occur in the early years of childhood, with notes on symptoms and when to seek a doctor's advice. Some of these ailments are contagious, and are therefore transmitted by close physical contact. In a day nursery or nursery school it is usual to exclude the child until he is said by a doctor to be free from infection. In the home, isolation is not necessary, provided treatment is being given and the normal rules of hygiene are adhered to (see page 116).

Disease	Cause	Contagious or not	Signs and symptoms	Treatment
Skin diseases Ringworm	fungus	yes (may be caught from family pet)	circular red, raised area with white scaly centre; itching; if on scalp – hair breaks off	doctor – usually antibiotic cream
Impetigo	staphylococci	yes	yellow, oozing sores with scab on top; itching; usually around nose and mouth	doctor – usually antibiotic cream
Scabies	'itch' mite (*Acarus scabius*); female mite burrows under skin and lays 20–30 eggs; eggs hatch out in 3–4 weeks and repeat cycle	yes	burrows visible as red raised spots especially between fingers; intense irritation; sleeplessness	doctor – Lorexane or benzyl benzoate lotion; all family members should be treated as instructed; sheets, pillowcases, blankets, clothing should all be washed thoroughly before re-use after treatment
Nettle rash URTICARIA	allergy to food, dogs or drugs, etc.	no	pink raised weals or blotches; may be swelling; itching	find allergen and avoid it; calamine lotion; doctor if associated with sneezing, raised temperature or runny nose
Sweat rash	heat too many clothes	no	pinpoint red spots; fretful baby	cool bath, calamine lotion; less clothing;

Disease	Cause	Contagious or not	Signs and symptoms	Treatment
Eczema	not always known, may be allergy	no	red angry rash, especially at backs of knees and in front of elbows; may be dry and scaly or moist; very irritating	doctor – special creams; stop child scratching; avoid use of wool in clothing
Intertrigo (sores in creases, e.g. neck)	insufficient drying after bath	no	sore red areas in neck creases or under arms or groin	zinc and castor oil cream; prevent, by drying child thoroughly after bath
Nappy rash	variety of causes: (1) faulty washing of nappies (2) dirty nappy left on too long (3) diarrhoea (4) insufficient fluids, leading to concentrated urine (5) infection, such as thrush (6) allergy to nappy liner/cream/softener in nappy, etc.	no	red area over buttocks and groin; may be scaly; may be blisters or raw patches	find cause and eliminate (1) wash nappies – boil or use sanitising powder; rinse very well; dry in fresh air (2) change nappy frequently (3) treatment for diarrhoea (doctor) (4) give extra boiled water to drink (5) treatment for thrush (doctor) (6) change nappy liner brand; stop using creams/lotions or washing softener in nappy; expose buttocks to air – leave off nappy as much as possible; Drapoline cream (medical advice)

Disease	Cause	Contagious or not	Signs and symptoms	Treatment
Verruca	?virus	?yes	wart on sole of foot – looks like a black speck – hurts when pressed	doctor or chiropodist for removal
Cradle-cap (scurf on head)	(a) inefficient washing of hair, especially rinsing (b) too much washing of hair	no	(a) brown greasy patches on scalp (b) flaky white patches	once a week: apply liquid paraffin or olive oil overnight; wash thoroughly next day; prevent by washing hair once a week – rinse very well
Eye conditions Blepharitis	not known	no	crusts (like scurf) on eyelashes; may be redness	bathe with cool boiled water and sterile swabs 5 times a day; doctor if no improvement
Conjunctivitis ('pink eye')	?virus ?bacteria	yes	itching and pain in eyes; red inflamed eyes; may be discharge	doctor isolation separate towel, flannel, etc.
Stye (abscess on root of eyelash)	staphylococci (poor health pre-disposes)	no	painful swelling at root of eyelash; pus collects (as boil)	doctor
Other conditions Thrush	fungus, via unsterile dummy or bottle teat	yes	white patches inside mouth; sore mouth; diarrhoea, vomiting may be present	doctor strict hygiene measures to prevent spread via dirty hands

Disease	Cause	Contagious or not	Signs and symptoms	Treatment
Threadworms	threadworms (1) egg swallowed (2) develop into worms in intestine (3) worms come outside anus at night to lay eggs (4) this causes itching (5) child scratches – eggs are deposited under nails (6) child licks fingers or sucks thumb – swallow eggs	yes	presence of threadworms in stool (white cotton-like pieces); sore anus; itchy bottom; sleeplessness; lack of appetite	doctor Pripsen all children in family should be treated; hygienic measures to prevent infestation: prevent scratching – tight pyjamas; nails cut short; scrub hands and nails before eating
Pediculi capiti (lice)	head lice	yes	head scratching; presence of nits (eggs) – white specks which are stuck to hair; presence of lice – small insects which move along hair	Prioderm lotion – follow directions; 'Derbac' comb – a metal comb used on hair to remove nits; all family should be treated
Constipation	various: poor diet – lack of fluid; lack of roughage; lack of vitamin B faulty habit training poor muscle tone emotional blackmail	no	hard stool painful evacuation headache listlessness abdominal pain	give extra fluids, extra roughage, extra vitamin B; encourage more exercise; encourage daily attempt to have bowels open

Disease	Cause	Contagious or not	Signs and symptoms	Treatment
Colic ('3 months colic')	air (wind) in bowels baby takes in air when feeding	no	screaming baby draws up legs in obvious pain often 6 p.m. to 10 p.m.	warm boiled water to drink; massage 'tummy'; comfort him; put baby on abdomen to sleep; 'Gripe' water may help; usually improves after 3 months of age; doctor, if severe
Hernia	weakness in muscle wall	no	(1) umbilical: bulge around umbilicus (2) inguinal: bulge in groin (3) hiatus: constant vomiting	(1) doctor – may correct itself – usually left until baby 1 year, then possibly surgery (2) doctor – usually surgery necessary (3) doctor; sit child up, especially after meals
Diarrhoea	various infection diet	yes no	loose, frequent stools abdominal pain	doctor within 24 hours if under 1 year old, 2 days for older child; boiled water only to drink for 24 hours
Vomiting	various may be infection may be feed wrong may be defect, e.g. pyloric stenosis may be regurgitation	yes no no	evacuation of stomach contents	doctor within 24 hours if under 1 year old; doctor if continuous in older child; boiled water only to drink

Disease	Cause	Contagious or not	Signs and symptoms	Treatment
Hypothermia	extreme cold	no	quiet 'good' baby; pink hands and face; body feels icy; later: unconsciousness	doctor; meanwhile: remove covers, raise temperature in room, cuddle baby; (try to prevent – warm room)
Infantile convulsions	high temperature	no	pale bluish colour; eyes turn up; twitching of muscles; unconsciousness; may stop breathing	doctor; meanwhile: cool bath or sponge down to bring temperature down; (try to prevent – see Nursing Sick Child)

Exercise 9

Multiple-choice questions

1. Which of the following is a description of impetigo?
(a) a wart on the sole of the foot;
(b) an eye infection;
(c) a septic finger;
(d) infected spots around nose and mouth;
(e) a fungus infection.

2. Which of the following diseases does not cause a rash?
(a) measles;
(b) chicken-pox;
(c) rubella;
(d) eczema;
(e) whooping-cough.

3. If a child has a temperature of 39.5°C (103°F), which of the following actions should you take?
(a) no action, just watch him;
(b) give him an aspirin;
(c) wrap him up to keep him warm;
(d) call the doctor;
(e) put him in a tepid bath, and call the doctor.

4. Thrush is caused by which of the following organisms?
(a) fungus;
(b) streptococci;
(c) amoeba;
(d) bacillus;
(e) staphylococci.

5. Which of the following diseases cannot be prevented by immunisation?
(a) measles;
(b) rubella;
(c) mumps;
(d) diphtheria;
(e) tuberculosis.

Essay questions

6. Why is diarrhoea such a serious disease in a young baby? What could be the cause of it and how can it be prevented?

7. Describe how you would care for a child aged five years, who is suffering from a feverish cold and cough.

Suggestions for further reading

Gerard Vaughan, *A Pictorial Guide to Common Childhood Illness*, Arcade Publishing Magazine Ltd

Eva Noble, *Play and the Sick Child*, Faber & Faber Ltd

James Robertson, ed., *Hospitals and Children*, Victor Gollancz Ltd

Stages in mobility: two to three months

Stages in mobility: four months

Chapter 10
Growth and development of young children

Whilst growth is an increase in size, development is an increase in ability. In practice, it is difficult to separate the two. The process of growth and all the different aspects of development interact with and are dependent on one another. For example, a baby will not start responding to his mother until he is capable of identifying her as a distinct person. However, for the purposes of study, it is necessary to separate these aspects but, at the same time, to note how the interactions take place. All babies follow the same pattern but, as they are all individuals with different environments and experiences, there are bound to be variations within this pattern, especially in the timing of the various stages. It is useful to know this pattern and its variation because it gives us a means of measuring progress.

For many years babies and children have been regularly weighed and measured and these results compared with a table of average weights and heights for various ages. But although this was a useful pointer to normal development, it was by no means a thorough guide.

Tests. The concept of developmental tests in conjunction with measuring was much slower to materialise. Hundreds of children were examined to determine the average ages for the various stages of development. Tests were devised to make use of this research. Now it is common for children to be examined at intervals from birth onwards for developmental assessment – that is to make sure that the child is growing and developing at an average rate. This has led to an earlier diagnosis of 'backwardness' or 'failure to progress' and enabled help to be given much earlier. A good example of this is the story of Michael. Michael was nine months old when brought for his first check-up, his very young mother not having thought it necessary before this time. He was found to be about three months behind in his development. His mother described him as a 'good' baby who never gave any trouble. Investigations revealed no physical reason for delay in development, but on talking to his mother it became obvious that Michael lacked stimulation. His mother expected him to lie in his cot all day. She seldom spoke to him because she herself was desperately unhappy and depressed. An attempt was made to explain to her Michael's need for attention and she was referred to her own doctor for treatment of her depression. Because there was very little improvement in the situation, Michael was admitted to a day nursery

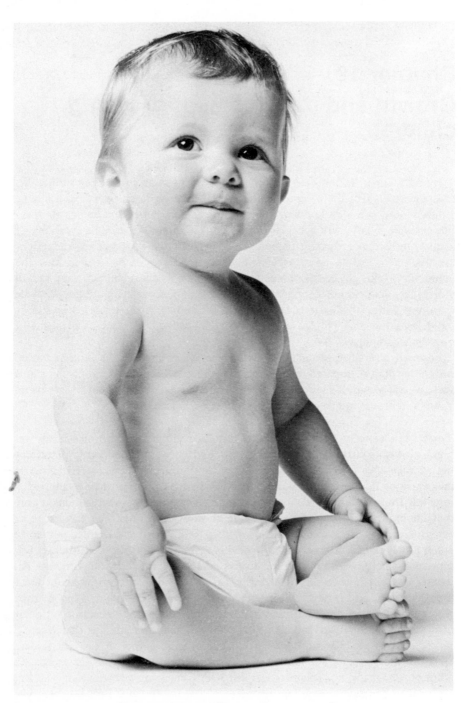

Stages in mobility: seven months

where he rapidly responded to the stimulating environment. Fortunately his mother formed a good relationship with his nursery nurse and began to take pride in Michael's achievements. At two years of age Michael was well within the normal range of development. But if the deprivation had continued, he could have remained backward all his life.

Hearing and sight. Impairment of hearing and sight are developmental defects which can be easily recognised by deviations from normal and by specific tests. The earlier this sort of defect can be detected, the sooner help can be given which can minimise the effect of the disability on the child's future life. For example, if a child is found to have poor hearing, he can be fitted with a hearing aid from about six months of age. This means that he will hear normal speech and therefore have a chance to learn to speak normally.

It is essential for the nursery nurse to know how a child grows and develops. She is often the closest person to a child and, by her knowledge and observation, she could be the first to notice that the child is not progressing as well as he should. So, as well as learning in theory what to expect at various ages, the student nursery nurse should also develop her powers of observation by watching children wherever she goes. There are always babies and children in shops, buses and parks, etc. as well as in the nursery or school. An interesting and useful exercise is to watch normal children playing and try to estimate their ages. This helps you to know what is normal, and is essential if you are to be able to detect what is abnormal. Your written observations, which are part of the NNEB course, are meant to help you develop these powers of observation.

Growth of children

If you compare a newborn baby with an adult, you will see that not only is the baby obviously a lot smaller, but he is a different shape as well. In fact his proportions are all very different. His head appears to be very large compared with his body; in fact it is just over half the size of an adult head. Although the baby's body is small, it is his arms and legs that are extremely short. Therefore it is obvious that most of his growth must take place in the long bones of his legs and arms. Indeed, by four months of age his limbs will already be beginning to lengthen and his proportions will have changed.

Long bones form early in foetal life as cartilage, a thick, rubbery substance which bends easily. During later pregnancy and childhood, calcium, phosphorus and vitamin D are gradually deposited on to the cartilage to form hard bone. The process is known as ossification and it continues until all growth ceases, which is usually some time between twenty and twenty-four years. Most of the ossification takes place during foetal life and early childhood – hence the need to ensure a good supply of calcium, phosphorus and vitamin D in the diet during the first five years of life.

The ossification of the long bones starts at both the extreme ends and the centre of the cartilage, and the patches gradually spread towards each other, eventually leaving a 'neck' of cartilage at each end which enables growth to continue (see diagram).

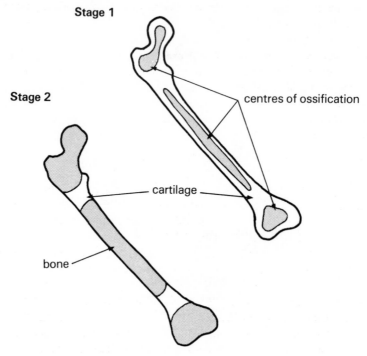

Development of bone

By studying X-rays of children's long bones, it is possible to estimate a child's age by the degree of ossification. This is known as the 'bone age'. It is a useful guide for estimating future growth. For example, if a teenager is very small, X-rays may reveal that there is still a fair amount of cartilage present so that the child can be reassured that he will continue to grow. But once the long bones of the legs and arms are fully ossified, then no more growth can take place. In most people this occurs at about twenty-one years of age.

Teeth develop in a similar way. Here the process of ossification is called calcification, and the outer surface of the teeth (the enamel) becomes much harder than bone. The first 'teeth buds' form in the gums by about four months of pregnancy and the buds of the second, or permanent, teeth form just before birth. The buds are small pieces of cartilage and, by birth, the process of calcification of the first teeth has begun. Some babies are born with one or two teeth, but more commonly they begin to erupt between six and ten months of age when they are fully calcified. The second teeth have already begun calcifying and they will begin to erupt from about five years of age.

The first teeth are usually complete by about two and a half years of age. There are twenty in all and they consist of eight incisors which are chisel-shaped for biting and are in the front of the mouth, four canines and eight molars which are flatter in shape to enable chewing and mastication to take place. They usually erupt in a definite order:

(1) two lower central incisors;
(2) two upper central incisors;
(3) two upper lateral incisors;
(4) two lower lateral incisors;
(5) four first molars;
(6) four canines;
(7) four second molars.

They are known as deciduous teeth because, like the leaves of deciduous trees, they are shed. Around five years of age the roots of the first teeth are gradually absorbed by the body so that they become loose because of lack of anchorage. At the same time the second teeth are pushing upwards. Eventually, one by one, the first teeth fall out and the new ones erupt. In most children these processes occur at the same time, but sometimes a child will have a gap for a while before the new tooth appears. There are thirty-two permanent teeth, consisting of four incisors, two canines, four premolars in each jaw, and they gradually erupt during the next ten years or so, during which time the jaw must grow forward to accommodate the thirty-two larger teeth which will replace the twenty small 'baby' teeth. This growth of the jaw is a gradual process from about six months of age but there is a spurt of growth between five and seven years of age and this accounts for the change from a 'baby face' to one with more adult characteristics.

Since the teeth calcify early in life, it follows that calcium, phosphorus and vitamin D are extremely important in the diet for the first five years of life. If fluoride is also given by mouth in the first five years, it will combine with calcium and phosphorus to make the enamel surface of the tooth harder and more resistant to attack from bacteria which leads to decay. Applications of fluoride after the teeth have erupted are not so effective because the fluoride must be absorbed through the surface of the teeth, which limits the amount available. However, this treatment will help to reduce the rate of decay.

Although most growth continues at a steady rate throughout the body, there are exceptions, the most striking being the brain, the skull and the reproductive organs.

Brain and skull. The growth and development of the brain, spinal cord, eyes and ears are very rapid until about two years of age, when sixty per cent of their development is complete. By the time the child is seven years of age, they are almost adult size. The skull also grows rapidly to accommodate the enlarging brain. At birth it is 33–35 cm (13–14 in) in circumference, while at one year of age it is approximately 45 cm (18 in) and by seven years it is about 50 cm (20 in). The average circumference of an adult head is 55.8 cm (22 in).

The skull is made up of flat plates of bone which join together to form a box-like structure. There are two gaps (called fontanelles) created by the spaces at the joints of the skull bones.

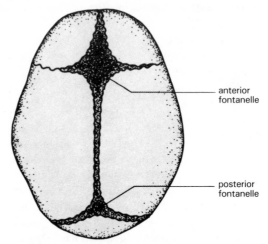

anterior
fontanelle

posterior
fontanelle

Top of head of young baby

The fontanelles are covered with membrane which protects the brain. They gradually close as the bones of the skull grow together. The posterior (back) fontanelle is usually closed by six to seven weeks, the anterior (front) one by about eighteen months. If the fontanelles are slow in closing it is an indication of poor bone growth, possibly owing to lack of calcium and vitamin D.

Sexual organs. In contrast to the rapid early growth and development of the brain and skull, the sexual organs grow very slowly until about the age of ten, and then, with the onset of puberty, there is a period of rapid growth and development, which begins earlier in girls than boys.

Weight. Weighing and measuring a child at regular intervals is a useful guide to his state of health, especially during the first year of life. If a baby is gaining weight steadily then we know that he must be getting enough food and making use of it for growth. If, in addition, he is happy, lively and active we can be sure that all is well. On the other hand, if a small baby does not gain any weight for two to three weeks it is an indication that something is wrong. It may simply be that he is not getting enough food or it could be that because of vomiting or some other reason he is unable to absorb the food. (If too much weight is gained, then it is an indication for the child's diet to be regulated to prevent obesity.)

However, weighing and measuring need to be carried out over a period of time at regular intervals so that the pattern of growth can be seen. The average new-born baby weighs about 3.400 kg (7 lb 8 oz) but his weight could be anything between 2.50 and 6 kg (5½ lb–14 lb), so when studying a baby's weight gain it is necessary to know his birth weight. Variations in the lengths of babies are not so big, the average length being 50 cm (20½ in) within a range of 45.5 cm–55.8 cm (18–22 in). Boys are usually slightly heavier than girls, although boys and girls tend to grow at much the same rate in the first seven to ten years.

Age	Height (cm)	Weight (kilos)	Height (in)	Weight (lb)
Birth	52	3.400	20½	7½
5 months	63.5	6.800 Double birth weight	25	15
1 year	71	10.000 Treble birth weight	28	22
1½ years	76	11.700	30	26
2 years	83.5	13.600 Four times birth weight	33	30
3 years	94	16.000	37	34
4 years	101.5	18.000	40	39
5 years	106.5	20.400 Six times birth weight	42	45
6 years	111.5	22.000	44	48
7 years	119.5	23.800 Seven times birth weight	47	52

These figures show that a baby grows very rapidly indeed during the first year of life. After this, growth slows down to a steady rate. This fact is important because it demonstrates how unreasonable it is to expect the one to five year old to eat as enormously as he did in his first year. He does not need such large meals because his growth has slowed down.

The child's eventual height will depend mostly on hereditary factors, bearing in mind that most children are slightly taller than their parents. A useful prediction of a child's eventual height is obtained by doubling his height at two years of age.

Factors which affect growth adversely are as follows:

1. poor diet, especially lack of protein;
2. poor general health, often associated with poor diet;
3. serious illness;
4. lack of exercise;
5. lack of sufficient rest and sleep;
6. lack of affection, security and stimulation;
7. lack of growth hormone which is produced by the pituitary gland (very rare).

1. It is no accident that the teenagers of today are larger than their grandparents. Increasing knowledge of diet, and the lessening of dire poverty, have meant that most modern children have the right foods for growth and good health. Before the Second World War it was possible to guess the social class of a person by his height and his health. People from the upper classes always had adequate food so their children tended to grow tall and strong. They also appeared to be, on

average, brighter and more active. This has led to the belief that a poor protein diet in the first two years of life (when the brain is growing and developing rapidly) will prevent a person reaching his full intellectual potential. Such a theory is difficult to prove because poor diet is often linked with so many other socio-economic problems in a child's life. But logically this may be the reason why many people in the newly-developing countries are unable to use their resources to their full advantage.

2. and 3. If a child has a series of minor illnesses or one serious illness, growth is often held back for a while, although most children catch up rapidly when they are fit again.

4. Lack of exercise will lead to poor muscle 'tone' which slows down growth.

5. Lack of rest and sleep tends to slow down growth.

6. Evidence suggests that emotional problems in a child caused by lack of affection, security and stimulation can result in a slowing down of growth.

The development of children

The process of development is continuous from conception to maturity. So the first observable signs are when the baby begins to kick in his mother's womb.

Although man is an animal, there are some differences that make him superior in some respects to all other animals. These differences can be summarised as follows:

1. the ability to stand upright and walk, thus leaving his hands free for food gathering, defence and other activities;

2. the ability to use his index-finger in opposition to his thumb. This enables him to perform fine movements and to use implements;

3. the ability to use a spoken language and to think abstractly – this allows him to communicate and reason;

4. the complexity of his emotions and social relationships.

The study of a child's development, therefore, is really observations of these aspects.

The human baby is one of the most helpless of creatures at birth, yet, by the time he is a year old, he has a rudimentary mastery of many of the skills necessary for his future life. By his first birthday he is mobile, in some way or other – either by rolling over, 'swimming' on the floor or by crawling, creeping or even walking. He has an understanding of speech and will be communicating his needs by pointing and/or using his voice. His manipulative powers are developing, so that he can pick up objects, examine them and discard them if not wanted.

Physical and motor development

The newborn baby has very little control of his body but he does have reflex movements which are essential to his survival. A reflex movement is an automatic response to certain stimulus – there is no conscious control. A good example of a reflex movement is seen when a person treads on an upturned drawing pin. The foot is removed very rapidly without the need to think 'I must move my foot'.

The baby's reflexes include the following:

1. 'rooting' reflex – when his cheek is touched he will turn his head and 'search' with his mouth for the nipple;

2. sucking reflex – when a nipple or teat or any other object enters his mouth he will suck strongly;

3. palmar and plantar reflexes – when an object is placed in the palm of the hand, the fingers will grip the object firmly. Similarly, if an object is placed on the sole of the foot, the toes will curl around it. This reflex was essential when the baby had to cling to his mother's hair. It is a throw-back to our prehistoric ancestry;

4. 'startle' reflex – in response to any sudden movement or noise, the baby will visibly 'jump' and spread his arms and legs wide whilst screaming;

5. stepping reflex – if you hold a newborn baby upright on a flat surface, he will make stepping movements with his feet.

In addition to these reflex movements, the newborn baby communicates by crying; he can wave his arms and legs and turn his head from side to side. When placed on his tummy, he can lift his head from the floor momentarily, but when he is held upright his head will fall back unless it is supported.

Gradually the reflexes vanish and are taken over by conscious controlled movements. His crying becomes more concentrated and more a demand for services.

Motor development. Motor development and control of movement follows a set pattern, the earliest development being the control of the eyes and lips. From then on development follows two principles:

1. The control of the head and back is followed by the gradual control of the rest of the body from the head downwards.

2. The control of the larger muscles and big movements must come before control of the smaller muscles and finer movements.

In addition there are various periods in a baby's life during which he is 'ready' to master a certain skill, such as sitting up or walking, because his body has become capable of doing so. And if the right stimulus is given at this time then he will achieve this skill easily. On the other hand, if stimulus is lacking then his development will be impaired. This means that a child cannot be 'taught' a motor skill until his muscles are capable of performing it. Therefore it is essential to supply the correct stimulus at the right moment for him.

Motor development follows a pattern, although the age at which a child reaches each stage varies quite considerably. Some stages of this development may be apparent for only a day or two, others may last for many weeks.

A chart to show the progression towards walking and dexterity follows:

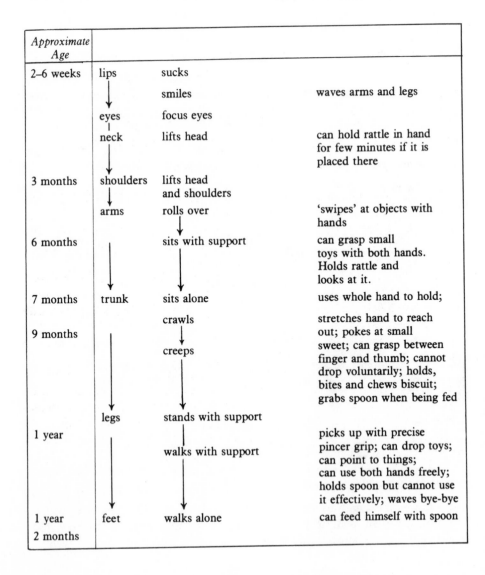

Approximate Age			
2–6 weeks	lips	sucks	
	↓	smiles	waves arms and legs
	eyes	focus eyes	
	neck	lifts head	can hold rattle in hand for few minutes if it is placed there
3 months	shoulders ↓	lifts head and shoulders	
	arms	rolls over ↓	'swipes' at objects with hands
6 months		sits with support	can grasp small toys with both hands. Holds rattle and looks at it.
7 months	trunk	sits alone	uses whole hand to hold;
9 months		crawls ↓ creeps	stretches hand to reach out; pokes at small sweet; can grasp between finger and thumb; cannot drop voluntarily; holds, bites and chews biscuit; grabs spoon when being fed
1 year	legs	stands with support walks with support	picks up with precise pincer grip; can drop toys; can point to things; can use both hands freely; holds spoon but cannot use it effectively; waves bye-bye
1 year 2 months	feet	walks alone	can feed himself with spoon

A baby starts to 'learn' to walk even before he is born. By kicking and other movements in the uterus, he is exercising his muscles and helping in their development. After birth the first stage towards becoming upright is the raising of his head, followed by the lifting of his head and shoulders. He must gain control of his back, trunk and arm muscles, so that he can sit up, before he gains control of the leg muscles so that he can walk. This is why it is important to give a baby plenty of opportunity to move from early days. Equally important is to let him walk in his own time and not try to force this development by putting him in a baby walker contraption.

Factors that will help him are:

1. good diet and good health;

2. opportunity to exercise – because this increases muscle tone which helps development;

3. plenty of freedom to move around and explore from early days;

4. bare feet – avoiding any restriction of shoes; better grip on floor;

5. stimulation – fun and encouragement from mother/nursery nurse;

6. push and pull-along toys.

Walking may be accomplished at any time between about seven months and two years. The average age is about thirteen months for a girl and fourteen months for a boy. The baby also learns to control his hands and use them purposefully, so that by the time he is eighteen months old he is usually walking well and is able to feed himself with cup and spoon.

From this age both developments proceed rapidly. From mastery of walking, he progresses to crawling upstairs to walking upstairs and climbing on furniture. By two and a half years he is running and jumping and kicking a large ball with some degree of accuracy. By the time he is approaching seven years old he will be able to run on his toes and will be active and skilful in sliding, climbing, swinging and hopping. He will also be able to dance to music.

The hands become more and more efficient, especially for finer movements, so that by two years he can unwrap a small sweet and pick up pins and needles. By two and a half he can pull down his own pants at the toilet, although he cannot always get them up, and can eat skilfully with spoon and may use a fork.

By the time he is approaching seven years of age he can use a knife and fork, print accurately and draw recognisable pictures.

Exercise 10

Multiple-choice questions

1. Where does the most rapid growth take place in a child during his first year of life?
(a) in the long bones;
(b) in the brain and skull;
(c) in the flat bones;
(d) in the liver;
(e) in the genital organs.

2. By what age should a baby have doubled his birth-weight?
(a) six weeks;
(b) seven months;
(c) eight months;
(d) one year;
(e) five months.

3. Fluoride aids good health because:
(a) it helps growth;
(b) it makes strong muscles;
(c) it combines with calcium to form strong teeth;
(d) it helps convert iron to haemoglobin;
(e) it helps the anterior fontanelle to close.

Essay questions

4. How does a baby learn to walk? What stages must he go through? How can a mother or nursery nurse best help a child acquire this skill?

5. Describe how a child acquires manipulative skills during his first two years of life. What part is played by the mother, or the nursery nurse, in helping a child develop these skills?

Observations

6. Observe a child of between three and six months lying on the floor. Describe his movements and attempts to become mobile. How does he respond when you talk to him, and when you offer him a toy?

7. In the same way, observe a child of between nine months and twelve months. Compare and contrast the two children's activities. Say how they differ.

Suggestions for further reading

Arnold Gesell, *How a Baby Grows*, Hamish Hamilton Ltd
Arnold Gesell, *The First Five Years*, Methuen & Co., Ltd
Mary D. Sheridan, *The Developmental Progression in Young Children*, HMSO
Mary D. Sheridan, *Spontaneous Play in Early Childhood*, NFER Publishing Co
Mary D. Sheridan, *Children's Developmental Progress*, NFER Publishing Co

Chapter 11
Intellectual growth and development

The human brain and nervous system

The way we employ our brains is commonly thought to be what chiefly distinguishes man from the animal kingdom. The adult brain weighs about 1.3 kg (3 lb), and consists of a pinkish-grey mass protected by the shell. It is cushioned against bumps and blows by shock-absorbing fluid, and is wrapped in three membranes. It is the headquarters of a most complicated communications network, and is fed messages via the millions of nerve fibres supplied to all parts of the body. Information received (for instance, seeing a potential accident and taking appropriate action to prevent it) is triggered by messages or impulses from the appropriate brain centre.

There are three main message centres in the brain; the medulla oblongata takes care of automatic functions like the pumping of the heart and breathing, the cerebellum controls the voluntary action of the muscles, while the cerebrum is the seat of consciousness, memory, reason – in fact learning and personality.

Relatively speaking, at birth the baby's brain is nearer physical maturity than most other organs of the body. In fact it is fully functioning before birth. Its growth will virtually be complete by the age of seven. Scientists are only just beginning to learn more about the relationship of the size and structure of the human brain to an individual's functioning, or intelligence. It is not a simple matter of 'the larger the brain, the more brainy the owner'. We do know that oversized or undersized brains do not work as well as they should. We also know that the brain can be damaged at birth, thereafter impairing the functions of mind and/or body. We now also believe that the development of the brain can be stunted by a diet deficient in protein, in the child up to the age of about two. It is a subject on which current and future research may furnish us with keys to improving every child's optimum brain development.

Learning and intelligence

The newborn baby is helpless and incapable. All he can do is cry and suck. All other skills and responses have to be learned, and the way he learns is first through the thousands of sense impressions his nerve cells receive and transmit to the brain, hands and eyes playing a particularly important part here. Very

gradually he will learn to organise all this stored information and make some sense of both his environment and his own body, and the way the one reacts with the other. For instance, he discovers through repetition that the sight and sound of mother's presence means that he is going to be picked up and probably fed.

He is almost ceaselessly active, while awake. He appears curious and interested in his surroundings. He can attend to things he wants to investigate further. Having discovered a new accomplishment, such as crowing, hand-clapping or raising his head, he proceeds to repeat and repeat it, and obviously enjoys doing so. Quite early on, he also imitates spontaneously. Thus he seems to possess inbuilt aids to learning, both motivation and means. The *enjoyment* will later develop into a sense of achievement and pride, the *repetition* into perseverance and persistence. *Curiosity* will remain an impelling urge to find answers, and *imitation* will bring him the benefit of adult and other models.

Thus equipped, the child begins to develop what we know as intelligence. A reasonable degree of intelligence is really proof of the effective functioning of the brain and nervous system, and the way this helps the individual to deal successfully with all the events and situations that arise in his life.

Intelligence covers a whole range of quite different abilities – for instance to perceive and recognise accurately, to retain and recall experiences, to solve problems with only one correct solution, to solve problems with a variety of possible solutions by applying recalled and relevant facts, to evaluate and criticise one's own solutions and seek to adjust them. Such abilities can undoubtedly be improved with guidance and help. Approximately one-third of these intellectual skills will have been mastered by the time the child is six. Nearly fifty per cent of the child's mental capacity will have developed between birth and the age of four, a further thirty per cent between four and eight, and the remaining twenty per cent between eight and seventeen.

Levels of thought

Intellectual development, however, is not a straightforward progression – the child acquiring more and more adult intellectual skills, from infancy and throughout childhood. In order to understand the child's intellectual development more fully we need to realise that the young child perceives the world in a very different way from adults or even older children. Jean Piaget, the Swiss psychologist, spent many years studying his own and other children's modes of perceiving and thinking, and his findings have greatly influenced teaching methods in recent years. Very briefly, he found that there appear to be four stages through which children pass in the development of their mental capacities. The age ranges for each period are the *average* ages at which children demonstrate the characteristics of thought of each period.

The stages are:
1. The sensory-motor stage from birth to two;
2. The pre-operational stage from two to seven;
3. The concrete operational stage from seven to eleven;
4. The formal operations stage from eleven to fifteen.

During the first stage, the baby and infant perceives and learns directly and entirely through his five senses, and his own actions – in fact he does not so much think as act. In the next stage, the child can think (helped by his growing acquisition of language) but he thinks intuitively. He does not reason, nor can he think in any abstract way. A child at the next stage can think logically about situations and events he knows about, and a child at the ultimate stage can think and reason abstractly – the prerequisite of formal intellectual study.

We need to look more closely at the pre-operational stage, and we must understand that the small child is an egocentric being, seeing the world only from his own point of view, and in relation to his own limited experience. We can see it in his total lack of understanding of 'long ago' and 'far away': how many of us have been asked if we were alive at the time of the dinosaurs, or have been asked to 'fix' the timing of a promised future treat by stating whether it is 'before my birthday'? Some of us still retain a mental picture of a setting we imagined for some far-off story we heard as infants; almost always it approximates – quite incongruously – to a place we knew in childhood. This story was obviously so far removed in time and distance from anything we could understand that in our mind's eye and memory we had to turn it into something we *did* know. We can see the child's egocentric thinking in the way he will hit out at a chair he has bumped into, or talk to a statue or shop dummy. Everything, it seems to him, must be possessed of life, as he is.

Because he cherishes ideas of things he would like to own, or roles he would like to play, he sometimes talks and acts as though they are real. He may even take the prized possessions of someone else because he has little concept of ownership. He cannot tell the difference between fantasy and reality, and may believe that things dreamed or daydreamed really happened. He believes that the adults who direct his life also direct the universe, and may cry angrily if mother 'lets it rain' on the day of a proposed picnic.

He attributes his own tastes and preferences to other people, as we can see in his choice of presents to those he loves. He will be confused about relationships, because he can think in one dimension only. Nursery nurses often have to answer the question 'Is that your Daddy?' when husband or boyfriend visits the nursery. It is also difficult for young children to realise that one person can play two roles – for instance mother and teacher. It is essentially a here-and-now world that the child at this stage inhabits. All his thinking branches outwards from himself and his own experience.

Yet, during this stage, if he is offered sufficient real-life experience, he begins to move towards the next stage of logical thought and reason. He makes discoveries about, for instance, the way materials behave, and he sees there is a

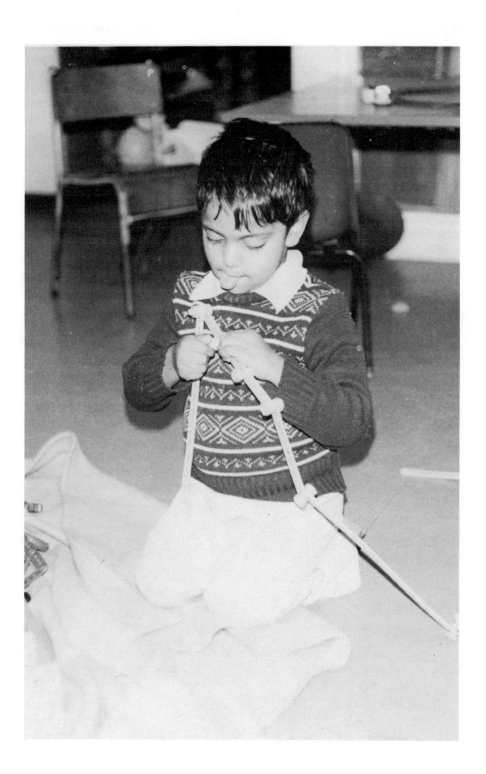

consistency and pattern in what happens. Thus he can form ideas (concepts) about, for instance, objects that float and sink. He 'knows' in a very real sense, because he has learned (not been taught) certain facts to be true; he comes to expect other things to follow. He can group objects together by some common characteristic. Such mental ability will later be very important in the more formal and advanced studies in his primary and secondary education.

Implication and application

Here, then, are the guidelines for all who are concerned with the healthy development of young children.

1.   The nursery years are clearly a crucial stage in the child's intellectual development.

2.   We should approach any testing of intelligence with caution.

3.   We should avoid labelling children intelligent or unintelligent; a child who at this age may appear to be either may simply be at a different stage of intellectual development from his peers.

4.   We should keep our expectations of children's intelligent behaviour very flexible.

5.   We should accept that we cannot artificially hurry children from one stage to another; the physical maturation of the brain may be involved. Undoubtedly the amount of stimulation and first-hand experience in a child's life so far has a great bearing on the stage he has reached.

6.   We can see that active first-hand experience (often in the form of play) is not a 'frill' or pill-sweetener to intelligent thought and development. It is an integral part and stage of learning.

7.   We should be aware all the time of the contributions we can make, depending on the stage the child is at, in stimulating mental processes and growth.

Play and language

Through play we stimulate interest and curiosity which result in learning. Enjoyment and activity are the keynotes of play, and they work with the child's inbuilt drive to learn. Novelty, variety and spontaneity are other aspects of play which accord with the child's mercurial moods and limited powers of concentration; they will also aid memory.

It is not enough, however, to set the scene for play and then just leave the child to get on with it. Play must be structured to exercise his developing intelligence and mental processes. (We shall deal with this aspect more fully in the chapter on play.) We need to watch and listen to each child's action and reactions so that we can offer material which all the time is challenging him and preparing him for the next step.

Most importantly, he needs help in developing the tool of language so that he can make his thoughts clear, put them in order and express himself. Language is a way of expressing happenings. Without it the child will never be able to deal with an abstract world (or even a concrete world) and so will be greatly handicapped in all later learning.

The three Rs

We cannot leave this subject without a brief word on a matter which troubles many parents of pre-school children.

If the nursery years are such a vital stage in the child's intellectual development, why is not more time spent on giving children a head start in their formal education? Surely this is one of the prime tasks of nursery education?

The answer is really both yes and no. Of course we are concerned at nursery with building a sound foundation for later literacy and numeracy skill. But our preparation for these is frequently not recognised as such by parents, who look only for superficial evidence such as counting out loud and writing names. Our preparation goes much wider and deeper. Educationists over the years have been able to analyse the skills required for mastery of the three Rs – and there are a great many of them. Visual and auditory perception and discrimination are two obvious examples. Spotting small differences and similarities between items or symbols is another. Matching, sorting, grouping, ordering, grading, cultivating a left-to-right eye movement across a page, are still more.

None of these skills will be attainable unless the child has developed reasonable co-ordination between hand and eye, control of the working of his body, and accurate small manipulative movements.

Furthermore, as we have already seen, children learn by doing. Before about five they cannot deal successfully – or for any sustained period of time – with abstract ideas or symbols. First-hand experience, in all its richness, must come first. Parents do not always realise the importance of language as a foundation for later learning. They are apt to say 'He talks all the time at home – there's nothing new about that!' What they perhaps do not realise is that the skill and expertise of the trained adults at nursery who, unlike busy mothers at home, have nothing to do other than concentrate on the children, can develop the art of communication to a far higher degree than is possible in most homes. This will happen through questions and discussions, books and stories, rhymes, finger plays and songs. Without a working vocabulary of some 2000 words, the child at five will be at a disadvantage, educationally speaking, when he begins 3R work at the infant school. Besides, many parents do not fully appreciate that a good nursery environment can give the child such self-confidence, grounding in learning skills, and such a positive and enthusiastic approach to school generally that he will indeed be off to a head start when he begins the next stage of his education.

Link with all-round development

We cannot separate a child's intellectual development from his physical, social and emotional state. To learn effectively, the child must be sufficiently well-fed, healthy, comfortable and wide awake. He cannot function mentally in a stuffy, dark, cold or overheated atmosphere.

Some less tangible obstacles to learning are insecurity, conflict and tensions, fear of making mistakes, hostile attitude to authority, discrimination, non-involvement with the other children, discouragement.

The child needs to feel relaxed, happy and secure in order to feel self-confident, and to welcome intellectual challenge. He needs to trust and feel at ease with the adults, and be accepted by his peers.

Exercise 11

Multiple-choice questions

1. An intelligent child is one who:
(a) has proved himself on IQ tests;
(b) has a large-sized brain;
(c) has clever parents;
(d) comes from a middle-class background and expresses himself well;
(e) one whose brain and nervous system function effectively, enabling him to interact successfully with his environment.

2. Only one of the following statements is true. Which is it?
(a) Intelligence is a fixed entity and cannot be improved upon.
(b) Almost all of a child's mental capacity will have developed by the age of four.
(c) Environment has no influence on a child's eventual intellectual ability.
(d) The growth of the brain will be virtually complete by the age of seven.
(e) There is no connection between diet and brain development.

3. A small child's thinking is egocentric. This means:
(a) he is conceited;
(b) he has no feelings for other people;
(c) he is eccentric;
(d) he sees the world from his own standpoint, in the context of his life experience so far;
(e) he is selfish and greedy.

Essay questions

4. Parents of a child in your nursery school group confide to you that they are worried because their son is not learning to read or write. How would you answer them?

5. Give examples, from your own experience if possible, of how learning can be hampered by physical, emotional, social or environmental factors.

Suggestions for further reading

Alice Yardley, *Young Children Thinking*, Evans Brothers Ltd
Jean Marzello and Janice Lloyd, *Learning Through Play*, Penguin Books Ltd
Vorna Hildebrand, *Introduction to Early Childhood Education*, Macmillan Publishers Ltd

Chapter 12
Language and communication

Development of speech and language

Scientists have discovered that some animals have their own systems of communication; different noises can convey such messages as 'Keep off! That's my
territory!' or 'Come here – I fancy you'. We all know that parrots and myna birds
can be taught to utter certain sounds at a given signal, and some domestic pets can
be taught to respond vigorously to commands or 'trigger' words. One corgi dog
becomes quite ferocious if he hears his most hated sounds uttered, even as
syllables of words with quite different meanings, such as 'catalyst' or 'octopus'.

But free, spontaneous speech and complete understanding – in other words
communication – is the prerogative of man. Communication is concerned with
both the physical production of speech – pronunciation, inflection, range,
auditory discrimination and so on – as well as knowledge and awareness of
language itself – using symbols, labelling, meanings, memory, sensing moods.

The baby's earliest sounds and communication

The newborn baby has what might seem a daunting task – to master all the
complexities of a communication system, particularly in the English language
which is unusually rich in vocabulary, and complicated in grammatical structure.

The baby's first sound is breathing, closely followed by crying. We might say
this in itself is a message which tells us he has been born active and healthy. When
he cries, his face will be contorted, the lips stretched wide, and a rather nasal 'a'
sound emerges. This might be called an *urgent cry*, and will be heard repeatedly
over the next few weeks when the baby wants something – food, relief from pain,
relief from discomfort, or from boredom or loneliness.

At the age of a few weeks he will begin to make other, less urgent noises,
sometimes called *comfort sounds*. These often occur after a feed, when baby is
replete, relaxed. There is still saliva present in the mouth, and the sound may
resemble a wet 'goo-goo', as the baby relives, perhaps, the pleasurable sucking
sensation.

By about two or three months, the baby's lip muscles have gained strength
from practised sucking, and we hear the *first definite sound* – M. A little later
comes a hard G sound, bringing the palate into play now, then possibly a nasal N.

161

About the sixth month, with the eruption of the first tooth or teeth, the baby happens upon the first *dental* sound – D. Soon after this, he begins to elongate these first sounds, so that we hear 'Ma', 'Ba', 'Na', 'Da'. These are the *root sounds* of babies all over the world, and from them, depending on how their parents, or those looking after them, select certain sounds to reinforce and shape to their liking, encouraged by smiles, hugs and repetition, the child's future language will grow.

These are the sounds, plus other blurred and indefinite noises that the baby will play with on his own. They form a sort of experimental play which we call *babbling*, and which is clearly enjoyable to the baby. Sometimes certain sounds seem to represent a call for attention, or delight on seeing mother. The pleasure of parents and their response sets up a two-way communication. Within a warm relationship, early attempts at communicating flourish. Baby says 'Da . . . Da' and mother hugs him, smiles, and says in an affectionate, proud tone 'Yes, Dada. It's Dada, isn't it? Dada's coming. Here's Dada!' and so on. Thus the baby learns to make certain sounds in certain situations.

Sometimes a slightly older baby, left alone, will imitate the general buzz of adult conversation in his babbling. This is good practice for him in using different inflections, and also helps to develop vocal cords and the mechanisms of speech.

Another game he plays which helps him to acquire speech is to put his fingers or a hand over or in the mouth of a loved adult who is holding him and talking to him. Through such investigation, he is learning, in a literally first-hand way, about movements of tongue, lips, teeth, reverberations through the lips from the voice box.

At this stage, between approximately five and nine months, his *understanding of and response to language* is just as important as his utterances. He hears 'bye-bye' and comes to associate it with all sorts of things happening – someone waving a hand, a hug, a kiss. The smell of perfume or aftershave, the feel of a soft cheek or bristly beard, a retreating figure, the sound of a door closing, a car starting up. Soon he has only to hear the word and he automatically waves himself. Thus we see that association and imitation are both going to play an important part in his powers of communication.

Other forms of communication in infancy

Of course, it is not only through crying and early vocalisations (utterances) that babies communicate. They have no difficulty in letting us know what they do not like – for instance, puréed spinach or minced liver. Joy at being picked up or played with will be expressed in laughs and smiles and bouncing up and down. Resentment at being held by a stranger, or held when he wants to be left alone, will be expressed by pushing, kicking and rejecting with arms and legs. From about nine months he will also point at objects he wishes to make contact with. By about nine months, the baby often has about *four or six recognisable words*. Parents will have fashioned whatever, in their own language, are acceptable baby versions of 'mother', 'father', 'baby', 'good-bye', 'grandmother', perhaps 'dog' or 'cat'. They will have identified themselves with one of these early words, and will attach meaning, for the baby, to the others. Parents are thrilled when the baby progresses as far as this; he seems to be on the threshold of real speech.

At about this time, however, there often comes a period of apparently little progress. This is because baby is concentrating on the absorbing business of crawling, standing, walking. All his energy and efforts are going into these skills, and his concentration engaged in the fascinating world he now finds he can investigate. Like any other human being, he cannot devote himself wholeheartedly to several different things at once.

Progress with speech and understanding

Between one year and eighteen months his vocabulary begins to expand noticeably. He copies from adults, especially mother, labels for things (nouns) in his world, the things that are of most importance to him – dinner, bath, sweets, biscuits, potty, ball, garden, pushchair. He will use one word, helped out with gesture and facial expression, to mean a variety of different things. For instance 'ball' (which will probably sound like 'baw') may mean 'I've got a ball,' or 'There is a ball,' or 'Bring me that ball,' or 'Play ball with me,' or 'Look at my ball and admire it,' or 'There is something resembling a ball,' (pointing to an orange, for example). Now, as throughout the whole period of language acquisition, the child understands far more than he can express.

Between about eighteen months and two years, a few simple verbs appear – 'go', 'come', 'eat', etc. Then when we hear him put together some of his nouns and verbs, for instance 'Daddy come' or 'doggy eat' and then later 'doggy eat dinner', we say he is talking in sentences, in fact he is *really talking*. Of course, he often gets the word order wrong, and does not yet attempt pronouns, prepositions, adjectives or adverbs. Nor can he cope with tenses or noun/verb agreement. This stage of talking is often called *'telegraphese'*, because it is rather like the brief, simple style of telegraph messages; but, whereas adults deliberately leave out the small linking words, the infant has not yet learned them.

The negative appears very early on, always before the positive, and pads out meaning very effectively – for instance: (sadly) 'No Daddy come', (looking out of the window) or (defiantly) 'no go play toys'.

Often these early sentences express commands or requirements. Another interesting development at about this time is that the child begins to substitute words for actions or things, whereas before he always used them together. Now, if you ask him, 'Where is the ball?' when none is in sight, he will look round for it, showing us that he has truly grasped the word and its meaning, and can visualise the real object from the heard symbol alone.

Individual children vary greatly at this stage in the size of their vocabulary.

Gesell found the extremes to be as low as five, and as high as 1200 or more words. Much depends on encouragement to talk, and how much adults reinforce and expand the child's utterances. When a cat enters the room and Timothy says 'Look! Kitty!', one mother may say 'Yes' or 'Mm' abstractedly, or ignore him completely, but another may say 'Yes, here's Kitty. She wants us to stroke her; oh isn't she soft and smooth?'. Of course, the child will not understand every word, but grasps the gist and can guess at meanings of new words, because he hears them in context; he also hears intonation used appropriately, and senses interest, and is given the impetus to go on.

The child's third year sees a tremendous expansion of vocabulary and progress also in sentence length, and general confidence. Questions will arise, often the favourite being 'What's that?'. Word order will be strange, and grammar comes only with difficulty, but intonation will help to suggest the meaning.

By the age of three, he may have a vocabulary of 800 or more words. He will now know many more verbs, which will widen his use of language. He will be able to converse very simply with other children, without adult help. His memory comes into play about this age, indicating that we need language in order to store information and experiences. If we look back to our earliest remembered experiences, we usually find they occurred about three. The three-year old asks many questions; 'What's that?' is still a common one, though it may refer to objects already known to him. He is talking for the sake of talking, and of staying in verbal contact with loved adults. He has now grasped pronouns – 'I', 'Me', 'you', which are confusing – some prepositions – 'in', 'on', 'at', 'to', etc. – and plurals. He can name many of the parts of his body, and knows some colours. He has grasped the idea of changing the present tense into the past where necessary. The appealing (to adults) and indiscriminate way in which he usually adds 'ed' to form the past tense of verbs, shows that he is absorbing some rules of grammar, and applying them in a logical manner. He will say 'Daddy digged the sand', 'I runned all the way'. His acquisition of language is clearly not a simple matter of imitation alone.

By about four, his vocabulary may be about 1500 words. His sentences noticeably lengthen, with more adjectives, and also adverbs. This is the classic age of asking questions, but now they will be 'why?' and 'how?' questions, showing us that he is probing for more complicated information – for reasons and explanations. A four-year-old can ask some disconcerting questions, 'Who made the clouds?', 'Where does the sun go at night?', etc, in this way constantly adding to his knowledge of the universe. He enjoys nonsense language, too, repeating a word several times with alterations to make it sound sillier and sillier, and chuckling heartily at the joke. He revels in exaggerations and tall stories. He is apt to fall over himself (verbally) in his haste to convey something; he may even appear to stutter. He leaves off beginnings of words, saying 'cause' for 'because' and may repeat such a word several times while he gathers his thoughts in order to deliver the next part of the speech with sufficient impact. He mispronounces many words and still uses some baby forms of words. He will often keep up a private and totally unselfconscious commentary on what he is doing; this could be said to be thinking aloud, and it will soon develop into silent worded thoughts.

The five-year-old's vocabulary is usually about 2000 words strong. His speech is clear and distinct, and he can make himself understood by strangers. He may still confuse R and W, S and TH, as foreigners do. But his word order, tenses, subject and verb agreement, plurals, etc. are usually correct. To all intents and purposes, he has mastered his mother tongue.

The uses of language

As adults, we know that it is very largely through the tool of language that we organise and arrange our lives. Through language we come to understand more and more of the world about us. With it we initiate and sustain relationships. We select and manage events and people to our advantage (as in pay negotiations), convenience (as in domestic arrangements), pleasure (as in social invitations). Language allows us to discuss and resolve problems, effect compromises, and gives us the key to the delights of literature and intellectual challenge. We therefore use language in a variety of ways – ways so different that the style of the language itself changes enormously. Compare, for instance, the language employed by barristers in a court of law, and that used by teenagers chatting on the telephone. Yet all are using their mother tongue, and using it appropriately to the particular need. Without the power to talk and make ourselves understood, we should probably be ineffectual, passive, ignorant, friendless, exploited, boring and bored individuals. We might even be pugnacious, because clashes of will must be resolved somehow.

It is interesting to watch the young child develop his use of language, so that eventually for him, too, it becomes this invaluable tool.

If we listen to any short snatches, or longer sustained conversations at nursery, we are soon aware that from the third year onwards all children seem to use language for:

1. protecting their own rights and property ('Get off! I had it first!') and ensuring their own comfort and pleasure ('I like this swing. I'm going to stay here all day.');

2. initiating and maintaining relationships with other children and adults ('Will you be my friend?');

3. reporting on present experience ('I'm painting a big, big lorry.');

4. directing their own and others' actions ('You're the baby and I'm the mummy.');

5. asserting their own superiority ('My one's better than yours.').

The following, more adult, uses of language, however, are noticeable only in children who are cared for by adults who actively encourage the child to communicate:

1. reporting on past experiences ('When I went to Longleat');

2. co-operating with others towards agreed ends ('I know! Let's be spacemen!');

3. anticipating and predicting the future ('It might fall down if we do it like that.');

4. comparing possible alternatives ('Glue's better than sticky tape.');

5. seeing cause and effect, and connections between events ('Now it's raining, so we can't go outside.');

6. explaining how and why things happen ('He pressed it too hard – that's why the wheel fell off.');

7. attending to abstract problems (for instance, of a character in a book) and suggesting possible solutions ('*I* would have chopped the dragon's head off!');

8. referring to symbolic uses of materials in imaginary games (while placing grass on small plastic plates): 'This is our supper. It's spaghetti. Umm, lovely!';

9. justifying behaviour ('Anyway, *he* pushed *me* first!');

10. reflecting upon his own and other people's feelings ('When our Gran died, my mum cried all day, she was so sad.').

It is not difficult to see how these latter uses of language give the child a much more powerful grasp of events, and much greater depth as a thinking, self-regulating individual, bound up as they are with thought, learning, understanding, reason, choices, emotion, and empathy with others.

How, then, can we fulfil our role during the nursery years in enriching children's language skills?

The role of the adult

1. First of all, we must be approachable in ourselves, and our attitudes. We can help to create a relaxed friendly atmosphere in which the child will feel free to talk.

2. We can cultivate our own listening skills – *really* listening to what each child is saying, and showing our attentiveness by concentrating on him alone, staying still, looking at his face – preferably on the same level – refraining from interruptions, letting him finish, giving the response he is looking for, whether it be amusement, mock horror or admiration. Only in this way will he grow in self-confidence as a talker – and a person.

We can encourage listening skills in the children, by *telling* stories, introducing *listening games* with instruments, domestic sounds, the sounds in nature, etc.

3. We can provide stimulating surroundings which will give children plenty to *talk about*. A bare, drab, or unchanging room or play materials will not inspire conversation.

4. We can particularly encourage all forms of dramatic play which involve much talking. Puppets, dolls, masks, two telephones, a well-equipped home corner and dressing-up clothes are good starting points.

5. We should show our own interest in and enthusiasm for the content, the beauty and fun of language. Books, stories, finger plays, poetry, word games, songs all have an important part to play.

6. We should always give a good example in use of language, with correct grammar and pronunciation, word endings, etc. We should modulate our tone pleasantly, avoiding shouting, whining, snapping or hectoring. We should employ different sentence forms, and introduce new, lively and relevant vocabulary wherever possible.

7. We should direct children's attention to potential talking points whenever they occur, in pictures, on displays, the birds on the bird table outside. We should always be ready to carry on a short discussion that has arisen spontaneously – for instance, about some cakes that a group of children have just made.

8. We should be alert to fresh ideas from outside the nursery as a stimulus to conversation. These may be suggested by interesting items the children bring in, visitors to nursery, or visits out which can be organised. Even the shyest child will respond well to such fresh impact.

9. We should make our questioning thought-provoking, and requiring a properly formulated sentence as reply, rather than a straight 'yes' or 'no' or one-word factual answer like 'red'. We should ask 'how?' and 'why?' questions. Some children not used to being talked to much may need some help here – for instance, 'How does our hamster eat his food? He takes it in his front paws . . . etc. That's how he eats, isn't it?'. We can frame our questions thus: 'I wonder what will happen if . . .', 'How would you feel if . . .' and then show we value what the children offer in reply.

10. We should be quick to spot specific speech defects, difficulties, or lack of progress, talk about these to our superiors, note what steps are taken, then do all we can to help to overcome these problems.

11. We should accept the children's verbal contributions, including mistakes, but where necessary, rephrase and give him back the correct version in an uncritical, oblique way, so that he does hear the correct version. For instance:
Martin: We wen over my Nan's Sundy and dun fruit pickin'.

N.N.: You went to your Nan's on Sunday, did you Martin? And you did fruit picking? That was exciting!

We should also encourage children to talk descriptively and precisely. For instance, 'You know, it was a thingummy' does not adequately describe a small black beetle.

12. We should answer children's questions simply and honestly, even when they concern something we find embarrassing. For instance 'Are you going to die soon, now you're quite old, Mummy?'. We must bring up the child to trust words spoken by trusted adults.

13. We can use the media whenever appropriate to extend and stimulate language. Some children's television programmes (properly used and shared by adults, never as a *substitute* for talking), and the use of tape recorders can offer much lively and original material.

14. In our semi-formal talking times we should constantly be aware of bringing in *all* members of the group, and leading them into the more advanced uses of language. Some talking times can be rather unprofitable if one or two confident and forthcoming children monopolise the conversation. They probably already enjoy plenty of opportunity and encouragement to talk at home, whereas others, who would have benefited from such a nursery session, will in consequence hang back and be reduced to silence.

15. We can make the best use of mealtimes, so that they are truly social occasions.

16. We should avoid talking *down to*, or *at* children, and, most important, should avoid *talking all the time*. Pauses are a most effective part of speech, as any public speaker or actor knows, and quiet periods throw into sharper focus the periods when we have much to share verbally. Children quickly learn to 'switch off' a constant verbal barrage.

17. We should aim at spending about ten minutes a day, on a one-to-one basis, with children experiencing difficulties.

18. We should use singing, music, rhythm and other forms of expression to encourage communication and confidence. It is no coincidence that often the only remnants of a foreign language we once half-learned when young, which we later either remember or would dare to utter, are the words of a song.

Difficulties in language development

There is an important difference between the child who has poor speech, and the child who has poor language, although the two conditions are sometimes found together.

If it is purely a problem of articulation, probably stemming from defects in the speech mechanisms, the child will require expert professional advice and help, probably regular sessions with a speech therapist.

A failure to develop communicable language, however, is a much more complex and common problem. The reasons will probably involve physical, environmental and emotional factors. When seeking reasons, it is often possible to eliminate or identify certain *physical factors*, which will go some way towards helping the situation. It is thus very important that every young child should have a physical examination by a doctor, including a hearing test, before adults assume that language difficulties must be due to environmental reasons. The sort of conditions which may be present include:

1. hearing loss due to a permanent condition;

2. periods of hearing loss due to past or present catarrhal conditions affecting the ears, or enlarged adenoids, etc.;

3. autism;

4. mental subnormality;

5. malformation of palate or teeth;

6. cerebral palsy.

Environmental and emotional factors which may explain language retardation, as it is called, include:

1. history of battering, accident or illness;

2. immaturity;

3. shyness;

4. deaf parents who do not talk to child;

5. parents of low intelligence;

6. background lacking in stimulation (the child may have been kept for hours in pram or cot, or may have very young mother (or a mother suffering from depression) who does not realise the importance of talking to baby;

7. mixed-language home, or home/nursery situation;

8. over-indulgent home where all child's needs are met by others without need for him to talk (perhaps a child of elderly parents, or last in a big family);

9. twins;

10. history of unhappiness and instability in home background;

11. lack of maternal affection (may be from home of care or unsatisfactory fostering or child minding);

12. temporarily unsettled state (caused by starting nursery, moving house, etc.).

Any or all these reasons may be compounded by emotional difficulties when the child feels different, inadequate, or excluded from peer contact. Unhappiness may reveal itself in withdrawal, aggressive behaviour, finding unacceptable outlets for frustration.

How the adult can help

For the child with communication difficulties, more so than with the 'normal' child, we must begin at the point the child is at. For instance, it is useless to fire 'open-ended' questions at a Chinese child who can barely speak any English, or to expect a desperately shy child to enter instantly into jolly finger play groups. Relationships come first, as with all things. Quiet, casual looking at pictures or books together for a few minutes at a time may well be the beginning stage. We should never underline a child's difficulties by drawing attention to him in a group or forcing him to talk. On the other hand, occasionally we may have to 'act dumb' if a child who can talk but has not experienced the need at home continues to try and make himself understood at nursery by merely tugging at our skirts and pointing.

We can introduce simple tongue-twisters and other articulation games to a group which includes a child with difficulties of this kind. We can select stories which involve participation by the children in repeated phrases etc. Bubble blowing is helpful to children who are tense and communicating poorly because it relaxes the throat muscles. Rhymes involving actions of any sort are effective in reinforcing meanings and aiding memory. Music, movement and other forms of expression, such as painting, offer alternative avenues of communication; success and enjoyment in these often spills over into greater success in verbal communication, and breaks down self-consciousness and reserve.

In summary, we might say that for children with communication difficulties, we need to abide by all the guidelines set out on page 166, but we must do so more consciously and intensively, without, of course, letting the child know that he is the focus of concern. Nursery nurses, because they frequently deal with the individual child in a personal way more than teachers, are in a better position to help him communicate. They should take every opportunity during the day that lends itself to establishing communication, suiting it to the individual child's needs and abilities.

Our aim, working through warm relationships, stimulating surroundings, activities and approaches, is to produce children who are eager, self-confident, competent, interested and interesting communicators. As a foundation for the whole of their future education and future life, we can do them no greater service.

Books and stories

Books and stories play such a vital part in a child's language development that we need to give them separate consideration. They are at the same time a means to growing competence in language, and a source of pleasure in themselves.

We who probably derive great pleasure from books might be surprised to learn that a survey (Plowden Report, 1967) showed that nearly thirty per cent of homes in Britain possessed five books or fewer. We should, therefore, not assume that all our children will come to nursery with a ready-made interest in books, or knowledge of how to care for and respect them. Unless we can encourage such an approach, however, and sustain the interest already present in our more privileged children, we shall be doing our charges a disservice.

Despite the extensive use of audio-visual aids in teaching at all levels today, books are still indispensable, and an essential component of learning throughout life. They can be sources of practical information, aids to our powers of expression, and a window on other worlds we might never otherwise know. They offer emotional release and comfort, escape from dreary reality, insight into human relationships, companionship, entertainment, beauty, humour and uplift. We should try to share with others – rather like the evangelists of old – this precious world we possess.

Choosing books

1. About one year. From the age of about one year or even earlier, the infant's perception will have developed enough for him to take pleasure in sharing of a short, simple picture book, with his mother or the person who looks after him. The book itself should be tough, wipeable, light and easy to handle on a lap, with rounded corners. It should feature familiar (to the infant) objects, drawn with clear outlines, bright colours (red is the first colour children take notice of), uncluttered by background detail, shadows etc. Print is not necessary at this stage. The objects must mean something to him – for instance, the mug or plate he drinks and eats from, the teddy bear he plays with, and so on. Thus each picture is a talking point. Mother says, for instance 'Car. Yes, a car. It's like Daddy's car isn't it? How does Daddy's car go? It goes brrm, brrmm, doesn't it?' In this way, the child learns to identify the picture symbols he sees with a real object in his life, and the spoken and heard word. He also learns to set each object in its context, knowing what it is like and what it does. As well as gaining in language, he is coming to associate books with pleasure and the pleasurable close contact with those he loves. This close contact, 'special' time devoted solely to him and books, will continue, probably at bedtime, for many years.

2. During the second year. He will now like to spend a little longer on a book than the few minutes his first picture book took, and now that he is independently mobile and upright, his knowledge of his surroundings has become wide enough for the subject matter of the book to be slightly less domestic.

3. By about two. He will now be able to follow a simple unfolding of events he knows about – *Timmy's day* or *Jennifer's Birthday* etc. These will not contain a plot as such, but there will be a little action, and maybe a kind of climax – for instance when Jennifer blows out the candles on her cake. Such a book will have a few words with each picture, but mother will probably still expand content and meaning ('Let us blow the candles out, shall we?' and so on). A slightly more advanced version of this kind of book might be *Shopping with Mother* or *Andrew Goes to the Zoo*. Now there is more action, and it takes place outside the home, but it is all very much based still on a character and events the child can identify with, and, of course, there must always be a satisfactory ending. Pictures will continue to play an important part in the book, and they will be bold, clear, bright, easily recognisable, and free from sentimentality.

4. At about three. The child should now be ready for a simple plot, and the central character may now be an animal or animated vehicle (train, truck, etc.). Children of this age happily accept the idea of this talking, thinking, feeling 'hero'; this is because they do not yet differentiate between reality and fantasy. But they cannot yet cope with pure fantasy, such as goblins and witches. The idea of such creatures as these will be alarming and may even give them night terrors, because they do not *know* that, for instance, goblins will not visit them in the night. Events and characters should still be familiar and wholesome, and should reinforce the child's sense of security and his place in the world. Hence tales of rejecting stepmothers, etc. should be avoided. Now that the child is more competent in expressing himself, he will love a story that invites participation in a repeated phrase, and an element of predictability, since his imagination and memory are both developing. There can be more print per page, but it is important that illustrations reflect directly the main sequence of action, so that the child can 'read' the story on his own, or to his friends, away from the adult.

5. Between three and five. For children between three and five, books can begin to feature characters and events slightly outside the child's first-hand experience, thus broadening his horizons. The setting of a simple tale may now be on a boat, or on a farm, for instance. There will be more than one central character now, and these characters will be more three-dimensional, thus feeding the child's capacity for greater self-awareness and awareness of others. They may even do 'naughty things', or undergo some disconcerting experiences, but all will be well in the end. They may be involved in emotionally charged real-life situations, and, through an enlightened exposition of, for instance, going into hospital, moving house, accepting a new baby in the family, the child listening is helped to come to terms with them himself; he is a little better prepared for such an eventuality; he is comforted to be assured that other children have experienced disquieting occurrences, but have come through unscathed.

Humorous books now come into their own. The humour may be of a slapstick kind, or it may be based on a topsy-turvy situation, the discomfiture of an unlikeable adult, or a triumph of small creature over large and powerful one. Taste for such humour shows us that children of this age now possess a good grasp of what is and is not likely or possible in the real world, and also how satisfying it must be to them when small and defenceless wins the day.

6. After the age of about five or six. The child is beginning to differentiate between fact and fantasy. He is also beginning to reach out more, in mind and imagination, to the world of long ago and far away. This, therefore, is the stage when we can introduce some of the rich inheritance we possess of fables, fairy stories and traditional tales. Such stories embody many age-old values and themes we still try to uphold today: goodness brings its rightful reward; appearances can be deceptive; crime does not pay; perseverance brings results; money does not necessarily bring happiness; life is full of 'alarums and excursions', but things usually work out all right in the end. Set down thus, they read like a string of truisms, but children respond well to such themes, wrapped up as they are in colourful characters and flamboyant settings. Stories which labour a moral point – so popular with the Victorians and after – are generally not appreciated today. 'Lessons for life' should come through naturally in the characters and events themselves. Traditional tales also possess a pleasing symmetry, and well-balanced elements of predictability and surprise; there is usually a climax, and a happy ending.

Children of this age can also begin to appreciate tales of some historical and Biblical characters, and tales of children from other lands.

Five- to seven-year-olds will be able to cope with more adventures in a story, several twists and turns of the plot, numerous characters, 'baddies'. They like the titillation of a scare, as long as it is of manageable proportion, and is either resolved happily in the end, or is presented in a humorous way. For instance, there are some delightful books on themes like burglars and ghosts, in which elements of fear and thrill are finely balanced by rational explanation and humour. This is not true of some of the more horrific fairy tales, however, which, we should remember, began in an age when death was much more a fact of everyday life than it is today, and also when the virtue of courage (we might call it brutality) was prized much more highly than that of humanitarianism.

7. Factors governing choice. In selecting books for children of all ages, we need to consider above all whether *we* like them. If we do, our enthusiasm will be evident and the story will be a success. We should guard against the understandable temptation to introduce automatically stories we ourselves liked as children; memory can play tricks on us; we were probably older than we realise when we enjoyed a certain book so much. Our own background, too, may have been very different from that of the children we care for today, thus influencing taste. For instance, does the idea of a 'nanny' insisting that a six-year-old puts on smart gloves to walk into town mean much to multi-culture working class children living on a council estate?

We should naturally consider the age, understanding level, backgrounds, tastes and interests of the children for whom each book is intended. We need to consider the language content – imaginative? enriching? or oversimplified, sentimental or boring? – the length, the illustrations, the lay-out, the cover and general appeal of the book's appearance, the durability, and the price in relation to all these other factors.

Reading and telling stories

We should try both to read and tell stories to our young children. Each approach has its merits, the first directly introducing the charms of a book, complete with relevant illustrations, the second enabling the adult to enter into a direct, dramatic situation with her listeners, using facial expressions, gestures and voices, unhampered and to best effect. Both approaches need preparation, beginning with selection.

About ten minutes is a long enough story session for the under-fives; the over-fives can concentrate a little longer. The children should ideally be in a small group for intimacy, and should all be seated comfortably where they can see and hear clearly. Potential disruptors should be separated and placed strategically at the outset. The whole group should be contained (not squashed) into an area like a book or home corner. If the children are not in a quiet receptive mood, they should be calmed down with a few finger plays or similar activity at the beginning of the session. Visual aids can be used if the story is told, and can add greatly to the interest, provided they are introduced at an appropriate point and all the children can see or touch them without breaking into the flow. Different and interesting voices should be used for different characters, and volume, tone, pace and pitch all varied, to avoid monotony and make the story truly come to life. If this is happening, there will be few interruptions. Questions and comments should be woven in – and answered fully at an appropriate time if possible – but not allowed to spoil the continuity. When the story has ended, if it has been a success there will probably be a few seconds' pause while children come out from the spell. Then there may be the sound of a thumb coming out of a mouth, and a request 'Can we have it again?'. The story teller should avoid the mistake of putting the children through a comprehension test on the story. If she feels questions and discussion are called for, she should make her questions open-ended. 'I wonder what *you* would buy your Mummy if you wanted to give her a special treat?', etc. The acting out of stories heard, or the suggestion that all 'draw me a picture' of it, are not appropriate follow-ups for nursery age children, and may even dampen enthusiasm for future story sessions. If the story has been a success, it has been an immensely worthwhile experience in its own right, and will live on in the children's imagination where it took root.

1. A love of literature. This is probably caught rather than taught, and a great responsibility lies with us as the adults who are in a position to influence children's developing attitudes.

2. The adult's enthusiasm. Our own enthusiasm or lack of it, will come through all our dealings. We can show interest and enthusiam in such matters as books brought in from home by children. (These are frequently not to our taste, which calls for tact.) The arrival of new books for the nursery can be happy occasions, with the pleasure of anticipation. We can let the children see us refer frequently to books for information, for instance in cookery. We can make story times intensely enjoyable occasions for all.

Using and caring for books

We can demonstrate and teach *care and respect in the handling of books* (hand cleanliness, method of page turning etc.) and involve the children in setting aside and repairing damaged books, so that they remain attractive and appealing for a long time.

We can include books in *displays*, and in *follow-up* work to visits, themes or projects going on in the room.

We can teach the children the use of simple *reference books*, and for older children who can read, the mastery of an index.

We can suggest *making class or group books* about, for instance, autumn, our bodies, or whatever is the current interest.

We can provide and maintain an attractive, well-sited and laid out *book corner* where the children can enjoy books individually or in small groups, sitting in comfort, quiet and a good light. For young children at home, books should be kept on proper shelves, not thrown in boxes with toys.

We can frequently *change the selection of books* available to the children, inside and outside the book corner, and display them in new and eye-catching ways.

We can keep ourselves informed of *newly-published children's books* and constantly be appraising them, with the next book allocation allowance in mind, or as ideas for forthcoming Christmas and birthday presents for nephews and nieces, godchildren and so on. About three thousand new children's books come on to the market every year. This is why we have not attempted here to give examples of different points made. Some authors and fictional characters go on for ever, but many date quickly and are superseded by new trends. It is dangerously easy to get in a rut, so we must keep an open mind.

We can be enthusiastic and helpful both in the children's use of the *local public library*, if visited, or school lending library, and encourage interest in book fairs or similar exhibitions held for parents' benefit.

We should always be ready to *talk to parents about books* if they want advice or suggestions for children's books at home.

We can select, collect and introduce the children to *poetry*. We can share with them the beauty of ideas and language, the humour, the fun of play with words, the stimulus of seeing something familiar through the eyes and mind of another individual, who is observant, sensitive and has the gift of expression. In this way, poetry will not seem something apart from everyday life, but another vivid means of communication, intense and living.

Exercise 12

Multiple-choice questions

1. A three-month-old baby communicates:
(a) not at all;
(b) by crying only;
(c) by crying and gurgling;
(d) by gestures, facial expressions, actions, cries and some verbal utterances;
(e) by vocalisation only.

2. Children in their second year, hearing language around them, understand:
(a) more than they can express themselves;
(b) almost everything;
(c) almost nothing;
(d) only sentences spoken to them directly;
(e) only sentences used in conjunction with objects or actions.

3. If a child of nearly five has far fewer than 2000 words at his command, it means:
(a) he must have special attention if he is not to be at a disadvantage, socially and intellectually, when he begins infant school;
(b) he must be mentally subnormal;
(c) he must see a speech therapist;
(d) he must have a hearing loss;
(e) his parents must be of low intelligence.

Essay questions

4. A child of four in your nursery group has articulation difficulties. He is receiving treatment through speech therapy. How might you be able to support this treatment and help him generally?

5. How might language retardation in a five-year-old give rise to difficulties?

Observation

6. Over a period of time, at three different intervals, observe the same child's ability to communicate (0–6 months, 6–12 months, 12–18 months are suggested ages).

Notice:
(a) early vocalisation and jargon;
(b) use of gesture, facial expression, tone of voice;
(c) clearly articulated words;
(d) length of phrases and sentences;
(e) word order;

(f) new and interesting vocabulary;

(g) confidence and spontaneity when talking to adults or other children.

Questions on books and stories

Multiple-choice questions

7. The most suitable content for a book for two-year-olds would be:

(a) pictures of familiar, single objects, named;

(b) fairies, elves and pixies;

(c) cautionary tale of a 'bad' boy;

(d) simple tale, based on familiar domestic happenings with a happy ending;

(e) ghosts in a haunted house.

8. Illustrations in story-books for three to five-year-olds should be:

(a) plentiful, clear, recognisable, pleasing to the eye;

(b) much more important than the text;

(c) very detailed to encourage the child to look intently;

(d) few and far between, to give appropriate importance to the text;

(e) mostly funny caricatures and cartoon-type figures.

9. What is the most important prerequisite for a successful story session with nursery children?

(a) that the story is very short;

(b) that the adult tells, rather than reads the story;

(c) that the story is accompanied by visual aids;

(d) that the adult tries to put on as many different voices as possible;

(e) that the adult likes the story herself.

Essay questions

10. (Suitable for students after approximately one year's training.)
How have you, during your training, tried to encourage children to love books?

11. Draw a plan, or a picture, of an ideal book-corner for a nursery school classroom, and list the types of book with which you would equip it.

Project

12. Visit some book shops near to college or your home. Concerning the children's department, collect information on:

(a) size of stock kept;

(b) methods of display;

(c) any sales promotion;

(d) current best sellers or latest publications;

(e) prominence of 'old favourites';

(f) numbers of children browsing, or adults looking at children's section;

(g) attitude of staff to children browsing or asking questions;

(h) titles and authors of new books which appealed to you (give reason for appeal);

(i) variety of simple reference books, poetry books, simplified vocabulary books for early readers.

Project

13. Make a simple first book for a child of approximately one year old, using improvised materials as far as possible, but incorporating all necessary features.

Suggestions for further reading

Joan Cass, *Literature and the Young Child*, Longman Group Ltd

Hazel Bell, *Situation Books for Under Sixes*, Kenneth Mason Publications Ltd

Alice Yardley, *Exploration and Language*, Evans Brothers Ltd

Joan Tough, *Focus on Meaning*, Unwin Education Books

Joan Tough, *Listening to Children Talking*, Ward Lock Educational Co. Ltd

Andrew Wilkinson, *The Foundation of Language*, Oxford University Press

Chapter 13
Social and emotional development

The newborn baby is an entirely self-centred creature. His emotions are few but extreme – rage or satisfaction – and in so far as he perceives other people at all, it is only in their degree of usefulness in administering to his needs.

Over the next seven years these two extreme emotions are refined and diversified and he becomes better able to handle and control them. His social development leads him to interact in an acceptable way with other people, and in the end to take his place in society on his own or as a member of a group.

The whole process is slow and gradual. There will sometimes appear to be reverses or periods of no progress, but these are perfectly normal; no aspect of learning or development proceeds at a uniform, uninterrupted rate. It must be borne in mind what a great deal of discovering the child has to do, both about himself and the world he finds himself in; moreover it all happens during a period of tremendous physical growth.

To set down ages and stages in this, as in any other aspect of young children's lives, is artificial. Likewise, generalisations can be foolish, even dangerous.

What we have to do is build up a picture of what, for many children, is *often the sequence of development*. For the purposes of clarity, we have divided the sequence into age bands.

Infancy

The newborn baby is entirely dependent on the person who looks after him – usually mother – for all his needs, food and comfort. Rage or contentment are clearly visible – and audible – and are mainly associated with feeding and elimination. Therefore he lives in a very sensuous and self-centred world.

By bringing pleasure and relief the mother or nurse becomes familiar and from early days the child realises, through his senses, the pleasure she takes in caring for him, her loving and sure handling of him and her voice. As soon as his eyes focus, he will see her eyes and her face and their relationship forms. With a normal, happy mother and baby these happenings bring about *bonding*. Midwives and obstetricians believe that this process is given a positive start by the baby's being placed into his mother's arms as soon after birth as possible. Some even place the naked baby on his mother's abdomen.

If bonding, or emotional attachment of mother to baby and baby to mother, does not take place in the early weeks (and there could be many reasons for this), all sorts of other things can go wrong. From the experience of this first relationship the child builds all his other relationships. From his mother's demonstrated love for him he begins to feel secure about himself. This knowledge is sometimes called self-image, or self-concept, and is not to be confused with conceit or inflated ideas of one's importance. If a child feels at ease with himself and secure in others' love for him, he is able to face life confidently and cope with challenges and limitations both within and outside himself.

This bonding process, then, becomes more established during the child's first months of life. By about six weeks the baby can recognise his mother as a separate person from himself, and will smile and respond to her. Play, encouraged by parents, makes him smile, kick and respond happily. By the age of three months, just the appearance of his mother often produces a joyful response. About this age he begins to chuckle, and at four months or so he laughs out loud.

The baby is thus already responding socially. His perception ensures that moving, changing sights, such as people, attract and hold his attention more than inanimate objects. From about three months, the father will elicit a special response, and soon after, the baby will welcome the attention of strangers, although still keeping his own special reactions for parents, brothers, sisters and familiar adults, such as grandparents. This distinguishing between familiar and strange adults shows us that his awareness of the world is widening.

Between about six and nine months he will make determined efforts to communicate by smiles, babbling and gestures. His ability to laugh at funny situations will play an important part in his later social life, as laughter is a useful safety valve. The baby of this age enjoys games with less familiar adults, and even deliberately tries to start them by dropping objects repeatedly out of his pram when out with mother. His understanding of speech, especially the word 'No' and tone of voice, influence his behaviour. Again, we see that his social development proceeds from his close family outwards.

His range of discernible emotions is widening too. Because he has developed **trust** of his parents, he can withstand a certain amount of delay, restraint, withdrawal of satisfaction, frustration. Weaning and toilet training, both of which he will experience in some measure before he is one, are built on this trust, leading to compliance with mother's expectations. Pleasure in giving pleasure to his beloved mother also aids the process. He may, at other times, display defiance, or jealousy, as for instance when father is taking too much of mother's attention away from him.

The mother's temperament and quality of care will be influential factors in his early social and emotional responses. But even at this tender age babies differ widely one from the other for no apparent reason. Some are friendly, happy and amenable from the first; others are fretful, demanding and unresponsive. It is undoubtedly true that certain personality characteristics are laid down at or, more accurately, before birth, some inherited from several generations back. The accommodation of these characteristics with the child's early environment –

which includes most importantly the personalities of those looking after him – the interaction which takes place, and the modifying or otherwise of the characteristics, results eventually in the emergence of his adult personality.

This is why we say, rightly, that all babies – and all children and all people – are individuals and should always be recognised as such.

One to two

The importance of the baby's relationships with his parents continues into his second year, and will colour other relationships. Security, affection and trust are essential in his emotional background, and will provide the safe harbour from which he will increasingly sally forth to meet the world.

As he becomes more and more mobile, he will spend a great deal of time exploring his surroundings, but he still very much needs mother's presence around all the time, and will constantly return to her if puzzled or frightened.

Research in the past thirty years has alerted people who care for children to the important role of the mother in these early years. Not so long ago it was believed that the lack of such a background of consistent, loving handling by the same mother, or even the experience of an interruption in this relationship (such as in the case of a spell in hospital), could cause the child to grow up scarred for life. We now believe, however, that such damage may not be irreversible, and that skilled, sensitive handling of separation by all concerned can do much to minimise emotional damage. But it is thought, nevertheless, that handling by too many different people who are caring for the child (as for instance in homes of care) can result in little bond formation, whereas too few contacts with strangers can lead to later narrowness of outlook or shyness.

The relevance of this research to our discussion here is that ideally the under-two-year-old should be cared for by one or two consistent loving parents, but also be exposed to contacts with friends of the family.

During his second year, the child's sense of his personal identity begins to develop. Because of this, and aided by his growing acquisition of language, he begins to be interested in other children. He will not be able to play with them in any real sense, of course, but if put together with another child about his age, he will reach out, stare, touch, circle, possibly hand out temporarily a plaything, which will then quickly become the focus of a tug-of-war. There will probably be squeals and tears, and little talking, apart from frequent claims of 'mine'. Such early battles, trying as they are to mothers, are unavoidable and healthy because they are situations from which the child will learn. In such clashes, the child is asserting himself and his rights in the only way he is able. As adults, we control or hide such feelings, mutter darkly to ourselves or tell a friend later what we would *like* to have done. But a child of this age has no such outlet. He simply lashes out as the occasion demands. He *understands* adult restraints, although they may have little effect. However, he is quite easily distracted, which means that his aggression may soon die down.

It has been found that, limited though interaction is at this stage, companionship from the second year on has a stimulating effect on development generally.

Often during this period the child goes through a phase of refusing to conform in some way to the routines of his day; he may refuse to eat, sit at table, use the potty, or go to sleep at bedtime. This worries many mothers who previously took pride in their child's compliance. Because his growth rate has slowed down, his physical needs are changing. The comparatively new exercise and satisfaction of asserting his individual will, aided by growing language ability and the power of the negative, all combine to make this refusal a normal part of growing up. Usually, the less fuss that is made, the sooner will the phase pass. If, however, his refusals are allowed to become the centre of pitched battles between himself and a fraught, tense mother, their once-happy relationship may be temporarily affected.

This relationship becomes more complex during his second year. Although the child loves mother and wants to please her, sometimes he hates her for thwarting him. Then he feels guilt and a torment of doubt about her continuing love for him. He cannot release this build-up of emotion as adults do, by words. (We call this mixed-up state of love and hate ambivalent feelings; they are present in most intense relationships – for example marriage. To accept this fact is to go a long way towards understanding a great deal of human behaviour.)

The child of this age can also be possessive of his mother. He may accept the fact that she has household tasks, but hates her to read a book, for instance, go by herself to the bathroom, or maybe make a fuss of another child. This is when he will appear demanding or draw attention to himself. Father will play a more active role in his life now, and he will enjoy Father's special rough and tumble, humorous or gentle tactics. From such experience he will learn about special male characteristics and qualities, which lays the foundations for understanding of the male role.

By the end of the second year he is no longer a baby. He is a confident young child who works hard at establishing and demonstrating his independence. However, he can easily return to baby dependence when frustrated or ill. There is a possibility that we may expect too much of him because he can appear so competent.

Two to three

These various trends continue into his third year. Particularly noticeable are the eagerness and unpredictability of his exploring, and his self-assertiveness. His own possessions mean a great deal to him; their positions at bedtime or around the home are an integral part of his security. His emotional base is still very much the home, and any weaning away from it should be gentle and gradual. He may be willing to stay an occasional night with grandparents or a favourite aunt.

As he becomes more and more aware of all the possible choices in his world, he may feel some confusion, and also change his mind and direction suddenly and frequently. He does not like adult interference in his schemes, and sometimes does not welcome friendly advances by adults. Sometimes he goes through a very shy or clinging phase, which can be a great trial to parents, particularly his mother.

This is the classic age of temper tantrums – the natural consequence of his self-assertiveness, exploratory impulses, inability to get inside the feelings of other people, or understand cause and effect. His rage and distress, when aroused, can be formidable. The overwhelming nature of them can be frightening to him.

Because his outlook on life is inevitably so self-centred and limited in understanding, he may think he is to blame for unhappy incidents such as his mother's temporary absence. Because he does not distinguish between reality and fantasy, he may have occasional nightmares or irrational fears.

With other children, he will still play side by side and although there will be more conversation, there will still be many clashes of will, snatching and grabbing. Given the choice, he will often choose to play alone.

Through his developing mental perception, he is observing and absorbing more and more about what is acceptable behaviour, and he learns this almost entirely from those within the family circle. Because he wants to feel accepted and loved, he will gradually learn to conform to these ideas, and so by the end of the third year he will be complying with many adult expectations.

Towards the end of this period one can also see tendencies which will be important in his adult personality – characteristics like leadership or submissiveness, gregariousness or detachment, dependence or independence.

Three to four

By this age the child starts to look at the world in a less self-centred way, and this stage sees the beginning of social relationships with his contemporaries. He is now aware of himself as a separate person, and therefore he can look with more interest at other people. He is interested in the actions and reactions of other children, and this forms the basis of real play. He will make friendly overtures to other children and want to sustain periods of play with them. He can, literally, give and take in a limited fashion, and can wait a short while, but, of course, he is still mainly concerned with getting his own way. However, he begins to learn that to acquire and keep companions, he sometimes has to compromise over this. He has greater emotional control, and also more 'know-how' about life and its limitations. Although there will still be occasional clashes with other children, clashes with adults will be fewer.

Jealousy, rivalry and bickering among brothers and sisters (siblings) are commonplace during this period, if not before. This can be another trial to parents, particularly, again, the mother who is often surrounded by apparent discord for hours each day, and it sometimes goes on for years. There is good and bad about every child's position in the family, and all, in a sense, are rivals for their parents' love. Within such a close-knit group in restricted premises there is bound to be friction. Through it, however, the siblings build their relationships from which they derive much happiness and security. Loyalty between family members in the face of criticism or threats from outside is also built up by such interaction. It is interesting to note how often childhood warring between two siblings grows into close enduring friendship and love in later life.

By this age the child can work out, through play, many of his aggressive feelings and distressing experiences. He likes rough and tumble play with an adult. This is particularly true of boys. Exasperating though it can be to mothers, especially just before bedtime, it is a normal and healthy testing out of his own strength, and outlet for exuberant spirits. He likes also to order his parents about in a playful way.

Adult patterns for acceptable social behaviour and harmony in the home are very important now. He needs practical, consistent demonstrations of affection, care, truthfulness and patience. The limits set on his behaviour in the home and the way these are put into practice should help him to conform, feel safe and be liked. He should be building up a good image of himself, but he cannot do this if overstepping the boundaries is linked with guilt. He will understand most logical explanations for limits, but will need constant reminders of abiding by them. Simple courtesies are learned from parents and mean little at first, but gradually the child will come to see them as signs of thoughtfulness to others.

During this stage the child may show curiosity about sex; children will explore one another's bodies and perhaps indulge in mutual genital manipulation; no emotions except sensuous pleasure are involved, and guilt is often only introduced by a worried parent.

Also during this stage, the child may invent an imaginary friend. This is an interesting, and often long-remembered development. It fulfils not so much a need for companionship as for someone on whom the child can project the other side of his personality. For instance, the 'friend' (one small boy's was 'Dob' who always had to be spoken to in a very gruff voice) may do all kinds of dreadful things, when the real child is feeling particularly good and conforming, while at other times the 'friend' may be a paragon of all the virtues. Thus the child is helped to handle his ambivalent feelings. Parents can play along with this fantasy without fear of rearing a neurotic, but, of course, it should not be carried to ridiculous extremes. When the child is emotionally ready to abandon the 'friend', he will.

Four to five

The imaginary friend will probably survive into his fifth year, but the four-year-old's own real life personality is by now well established. Through the examples around him, and his greater life experience, he has standards by which to judge his own behaviour and that of others. He will begin to rely on his own judgements.

He will alternate between dependence and independence, but will on the whole be self-confident and often boisterous. He is fairly amenable to reasonable adult demands, and fairly good at controlling his feelings. He can show patience if there is delay.

Four-year-olds are often happy to play together for long periods in groups. The groups frequently break up and form again, or there may be one pair of close friends within or outside it. Four-year-olds like to know that adults are dependably in the background, and while not liking the adult to interfere, they will turn to her for advice, approval or material help.

Nevertheless, they are essentially acting as individuals within the group. The first signs of genuine concern for others usually appear during this stage. A child will inform an adult about one of his group who is in trouble. On the other hand, four-year-olds are quick to condemn or reject a child they do not like.

Imaginary and imitative play flourishes, reflecting the child's observation of real life as well as the fulfilment of his desires. His heightened imaginative powers are evident, too, in his boasting about his family and possessions and the telling of tall stories. He constantly demands our praise and recognition: 'Watch how fast I can run!' and so on. He is asserting his own ability, and this 'showing off' as it is sometimes called, is a natural step to building skills and self-confidence.

Sometimes adults, particularly parents, are concerned at an apparent change which comes about in the child's behaviour between four and five. Boys may swear, shout, defy adults, show off ostentatiously. Girls may giggle secretively or become pert or insolent. Both may dawdle or talk among themselves to avoid complying with adult requests. There may be several explanations for this. The adults may not be acknowledging the child's need for greater independence as he is becoming more grown up. The child may be ready for more stimulation than home, play group or nursery can supply. The child may also be apprehensive about moving to 'big school' soon.

Five to six

This is the stage when the school years begin and it is a widening experience away from the family which will bring the child both happiness and unhappiness. He will welcome the new social contacts, but he will expect to be liked and valued by all, and if this does not happen, can feel hurt. Girls usually take to their new role more happily than boys; being eager to please the teacher, and being more mature as a rule, girls tend to get off to a good early start with literacy and numeracy skills. Boys often find the break from their mother more upsetting than girls. Some people think this may be because girls have much more practice than boys in learning about their future role in life, through close contact with their mother in the home, and are therefore more confident and independent.

Five-year-olds find apparent failure of any kind difficult to accept. They regard their contemporaries largely as rivals rather than friends, and as yet there is little real interest in team enterprises. Quarrelling and teasing can arise out of aggression, but some aggressive behaviour is inevitable as the child comes to terms with the outside and more grown-up world. Five-year-olds sometimes revel in destructive acts, through which they test out their own power and strength.

Five-year-olds will play in groups, but the groups are quite fluid. They are often happiest playing in pairs; if there are three, invariably one will be left out and hurt feelings will result, particularly among small girls who, by this age, are choosing 'best friends', who themselves change frequently. Separate boy and girl groups begin to form for play at about this age, with separate interests. Boys may appear outwardly more aggressive in play and conduct, but research has shown that this characteristic, in the early school days, masks greater anxiety and lack of self-confidence than girls experience.

Early school experience can be tiring and stressful, making for irritability or sullenness at home. Eager parents, interested in their child's new step, will frequently be disappointed or mystified at the lack of communication from the child about all that he has done. His 'cuddly' or comforter may still be much in demand at bedtime.

With skilful adult help, a group of children may stay together, perhaps for several days, and work for a common purpose. There will be many quarrels along the way; one child will appear content with a minor role, then suddenly demand a major one. Group leaders can be clearly identified by now. The children's developing sense of humour, growing out of a knowledge of what is real and what is ridiculous, will help to promote a happy atmosphere within a group of five-year-olds.

The five-year-old is still very much an individual, however. He can make deliberate independent decisions and put them into effect. In this sense, he has taken a big step towards becoming a self-directing person. He is still building up his own image of himself, and because he wants it to be a good one, he constantly asks questions and seeks praise about himself, his past, his abilities, etc. He cannot accept self-blame, although irrationally still feels guilty at things for which he is not to blame, thus revealing his muddled ideas on reality and fantasy. Despite his apparent move towards independence, he still needs his mother's support and companionship a great deal, especially in times of stress. He likes the familiarity of routine in the home.

Six to seven

By six, most children have become adjusted to the greater demands of school. Belonging to a group, and being accepted by their peers, means a great deal to them. They dread being rejected, and it is rare to find six-year-olds playing alone.

Groups have grown bigger, and sometimes they become very over-excited, and play, including much 'horse-play', becomes uncontrolled. Sometimes a scapegoat is created. Six-year-olds often make up their own rules for group play as they go along. They can take part in organised games – for instance, party games, which involve competitiveness – but the games must allow each child to have his chance to shine. There is a good deal of rivalry and jostling for positions of influence in their social setting, and sometimes the strain brought about by this results in silly behaviour at home.

Changes of mood are very common in six-year-olds. They may be in turn dogmatic and impulsive. Some children of this age present entirely different personalities at home and at school. To all appearances, the teacher tends to have more influence than the parents, therefore the degree of co-operation with each varies, and can cause irritation at home. Fluctuating feelings make choices difficult, and sometimes six-year-olds let their parents down in a social setting.

They are highly imaginative, and although they enjoy fear and titillation of manageable proportions in stories, they may be a prey to imagined terrors, such as burglars breaking into their home. Nightmares accompany such fears.

They are very proud of their possessions, and only reluctantly allow others to play with or use them. They begin to be critical of their own achievements.

Although not generally outwardly affectionate, they do appreciate scope for happy activities and things of their own, as provided by adults. They can also usually be trusted not to hurt younger brothers and sisters if left in charge for a short period.

This stage probably sees the height of individualism. Sometimes adults assume a greater degree of maturity within the six-year-old than is really there, particularly if the child is well developed physically.

Age seven

The set of friends, though transitory, of which the six-year-old was aspiring to become an accepted member, now merges into a gang or club. With groups of boys, sometimes there is one shared predominating interest, nowadays often football. In other settings, it may be Cub Scouts, cowboys and Indians, space travellers, or secret societies with dens. Having friends with interests in common who like and respect one brings satisfaction and builds self-confidence at this stage. Girls will often stay together in a less formal way; sometimes a shared passing interest in, say, skipping or knitting is the reason for these groups. 'Best friends' are still important. The groups will invent and pay lip-service to rules, but individuals still find it difficult to apply the rules to themselves, and one child may quickly walk off in a huff if tackled by others, and be stubborn about admitting his wrong.

Seven-year-olds can also be very sensitive to teasing and being made to look silly in front of their peers. They will tell tales about each other because they like to feel righteous. This shows that they have adopted adult standards of what is acceptable behaviour. Brothers and sisters of this age will complain to parents of unfair treatment when they feel adults have deviated from these standards.

In their activities at home and at school we can see other typical seven-year-old characteristics – a striving towards perfection, through self-criticism which now becomes very marked. Children of this age can be very persistent in working towards their goal, and get angry at interference or interruption, especially by younger siblings. Gesell calls this 'the eraser age', meaning that the seven-year-old is forever rubbing out things he has written and drawn because 'I'm no good,' or 'It's rubbish,' – both common enough cries during this phase. At other times, however, the seven-year-old will be full of exuberance and enthusiasm for life. Moods change from exuberance to depression, brooding and preoccupied behaviour are very common.

About this age the child begins to feel genuine appreciation of others' efforts. Team games and competitive sports can now be enjoyed, although feelings may run high at times.

Sometimes a seven-year-old will fall in love for the first time. This is an interesting development, because it represents a move away from individuality and a recognition of the need for companionship. One small seven-year-old boy, who admired a girl twice his size, bestowed a ring case on her in the playground, assuring her that the ring would follow later. His gesture could be said to anticipate the more sophisticated, complex world of emotional and social experience which the child at seven is about to enter.

Exercise 13

Multiple-choice questions

1. Bonding between a mother and her baby means:
(a) the umbilical cord;
(b) emotional attachment;
(c) naked newborn baby being placed on mother's abdomen;
(d) their eyes looking at each other, for the first time;
(e) interaction between the two.

2. The older baby, six months and onwards, learns to withstand a measure of frustration, delay and restraint in the gratification of his desires, because he has developed:
(a) self-control;
(b) a smaller appetite;
(c) bladder and bowel control;
(d) trust in his mother;
(e) wider interests.

3. One of the following factors is crucial in how damaging or otherwise separation between a mother and her child of under two may be. It is:
(a) how long the separation lasts;
(b) whether or not the mother explains fully to the child beforehand about the unavoidable separation;
(c) reason for separation;
(d) quality of relationship between mother and child before separation takes place;
(e) age of child when separation takes place.

Essay question

4. How does the environment of a good day nursery *or* nursery school help children between three and five to develop in social and emotional adjustment?

Observation

5. Observe a group of friends at the nursery. Note the number of children, ages, sexes, whether group is fluid or fixed, whether there is one obvious leader. Do they use language – discussion and compromise – to sustain the group, or action – show of strength, bullying, etc.? Are there frequent quarrels? How do they show their liking for each other?

Suggestions for further reading

Joseph Church, *Understanding Your Child from Birth to Three*, Fontana
Rudolf Dreikurs and Vicki Soltz, *Happy Children*, Fontana

Chapter 14
Difficulties in the pre-school years

Susan Isaacs, who made a detailed and valuable study of the social and emotional development of pre-school children, states:

> In the period from one to five years in particular, emotional difficulties occur so frequently that they may be looked upon as a normal phase of early childhood. Few, if any, children do not manifest some sort of difficulty, although these vary very much in degree and persistence.*

Because social and emotional development are so closely bound together, inner emotional difficulties will reveal themselves in disturbed behaviour. This being so common and normal a part of development, it is dangerous to label one facet of a child's behaviour as a 'problem', still worse to label the child a 'problem child'. Even if one does this only inwardly to oneself, it must inevitably colour one's attitudes towards and expectations of that child, and we know how most children live up to others' expectations of them. 'Naughty' is another word still used a good deal to and about children. We should be wary of branding the child with this. For one thing, it has a slightly wicked connotation which some children find attractive. More important, it is a vague, all-embracing word used to cover many different kinds of behaviour. Often it is behaviour which we, at that moment, with our superior knowledge of that situation and possible consequences, and sometimes – let us admit it – partly because of the mood we are in, find irritating or inconvenient. When three-year-old Darren suddenly smashes all the stickle bricks from the table where he is sitting, with a resounding crash on to the floor, to the shocked delight of his companions, he is not to know that a VIP visitor to the day nursery is expected in the room at any moment, nor that his nursery nurse is experiencing pre-menstrual tension *and* has just applied for a promotion. All he knows is that he has been waiting an interminable time for his dinner; he is hungry, bored and irritable. For the nursery nurse to round on this as 'naughtiness' is therefore irrational and unjust. This is not to say, however, that small children are never trying, nor a great test of our patience and self-control. It is inevitable that they should be so at times, when we consider that they are far from ready to meet all the demands that life makes on them. Their feelings are

---

* Susan Isaacs, 'The Psychological Aspects of Child Development', p. 26, *Year Book of Education*, Section II, 1935.

intense and rapidly changeable. They want instant gratification of those feelings, and lack, on the whole, the ability to control them if met with frustration or denial. They are surrounded by big, powerful adults who can dictate events, while they, the children, have to allow events to happen to them. Inner frustration will surface in one way or another. Sometimes their expression, and the consequences, give rise to guilt and emotional turmoil which, unless handled wisely, can perpetuate the undesirable conduct.

The maintenance of a stable, consistent and happy atmosphere at nursery will go a long way towards reducing emotional and social difficulties. Surrounded by adults who care about him, and with absorbing activities to take part in, the child will gradually learn control and a measure of conformity.

If disturbed behaviour is very frequent, persistent, continues well after five, or suddenly manifests itself out of nowhere, there are certain questions we can ask ourselves:

1. Is there an upset in the home? For instance, has the father deserted or a new baby arrived?

2. How is the child's physical health? Is he sickening for something? Has he an undetected defect, such as hearing loss, which may make him appear unco-operative? Is apparent 'clumsiness' part of his difficulty?

3. Is he getting enough sleep?

4. Is he getting enough attention and affection at home?

5. Is he comfortable at nursery?

6. Is the pattern of his life a satisfying one? (or does he, for example, have too long a day at nursery, or too little contact with mother?)

7. Is he getting enough or too much stimulation? Is he bored?

8. Are we allowing him gradually to become more independent?

9. Are we expecting too much of him?

By endeavouring, without prying into the family's private affairs, to understand possible reasons for disturbed behaviour, we can begin to help the child.

Here *consistency between home and nursery* is vital, as in so many other matters. Inconsistent reactions to his behaviour will only confuse the child and increase his difficulties. Nursery staff and parents should all be pulling in the same direction, that is to help the child back to a happy, tranquil state of mind and reasonably conforming behaviour. Two-way information can be most helpful, provided the child is not aware that he is the focus of much attention and concern.

If parents are deliberately unco-operative and unapproachable, the nursery staff can only do their best, bearing in mind that, if the reasons for the disturbed behaviour lie entirely in the home, their influence will probably be greatly outweighed.

We should remember that most parents want to do, and indeed do, the best they can for their child. The fact that their best is not good enough, or that all their good intentions are rendered useless by circumstances in their personal lives, should not be held against them. Indifference, defensive attitudes or denials about difficult behaviour mask feelings of guilt, failure, anxiety, or fear that the child will lose his nursery place. Some parents need to offload their worries about the child to staff at nursery. Others are helped to handle their feelings of failure by nursery staff agreeing with them (out of the child's earshot) how difficult he can be, or telling the mother that he had a particularly trying day. Much can be done by tactful and friendly approaches.

Some common difficulties

Between toddler stage and approximately age seven, the following forms of behaviour are commonly seen from time to time:

1. tantrums;
2. destructive and aggressive behaviour and bullying;
3. negative, stubborn or defiant behaviour;
4. 'lying' and 'stealing';
5. withdrawal and shyness;
6. aimless activity and lack of concentration;
7. fears and anxieties;
8. jealousy;
9. sucking.

There are other difficulties which worry parents and nursery staff which could be described as *comfort-seeking behaviour habits*, such as thumb-sucking and masturbation. Sometimes these habits accompany the emotional states and difficulties listed above.

There are no magic formulas or glib solutions to any of these difficulties. All we can do here is to suggest possible underlying causes, general guidelines and a few practical tips gleaned from experience.

We also remind the reader that no two children react to the same approach in exactly the same way. Neither does the same highly commendable approach work as well for one adult as another. We must all be true to ourselves. All successful handling techniques rely on this, and equally on knowledge of the child, and a good relationship with him.

1. Temper tantrums. The classic stage for temper tantrums is the year between two and three. The child by now is fully mobile, is increasingly able to explore his environment and gratify his curiosity and his desires. Yet, while wanting to assert his developing personality and his will, he is conscious of apparently being frustrated at every turn. 'No' is all too familiar to him, as is having exciting-looking objects removed from his grasp or path. Physically, he attempts more than he is able to accomplish, in manoeuvring objects and so on. Although he can understand much more than he is able to express, he as yet cannot understand explanations about, for instance, why he may not help himself from the tempting sweet display in the supermarket – all within easy grabbing reach. His reaction on not getting his own way is often to throw himself on the floor, perhaps with arms and legs flailing, and scream until he is red in the face, by which time both he and mother are the centre of a part-sympathetic, part-critical crowd of onlookers. This, in itself, often complicates things, as does the problem of a trolley full of shopping to be dealt with somehow at the same time!

Children older than three often revert to these tactics in very 'fraught' moments, or if they have found in the past that they can get their own way by such means. Children of low intelligence may be specially prone, because they do not understand about limitations; but highly-intelligent children may also be given to such tantrums because they want to do so much more than their limited physical skills will allow.

Although it is much easier to say rather than do, the important thing is for the adult to keep calm and maintain an atmosphere of firm, patient affection. Do not give in to the child 'for the sake of a quiet life', but do not, either, turn the tantrum into a pitched battle between you; screaming back at him will do no good at all. The child is temporarily out of control and you must help him to regain that control. He will probably need to be removed bodily from the scene, away from staring or frightened children, or anyone who is likely to get physically hurt. Restraining the child, in a firm hold, from damaging property or himself will gradually have a calming effect on him, and will make him physically aware of your strength and resolve. If the tantrum lasts any time, he should not be left alone, so stay with him while these frightening, overpowering feelings last. When he has calmed down, quiet, comforting talk and a wash will all help him feel better. The nursery nurse will probably need to involve him in a quiet activity or chore she is doing so that he recovers his composure gradually, before being reinstated with the group. Do not refer to the episode again, and certainly do not adopt the attitude 'Miss P. doesn't love you when you do that'. The alarming experience he has gone through will be all the worse if you threaten to withdraw your friendly feelings towards him.

Prevention is always better than cure, and an observant nursery nurse can do much to foresee possible 'trigger-points'. Fortunately the two-year-old child is easily distracted by, for instance, something unusual you 'thought you saw' out of the window. Remove obvious and unnecessary frustrations from his environment, for example, treasured adult ornaments he must not touch. We all have to endure frustration in our lives, but the two-year-old's life abounds in it, so you need not fear that you are smoothing his path more than is good for him.

2. Destruction, aggressive behaviour and bullying. We all have aggressive feelings and impulses, particularly, the authors believe, boys and men. How far and in what ways we channel this aggression depends very much on the society we live in, and our early environmental influences. In wartime, for instance, we praised the young men who boasted about shooting down Germans; in peacetime, we condemn similar young men who vent their aggression on the football terraces. If a child has, from birth, seen arguments settled by physical blows or vehement abuse among those closest to him, this behaviour will probably be reflected in the child at the nursery. As civilised adults, we curb our destructive impulses – for instance, to throw a brick through a plate-glass window. We respect others' property rights; we can foresee consequences. Small children do not possess these adult attributes. Moreover, they need to destroy before they can create.

Boredom often leads to aggressive behaviour. It is small wonder that there are so many minor fights between children in ordinary primary school playgrounds – there is so little else to do. We should always ensure that small children's surroundings and routine give them enough stimulus. Variety in play material, the arrangement of the room, visits and visitors, new games introduced out of doors, all go a long way to prevent boredom. Older boys at the nursery or playgroup who have gone through all that the establishment has to offer, and also those at the top of the infants school especially need these stimuli.

Children with abundant physical energy, and often strength, need constant outlets if these are not going to be used for disruptive ends. An exciting garden, well equipped, and the opportunity to use it in an unhampered way, will use up a good deal of energy. Wet weather poses a problem for such children, and then they will require alternative vigorous activities such as movement and music-making and building with blocks. Play material which gives outlets for banging, cutting, pinching, tearing, destroying legitimately (such as woodwork, clay and dough, papier mâché, sand, painting, rag dolls) all channel destructive impulses, although needing careful supervision, especially where a potentially aggressive child is using tools or scissors. A home-made cardboard or wooden target figure on a pivot, to be aimed at with bean bags or something similar, is a popular toy for outside play. Play and cleaning jobs involving water can have a soothing effect on an aggressive child.

Sometimes an aggressive child is literally 'hitting back' at life which has been less than kind to him, and is making his mark and seeking attention. To let him see what a nuisance he is, or worse, how much he is disliked by one and all, will only satisfy his perverse impulse. The chances are that he will then go on making life more and more uncomfortable for everyone, living up to his bad reputation. Instead of taking a negative attitude to him and his behaviour, try to make him feel good about himself, by praising anything that can possibly be praised, and letting him help and take small responsibilities. Perhaps a disruptive six-year-old can be put in charge of collecting litter from the school field, or fetching the milk crate, so using his energy and love of power to the good of the community.

Experienced staff recommend what they call 'catching' such a child first thing in the morning, by involving him straight away in an interesting, demanding activity.

Aggressive behaviour, although it will occur frequently in minor ways, cannot be tolerated incessantly or in severe forms. The child must realise that he is inflicting harm and hurt, and that you care enough about all the children to protect them from this. 'Hitting back', of course, cannot be recommended, nor can corporal punishment by the adult, although we are aware that when a child is punished in this way at home, our approach will seem weak and ineffectual. Learning to settle differences, or manipulate a situation through words rather than actions, is a very important part of the socialising process which all nurseries must work towards. Give reasons why a certain kind of aggressive conduct cannot be tolerated, and make it clear that you are condemning the deed, not the child. Although it often does not appear so, he badly wants to retain your liking for him. Take him to task quietly but firmly, away from other children. Shouting or emotional reactions on your part will only incite him to further unsocial behaviour; the presence of his friends around will encourage him to make the most of this attention. Where practicable, let him suffer the consequences of his actions, not as a punishment but rather as an unemotional matter of cause and effect. If he has deliberately 'flooded' the bathroom, supervise him calmly while *he* mops it up. He may think this fun at first, but the novelty will soon wear off, and he will probably think twice before doing it another time.

Cruelty → The emergence of both a bully and a victim figure must be quickly observed
to and steps taken; otherwise real harm could be done to both children, and trouble
Other will arise in nursery/home relationships. Supervision outside must be very close,
Children and possibly excuses found for keeping the children concerned in different parts of the outdoor area. The victim should be given opportunities to succeed and win praise in all sorts of activities, so that his self-confidence is boosted. The aggressor should be kept busy with all the various activities already suggested. Acts of kindness, sharing, etc., however small, should be noted and praised. Sometimes an aggressor will be helped by involvement with the nursery pet, but close supervision will be necessary. Incidents of bullying must be stopped and condemned, but soul-searching sessions of 'Why did you do it?', 'How would you like it if . . .?' or 'You're to wait here till you've said sorry' and so on avail little. The egocentric pre-school child cannot sufficiently think himself into another person's feelings; moreover the incident is past and forgotten as far as he is concerned. If there ever was a reason for his action (which is not always the case) he has probably forgotten it by now, or at any rate will not be able to put it into words. 'Sorry', if it is forced reluctantly out of a child, means little. What is worse, if he utterly refuses to say it, you have placed yourself in a position from which you will have to climb down – never a desirable course for an adult in charge.

3. Negative, stubborn or defiant behaviour. The child who exhibits this type of behaviour may be used to getting things all his own way at home, and be protesting about demands made of him at the nursery. He may be going through a self-assertive phase and feels he can best make his mark by negative gestures. Or negativism may mask fears and uncertainties.

The nursery nurse may be best advised to ignore his negativism over little matters. She should practise a positive approach in her voice and manner when requesting the group to do something. 'Now we're *all* going into the garden to hear a Topsy and Tim story.' Imply in your voice that you confidently expect everyone to participate in this delightful prospect.

If the child has objected to particular routines – for instance putting on his coat to play outside in winter or getting undressed for movement or PE – make the point of the exercise clear to him, not in a wheedling way but as a simple matter of fact. 'We must put our outdoor clothes on because it's so cold today.' Leave it at that. Do not make his refusal the focus of a scene, but let him experience the results of his action. If he sees everybody else having a good time outside, he will probably change his mind eventually and sheepishly join them – with coat. Do not make him feel he has given in.

Not making unreasonable demands on him, not blowing up a refusal into a confrontation between himself and you – all these will help. Giving him a choice of two definite alternatives often distracts him from the fact that he does not really want to do either. Try to find something he is interested in and encourage him to join in. Praise his efforts in group activities; if he wants to remain one of a group he will have to accept some orders.

We should remember that obedience as the Victorians practised it (and many cultures today still expect and obtain utter obedience from their children) was an end in itself. For us, it is only a means to an end. Our goal is for the child to derive the maximum benefit from the nursery, and become a social being.

4. 'Lying' and 'stealing'. We have put these words in inverted commas, because to use them in the usually accepted sense presupposes that young children can distinguish between truth and fantasy, yours and mine. We know from their enjoyment of stories and books which constantly step in and out of the real world (for example, engines that talk and have distinct personalities) that they cannot make such distinctions. Therefore, why should they not make up their own 'tall stories' about, for instance, seeing an alligator on the way to the nursery? Adults should never react sharply to this as telling lies, but enter into the spirit of the story, while letting the child see by their facial expression that it is a shared joke. This will help the child to know that it is only a joke, without demeaning him.

If tall stories and boasting persist well into the infant stage, it may be a sign that the child is not getting enough opportunity to succeed and win praise and admiration in other fields. Children also lie when they are afraid of the consequences of telling the truth, so that it may be a sign that we, or his parents, are being over-strict, or expecting too much of him. We have to help him understand, in a quite unemotional way, that it is important for us to feel able to believe him; otherwise we shall not know when he is telling the truth. Lying can also denote an escape from an undesirable world. Sometimes boasting about heroic acts and so on can represent what the child *would do* if the need arose, or what he would like to do. We should remember that there are many different kinds of truth, as well as untruths.

In the case of 'stealing', we should remember that moral principles of right and wrong are not really grasped until children are about seven or eight. We should also remind ourselves that the little child lives entirely in a here-and-now world, and that his feelings and impulses can be quite overwhelming. If he sees a lovely rosy apple in a friend's coat pocket, and he is feeling peckish, the fact that he can have three or four of his own at home that evening does not enter into it; he wants it there and then, and the temptation is overwhelming.

It is even greater for children who have little in the way of treats and personal possessions at home, particularly where they may be a division between 'haves' and 'have nots' at the nursery or school. Children who are experiencing emotional upsets, lack of affection or loneliness in their personal lives – and this applies particularly to the fives-to-sevens – may help themselves to tempting items as a form of compensation, much in the same way that we gravitate to the biscuit tin, refrigerator or chocolate box when we are feeling let down or miserable.

Parents are often unduly horrified and upset by the fact that their child is taking things. Emotive words like 'pilfering' and 'thieving' spring to mind, with an apparent future of juvenile delinquency. What the neighbours know or think about it also clouds the issue. It is important that if the child is taking things which do not belong to him, certainly for the five-to-seven-year-old, his parents and school staff should consider whether it may be a distress signal. The authors believe that children of this age should have a sensible amount of regular pocket money, freely and gladly given, as evidence of the parents' love for the child, and his growing independence. Pocket money should not be attached to chores like cleaning the car or doing the washing up; earnings for such tasks, if performed, can be extra. Some parents have been surprised to discover that, where punishments and deprivation of pocket money fail to solve the problem, extra love and attention, and possibly extra pocket money, help considerably.

If we know we have in our care a child who has this tendency, we should take sensible precautions not to leave tempting items in his path. Avoid asking the children to bring money to school whenever possible. Certainly never leave money around the room, or in an adult's desk. Snacks and special birthday presents, toys, etc. can be admired and then put on a high shelf for safe-keeping. If we find items belonging to other people, we should return them to the owner, explaining casually to the child. We should never 'frisk' children (parents could accuse us of physical assault if they chose), or turn the search for a missing item into a witchhunt, with a demand for confessions, and so forth.

As realists, we have to face the fact that regrettably there is a whole so-called grey area between the black and white extremes of honesty and dishonesty. How many people declare every penny of their earnings to the tax man, or return to a shop with excess change? How many of us exaggerate anecdotes slightly to make a better or funnier story? Then there is evidence in certain homes of items like tins of paint which have 'fallen off the back of a lorry', teaspoons, towels and ashtrays marked with name of public houses, hotels and transport companies in various parts of the world. This is to state facts, though not to condone.

Children are not deceived. They practise what we practise rather than what we preach.

5. Withdrawal and shyness. These two manifestations appear similar, but may be fundamentally different. A child may be severely withdrawn because of distressing circumstances or events in his early life; he has literally retreated, mentally and emotionally, from the possibility of further hurt and disappointment over relationships. Such a child may also withdraw physically, perhaps constantly to the book corner, home corner, or in small dens he finds or builds for himself. This is a very difficult child to help, and all approaches must be made exceedingly sensitively, gently and gradually. Forcing him to join in things, or badgering him with questions, will only make matters worse. Try to notice anything that seems to arouse his interest and this may lead into communicating with him and drawing him more out of himself and eventually into the group, but it will certainly not happen overnight. If withdrawal seems total, or persistent over a period of time, this child may need expert help, or it may be that he has started at the nursery too early.

Shyness is present in many of us, and to a certain extent can be hereditary. It may be a result of the child's not having mixed much with other children in the early years. It will be more helpful to this child to experience playing with other children on his home ground before being plunged into a larger group away from home. He should never be forced to join in something, or have attention drawn to his shyness, with, for example, apologies made for it. His mother may need to stay with him for a long time, even over a number of days, before he is able to be left happily at the nursery school. Direct close physical contact with strangers will paralyse him with shyness, so at first, contact needs to be oblique and indirect – a sideways, gradual drawing of him into activities, slowly merging into a warm, gentle relationship with adults and others. Praise will boost his self-confidence.

6. Aimless activity and lack of concentration. A child who flits from one group or activity to another can be a disruptive influence in a nursery group, and a trial to adults. Such a child may come from a high-rise flat where he is not allowed to run about or make a noise and where play opportunities are few. On the other hand, he may be over-indulged and overstimulated at home, so that his attention is constantly being distracted from one thing to another.

He will need to channel his energy into vigorous play for a good deal of the time, but he can also be gradually introduced to a more alternating pattern of vigorous, moving-around play, and quieter, relatively static activities. It will help him if a nursery nurse can sit with him, involve herself in his play, encouraging and praising the smallest sustained effort, endeavouring to extend his brief span of concentration in a gradual process. If he sees results achieved by, for instance, effort and time spent on a jig-saw, he may be more willing to settle next time. Strategic placing of this child near the adult at story, group or meal times may also have a calming, restraining influence on him.

7. Fears and anxieties. A child who is under pressure at home, perhaps by over-ambitious parents, or threatened domestic relationships, may appear generally anxious and 'nervy', afraid to accept the smallest new challenge. We can help by providing a happy and stable atmosphere at the nursery where he receives much praise, encouragement and affection.

Specific fears are very common, especially around three years of age. A fearful response to danger, real or apparent, and appropriate evasive action is part of our physical self-preservation mechanism, and is therefore a normal phenomenon. In dealing with young children's fears we should also remember the scale of the adult world as it appears to them. An Alsatian dog must appear as a large horse does to us, the sea an over-powering and endless expanse. Then, too, with our greater knowledge of the world we can rationalise and reassure ourselves that certain fears are groundless; we *know* that the dark corridor does not contain hobgoblins, nor is a clockwork spider really alive and threatening us. Young children are still finding out about such things.

Sometimes we actually *create* children's fears, for instance by squealing about a slow worm (legless lizard), looking frightened in a thunderstorm or, as parents, giving children the impression, through open quarrelling, that their home is about to break up.

To understand the reasons for and the intensity of children's fears is to go some way towards helping because then, clearly, we will not ridicule, tease, or force the child to 'face his fear'. A *gradual* facing and coming to terms with feared objects or situations will be necessary eventually, and often children set the pace themselves. A nursery pet can help a child with the fear of animals; singing songs about thunderstorms and rain can overcome, in a positive way, the distressing sound effects outside; water play and paddling pools can gradually familiarise a child with water as a non-threatening element. Masks or dressing-up clothes can help a child literally play out a fear. Funny books about ghosts or burglars can help to keep such subjects in proportion, although just before bedtime may not be the best time. One small girl who was terrified of fireworks but nevertheless watched a whole display, tightly clutching an adult's hand, was taken aback, then thrilled at an invitation to hold a sparkler for a few seconds. Her delighted recounting of this incident was proof enough that she had truly overcome her particular fear. Elements of fear in manageable (for small children) proportions can add much to the excitement of life.

8. Jealousy. Jealousy can arise at many times in a young child's life. Probably the classic occasion is when the child has to accept the arrival of a brother or sister. This can certainly give rise to deep-seated jealousy and we have tried to offer help over this in Chapter 4.

But other circumstances, too, can produce feelings of jealousy. A child with few possessions of his own can be very envious of peers with more. A child less intelligent, attractive or agile, or less obviously loved than his brothers or sisters may feel extremely jealous of them. Children without fathers can envy those with them.

Jealousy is often linked with lack of self-confidence and inner security. Therefore the adults caring for such a child need to bolster his confidence in himself. He needs a great deal of affection and opportunities to succeed and excel in all kinds of activities. If his jealousy is expressed in aggression, suitable play material can do much to channel these impulses into acceptable forms. A large rag doll can be thrown about and punished mercilessly; clay can be pounded, and nails hammered energetically. Baby doll play and looking after the nursery pet can awaken ideas of tender care. Books and stories about fictional children with similar feelings can help the child to see, in an indirect way, that his situation is not unique. This alleviates the guilt which may be complicating his jealous feelings. Mental notes can be made by staff of coveted things that other children possess, with a view to Christmas presents. Tactful approaches can be made to parents about the child's abilities and likeable characteristics, if it is the case that the jealousy stems from favouritism in the family.

9. Sucking. A baby has a natural instinct for sucking and it is essential for his survival. Besides being a means of getting food, sucking, or touching things with his lips, is a means of finding out the shape and texture of an article. It is also very comforting. As soon as a baby is able, he will put his hand or foot into his mouth to suck. Despite what people say, sucking does not cause a misshapen jaw or overcrowded teeth. From about six months, many babies will suck a thumb or two fingers as they go off to sleep and as this is a very comforting, soothing habit babies continue to do this, sometimes until they are three, four or even five years of age. Some children will, at the same time as sucking, stroke or pick at a small blanket or 'cuddly'. Others will just carry a blanket around with them. Other variations of these comforting habits are nailbiting, which is often a continuation of thumb-sucking, and masturbation. Of all these habits, masturbation (stroking and rubbing the genital organs) is the one which upsets adults most. But all babies find their genital organs and handle them in the same way as they find their hands or feet. The fact that masturbation is pleasant and comforting encourages the child to continue.

If these babyish habits continue well into the second and third years, one must ask oneself why the child is needing so much comfort. Does he need more stimulation or more demonstrated love? Is he happy? Are all his needs being satisfied? Perhaps a change in routine would help. Other than that it is best to leave him alone. As he gets older he will find other interests and satisfactions and should gradually drop the habit. If it disturbs you, then try distracting the child by giving him something different to do, or perhaps doing some activity with him. Nailbiting can sometimes be checked by giving the four-year-old a manicure set and helping him to smooth his nails so that there are no jagged edges to bite. Also oil around the nail will help to prevent jagged bits of cuticle forming.

If a baby admitted to the day nursery is used to sucking a dummy, or if a toddler still needs bottles, then care and judgement should be used to wean them gradually away from their comforters. The best method is to try to give them enough stimulation and care so that they no longer need the comfort of these things to suck.

Exercise 14

Multiple-choice questions

1. Your two-year-old suddenly throws a violent screaming tantrum because a friend's child has taken his favourite toy. You should:
(a) try to reason with him;
(b) scream back at him to be quiet;
(c) effect a compromise between him and his friend;
(d) put him in a room on his own to 'cool off';
(e) remove him from the scene and remain with him until he has calmed down.

2. You are fairly certain that a child of six at your infant school is taking things that do not belong to him. You should:
(a) set a trap for him to confirm your suspicions;
(b) try to ascertain why he needs this consolation by talking casually with his parents;
(c) speak to him privately, explaining about right and wrong;
(d) send a note home to his parents saying he is pilfering;
(e) search all the children and their clothing next time it happens.

3. A child of four displays a preoccupation with anecdotes about 'ghosts' he has seen. You should:
(a) tell him there are no such things;
(b) encourage him to get it all out of his system in great detail;
(c) casually add a couple of humorous books about ghosts to your normal book-corner supply;
(d) ignore it and distract his attention to other matters;
(e) ridicule him in front of the other children.

Essay questions

4. Describe a child of under seven you have known to experience behaviour difficulties. Were there explanations for his conduct, and how did you and/or other adults help him?

5. A child of three at the nursery seems either painfully shy or unusually withdrawn. What might be some of the possible reasons for this, and how would you try to reach him?

Suggestions for further reading

Martin Herbert, *Problems of Childhood*, Pan Books Ltd
John Gabriel, *Children Growing Up*, Hodder & Stoughton Ltd

Chapter 15
Play and development

What is play?

If we seek dictionary definitions of the word 'play', or think of adult forms of play, we gain an impression of an activity that is pleasant, light-hearted, even trivial – a pleasant contrast to 'work'. Yet these aspects of play are, for young children, only a very small part of its total significance.

Play *is* a child's work; in fact it is the business of childhood. Through play, the child will develop in body and mind. He will come to see some order in the confusing world around him. Because play seems to come naturally to children, and their enjoyment of it is so self-evident and spontaneous, it surely must be a natural way of integrating and exercising their curiosity, energy, vitality and capacity for learning in its widest sense.

Man has by far the longest period of immaturity (childhood) of all the animals. There is more that he must learn, therefore he is given longer in which to do so. It is through play that a great deal of this learning and preparation takes place. Think of how such attributes and abilities as perseverance, ingenuity, enthusiasm, co-operation, decision-making are all fostered during play.

We have seen in a previous chapter how small children cannot truly learn other than through first-hand experience; it is this same experience that we set out to offer them at nursery.

Play can be entirely undirected and unstructured, or it can be structured according to the child's evolving needs and developing powers. This is something that is sometimes difficult for parents to understand and recognise, but a good nursery is not simply a paradise of 'toys' on which the children are let loose. There should be provision for progression in every form of play, and this is where the expertise of the staff will ensure that the child is constantly moving forwards, but at his own rate.

With all new play materials, children pass through certain stages in their approach; first, they explore the material with their senses – and whole bodies, where possible. Then they experiment with it to find out its possibilities, potential and limitations. Later they imitate what they have seen other children do with it, or adults do with a similar substance. Ultimately, they play with it according to their own creative and original ideas.

Of course, the stages have little connection with the age of the child. A three-year-old, through frequent opportunity, may have passed through to the creative stage with sand play, whereas a five or six-year-old presented with clay for the first time will begin with the exploratory approach. Opportunity and discreet encouragement are key factors in children's working through the stages.

There are also definite stages through which children pass with regard to the social aspect of play. The very young child, or the child who has had little experience of mixing, will play first – with whatever materials – in a solitary way. Later, he will act as a spectator to others' play, which will lead to parallel play, where he and another child play side by side with similar material, but still essentially as separate individuals. Then the child will begin to associate himself with the other child in a momentary or tentative way. Lastly he will involve himself fully in co-operative play with a group; he will give and take, share, take turns, submit and lead as the occasion demands.

Types of play

It is impossible here to do more than outline essentials about the various types of play we offer small children. There is a good deal of overlap between the different types, which makes categorisation somewhat artificial. The tables on pp. 211–224 are intended as starting points for further reading and discussion. They may also be used as a basis for re-examination of what play opportunities we provide, how we do it, and – most important – why.

Although nursery space and resources are assumed, and in some cases are essential, in what follows, a good deal is easily adaptable or improvisable by enterprising play group leaders and mothers at home in more restricted premises, and on a far slimmer budget.

Music and movement. Musical experience is one of those activities arranged by adults, and though it cannot be called 'play', it greatly enriches the life of young children. They are surrounded by it for much of the time on television and radio, but we can make it far more than 'audio-wallpaper' for them. We can transform music into another avenue of expression.

Enjoyment and participation by children and adults should be the keywords in all we do. Music for young children should not be regarded as either a spectator or performer art; rather it is an action art.

The adult does not need instrumental skills or a good singing voice herself. If she looks to her own creativity and tries hard to overcome any lack of self-confidence, she is well on the way to success. Intelligent use of a record player and tape recorder, for example, will also more than compensate for lack of skill in piano playing.

Music has been said to be a blend of mathematics and magic, and both strands have a part to play in the musical experience we offer young children.

Four main aspects of musical experience

(a) *Cultivating auditory discrimination through attentive listening*: activities here will include collecting sounds, using tape recorder (for example, all morning sounds: kettle boiling, Dad shaving, milkman delivering, etc.); matching sounds (in the environment and using tapes); making sound patterns, alerting children to intensity and pitch. Full use should be made of children's natural response to rhythm. Remember, our very bodies function to rhythm – heartbeat, etc. Simple time-beat can lead to definite rhythm. A climax will also be satisfying in our sound pictures;

(b) *Developing vocal skills*: activities here can include 'mouth' music, humming, singing individually, singing together (which entails discipline of stopping and starting, etc.). Remember, however poor you think your voice is, or however embarrassed you are to perform in front of another adult, the children will be impressed and will not laugh at you. When introducing a new song, first sing a couple of familiar ones, then sing the new one through twice or three times (if short). Do not separate or teach it line by line. If you like it and are putting it over well, the children will soon be joining in;

(c) *Developing instrumental skills*: activities here might include making instruments (for example, from shells, coconuts) and household junk (painted and filled squeezy bottle shakers, date-box and sandpaper scrapers, etc.), experimenting with these, using them as sound effects in stories and songs, playing *some* together with melodic music; being aware of commercial instruments and the most suitable buys for the nursery (big cymbals and xylophone?); encouraging children to join in songs, etc. with single notes of tuned instruments as appropriate; providing a music workshop, or trolley, with pictures of adult instruments, etc.; letting children see and hear live instrumentalists, for example, a father who plays guitar? maybe get close enough to feel vibrations;

(d) *Adding to our repertoire of songs and music, and improving techniques*: there are many books of lively songs suitable for young children on the market today. Funny songs, rousing songs, gentle lullabies all have a place. We should make use of children's familiarity with TV jingles. Compose our own songs and musical phrases to accompany everyday actions like dressing, going upstairs, clearing bricks away, etc. because this can be fun. 'Children's' records can be evaluated, but tend to be limiting; we should make use of adult music – traditional, classical, modern, popular – which creates a mood, or is characterised by a strong beat.

Movement

Joy in music will lead quite naturally into movement and dance. Small children are rarely inactive, and response to beat and rhythm will be expressed in activity. Some children, in fact, are unable to stay still when music with a strong or

'catchy' beat is being played. We should welcome such a response and encourage spontaneity of expression.

Of course, music is not essential for children to enjoy movement. With a skilled adult to guide them, young children can move imaginatively, stimulated by experiences such as having watched snails move, or a piece of machinery in action.

Children must have adequate space in which to move, and a prearranged signal – not a shout – will be needed to attract their attention for each fresh activity. Uniformity in how children move is not the goal; we should encourage individual experimentation and expression.

Creative movement brings the emotions into play – sadness, solemnity, joy. It helps children to gain control over their bodies, and develops body-awareness, which we now know to be of vital importance for many reasons. Co-ordination and control bring poise, grace and economy of movement. An uninhibited, joyful approach at this stage will lead naturally into creative dance and drama later on.

Fields of discovery. Children are born explorers. They explore through their five senses and through their bodies. Much of their exploring will be of play materials that we provide for them, but much will also be of objects they meet in their daily life. Some objects will be living, some inanimate. Some they will find on their own – in the nursery garden, on their way home, at Grandma's. Others we will deliberately bring into the nursery for them to look at, handle, manipulate, ask questions about.

Perhaps these processes can be better described as *investigation* rather than play. Such investigation performs the following functions:
(a) It satisfies and also feeds a child's curiosity and spirit of enquiry.
(b) It encourages powers of reasoning, memory, classification, association, problem-solving.
(c) It promotes language development through discussion, and through 'how', 'when' and 'why' questions and answers.
(d) It encourages use of reference books.
(e) It sharpens observation skills.
(f) It fosters ideas of caring, reliable tending, personal responsibility (e.g. for pets, plants).
(g) It teaches patience (e.g. waiting for bulbs to appear).
(h) It extends the child's knowledge and understanding of the world around him, including dangers (poisonous berries, etc.).
(i) It teaches respect for forms of life other than human.
(j) It builds a foundation for later formal scientific experimentation; in the same way, later recording, ordering and measuring of findings (mathematics) will also stem from this. Life in an increasingly complex technological society makes these aspects of education more and more important.
(k) It fosters a sense of wonder, and appreciation of patterns and order in the world around the child.

(l) It teaches awareness and understanding of life cycles – birth and death.

If we are to care effectually for the environment of the present and the future, and find ways of making life on earth better for *all* mankind, then surely we need to give young children plenty of opportunity to begin developing these skills and attitudes as early as possible.

Starting points for investigation

We have to decide how much of the animate and inanimate world we can bring into the nursery, or take the children to visit. Here are some ideas:

(a) *keeping pets* (but *do* inform yourself fully *beforehand* on care and possible difficulties, health hazards, etc.), also wormery, aquarium;

(b) *gardening* activities (quick-maturing vegetables which can later be made into sandwiches or soups are especially good);

(c) keeping *plants and flower arrangements*;

(d) growing *spring flowering bulbs* indoors;

(e) taking children on frequent *walks*, particularly to see trees, wild flowers, ducks, animals, etc., fostering ideas on conservation;

(f) using natural materials in *displays* (e.g., leaves, bark, shells);

(g) using natural materials in *activities* (e.g., collage, leaf prints);

(h) making a *bottle garden*;

(i) making a *bird table* and observing activities on it, providing winter foodstuffs for birds, 'Christmas pudding' etc.;

(j) drawing children's attention to changing *weather, clouds, seasons, temperature*;

(k) keeping *seeds* and watching them germinate indoors;

(l) following up interest aroused by discovery of *beetle, snail* etc., in garden;

(m) keeping a *'discovery' table* ('things which work') with changing assortment of such items as bells, clocks, locks, taps, washers, pumps, syringes, egg-timer, springs, pendulums, cogs, levers, pulleys, springs, mirrors, magnets;

(n) organising walks to watch *work of all sorts* being carried out, for example, cranes at the docks, concrete mixer in the road;

(o) drawing children's attention frequently to different means of *transport*, in books, pictures and real life; different sources of *power* (light, heat, water) and different types of *construction* (bridge, flats, tower, etc.);

(p) encouraging *inventiveness* in many different forms; junk modelling is a favourite means of expressing this.

TYPES OF PLAY

Type	Value	Provision	Role of the adult
1. *Vigorous physical play*, often on large or small equipment, mainly outdoors	Enjoyment Release of surplus energy Offers new freedom from tensions and restrictions Stimulus to: appetite, digestion, circulation, sound sleep, mental alertness, skin health Promotes: muscle tone, bodily co-ordination, manipulative skills, balance, control, body awareness, resistance to infection Develops such skills as: running, stopping and starting, hopping, aiming, climbing, swinging, steering, carrying Offers element of challenge and adventure Builds concepts of: height, width, speed, distance, spatial relationships Fosters social adjustment: levelling of abilities in new setting, sharing, collaborating Builds self-confidence. Stimulates intellectual curiosity, powers of observation, aesthetic awareness and sense of wonder (insects and birds,	A well and imaginatively-planned garden with paved area and grass, different levels, paths, trees, digging and growing areas, possibilities for dens and privacy, storage for equipment, easy access to nursery Large but manoeuvrable apparatus, such as: climbing frame, see-saw, rockers, rope ladder, trestle units and plank, hollow cubes, packing case boxes, tyres, barrels, space hopper Small apparatus such as: hoops, skipping ropes, balls, bean bags Wheeled vehicles such as: trucks, carts, scooters, tricycles, wheelbarrows	Exercise constant watchfulness in supervision for safety (of equipment and children). Undertake arrangement and rearrangement of apparatus. Encourage child in his activities, without directing or goading him to try feats beyond his capabilities. Inject new ideas. Maximise language opportunities (with children, not other adults). Introduce idea of fair play, and 'police' for bullying or dangerous quarrels. Train children in tidying away. Initiate ring games, singing games etc. as occasion demands. Sharpen your own and children's powers of observation. Keep informed of new equipment available; offer suggestions for new buys based on critical evaluation and consideration of your children in your available space.

Involve parents in play and other learning

Involve parents in a group for young child...

Work with colleagues in a team (78...

Plan, implement and evaluate activities and development (78...

P.3 P.5 M.4 M.7

Type	Value	Provision	Role of the adult
	changing seasons, rainbow, reflections in a puddle etc.) Feeds the imagination and leads into imaginative play.		
2. *Play with basic materials* (a) Water	Enjoyment Fascination of primitive element Sensory experience Release of tension Outlet for aggression Soothing effect Language opportunities (very rich here) Encourages manipulative skills (e.g. pouring accurately) There is no right and wrong way, therefore endless scope. Link with imaginative play (e.g. tea parties, bathing the doll etc.). Mathematical and scientific discoveries concerning: volume, capacity, gradation (big, bigger, etc.), floating and sinking, absorbency, changes, of objects when wet and dry, in textures, colour, shape, water finds its own level, displace-	Play with paddling pool, water painting, hoses, etc. outside Equipment for washing dolls and dolls' clothes Suitable size water bath, preferably transparent Equipment for water bath: tubing, squeezy bottles, graded jugs and cups, beakers with holes, sponges, loofah, spoons and ladles, household articles such as colander, plastic dishes, lids, cotton reels etc., rubber ball, golf ball, table-tennis ball, bubble blowing equipment Protection for floor (newspapers on top of plastic sheet?) Protection for children, overalls on stand (number available can be way of restricting numbers) Table or similar nearby to hold categorised equipment Tepid water, sometimes coloured (vegetable colouring or	Site and plan water play for safety, comfort, accessibility of tap and sink. Supervise protection of children, looking out for wet sleeves, socks etc. Vary, perhaps limit equipment provided each day. Observe children closely for scientific discoveries, asking meaningful questions and giving extending suggestions. Maximise language opportunities. Intervene if play becomes over-boisterous. Constantly watch small children in paddling pool. Involve children in clearing away.

Type	Value	Provision	Role of the adult
	ment of water, force and pressure, conservation (of quantity irrespective of shape of container), proportion, evaporation, syphoning, condensation, dissolving, properties of: cleansing, sustaining life, metal corrosion Categorisation (of equipment) Standard units of measurement	washing 'blue'), sometimes bubbly Opportunities to join in cleaning chores with water (washing furniture) and life-sustaining functions (watering plants, changing pets' water)	
(b) Sand	Enjoyment Pleasurable link with seaside Outlet for aggression Opportunity to destroy legitimately Language opportunities Creativity Sensory experience Link with imaginative play There is no right and wrong way (see column 4) so endless scope Scientific discoveries concerning: properties and contrasts of wet and dry sand, weight, capacity, grains, moulding, imprints	Sandpit outside, away from trees, to afford children body contact Sand bought from builders' merchant (cheaper if fetched) Equipment for sandpit: variety of spades, buckets, cups, cartons, rake, shells etc. Sand container(s) inside for wet and/dry sand Equipment similar to that for sandpit For dry sand, also: funnels, colander, sieve, flour sifter etc. Protection for floor	Supervise children for safe and non-wasteful play (no throwing or removing it permanently). Supervise sandpit for foreign bodies, dangerous items, fouling by animals and litter. Check condition of equipment. Wash or replace regularly sand used indoors (sun and fresh air cleans outside sand). Maximise language opportunities, and inject new ideas. Involve children in sweeping up and caring for equipment. Observe stages children are at (exploratory play, through to creative building).

Type	Value	Provision	Role of the adult
(c) Clay and dough	Enjoyment	Protection for children (aprons)	Site clay tables intelligently, near tap and sink, and supervise for undue mess (e.g. door handles, clothes, hair).
	Endless possibilities, no right and wrong way	Protection for floor and chairs	
	Legitimate 'mucky' play	Tables and chairs of suitable height, to allow of banging and rolling with some force	Maintain clay by storing in grapefruit-sized balls, with small water-filled indentation. Place on brick or hessian rag inside airtight container, and cover with plastic sheet or damp rag. Inspect regularly, particularly before and after holidays. Keep in cool place. Well maintained, it will last indefinitely.
	Emotional benefits: outlet for aggression (prodding, poking, cutting, banging)		
	Therapeutic effect of handling plastic material	Sufficient amounts of red and white clay (best bought in ready-to-use state from local pottery) and kept in perfect condition	
	Sensory experience		
	Novelty of clay (too messy for most homes)	Plain and different coloured dough, made about once a week	
	Link with home of dough	Equipment for each	Mix dough to preferred recipe (often three parts flour to one part salt, water, oil and colouring optional) but experiment with other sorts of flour. Keep in airtight plastic bag.
	Scientific discoveries about properties of both (elasticity, contrasts of wet and dry etc.)	(a) Clay (keep equipment to a minimum): wire cutter, blunt knives, boards, spatulas	
	Satisfies and externalises children's curiosity and preoccupation with bodily products, play with which is taboo	(b) Dough: rolling pins, boards, flour sifters, patty tins	Vary materials offered.
			Introduce relevant and enriching vocabulary.
	Language opportunities (cool, moist, stretchy, etc.)		Refrain from making objects or models 'for' child.
			Value the doing more than an end product. Carefully dry older children's models, and

Type	Value	Provision	Role of the adult
(d) Wood (wood can also be considered a creative and constructional play material)	Enjoyment Sensory experience Link (especially for boys) with father and grandfather Fosters manipulative skills and eye/hand co-ordination (e.g., banging in a nail) Language opportunities (names of tools, grains of wood, etc.) Emotional benefits: outlet for tension and aggression, satisfaction of making a noise legitimately, sense of power, sense of achievement Avenue of creativity, perhaps leading to adult interest Mathematical and scientific experience: length, breadth, angles, stress	Suitably-sized rigid woodwork bench Scaled-down real tools (toy tools break and cause accidents and frustration) such as: hammers, tenon saw, screwdriver, awl, vice, spanner Suitable storage for tools (e.g. on pegboard, with jubilee clips and silhouettes of appropriate tools) Assortment variously shaped and sized soft wood pieces Materials suitable for wheels (tins, lids, bottle tops etc.) Assorted nails and screws in transparent containers with lids	encourage painting, displaying, firing if possible. Plan and site woodwork bench intelligently so that it gives least disturbance to others (e.g., noise-deadening flooring underneath it, or piece of blanket nailed firmly on top. Consider siting it outdoors or in corridor). Supervise closely and constantly for safety (small numbers, spectators to keep well back, no distractions to allow children's concentration to wander). Intervene and offer help and suggestions where necessary, without 'taking over' play. Discuss work in hand with children and offer relevant and enriching vocabulary. Observe and cater for stage each child is at (just banging nails into bench or making preconceived models). Offer more advanced children opportunity to paint, display, use models.

Type	Value	Provision	Role of the adult
			Value the 'doing' more than the end product. Train children in safe and correct method of handling and storing tools.
3. *Construction play* (a) with large junk	Enjoyment Feeds imagination Language opportunities Encourages social play First-hand experiences in spatial relationships (next to, underneath, on top of etc.), also three-dimensional shape Sometimes takes place outdoors, involving all health benefits as set down in 1 Emotional benefits: outlet for vigorous action, sense of achievement, sense of power from making life-size models Link with group interests, e.g. robot, shop, and imaginative play	Sufficient time and space Large cardboard boxes (including TV and refrigerator packing cases) Sheets of corrugated cardboard Spools from paper bales etc. Sugar paper Newspapers Brown paper Materials, fabric as needed String Strong glue Cellulose tape Paint Scissors Any other suitable discarded material 'Large junk' is also sometimes used to describe packing cases, tyres etc. used outside. See section 1.	Take up children's suggestions for constructions, or discreetly introduce ideas. Discuss practicalities with children. Sustain ideas begun. Introduce relevant vocabulary. Supervise for safe use of tools and materials. Use or display constructions as intended.
(b) with small junk items	Enjoyment Feeds imagination	Large assortment of household and other junk (sometimes cal-	Initiate and maintain a successful system for collecting junk.

Type	Value	Provision	Role of the adult
	Promotes resourcefulness Embodies conservation principles (of using others' scrap to good purpose) Cheap to provide Involves parents and children in provision, thus fostering greater understanding and appreciation Link with group interest (boats, engines etc.) Language opportunities (names of containers, former contents, sources of origin, parts of models made etc.) Sensory experience Encourages small manipulative skills (fixing, gluing, etc.) Awareness of three-dimensional shape Experience in comparing, matching, sorting	led 'treasure') such as cereal packets, egg boxes – not polystyrene type (the particles are very dangerous if inhaled), lolly sticks, bottle tops, margarine tubs Strong glue Paste brushes Paper Paint Scissors Storage systems for all materials (e.g. wallpaper – covered large boxes with labels) so that there are separate categories, and children can select easily. Appearance of containers is also important to look of room Tables and chairs to work at Protection from glue (aprons)	Keep it neatly stored, throwing out useless or spoiled items. Discuss work with children, introducing relevant new vocabulary and suggestions where needed. Encourage, and offer help where necessary. Arrange attractive displays, where practicable. Use reference books whenever possible (e.g. to find out, with child, number of funnels on ship, or what a lighthouse looks like). Involve children in care and use of equipment, checking numbers of scissors returned, etc.
(c) with blocks	Enjoyment Sensory experience (blocks are clean, pleasant to touch, non-threatening) Emotional benefits: outlet for	Adequate time and space Sufficient large wooden blocks, made in geometric proportions (e.g. two shorts = one long) Sufficient small blocks varying	Site block play where children will not be disturbed by through traffic, or boisterous activities, and where they will give least disturbance (by noise to quiet activities).

Type	Value	Provision	Role of the adult
	aggression, satisfaction of making loud but legitimate noise, and destroying	in shapes and sizes, colour, textures, grains of wood (possibly home-made from offcuts)	Check blocks for splintering and shortages.
	Feeling of power (especially of making life-sized models, walls to hide behind etc.)	Interlocking plastic bricks	Discuss children's constructions with them, feeding in enriching vocabulary and ideas where relevant.
	Encourages perseverance	A corner, or at least a wall, against which to build	Remember that many children like to build for long periods on their own, undisturbed.
	Fosters eye/hand co-ordination: balance, control, precision	Noise-deadening carpet or rug if liked	Give adequate time warnings about dismantling constructions. Come to reasonable and individual arrangements about large or ambitious constructions.
	Develops muscle tone in: stretching, lifting, carrying	Table where children can play with small bricks	
	Feeds imagination, often leading into imaginative play	Accessibility of 'small world' – dolls, furniture, vehicles, animals, etc.	Supply additional play aids as required, e.g. blanket for a roof.
	Language opportunities (names of shapes and constructions etc.)	Adequate and systematised storage facilities	Prevent deliberate untimely destruction by other children.
	Mathematical experience: height; weight, proportion, spanning, symmetry, three-dimensional shape		Involve children in clearing away (NB can be done to music).
			Make it a mathematical experience.
4. *Creative and imaginative play*	Enjoyment	Easels and/or tables	Site facilities intelligently (in good light, with easy access to
	Avenue of expression	Brightly-coloured paints of	

Type	Value	Provision	Role of the adult
(a) Painting and visual arts	Novelty for many nursery children Feeds imagination Language stimulation (colours, objects, etc.) Creativity Sense of achievement End product admired by adults Appeal of colour Experience in depicting and interpreting meaning of symbols on paper (foundation for later reading and writing) Control Emotional release (of frightening experiences, etc.) Fosters taste and personal preferences Perception of shape, spatial relationships Scientific discoveries about: textures, consistencies, mixing colours etc.	creamy consistency (mainly primary colours) Long-handled brushes, of different widths Paper of varying textures, shapes, sizes, colours (including textured paper like wallpaper samples) Non-spill paint pots Objects for printing (leaves, string, pastry-cutters, etc.) Non-fungicidal thickening agent for paint Washing-up liquid for bubble painting Candles for 'magic' painting Protection for floor, where necessary Aprons on hooks Provision of drying rack or similar Space to display work Large chalks, board, chubby crayons	water and sink). Maintain appeal of materials and equipment (no 'gunged up' easels or paint pots). Supervise children for protection. Talk to child about his work if he wants to, but not relentlessly, nor seeking representational likenesses. Occasionally introduce different techniques using paint in a semi-directed way, e.g. marble rolling, butterfly painting. Involve children in clearing up. Allow children to take home paintings (put names on backs as soon as possible after completion). Arrange frequent displays of *all* children's work. Observe children's progress from exploratory stage to preconceived ideas stage.
(b) Collage ('sticking' with a variety of materials)	All the values listed for painting apply equally here	Adequate supply of scrap materials, fabrics, wool, pasta, bottle tops, natural materials (bark etc.)	Similar to that for painting

Type	Value	Provision	Role of the adult
	ALSO Promotes resourcefulness Lends itself readily to group projects, current themes, etc. Sensory experience (comparison of textures) Invites judgements on suitability Encourages choice, personal preferences Involves small manipulative skills (using scissors etc.)	Methodical and attractive system of collecting, storing, sorting materials Glue Paste brushes Scissors Protection for children Protection for table	ALSO Initiate themes for group collage work. Organise execution of large pieces (on floor, etc.). Sustain ideas and incorporate children's suggestions.
(c) Dramatic play	Enjoyment Role play Helps children project into feelings of others Helps children relive happy experiences (e.g., wedding), come to terms with unhappy ones (e.g., witnessing road accident) Language stimulus (boundless opportunities here) Encourages social co-operation Offers wish fulfilment and escape Involves small manipulative skills	Adequate time and space Dressing up clothes (boys' as well as girls') Props (shopping bags, purses, jewellery, steering wheel, blanket) Masks Variety of puppets (sock, glove, finger, etc.) Storage for all the above (clothes should be hung up)	Set the scene and provide an encouraging atmosphere. Allow privacy if children require it. Give adequate time warnings. Allow play to spread outdoors if possible. Involve oneself through question and discussion. Keep clothes in good state of cleanliness and repair. Inject fresh ideas and fresh 'props' to suggest new play. Supervise, and intervene when necessary for reasons of safety and noise level.

Type	Value	Provision	Role of the adult
	Exercises the imagination Sensory experience (textures and colours of dressing-up clothes) Outlet for tensions and aggression Insight for adult into thoughts and feelings of child		Observe for signs of increasing co-operation.
(d) Domestic play	All the values listed for dramatic play apply equally here ALSO Link with home Greater knowledge of functioning of a home Mathematical experience (laying the table, etc.) Fosters social skills (e.g., being hostess)	Home corner, preferably large enough for sleeping and living areas, affording privacy and a sense of self-containment Bed and bedding Rug or carpet Table and chairs Cooker, saucepans, kettle Sink Cupboards Cutlery, crockery Cleaning equipment Telephones *NB*: Home corner may be temporarily converted into hospital, shop, hairdresser's, cafe, as occasion or current interest demands)	Similar to that for dramatic play ALSO Allow child to become involved in domestic chores of nursery (spring cleaning home corner, looking after nursery pets, plants, etc.)

Type	Value	Provision	Role of the adult
(e) Dolls	Enjoyment Avenue for projection into others' feelings Awakens ideas of caring, tenderness Outlet for tension and aggressions (e.g., if new baby is at home) Knowledge of baby care Knowledge of mother's role Mathematics involved in dressing dolls (comparative size, gradation, counting, pairs, matching, 1:1 correspondence, categorisation) Language stimulation Sensory experience (texture of dolls' clothes, etc.) Knowledge of principles of laundry	Variety of different dolls (large rag doll, baby doll, black doll) 3 matching size-graded dolls with identical clothes Variety of clothes for outdoor, indoor and night wear Doll's bed, pram Bath, soap, talc, bottle etc. Provision for washing doll's clothes Open dolls' house, and small-world dolls Road layout, farm, railway station etc. for small-world dolls	Observe intelligently children's play and reactions with dolls. Make the most of language and mathematical opportunities. Allow children to make dolls and dolls' clothes. Allow children to wash dolls and dolls' clothes. Encourage progression from simple handling and undressing, through to more complex and creative play. Involve children in systematic clearing and tidying away.

Type	Value	Organisation and role of the adult
(f) Cookery An adult-directed activity	Enjoyment Link with home Sensory experience (feel, smell, taste) Emotional release (in beating, kneading, cutting, whisking) Satisfaction and pride in end-product Language opportunities (names of utensils, origins of ingredients, descriptions of consistencies, etc.) Education in need for hygiene and home safety Social activity – working with a group towards joint goal, waiting turns, consulting with adult, handing round end products Social graces, contributing to special occasions (Christmas, school coffee morning, etc.) Education in nutrition (emphasis on savoury and wholesome foods) Encourages concentration Scientific and mathematical experiences: shopping, standard units of measurement,	Link it to an occasion, story, topical interest whenever possible (e.g., Shrove Tuesday, 'The Gingerbread Man', blackberries found in field.) Involve children in shopping; discuss requirements, allow them to select items, proffer money, look after change. Organise time, place, use of cooker, utensils, ingredients, etc. well beforehand. Prepare illustrated recipe card, or find place in book. Select group (of approximately 4) and keep a record of who makes what. Pre-heat oven if necessary. Make sure children go to toilet and wash hands, girls tie back long hair. Give clear instructions and demonstrate what you mean (e.g., 'cream the margarine'). Keep every child occupied all the time as far as possible, and let each have a turn at every process. Supervise and give advice and suggestions and invite comments throughout. Make the most of language opportunities (e.g., 'risen', 'golden brown', 'crunchy', etc.) Involve all children in clearing up. Give out or sell goods fairly, remembering 'sisters' or headteacher, and any visitors. Encourage cooking group to share experience with others.

Type	Value	Organisation and role of the adult
	passing of time, weighing, balancing, capacity and volume, counting, dividing, fractions, one-to-one correspondence, classification, judging, effects of heat, introducing air bubbles, absorption, changes in texture, pressure Link with reading: labels on goods, using recipe cards (left-to-right eye movement), seeing adults consult books, making own recipe cards, or pictures and records in class book	*N.B.*: 'Cooking' need not involve use of a cooker. Novelty sandwiches, bridge roll and cheese 'boats', peppermint creams, icing biscuits, etc. can all be made without a cooker.

Exercise 15

Multiple-choice questions

1. Children of three to five are becoming silly, boisterous and very wet at the water-play equipment. You decide to:
(a) pack it all away for a few weeks;
(b) ban all those concerned from water-play for the rest of the term;
(c) tell them not to be naughty;
(d) protect them more completely with overalls, cuffs, wellington-boots, etc.;
(e) ascertain what was causing boredom, e.g., unchanging equipment, and try to remedy it.

2. Nursery children are showing little interest in clay at present. Your best course is to:
(a) try sitting at the clay-table yourself, and working a piece of clay;
(b) pick a few children and bribe them to go to the clay table;
(c) make a model for a small group to copy;
(d) substitute dough for it for the rest of term;
(e) organise a competition for the best animal model.

3. A child of eighteen months encounters a sandy beach for the first time. It would benefit him most if you:
(a) let him pat and prod it, run hands and feet over it as he chooses;
(b) make a series of sand-pies for him;
(c) teach him how to make sand-pies himself;
(d) keep him in a pushchair out of direct contact with sand in case he does not like it;
(e) pour sand repeatedly over his hands and feet to show him how lovely it is.

4. One of the following is a 'golden rule' for woodwork with young children.
(a) always nail a blanket to the woodwork bench to deaden noise;
(b) always site in corridor or garden so that noise will not be a nuisance;
(c) never provide real tools since they can cause so much injury;
(d) insist that children do not waste wood, but set out to make real models;
(e) ensure constant supervision.

5. Children gain a great deal from play with blocks. Which would you say is the most significant and unique contribution block-play can make to children's development?
(a) practice in counting;
(b) training in clearing away tidily;
(c) pleasure in destruction;
(d) knowledge of adult construction techniques;
(e) experience in three-dimensional shape and spatial relationships.

6. The most suitable doll for a two-to-three-year-old girl would be:
(a) soldier doll, with equipment etc.;

(b) teenage doll, with appropriate outfits for different occasions;
(c) baby doll, with a few simple garments;
(d) walkie talkie doll;
(e) paper cut-out dolls and clothes.

7. The most valuable addition to imaginative play for two-to-three-year-olds would be:
(a) a uniform hat;
(b) jewellery;
(c) buttoned tunic;
(d) hairdressing equipment, rollers, etc.;
(e) set of make-up.

Essay questions

8. Draw a plan of nursery garden and list features and equipment.

9. Imagine you are creating and equipping a moveable home-corner for a playgroup. Cost must be kept to an absolute minimum.

10. Why is play with water so enjoyable for children? Describe some children of different ages you have seen playing with it, and say how you think they were benefiting.

11. Describe a cookery activity you have seen children take part in, remembering organisation, and the value of the exercise.

Project

12. From looking around in shops, decide on a suitable item as a fourth birthday present for a nephew, spending less than £2.

Observation

13. Observe children constructing something (out of blocks, wooden or cardboard boxes etc.), which they afterwards play with imaginatively. How did the idea arise? How many children took part? Is there a clear leader? Notice changes in direction as play proceeds. Record children's comments. Did an adult play any part?

14. Observe children painting spontaneously. Compare the approach, technique and skill of an older child with that of a younger child. What different opportunities are available, and how do children react to them?

15. Observe how children use large equipment for physical activity. Describe opportunities available to them and how they take advantage of these. Notice different approaches, and degrees of confidence and skill in such things as balancing, climbing, swinging, jumping.

16. Observe three different instances where children of varying ages were taking part in domestic play. How do you think each was benefiting?

Suggestions for further reading

K. M. Chesterfield and P. A. Binns and V. M. Robins, *Music and Language with Young Children*, Basil Blackwell Ltd

Beatrice Harrop, *Apusskidu*, A. & C. Black Ltd

Beatrice Harrop, *Okki – Tokki – Unga*, A. & C. Black Ltd

Marianne Parry and Hilda Archer, *Two to Five*, Macmillan Education Ltd

Kenneth Jamieson and Pat Kidd, *Pre-School Play*, Studio Vista Publishers

E. Matterson, *Play With a Purpose for the Under 7's*, Penguin Books Ltd

Donald Baker, *Understanding the Under 5's*, Evans Brothers Ltd

Catherine Lee, *The Growth and Development of Children*, Longman Group Ltd

Alison Stallibrass, *The Self Respecting Child*, Pelican Books

Alice Yardley, *Discovering the Physical World*, Evans Brothers Ltd

Katherine Read, *The Nursery School*, W. B. Saunders Co. Ltd

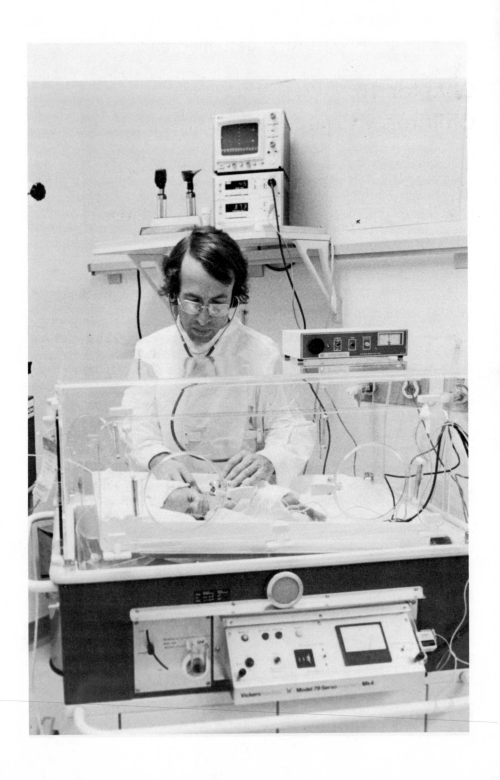

Chapter 16
Children with special needs

The premature baby

In Great Britain about eight per cent of all babies born each year are premature. The international definition of prematurity is a baby weighing less than 2.500 kg (5 lb 8 oz).

In practice these babies can be divided into two main groups:

1. *dysmature* (light for dates): a baby born after thirty-seven weeks pregnancy weighing less than 2.500 kg (5 lb 8 oz). *[handwritten: 9 mths]*
2. *premature*: a baby born before thirty-six weeks pregnancy weighing less than 2.500 kg (5 lb 8 oz). *[handwritten: 9 mths]*

N.B.: By the end of the twenty-eighth week of pregnancy a baby has become 'viable'. This means although he may weigh less than 1 kg (approx. 2 lb) he is capable of a separate existence. *[handwritten: 7 mths]*

The causes of prematurity are not always known, as there are many contributing factors. The dysmature baby has suffered a reduction in his food and oxygen supply during pregnancy which may be due to failure or malfunction of the placenta. This could be caused by toxaemia of pregnancy or by a rapidly ageing placenta. Heavy smoking by the mother can also be a contributary cause. Another reason for dysmaturity could be a multiple pregnancy, where one baby takes most of the food at the expense of another baby.

The truly premature baby is more common in the lower socio-economic group and this may result from many factors, including poor general health in the mother, especially when this stems from poor nutrition. Lack of regular ante-natal care aggravates to the problem. Again, multiple births are often premature. Further, if there is any abnormality in the baby, he may be premature.

The proportion of premature babies who are subsequently found to be handicapped is higher than in full-term babies, despite the expert care they receive in special care units. So the best treatment is the prevention of prematurity and, of course, this is one of the main aims of good ante-natal care. First, it is necessary to ensure that the mother is as healthy as possible, by making sure that she has a good diet and by giving her advice about her general health.

Secondly, it is necessary to examine mothers at intervals (so that if there are any signs of developing toxaemia it can be treated immediately) and to check that the baby is growing at the normal rate. If a mother does start to have her baby too early, then if at all possible the labour should be stopped.

The appearance of a premature baby will depend on its size, but the very tiny babies are extremely thin, because they have very little fat under the skin. They are wrinkled and have a worried look on their faces, like wizened old men. The limbs of such a baby are thin but the abdomen is large and the head appears to be very large in proportion to the body. Fontanelles are large and easily palpable. There may be fine hairs on the body, and fingernails are very soft.

The dysmature baby's problems are mainly the need to 'catch up' with the normal baby by feeding and putting on weight, so if the baby is over about 2.350 kg (3 lb) in weight he has a very good chance of survival. The truly premature baby has problems, because he has missed the last few weeks in the uterus and the more weeks he has missed, the smaller he will be and the greater his problems. Towards the end of pregnancy a lot of development takes place to equip the baby for the outside world:

1. The respiratory centre in the brain matures.

2. The baby learns and practises the art of sucking and swallowing.

3. The heat-regulating mechanism centre in the brain begins to mature.

4. Fat is laid down under the baby's skin.

5. Calcium is being deposited in the bones.

6. Iron is being stored in the liver.

7. Antibodies against infection are being passed over from mother to baby.

So his problems can be as follows:

1. poor respiration (breathing) due to immature respiratory system;

2. inability to suck and swallow;

3. inability to regulate his temperature;

4. inability to keep warm;

5. soft bones owing to lack of calcium – this may lead to damage to the brain at birth as it lacks the protection of a hard skull;

6. anaemia owing to lack of iron;

7. poor defences against infection.

The majority of these babies are placed in an incubator and cared for in a special care unit for premature and sick babies. The incubator is a transparent box-like structure with 'portholes' so that the baby can be attended to without being taken out of it (see illustration, p. 228). Inside an incubator, the environment can be controlled and made to resemble the conditions in the uterus. Very warm, humid air with the correct amount of oxygen is supplied. The warmth enables the baby to be nursed without clothing, which might restrict his breathing. He is protected from droplet and airborne infection by being in the incubator, and strict hygiene measures are taken by doctors and nurses to minimise the spread of infection via their hands. He can be fed by means of a tube into his stomach, or fluids can be given into the veins. Iron, vitamins and possibly calcium can be given via the tube or by injection. Handling the baby is kept to a minimum to avoid trauma.

The larger premature baby with fewer problems may be nursed at home under the supervision of the doctor and health visitor. General care of this baby will be similar to that of the normal newborn baby, but extra special care must be taken over all aspects.

1. *warmth*: the room must be kept to 21°C (70°F) and some humidity may need to be supplied by putting bowls of water near the heat source;

2. *lightweight clothing* which will not restrict breathing or irritate baby's delicate skin;

3. *cleanliness and prevention of infection*: no visitors; one person to care for baby; hand washing; use of gown when attending to baby;

4. *care with feeding*: the baby is usually fed three-hourly with small feeds because he can become very tired from the effort of sucking. Some babies may need a special bottle so that the milk can be squirted into the mouth, e.g. a Belcroy feeder.

Because of the inevitable early separation, premature babies and their mothers often lack the feeling of belonging to each other (bonding) and this may lead to emotional problems. Efforts are being made to counteract this by giving the mother access to the special care unit so that she can sit beside her baby and put her hands in the incubator to touch him.

Premature babies are now sent home much earlier than was once the case, so that the mother will have closer contact. In the past the baby was not allowed home until he weighed 3.17 kg (7 lb) which could take months. Now, in many areas, there are specially trained health visitors called Premature Baby Visitors who can supervise the mother and baby by visiting daily. Because of this service, it is possible to send the baby home once he is out of immediate danger.

Children with handicaps

The definition of a handicapped child is one whose development is impaired by disease or injury. One in every twenty children born will have some abnormality or defect, but many of these will be minor ones, such as a birthmark, webbed fingers or toes or an extra finger. Others will be of a more serious nature such as cleft palate or spina bifida. The known causes of handicaps can be classified as follows:

1. an inherited defect – e.g., haemophilia;

2. injury to the foetus – e.g. deafness caused by rubella;

3. injury at birth – e.g., failure to breathe immediately after birth causes brain to lack oxygen, causes brain damage – cerebral palsy;

4. disease after birth – e.g., jaundice in new baby can cause brain damage – cerebral palsy;

5. injury after birth – e.g., head injury causing brain damage – mental deficiency;

6. severe deprivation – e.g. child never stimulated – mental backwardness.

A congenital disease is one which originates before birth, so it may be either inherited or a result of injury in the uterus.

Although all babies are examined at birth by a midwife and a doctor, and during the first two weeks of life, many of these handicaps are not obvious and are therefore not detected at this time. Some defects can be found by using special tests. For example, all babies have a blood test for phenylketonuria, a rare inherited disease which, if not treated within the first two weeks of life by putting the baby on a special diet, leads to mental handicap. Another test commonly carried out on newborn babies is that which detects congenital dislocation of the hips. This is a condition which, if treated early enough, can usually be completely cured.

The majority of handicaps only become obvious as the baby grows and often developmental assessments during the first five years of life reveal that the baby is not progressing as he should. In other cases the parents of the child suspect there is something wrong and take him to their doctor. In many areas there are diagnostic units where the child can be examined by various consultants, and investigations can be carried out to discover the nature of his handicap and either cure it or alleviate some of the associated problems. Otherwise the child may be referred to a paediatrician at a local hospital.

The effect on the family

Discovering that their child has a handicap is a terrible shock to most parents. Despite the fact that a mother's first question after her baby is born is often 'Is he all right?', mothers and fathers expect their babies to be normal and fortunately this is usually the case. If the defect is obvious at birth, then the mother should be told immediately, so that acceptance and adjustment will occur as early as possible. Usually the father is present, so that both parents can be told together. They will need to be told again after the initial shock is over, so that plans can be made as early as possible about the baby's future. Similarly, should a handicap be detected later in a child's life, his parents should be told as soon as possible.

Reaction to the fact that a child is handicapped can range from a rejection of the child to a complete refusal to believe that there is anything wrong at all. Fortunately, most parents do eventually accept their child as he is and do their best to help him. But nearly all parents ask themselves 'Why should this happen to me?' and there may be a tendency for one parent to blame the other, especially if the disease is hereditary. The arrival of a handicapped child can cause much marital stress, and the ability to cope will depend on the maturity of the parents and the strength of their marriage. Another factor in the acceptance of the handicap is the child's position in the family. If the parents already have a normal child, then it will be easier to accept a handicapped child.

It is difficult to understand how a mother can reject her own child, unless we are aware that we are animals and it is usual for animals to reject the abnormal. If, for instance, a mother cat has a litter containing a deformed kitten, she will ignore it and concentrate on the healthy kittens. In fact she will allow the kitten to die.

Sometimes the child is not rejected, but the handicap is. The parents ignore the handicap altogether and expect the child to behave like a normal one and to achieve the same standards. This can place a tremendous strain on the child.

Over-protection is another parental reaction to a handicapped child and can bring problems both for the child and for his brothers and sisters. They will resent the attention given to the child.

Brothers and sisters may be embarrassed about a handicapped child and will not bring friends home. Family friends and relatives often keep away, because they do not know how to deal with the situation; consequently the family may become isolated. Conflicting medical opinions as to the degree of handicap and frequent visits to hospital with long waiting periods can be physically and emotionally exhausting. Many families lack the financial and emotional resources to cope.

The care of the child places a burden on all the family; the mother in many cases is unable to work because of the demands of this child. Holidays are difficult, because the child may need special facilities. The child may be incontinent, which causes endless washing and cleaning. Babysitters are difficult to get. In such circumstances even everyday chores such as shopping for food may become an insoluble problem because of the necessity of caring for the child.

The majority of parents eventually come to terms with their child's handicap and many handicapped children have special qualities which contribute to family life. It should be remembered that this is a child (first) with a handicap (second) because his physical, mental and emotional needs are exactly the same as those of a normal child. Handicapped children and their families benefit if they are able to attend a day nursery, nursery school or playgroup and mix with normal children. Under the guidance of trained staff, with space to play and a variety of play materials, their experience can be widened and confidence can be gained.

Education for the handicapped child

It is the responsibility of the local education authority to assess these children from the age of two years and to provide special education according to their needs. Children are placed in one of the following categories:

1. blind;

2. partially sighted;

3. deaf;

4. partial hearing;

5. speech defect;

6. physically handicapped: includes children with spina bifida, cerebral palsy, muscular dystrophy, etc.;

7. delicate: includes some diabetics, children with asthma, etc.;

8. epileptic;

9. educationally sub-normal: children with limited mental ability;

10. severely sub-normal: children with very limited mental ability;

11. maladjusted: children with severe behaviour difficulties.

In addition to these categories, there are children with multiple handicaps, such as blind/deaf children and those with rare handicaps, such as autism, which are difficult to categorise.

In many areas a special day school is provided for each category, or a special class in a normal school. In the case of some rarer handicaps, such as blindness, there are not enough affected children in one area to justify a day school, so there are a few boarding schools scattered over the country in which specialised teaching can be given. There are also residential schools for children with other handicaps whose parents are unable to cope at home. Alternatively, in many areas, home tutors are available to visit the house and assist parents in the care and education of their child.

In the past a handicapped child was nearly always placed in a special school, but since 1954 the principle has been laid down that no handicapped pupil should be sent to a special school who can be satisfactorily educated in a normal school. However, this is not always possible because of the design of school buildings (for example, too many stairs for the physically handicapped) and because some children need more specialised help. Moreover, some teachers feel unable to cope without special training. In some areas this is overcome by employing a nursery nurse specifically to care for a handicapped child placed in a normal school. If a child is to be placed in a normal school, then it is important that the staff should be fully prepared and informed. There are advantages and disadvantages to both special and normal schools for a child, so each side should be considered carefully when a decision is being made about an individual child.

1. Special schools

Advantages
(a) The ratio of adults to children is laid down in the Education Act and ensures that classes are small, e.g., for physically handicapped pupils the maximum number of children in a class is twenty.
(b) This means that each child can work at his own pace.
(c) Staff may have special training and experience.
(d) Free transport is provided as of right.
(e) School meals are cheaper.
(f) Milk is provided free for all age groups.
(g) Emphasis is on mutual care and support.
(h) The child has an opportunity to excel when surrounded by children with similar disabilities.
(i) The building will be adapted to the children's needs, e.g.:
    (i) toilet facilities for disabled in wheelchairs, encouraging maximum independence;
    (ii) ramps instead of stairs for physically handicapped.
(j) Special equipment and facilities may be available, e.g., heated swimming pool with hoists.

School nurses, physiotherapists and speech therapists are usually on the premises, ensuring regular treatment and any necessary medical attention available without too much loss of schooling.

Disadvantages

(a) Child grows up surrounded by handicapped people so that his social life is restricted.
(b) He may be so protected that he cannot cope with normal adult life.

(c) Segregation leads to ignorance about the needs of handicapped people by general public.
(d) School is usually some distance from home, so travelling makes a long day for child.
(e) Because of distance, school friendships are difficult to sustain at home.
(f) Special schools are costly to maintain.

2. Normal schools

Advantages:

(a) Mixing with normal children benefits both normal and handicapped children and adults – normal people become aware of other's needs.
(b) Child's social life is widened.
(c) Child's day is shorter because less distance involved.
(d) Most parents prefer to have their child in normal school.
(e) Child can go to same school as brothers and/or sisters.
(f) The ratepayer is saved the expense of maintaining a special school.

Disadvantages:

(a) Lack of any special facilities, e.g., toilet.
(b) Lack of specially-trained teachers and helpers.
(c) Medical treatment may not be available on the spot.
(d) School building may be unsuitable (too many stairs).
(e) High ratio of children to adults.
(f) Child may have to strive very hard in order to keep up with work and appear normal.

Help available

Parents need a good deal of support and encouragement if their child is severely handicapped. The family doctor, health visitor and local authority social worker can all provide that support and also put the family in touch with other agencies which may offer specific help.

1. Residential homes. These are for children under five years old whose parents cannot cope with them.

2. Attendance allowance. This is a weekly sum of money for adults and children over the age of two years who are severely handicapped, either physically or mentally, and need to be looked after for six months or more. There is a rate for day attention and a higher rate for those who need constant attention day and night.

3. Invalid care allowance. This is a weekly allowance for a person of working age unable to work because he or she is needed at home to care for a disabled relative. This is only available to married women if they are unsupported by their husband.

4. Mobility allowance. If a child aged five years or over is unable, or virtually unable, to walk, then a grant of £12.00 (in 1979) a week is made to enable him to be taken out.

5. Car tax. Since December 1978 recipients of the mobility allowance have been excused car tax for their vehicles (in the case of a child, the parent or guardian's vehicle which is used to take him out).

6. Car badge scheme. Parents of a physically handicapped child can obtain a badge for their car which entitles them to free parking.

7. The local authority social service department. This department may provide any or all of the following free:
(a) telephone;
(b) incontinence pads;
(c) disposable nappies;
(d) laundry facilities;
(e) night sitters;
(f) home helps (there may be a charge for this service).

8. Housing. The local housing authority may provide a specially-adapted council house for the family. If the family owns a house, the social services department can make money available for alterations to the house, for example the installation of a lift and/or ramps instead of steps, or a shower instead of a bath.

9. The family fund (Joseph Rowntree Memorial Trust). This is a trust fund set up to help disabled children and their families. The aim is to fill in the gaps of statutory care, so help depends on individual needs, e.g., provision of a washing machine for parents of an incontinent child.

10. Appliances. Wheelchairs, crutches, glasses, hearing aids and other appliances are provided free under the National Health Service.

11. Voluntary organisations:
(a) Many parents of children with specific handicaps have formed their own societies for mutual help and support and collect funds for research into their children's disease. One example is The Muscular Dystrophy Association.
(b) The local Red Cross Society, Women's Royal Voluntary Service and others will often give specific help to handicapped children and their families, for example holidays.

12. Genetic Counselling Centre. This is a special centre where advice on hereditary diseases is available to parents and relatives.

The deprived and disadvantaged child

This child has been denied one or more of the fundamental rights of childhood, which are normally supplied in a happy family life. We believe those rights to be:

1. a stable home;

2. a well-organised, loving mother;

3. a supportive father who provides for the child's material needs, such as protection, clothing, adequate diet and play space;

4. fresh experience to stimulate language and mental growth, which is allowed to proceed at its own rate;

5. recognition and an encouraging atmosphere;

6. contact with other children and adults.

Because one or more of these rights has been denied and a basic need left unfulfilled, there is a chance that the child will develop in an uneven, unbalanced way. His personality may present obvious gaps, or even be scarred for life. Because the first four years are critical and a period of tremendous growth and development, all children should enjoy 'an abundant environment', as Willem van der Eyken calls it.

We sometimes separate, as in this chapter, the various aspects of deprivation into material, social, environmental, intellectual, cultural, educational and linguistic. We have to do this to identify problems and needs, but it is an artificial practice; one 'lack' invariably goes alongside, or creates, others, as we hope to show further in this chapter.

Some people draw distinctions between the various terms used, for instance claiming that 'disadvantaged' refers to the inner condition of the child, resulting from an outer deprivation. Other people regard it as a matter of degree or severity, deprivation referring to the most basic and urgent 'lacks'. 'Underprivileged' is another term employed, usually to describe children lacking in material things.

It is possible, even easy, to become too bogged down by these various terms. It is dangerous to bandy them about indiscriminately, to label children, to make judgements (that deprivation is the 'fault' of the parents) and certainly to make spoken reference to such terms in front of children or parents.

One other fact needs to be borne in mind while considering this subject. Deprivation is not confined to low-income groups. One meets examples of deprivation in all classes and kinds of families. It is easy to recognise material deprivations – if, for instance, a child wears obvious hand-me-down clothes or looks undernourished. But the invisible, difficult-to-recognise forms of deprivation are usually more serious and lasting in their effects.

Material, environmental and social deprivation

1. Manifestations and reasons. Unemployment, poverty and mismanagement of money; shared or inadequate facilities for washing and cooking; poor housing; poor clothing; poorly-balanced diet; inadequate medical care, including preventive measures; lack of cleanliness, space, play material, protection. The 'typical' deprived child looks pale, undernourished, often has a runny nose and never seems to be really fit.

2. Possible effects. Ill-health (physical and mental) and lack of resistance to disease, undiagnosed defects, infestation; road and other accidents; becoming a social outcast; fatigue owing to cramped sleeping arrangements; apathy and lack of response to stimuli; depressed height and intelligence (through poor, low-protein diet in early years); envy and resentment of others with more; over-boisterous, aggressive or attention-seeking behaviour at nursery or school; lack of concentration and physical co-ordination.

3. How the nursery nurse can help. The nurse must understand the child's difficulties and make allowance for the child arriving late, in a dirty, ill-clad or unkempt state. He may need nursery clothes, bathing, possibly first-aid of some sort. He may need additional food, or rest. He will need space and opportunity for vigorous play, and also help in care of play materials.

It is vital that the nursery nurse acts in a tactful manner, both with child and parents. The child is an individual and has his pride. Parents may need to be referred to other social agencies for help in coping with their problems, but this must never be done in a patronising or condemnatory manner. She may be able to suggest ways in which parents can help a child, for example, a different bedtime arrangement. The child needs to be helped to feel good about himself, so praise and encouragement, one-to-one, are beneficial. Care must be taken that the child does not sense criticism of his background, making for divided loyalties.

Emotional deprivation

1. Causes:
(a) Child has been deprived of mother's care and love (this is called maternal deprivation) either through death or separation.
(b) Child has been rejected, is unwanted or unloved (because he is handicapped,

illegitimate, 'wrong' sex, or parent is, irrationally, unable to feel love for him).

(c) Child has experienced seriously unsatisfactory family relationships (absent father, parent mentally ill, violence in the home, etc.).

2. Possible effects. Any one of these causes may result in the child's needing to go into substitute care (residential home, fostering, adoption). Adoption and long-term fostering arrangements often work out successfully and may supply the child with more emotional and material benefits than he would have had in his natural home. But disturbed arrangements and long-term care in a residential home can result in the child's growing up with little sense of his own identity, individuality or personal worth. Through lack of personal involvement by parents in his all-round development, his past and his future, he may experience problems of personality, language or learning.

For a child who stays within his family unit, but experiences any of these three causes of emotional deprivation, there is a danger that if he has never known continuing personal love and involvement from one person close to him, he may be unable to give it himself. He may grow up with warped or idealised concepts of the opposite sex which may lead to immature and indiscriminate choice of friends and marriage partners later. He may withdraw from relating to others, to protect himself from further hurt. He may mistrust adults, and in particular those who represent authority. He often indulges in attention-seeking behaviour, of an obsequious, clinging, or anti-social nature. He often lacks concentration, frequently needs reassurance and encouragement to meet new challenges. The insecure young person may drift from one job to another, or hit back at life which has been less than kind to him, and make his mark by vandalism or hooliganism.

3. How the nursery nurse can help. This child needs adult interest, concern and affection, even when he appears to reject it in a most unlovable way. He needs to build up a good self-image, and so he must be praised not just for results, but for effort and progress – for *him* – whether it be a small act of kindness, one minute longer of concentration, one little bit of co-operation. If nothing else presents itself, then a brightly coloured jumper or well-brushed hair can be the focus for compliments. The nursery nurse should always stress the positive. If the child is withdrawn he will need very gentle approaches, on a one-to-one basis. Casual showing of books, or an invitation to help the nursery nurse with chores, can provide the occasion for gradually building up a good relationship. Such a child should never be forced to mix or join in or contribute in front of others. Wild behaviour, although it cannot be permitted in nursery, must be understood, and acceptable alternatives provided as outlets for aggression, such as woodwork, blocks, clay, water.

Intellectual, cultural and educational deprivation and disadvantages

This is a confusing and controversial area.

1. Recognising the different facets:

(a) On a straightforward level, a child who has been denied the opportunity to develop mentally at his natural rate because of lack of stimulation in the home (for instance, if he has been kept in a cot, or one room most of the time, or if his parents are deaf and dumb or of a very low intelligence) is disadvantaged *intellectually*.

(b) So, too, is the child who is subjected to a bombardment of over-stimulation, either from too much, or unsuitable television, or from ambitious parents with unrealistically high expectations.

(c) Both children could also be said to be *educationally* disadvantaged, because they will not be able to benefit to the full from the education system. But neither will children who travel around a great deal with their parents – it could be abroad with Service personnel, or around the country with rising company executives, motorway labourers or gypsies. Also educationally disadvantaged are those children who evade much schooling (through parents' convictions, or truancy) or who have very poor schooling (fortunately rare today).

(d) Another category of educationally disadvantaged children is those with perceptual or learning difficulties, or physical handicaps such as poor co-ordination, or those who have lengthy spells in hospital. They will need special care and attention if they are to cope happily in a normal nursery or infants school, where they are usually kept until accurate assessments of their difficulties can be made around seven years of age.

(e) Much controversy exists over cultural deprivation. 'Culture' here is sometimes used to mean middle-class values and attitudes concerning behaviour, linguistic ability, books, music, etc. In this sense, many thousands of children may be 'culturally deprived'.

More precisely, if controversially, the term is also used with reference to children from backgrounds of different ethnic or national cultures from the British. Certainly these children may be at a disadvantage educationally in our schools, but it would be more sensible to say they are culturally 'different'; their culture may be a rich and lively one which can contribute greatly to their own and other people's lives.

(f) Linguistic deprivation may exist in any one of these cases, if the child is not talked to and listened to and encouraged to communicate in his early years. We may also use this term in referring to a child who has been confused in his attainment of one language by the use of two by the adults around him in his early years.

2. Possible effects:

(a) The under-stimulated child may appear lifeless, incurious, deceptively unintelligent. He will not reach the normal milestones of mental development (memory, small problem solving, etc.) at the usual times. He may also be slow physically.

(b) The <u>over-stimulated child may be jumpy and 'nervy'</u>, over-anxious about things he does, tense, a poor sleeper. <u>He may stammer</u>. He may easily become over-excited or distracted. He may feel himself a failure in his parents' eyes, and thus unloved. He may suffer from nightmares or irrational fears. He may play highly imaginative or imitative games which tend to get out of control and frighten other children.

(c) Children who miss continuity of formal schooling, for whatever reason, are likely to have learning problems which could cause them to 'drop out', or make their mark on society in a different way. They have difficulty in forming relationships which may make them into 'loners'.

(d) A child with perceptual or learning difficulties may be unable to cope with quite simple forms of play, domestic tasks or memorising. Only very close observation will reveal the nature and extent of his difficulties. Because he cannot keep pace with other children, he may resort to boisterous, 'silly' or otherwise unacceptable behaviour. On the other hand, he may be excessively quiet and retiring, so that his difficulties can be easily overlooked. Sometimes a child who will later be termed 'educationally subnormal' looks noticeably dull, with lack-lustre eyes and open mouth; but, again, he may be possessed of a lively personality and animated manner which masks the extent of his lack of understanding.

Lack of co-ordination results in a child being 'clumsy'. He will be constantly falling over, or knocking into, spilling or dropping things. He may not be able to hop, skip or hold a pencil, and thus appears 'different' and possibly laughable to other children.

A child who has undergone long hospital treatment may have missed out whole chunks of everyday learning and social experience. He is therefore at a disadvantage in comparison with nursery or infant children who, we confidently assume, know all about such things as family meal times, involving as they do shopping, cooking, laying table, social conversation. Such a child's physical co-ordination and muscle tone could also be poor, through lack of exercise.

(e) Conventionally accepted standards of beauty in the environment – nature, art, music, books, poetry, creativity etc. – which most nursery staff take pains to introduce to their children, will be alien and uninviting to these children. They may as a result build up an anti-school attitude. This resistance may accentuate the difference between such a child and his more conforming peers.

(f) Lack of competence and confidence in expressing himself in one language often leads the child into behaviour problems arising from frustration and isolation, and also learning difficulties.

3. How the nursery nurse can help (*see categories (e) to (f) opposite*):

(a) Stimulation in the form of play materials, discussion points, stories, songs etc., must be introduced gradually to the under-stimulated child, with clear explanations and interaction by the adult. Games which foster mental alertness can be enjoyed, and praise will motivate the child further.

(b) The child who has been over-stimulated requires from the nursery nurse calm, stability, exposure to child-like rather than sophisticated pastimes and pleasures. He requires boosting in his own eyes if he has been made to feel 'slow'.

(c) The child who is destined to miss continuity of schooling is not yet an educational problem, but the disruptions in his life so far may have left him needing special care, an emphasis on one-to-one relationship, an encouragement to mix with other children.

(d) Children at an educational disadvantage because of handicap or long spells in hospital need special individual attention and encouragement, much praise for the things they *can* do, play materials, constructional and creative, which will let them experience success of all kinds, especially in large and small muscular skills, preferably within small groups. Good relationships with parents can help a great deal. Body awareness, leading to greater control and co-ordination, can develop from use of large and small apparatus for vigorous physical activity, and also from swimming. Music and rhythm, too, can be employed effectively to develop these qualities and break down barriers set up by feelings of inadequacy.

(e) This child must be accepted for what he is, and points of contact sought in subjects that are of genuine interest to the child, so that he can make his contribution to the group.*

(f) While understanding his frustration and the forms it may take, the nursery nurse must give this child outlets, first to vent his frustration, and secondly to build his self-confidence. Suitable forms of self-expression are painting, dressing up and music. She has also to build up his grasp of English, which can only be done within a warm relationship. Words concerning the child himself, parts of the body, clothes, etc., are an obvious starting point, and much playful repetition in the form of games, finger plays, action rhymes, will reinforce this beginning. Hearing himself on tape can intrigue and encourage this child. Play with basic materials is good for vocabulary building. All forms of dramatic play, particularly puppets, foster language. Visits outside the nursery can widen the children's experience of good, interesting vocabulary, as do stories and pictures. (See chapter on Intellectual Development and Language.)

* N.B.: See following section on child from minority ethnic group.

The child from an ethnic minority group

Often today, the needs of these children are overshadowed by racial tensions and politics. The fact remains that in Britain there are thousands of ethnic minority group families, and the children of these families require especially sensitive, kindly and intelligent care if they are to grow up socially adjusted, having benefited to the full from our educational system, and possessing a positive cultural identity.

The background

The great majority of these children will have been born in Britain, of parents who may have been settled here some time, and who in many ways have become westernised and anglicised. These particular children will find life much easier than will the children of recently-arrived families. This difference should be borne in mind when considering the various difficulties which may beset ethnic minority group families and their children.

Whether it was yesterday or some years ago, however, we should remember that the parents came here to better themselves and their families, in their careers, standard of living and educationally – much the same ambitions in fact which led Europeans to emigrate to Canada or Australia, and which we consider praiseworthy. Ambition for their children colours parents' attitudes towards all schooling.

Most of us are deeply ignorant of the cultural and even the geographical backgrounds of these families. It is impossible here to do more than touch on specific cultural differences, but it is of the utmost importance that everybody working with ethnic minority group children should read and find out all they can about this fascinating subject. Even a small amount of research will show how foolish many generalisations and long-standing prejudices are and it will lessen the risk of insensitive handling. To give but one small example, many British people do not realise that the custom of common law marriage, changing of partners, and acceptance of illegitimate children found in some West Indian families is an inheritance from the slave trade days, when marriage was inconvenient to the plantation owners, but children in large numbers were an asset.

The cultural background from which a family originally came will still, to a greater or lesser extent, be reflected in the home; in attitudes towards marriage or other unions, and children; in religious faith, practice and taboos; in language and folk lore; in dress; in cooking; in the pattern of the day; and in music and entertainment. The young child, therefore, is in the difficult position of absorbing both this and the western European culture to which we expose him at the nursery and infants school, during his most impressionable years. He will need to make constant adjustments from one to the other in the course of a normal week.

Factors affecting his parents' circumstances will affect the child. Some of these factors could be:

1. loss of extended family:

2. stress of adaptation;

3. need for mother to work;

4. ignorance of medical facilities;

5. poverty (resulting in poor housing and inadequate diet);

6. reaction to cold climate;

7. ignorance of domestic heating systems and hazards;

8. life-style or religious practice incompatible with British conventions.

Sometimes these factors lead to real problems:

1. physical or mental illness or depression;

2. unsatisfactory child-minding arrangements;

3. home accidents, especially by fire;

4. absenteeism or fatigue due to religious fasting or festivals;

There may be particular *health problems*:

1. infections due to low resistance;

2. illness due to first-time exposure to disease (e.g. TB in Asians);

3. inadequate ante-natal care resulting from ignorance, lack of communication, or modesty may cause premature or difficult births, even handicap;

4. anaemia caused by a diet deficient in iron, protein and/or vitamin B12 due to poverty, vegetarian diet, or traditional methods of cooking which destroy vitamin B12;

5. specific illnesses of a hereditary nature which may affect certain groups, e.g., sickle cell anaemia in West Indians;

6. rickets caused by lack of vitamin D, due to poor diet and/or screening of available sunlight from skin (by coloured skin, traditional clothes, or indoor life);

7. lead poisoning, caused by children chewing lead-based paint on old buildings or furniture (anaemic children are particularly likely to do this); damage to eyes from the use of traditional lead-based Asian cosmetics;

8. eczema-like rash, reaction of some coloured skins to different climate.

Contact with parents

Friendly contact with and acceptance of parents will help the child to settle within the group, but sometimes language barriers and other factors, such as working mothers and the shy Asian mothers who tend to stay within the home, make it difficult for nursery staff to get to know them.

Smiles and welcoming attitudes transcend some of these difficulties. First steps in this direction can lead to encouraging the mother or parents to spend some time in the nursery so that they are fully informed on the child's day. They may at first feel it is presumptuous to involve themselves in any way, as they usually have a high regard for the competence and status of the nursery staff. They may feel surprise, even disappointment or disapproval, concerning the play, particularly messy kinds, which takes place; they thought they were giving that child a head start in *formal* education, but this appears to be something quite different.

Care must be taken that friendly approaches are not made in a patronising way. Allowances must be made for the fact that limited communication can result in reasonable requests sounding like bald statements or demands. Tolerance should also be shown towards those parents who do not want involvement in the nursery; they may badly need this break from their children, or perhaps they do not like children in large numbers. Then there will be the parents who want to loosen their cultural links with 'home', rather than accentuate them by contributing towards ideas of the nursery staff.

To avoid misunderstanding and muddles, any regulations or announcements in written form from the school should be translated into the parents' first language if they do not possess much English (see *The Multi-Racial Playgroup*, PPA Publications). Older brothers and sisters at school nearby can also help here.

Helping the child

If possible, there should be more than one child of an ethnic minority group in a class or group. This will reduce the possibility of his feeling so different, or even being overloaded with attention – as, for instance, can happen when a beautiful little Indian girl, dressed enchantingly, enters an all-white Anglo-Saxon class.

Specific areas in which specific groups may need help could include:

1. West Indians. Children may need special guidance in handling and caring for play materials or books, as these are often lacking in their homes.

They find a great deal of choice bewildering, as they are not encouraged to be self-regulating at home. Strict discipline and sometimes corporal punishment at home can mean that softly-spoken restraints and explanations about behaviour limitations go unheeded at nursery; perhaps the children even regard the adults as 'soft' or weak.

West Indian children may appear to have a 'different' emotional make-up, and will cry and fight, laugh and love with equal energy.

Their responsiveness to music makes it almost impossible for them to remain still when music is played.

2. Asians. Eastern religious faiths govern the whole of many families' lives; taboos on food, for instance the meat of the pig or cow, need to be respected and catered for. This needs to be borne in mind in the selection of stories, rhymes, playground games and so on, as well as the more obvious business of menu planning.

Because girls are brought up to be exceedingly modest, getting undressed for movement, paddling, or PE is distressing to them. Likewise taking off their bangles and other jewellery with a religious significance goes against their upbringing.

Boys may not take kindly to being treated the same as girls. In the home a boy, particularly the eldest, is treated as someone very special. In the nursery, often the boys come in for less attention than the pretty little girls, thus creating a difficult reversal of roles. The inferior status of women may also affect Asian boys' attitude to teacher or nursery nurse.

Many Asian families are from rural areas, and the noise and bustle of the nursery may be overwhelming. The children may be missing the stimulation and companionship of village life and the extended family, now that in England the mother goes to work. Asian children may appear very passive and dependent on adults, as they are encouraged to be dependent and obedient in their families. Choices, again, can be confusing.

English food offered may seem very bland and unappetizing, and cheese may be unknown.

Names can be confusing – boy and girl Sikhs, for instance, with the same name – but if the second name is given as Singh it is a boy, and if Kaur it is a girl.

Young Chinese children may be involved in the family business if there is one, because this is their culture – that *all* contribute to the family income. If the business is catering, hours may not be compatible with ideal children's bedtimes, and in the nursery hours the children may appear fatigued.

Children are encouraged in the home to be docile and hard-working. Education is rated very highly. The children are often intelligent and learn quickly. They are usually quiet and extremely polite and well-behaved.

Language

Acquiring standard English will be vital to the children's whole future, but many are not yet competent in their own native tongue when they come to the nursery. This break of continuity in their acquisition of language, and possible enforced duality of language probably has an adverse effect on their thought processes and ability to learn.

Language, thought and actions are closely linked. While acquiring English, the child will at the same time be adopting and reflecting the English culture.

A certain amount of English will be absorbed by the child simply by being in a place where English is spoken. But he will also need adults to focus his attention on certain words and modes of expression. Other children may ignore a non-English speaking child; they do not recognise other sounds as talking; therefore the child is very much dependent on concentration by the adult.

A warm relationship with the child must come first, through smiles and touch, etc. All points of contact with the child should be made into language opportunities – greeting him in the morning, commenting on his clothing, etc., demonstrating with pictures and objects what are the talking points or interests of the day. The adult should look the child full in the face, let him see her mouth working, and use accompanying facial expressions and gestures. She should express herself clearly, simply and in short sentences. Newly-introduced words should be fed into later conversations to aid memory. Stories with illustrations, finger plays and action rhymes (but beware of confusion caused by fingers being presented as, for example, 'five little ducks', etc.) all consolidate language skill, as well as inviting the child to join in the fun, where it does not make undue demands on him, or make him self-conscious.

Understanding and using intonation, very important in the English language – for instance to express disapproval or sympathy – may be difficult for children to grasp. Intonation does not have the same importance in all languages as it does in English, and can be used quite differently in some.

Special one-to-one times with a friendly, skilled adult will help to offset the possible confusion of the 'enriching' language experiences that will be offered to English children.

A multi-cultural approach

This aims to give *all* children equal importance and acceptance in each other's eyes, but at the same time recognises the richness of what the different cultures can contribute.

Discrimination still exists in some story books and illustrations, where ethnic types are either caricatured or represented in a foolish or pathetic light. The extreme images projected by some third world relief charities, and, at the other end of the spectrum, the glossy pictures of travel agents are not suitable for nursery use either. We should try to offer books and pictures which show people of various races in a positive light, in everyday situations.

Puppets, home corner fitments, dressing-up clothes and items chosen for inclusion in displays should reflect a truly multi-culture approach. Rather than create specific displays and project work on ethnic themes – 'India' for instance – choose themes of universal interest. Food is a good example and all mothers could contribute items – those used in Gujerati cooking, Jamaican cooking, English

cooking and so on. Furthermore, this approach would be more suitable to young children's very limited concept of, or interest in, faraway places.

Some children from minority ethnic groups will require especially tolerant and patient handling. Let us always remember that every child has something to give, to learn and to be respected.

Abused children

These are to be found in all social classes. They are children who have received serious physical abuse from a parent or foster parent. At one time these children were called 'battered babies' but now they are usually referred to as cases of non-accidental injury or concealed parental violence (CPV).

There has been a progressive increase in these cases in the past twenty years. The exact number of children killed or injured is not known. The most widely quoted estimates for Britain indicate that between 2400 and 4600 children are seriously injured each year. The estimates of the number of deaths from these injuries range from 100–750 each year. The commonest injury from this sort of violence is bruising, especially on the face. There may be black eyes or bruising around the mouth caused by forced feeding with a bottle. Some children are found to have cigarette burns, others are admitted to hospital because of fractured skulls, or fractures of the arms or legs.

Bleeding into the brain has been found in some cases, where violent shaking has caused the jelly-like brain to bang violently against the hard skull. This can cause mental retardation or cerebral palsy.

Few people could fail to feel deep anger towards the parents when faced with a badly injured child, but evidence suggests that most of these parents love their child and are desperately in need of help. They are reacting to the whole circumstances of their lives.

The underlying causes of child abuse, however, are a study in themselves and they are many and complex. Apart from unsatisfactory living conditions and lack of money, many of the parents have acute problems of insecurity, inadequacy and possibly psychological damage during their own childhood. The isolation caused by new types of housing, especially high-rise flats and the separation from other members of the family, who in earlier times might have lived close at hand, and helped out in a crisis, also plays a part.

Investigation of a family where children have been ill treated does, in fact, often reveal that the parents themselves were neglected and badly treated by their own parents. Because of this they have grown up feeling unloved and unworthy of love. This can lead to difficulties in all their personal relationships, especially in marriage. In addition, these people have not had good models from which to learn about being a parent. Children learn by example and, if they grow up in a stable home with loving parents, the pattern is passed on to them. Even though children from a stable home may rebel against their parents in their teens, when they in turn become parents, they usually repeat the pattern of their own childhood. Similarly, children who have uncaring, neglectful parents tend to repeat that pattern when they, too, are parents.

Many of the unfortunate, abused children have young parents who have this sort of background and in addition are living in poor housing and poverty. There is nothing new in this – in Britain there has always been an underprivileged section of the community. However, in earlier times that section tended to be set apart, socially and geographically, from the rest of the population. Nowadays, when shops, magazines and colour television reflect the comfortable life-style and enviable luxury of better-off people, those who are struggling with poverty realise the great disparities, and understandably resent them. It does not matter that the pictures they may see are grossly exaggerated; they merely emphasise to the less able members of our society their inadequacy, frustration and inability to compete. They feel they are failures in today's affluent society. And with the pressures they have to bear, it is natural for the parents to become short-tempered and irritable and their children become the nearest convenient targets for their anger. Often the mother is pregnant or has had a baby recently, so that she is not physically fit. She may be overwhelmed by all the responsibility and the worry.

Usually an abused child is a 'wanted' baby and when he is born is showered with affection. But he will be expected, in return, always to respond lovingly. The parents have little idea of a baby's abilities or of his needs, and are liable to make unrealistic demands for obedience and to have high expectations of his progress. When the baby is wakeful at night, refuses food or cries, it is interpreted as ingratitude and a rejection of the parents' love.

Sometimes it becomes apparent why one child in a family is being abused – he may have been a premature baby or had a difficult birth, so that there was early separation of mother and baby and bonding did not occur. Other typical abused babies are handicapped or they are those babies whose early days were marred by constant crying, possibly because of feeding problems or colic.

Obviously, prevention is the best cure for this social disease, but measures which would help most must come from society at large. Ensuring that good housing is available to all and the abolition of family poverty would solve many problems, because these two factors – unsatisfactory housing and a very low income – are often the last straw to inadequate parents. Educating young people so that they understand themselves, the role of parenthood and the needs of children may also help to prevent some of these cases.

In Britain progress has been made in identifying families whose children are at risk and offering early help and support. Research suggests that picking out mothers likely to react to stress with violence during the ante-natal or early post-natal period may well be possible. These mothers could then be given extra help whenever stress is likely to occur. For example, a home help during the early weeks of a baby's life will enable the mother to care for and get to know her baby without the stress of coping with her home. Other help could be a day nursery place or nursery school place for the child for part of the day. In addition, if the parents have someone they can trust and to whom they can talk about their problems, it may act as a safety valve – health visitors, NSPCC Officers and social workers can all fulfil this function. When families lived in a close community, Grandma used to do this.

Many authorities have set up a life-line for these parents, similar to that offered by the Samaritans, so that they can ask for help when things get too much for them.

When a child has been abused, the aim of any treatment of the parents is to prevent a recurrence of the violence and also to keep child/parent relationships going, in an attempt to lessen the harmful effects. The child may be placed in a day nursery, or possibly in a residential nursery, under a 'care order'. In all cases efforts are made to keep parental links and the aim is eventually to return the child to his family, if at all possible.

The gifted child

A gifted child is more than just 'very bright'. Giftedness implies exceptional intellectual abilities, either of high intelligence, or in one particular sphere of activity – for instance music, ballet, art, sport. Less easily discernible, the special ability may be for creative thinking or innovation.

Recognising the gifted child

It is difficult to recognise gifted young children, for several reasons. The performance skills that are conventionally examinable have, on the whole, not yet been learned. We have, therefore, either to compare the child with his peers – a controversial and unfashionable pastime – or arrange for him to be tested by an educational psychologist. This course may produce an untrue picture of the young child, who may be affected by, for instance, hunger or discomfort in a strange situation. When they are tested, usually at seven, gifted children score approximately 140 or above intelligence quotient.

Gifted children are comparatively rare, and there are no national statistics on them. They are produced by parents of all social classes and all levels of intelligence; sometime they are found in families where one would least expect them.

In the nursery or the home, we may observe one or more of the following characteristics:

1. Extreme liveliness, often associated with less need for sleep than usual

2. Early mobility, linked with curiosity.

3. Advanced language development, and use of quite long and complex sentence

constructions. Also frequent and searching questions, of the 'how' and 'why' variety.*

4. Advanced manipulative skills, often shown in problem-solving.

5. Marked interest in topics usually associated with older children, e.g., prehistoric monsters, makes of motor cars.

6. Complicated imaginary games, with or often without props.

7. Response to music – melody or rhythm – or marked artistic talent.

8. Reading as young as two and a half or three.*

9. Understanding of mathematical ideas.*

10. Complete concentration on the task in hand; perseverance.

11. Initiative and originality.

12. Marked independence.

Writing – of letters, words or figures – is seldom learned at such an early age; it is too tedious for a quick brain.

Coping with a gifted child

Potential and performance can be two very different things. The child's gifts require recognition, understanding and skilful nurture. With these he can grow into a well-adjusted, happy individual who can contribute enormously to society – perhaps even change the course of history.

There may be problems and pitfalls. A toddler who is always on the go, exploring and investigating, particularly if he can find ingenious ways of reaching forbidden items, or 'escaping' from his place of safety, can exhaust a mother or nanny. It is worse if he cannot be relied on to settle down early to a good night's sleep. The adult may feel she is failing, or else may feel exasperated that, despite all her well-intentioned efforts, the child refuses to respond conventionally. Without reassurance and practical help, such a mother may even fear for her own sanity, or her fitness to be safely alone with so demanding a creature. She must be helped to see that her child *is* different, and has different needs. Tranquillisers from her doctor, or supposed words of comfort about this being 'just a phase' that he will grow out of, are little help. What she does need is a husband and/or reliable child minder to relieve the pressure sometimes in the day, and certainly during a long spell of disturbed nights. If there is an older child, he could be found a nursery or playgroup place. The toddler himself will need such extra

* Middle class children can be deceptively advanced in their language development, denoting background encouragement rather than exceptionally high intelligence.

outside stimulation at two or two-and-a-half; by the age of three, many typical nursery activities will be too babyish for him. Questions must be listened to and answered, interests followed, however tiring or trying this may be at times.

The child's 'differentness' may set him apart from his peers, whose company and interests hold little appeal for him. Yet older children will not accept him as an equal. At the playgroup or nursery he may evoke dislike because he appears superior, or else may try to organise the people there – including adults!

He must be helped to get along with his peer group, however uphill a struggle this is for the adults. Not only could failure here result in many years of miserable schooling for the child, but it could also instil anti-social attitudes for life.

His interests should be taken into account. He could be assigned an appropriate aspect of a group activity or project. For instance, if a model castle is being made out of junk material, perhaps he could research on vital facts and statistics for its construction and use. Freshly stimulating play material must frequently be presented to him. Home-made games, puzzles, etc., as well as improvised and borrowed materials, can supplement manufactured ones. New tasks can be set and lines of enquiry followed up, using basic materials such as sand and water.

At the same time as extending such a child's intellectual capacities, and working towards his social integration, the adult must recognise that the child's physical and emotional needs are as important as those of any other child. The stage these are at may even be characteristic of a younger child. For instance, his physical co-ordination may be poor. Parents, particularly, need help in being patient and acknowledging that his development may well be uneven. It may irritate them to watch a classic temper tantrum, staged after a narrow defeat at chess. It may also annoy them to find that common sense by no means always accompanies giftedness.

There are still some parents and teachers who regard gifted children as a nuisance, or even a threat. Some parents are ill-equipped to nurture their child's gifts. They may have little liking for music or mathematics themselves, or fear that their child is the 'wrong' sex to possess such a talent. They may play down their child's giftedness for any of the foregoing reasons, or else because they fear he will grow up conceited.

At the infant school, the child may find the activities and work tedious. He *may* even be held back in his progress in, for example, reading, because it is inconvenient to the class's programme. Frustrated and bored, he may develop anti-school attitudes very early. He may become excessively withdrawn, or indulge in disruptive or aggressive behaviour. He may take on the role of the class clown. He may attempt to hide his giftedness in order to be accepted more freely by the group. In an extreme case, he may have to attend the Child Guidance Clinic, and/or become one of life's misfits.

Joining with a group of older children to pursue his particular interest – for example playing an instrument – can ensure his active co-operation for at least a number of sessions per week. The Association for Gifted Children offers half-day activities and short courses. Total segregation at an early age is not thought, in our society at least, to be in the child's best interests. Other aspects of his development may be neglected in such a rarefied atmosphere, and it has been known for the gift itself to wither and die.

Rushing him through the infant school curriculum only delays his boredom with school. Mentally demanding activities must be found for him, and here one can draw on the experience common to the group as a whole and let him go further. But he does require individual attention to 'extend' his powers and should not be expected to work on his own for long periods.

Wisely handled, a gifted child can bring great joy, indeed excitement, to all who know him.

Exercise 16

Multiple-choice questions

1. The official definition of a premature baby is:
(a) a baby weighing less than 2½ kilos (5½ lb);
(b) a baby born two weeks early;
(c) a delicate baby;
(d) a baby born too rapidly;
(e) a baby in an incubator.

2. What is the best attitude a family should adopt towards a handicapped child?
(a) ignore his handicap;
(b) treat him as a normal child, making allowances for his handicap;
(c) indulge him, to compensate for his handicap;
(d) make him the central concern of the whole family;
(e) be light-hearted about the handicap and make fun of it sometimes.

3. You are told that a child in your nursery group suffers from maternal deprivation. This means:
(a) the child's mother goes out to work;
(b) the child misses his mother when separated from her;
(c) he lacks material possessions;
(d) he and his mother have been separated for a long period of time;
(e) he lives in a slum.

4. You are told that the four-year-old child of a newly arrived Asian family is to join your English nursery group the following Monday. By way of preparation, would you:
(a) find out all you can about the family's background, and casually mention the newcomer to the other children;
(b) prepare a project on Asia;
(c) do nothing until you have met the child;
(d) arrange a welcome party the first day so that the child will be the centre of attention;
(e) tell the other children that black people *can* be nice.

5. You are told that a child in your group at nursery is a gifted child. Which approach would you adopt?
(a) treat him just the same as all the others;
(b) play down his giftedness, for fear of making him conceited;
(c) treat him with the same care you show to all the children, but take steps to extend his special gifts;
(d) make him the central concern of your work;
(e) hope it's just a passing phase because he doesn't fit in with your plans for the other children.

Essay questions

6. Deprivation and disadvantage occur among children from all strata of society. Explain how this can happen among higher income groups.

7. How would you, as a nursery nurse in a nursery school, endeavour to make your group a happy and effective multi-cultural society?

8. What would lead you to suspect that a five-year-old child was being abused by his parents? How would you deal with the child at school, and what services could you call upon to help the family?

Suggestions for further reading

Mary Crosse, *The Pre-Term Baby*, Churchill Livingstone
Bowley & Gardner, *The Handicapped Child*, Churchill Livingstone
Mary D Sheridan, *The Handicapped Child and his Home*, The National Children's Home
Lesley Webb, *Children with Special Needs in the Infant School*, Fontana
Peter Wedge and Hilary Prosser, *Born to Fail?*, Arrow Books
Lorna Bell, *Underprivileged Under 5's*, Ward Lock Educational Co. Ltd
Mia Kellmer Pringle, *The Needs of Children*, Hutchinson & Co. Ltd
Edited by James Loring and Graham Burn, *Integration of Handicapped Children in Society*, Routledge & Kegan Paul Ltd
Ivor Morrish, *The Background of our Immigrant Families*, Unwin Educational Books
Calendar of Religious Festivals, Commission for Racial Equality (Shap Mailing, 7 Alderbrook Road, Solihull, West Midlands)
The Multi-Racial Playgroup, PPA Publications (Alford House Avelina Street, London, S.E.11)
Children's books: *My Brother Sean*
                  Dr. Sean
                  Sean's Red Bike
                  Sally-Anne's Umbrella
all by Petronella Breinburg, Bodley Head Ltd
                  The Snowy Day
                  Whistle for Willie
                  Goggles
all by Ezra Jack Keats, Picture Puffin
Sean Lyle, *Pavah is a Sikh*, A & C Black Ltd
Madeline Blake, *Nadha's Family*, A & C Black Ltd
Fiction:
Harper Lee, *To Kill a Mocking Bird*, Heinemann Ltd
Semi-fiction:
George Lamming, *In the Castle of My Skin*, Longman
Autobiography:
Camera Laye, *The African Child*, Fontana

Chapter 17
Accidents and first aid

Prevention

Accidents in the home or on the streets are among the commonest causes of death in young children of under seven years of age. Every year out of every 100 000 children approximately ten will die as a result of an accident in their homes, seven will die because of road accidents and about 6000 children will require hospital treatment following an accident of some kind. Many, if not all, of these accidents could be prevented with forethought, and much physical and mental misery could be avoided.

Children in the birth to four years age group are most prone to home accidents, and there are several reasons for this:

1. Children under four years lack experience and knowledge of what is dangerous and do not always understand verbal warnings.

2. Children of this age are natural explorers – impelled by their own curiosity.

3. Children put things in their mouths because this is how they explore and feel things.

4. Children have a poor sense of taste.

5. Children are vulnerable to adults' carelessness.

6. Children copy adults' actions.

7. Many adults under-estimate a child's reach and ability.

All adults in charge of children should examine the furniture and fittings in a child's surroundings and use their imaginations – and their knowledge of a child's ability – to detect potential hazards. Those hazards should then be tackled in some way. It is better to make the environment as safe as possible than to rely on saying 'No' or 'Don't touch'. Over-protection and constant warnings often cause children to become over-timid and unable to fend for themselves. As in all aspects of child-rearing, emphasis on the *positive* is always better than the negative.

Adults should themselves act safely at all times, especially when in charge of children, remembering that children will imitate their actions. For example, when crossing the road you should always use the proper crossing place, even if it means extra walking. Taking a chance and dashing across a road may be safe for an adult who can judge the speed of traffic, but could be fatal to a child who copies that action.

Good housekeeping and general tidiness will help to reduce accidents, and children should be taught to put away their toys and clothes. This habit is learned primarily by good example.

Children under seven should *never* be left alone in a house, not even for a minute when they are apparently safely asleep. There are many grieving parents who know, too late, how necessary this rule is. All dangers are multiplied many times when adults are absent.

We cannot discuss all eventualities here, but the following are some of the commonest accidents which happen to children (and in many cases cause their deaths) and routine preventive measures.

Cause	*Prevention*
Inhalation and ingestion of food – choking	
Baby left in pram or cot with bottle.	Babies should always be nursed when drinking from a bottle.
Baby vomits and inhales vomit.	Put baby on tummy or side to sleep, so that if he vomits he cannot inhale. Bring up baby's 'wind' before putting him down to sleep.
Child chokes on large piece of food.	Cut food into small pieces. Encourage child to chew properly. Never leave him alone when eating. Always make child sit down when eating – don't let him walk around.
Child inhales peanut.	Do not give young children peanuts.
Inhalation of other objects	
Small beads or toys in baby's mouth.	Do not give very small toys. Check eyes, etc. on fluffy toys.
Baby left in pram or cot with dummy.	Avoid using a dummy.
Suffocation	
Plastic bib flaps up over face – forms seal.	Do not use thin plastic bibs.
Plastic bag placed over head.	Destroy plastic bags when finished with. Never leave within reach of children.
Baby buries head in soft pillow.	Pillows are not necessary for a baby. Use 'safety' pillow made of foam rubber for older child.
Cat gets into baby's cot or pram – smothers baby.	Use a cat net. Discourage cats from getting on beds or entering bedrooms.
Child gets in refrigerator and closes	Remove doors from old refrigerators.

Cause	Prevention
door which cannot be opened from inside.	Ensure refrigerator has magnetic catches on door which will open from inside.
Burns	
House on fire.	Never leave child alone in house.
Child plays with matches.	Keep matches away from children.
Portable heater tipped over.	Use fixed heater and fixed guard.
Clothes airing near fire ignite.	Do not leave clothes to air too close to fire; supervise it.
Cigarettes left burning.	Make sure cigarettes are out before discarding.
Child's clothes are set alight when he leans over fire.	Use a fixed guard on all fires. Use non-flammable materials for clothing. Do not put mirrors or children's possessions on mantelpiece.
Child plays with bonfire.	Never leave a bonfire unsupervised.
Child plays with live electric plug.	Disconnect plugs from kettles and irons, etc. when not in use. Use short flex.
Iron pulled from ironing board.	Never leave iron, ironing board in position if child alone in room.
Scalds	
Hanging tablecloth pulled by child – hot tea pours on head.	Avoid use of tablecloth.
Child pulls saucepan handle – contents tip on child.	Use a guard for the cooker. Turn saucepan handles inward so that they do not overhang.
Adult drinks hot tea whilst nursing baby. Tea tips on child.	Always put baby down when drinking tea.
Child climbs in bath containing very hot water.	Always put cold water in bath first.
Child burnt or scalded by hot water bottle.	Do not use boiling water. Use a cover on bottle. Check rubber bottles before each use for wear and tear.
Falls	
Baby left on bed, settee or table – falls off.	If you have to leave the baby for a moment, put him on the floor.
Toddler climbs and falls.	Give child somewhere safe to practise climbing under supervision, e.g. firmly-fixed low climbing frame with rubber mat or grass underneath. Teach child how to come downstairs backwards.

Cause	Prevention
	Use a stair gate.
	Put ladders away when finished using.
	Make sure clothing and shoes are safe for climbing.
Child falls out of window.	Safety catches on all windows, or window guards.
Child falls from pram or cot.	Use safety harness in pram.
	Put child in a bed once he starts climbing rails of cot.
Child falls from top bunk bed.	Use a guard.
	Children under five should not sleep in top bunks.
Child falls or trips over:	
discarded toys;	Keep home tidy.
untied shoelaces;	Check shoelaces.
dressing up clothes;	Cut them short.
loose carpet;	Fasten carpets securely.
rugs on slippery floors.	Do not polish under rugs.
Poisoning	
Child takes tablets prescribed for adult.	Keep tablets and medicines locked up.
	Take unused drugs back to chemist.
	Do not take tablets in front of children – they may think these are sweets and try to get one.
Child drinks bleach, disinfectant, detergent or weedkiller.	Keep these things in a locked cupboard.
	Never put other liquids in lemonade bottles.
Child drinks alcohol.	Keep bottles locked up.
	Never leave glasses with dregs within reach of children.
Child sucks painted surface containing toxic substances.	Use lead-free paint on all surfaces.
Child eats berries or leaves from poisonous plants.	Remove these hazards from garden.
	Watch child when out on walks.
	Warn child.
Drowning	
Falls in bath.	Never leave child alone in bath.
	Use non-slip mat in bath.
Falls in goldfish pond, swimming pool.	Make sure these are guarded.
Electric current	
Child pokes something in plug.	Use safety plugs with shuttered holes.
Bleeding	
Child plays with scissors, knives,	Keep all these away from children.

Cause	*Prevention*
pins, needles, razor blades, etc.	
Toddler walking with drink in glass trips and breaks glass.	Make children sit down to drink. Use plastic cups.
Toddler falls against patio doors.	Use 'safety' glass.
Road accidents	
Child runs out of house into road.	Keep gates and doors locked.
Child runs across road.	Show by example how to cross a road. Supervise the under-seven-year-old. Teach road drill by use of games, etc. Never let young children play near busy roads.
Child in car accident thrown forward on to windscreen or through it.	Use seat belts or special seats. Do not allow a child to travel in front seat of car.

First aid

All accidents, however trivial, are accompanied by some degree of shock, and most children are very frightened when they are hurt. Fear increases shock, so it is important that the adult in charge should keep calm and appear to be in control, even if she is quaking underneath. A hurt, frightened child needs comfort and support and this is also the treatment for shock.

Sit or lie the patient down, hold his hand or cuddle him and tell him it is going to be all right. This must be the *first* action, whatever the injury and fortunately most mothers and nursery nurses do this instinctively. It is no use expecting a small child to report accurately on what happened, as he will not be able to tell you properly. Use your own observation and make a quick examination whilst you are comforting him. Is he pale or flushed? Is he bleeding? Is one of his limbs at an unnatural angle?

Potentially fatal conditions

The main purpose of a first-aider is to save life, so it follows that any condition threatening life must be dealt with first. There are four main causes of death following an injury:

1. shock – treat with comfort, reassurance and rest;

2. bleeding – treat by raising the affected part and by putting pressure on the bleeding point;

3. asphyxia – treat by using mouth-to-mouth resuscitation;

4. heart stops – treat by giving heart massage (this applies *only* to a trained first-aider).

In nurseries and schools there should always be someone available who is trained in first aid, because if a child needs mouth-to-mouth resuscitation or heart massage it must be started within four minutes to be effective. All these conditions need medical aid urgently, so send for an ambulance immediately – don't waste time.

Other conditions

The other purposes of first aid are to prevent the injury becoming worse and to aid recovery. Often the best way is to do nothing apart from treating shock and sending for an ambulance. Too much interference can sometimes make the injury worse.

1. Unconsciousness (for any reason). If the child does not respond to his name, apart from moaning, he is unconscious.
(1) Check whether he is breathing – put your ear to his mouth and listen.

If he is breathing:
(2) Turn him almost on to his tummy with his head on one side. This is known as the recovery position and it prevents his airway being blocked, either by his tongue falling to the back of his mouth or by the child's own saliva or vomit collecting in the back of his throat.
   Stay with him to support him and keep him in this position. Talk to him gently, because he may be able to hear you. (Hearing is the last sense to be lost in unconsciousness.)
(3) Send for medical aid.

If he is not breathing:
(2) Start mouth-to-mouth resuscitation.
(3) Send for medical aid.

2. A blow on the head:
(1) Comfort child.
(2) Cold compress can be put over injured part.
(3) Allow child to rest but watch his condition.
(4) Inform parents.
(5) Medical aid is needed if any of the following conditions is present:
   (i) any unconsciousness, even if only momentary;
   (ii) vomiting; (iii) confusion.

3. Fainting. Put head as low as possible – the easiest way is to put the child in recovery position.

4. Cuts and wounds. Large gaping cuts or wounds which bleed a lot will need hospital treatment.
(1) Stop bleeding:
 (i) Raise the injured part.
 (ii) Place a pad over the wound and apply firm pressure. If the wound is gaping, press edges together before applying pad. The only exception to this is a head wound where you suspect that there may be a fracture under the wound. In this case press edges of wound together only.
(2) apply a dry, sterile pad and bandage firmly – if blood comes through this dressing, add another pad and bandage.
(3) If a foreign body is present in the wound, leave it alone unless it is easily removed. It is rare for a wound to bleed heavily if a foreign body is present, because it acts as a plug. In this case leave it alone and cover loosely with a sterile dressing.
(4) Get medical aid.

Small cuts and wounds, grazes and scratches which do not require medical attention should be treated in the following way:
(1) Wash well with soap and water.
(2) Dry and leave exposed to the air.
(3) It may be necessary to apply a dressing for psychological reasons, but this should only be temporary and should allow air to circulate. Wounds heal much better when exposed to air. If the child is playing in a sandpit or mud, etc., then a temporary dressing may be needed to protect the wound from contamination.

Antiseptics and antiseptic cream should *never* be used in first aid work. This is in accordance with modern views and practice.

5. Cat and dog bites. Treat as any small cut or wound.

6. Insect stings:
(1) Remove sting if present.
(2) Treat as any small cut or wound.
(3) Medical aid is needed if sting is in the neck or face area, or if there is excessive swelling.

NB: When treating any break in the skin, the first-aider should enquire whether the patient is protected against tetanus. If he is not, then the patient or his parents should be advised to seek medical aid. Most children under five will have protection, because it is included in the routine immunisations. If the older child had a 'booster' immunisation before entering school, then he also is protected.

7. Nose bleed:
(1) Sit child down with head slightly forward.
(2) If child will co-operate, make him blow his nose in order to remove clots and mucus.
(3) Pinch the nose just below the bony prominence for three minutes (by the clock). This will control the bleeding.
(4) Sponge the child's hands and face and remove bloodstained clothing as quickly as possible.
(5) Encourage child to sit quietly and try to avoid blowing his nose for the next hour.

8. Bruises. These are due to bleeding under the skin and this is controlled by the increasing pressure of the skin, so that no first aid is necessary. However, a cold compress (cottonwool squeezed in very cold water) can be applied and the injured part elevated. If bruising is extensive, suspect further injury underneath and get medical aid.

9. Squashed fingers. Treat as for bruising.

10. Fractures, dislocations and sprains. Usually these are preceded by a fall, blow or twist. There is immediate pain and there may be swelling. Movement will be painful and difficult. No first-aider is qualified to differentiate between a sprain and a fracture so all these injuries should be treated as a fracture.
(1) Keep patient still.
(2) Call an ambulance.

11. Burns and scalds:
(1) Reduce heat immediately by immersing the affected part in slowly-running cold water for ten minutes – do not remove clothing or burst blisters.
(2) Cover with a sterile cloth and bandage.
(3) Medical aid will be necessary if blisters or a reddened area larger than a 10p piece are present.

12. Poisoning:
(1) If patient is unconscious – place him in the recovery position.
(2) If patient is conscious – give nothing to drink unless poison is corrosive, when sips of milk or water can be given. DO NOT MAKE CHILD VOMIT.
(3) Get medical aid immediately.
(4) Save any tablets, liquids, containers and vomit so that the poison can be identified.

13. Foreign bodies:
(a) lodged in eye:
      (i) sand or dust – can be lifted from white of eye with a piece of moistened cottonwool;
     (ii) if embedded – apply eye pad and get medical aid;
    (iii) if corrosive – wash continuously with water until medical aid arrives.
(b) lodged in ear or nose: do not attempt to remove foreign body. Get medical aid.
(c) lodged in throat: hold child head downwards and slap sharply between shoulder blades, or try to hook foreign body out with fingers. Mouth-to-mouth resuscitation is necessary if breathing stops.
(d) splinters – remove with sterilised needle; treat as any wound.

Mouth-to mouth resuscitation

All adults in charge of children should learn how to perform mouth-to-mouth resuscitation by practising on a dummy. The method used is as follows:
(1) Tip the child's head right back by placing one hand under the back of the neck and the other on the forehead. This will give a clear airway and may be all he needs to enable him to start breathing. Check before proceeding.
(2) Keeping your hand under the neck to maintain position, pinch the nostrils with the other hand.
(3) Take a breath in and then, covering the child's mouth with your own to make a seal, breathe into the child. Watch the child's chest rise.
(4) Remove the mouth and take another breath.
(5) Repeat this action about twenty times a minute.
(6) If the chest does not rise, the airway must be blocked, so check for any obstruction before continuing.

First aid box

The first aid box should be easily accessible but out of children's reach. In a car it should be visible. The box should be painted white with 'FIRST AID' written on it.

The Offices, Shops and Railway Premises Act 1963, Section 24 says that first aid boxes must be provided by employers and should contain the following equipment, in quantities according to the number of employees:

        1– 10 employees – No. 1 contents
     11– 50 employees – No. 2 contents
    51–150 employees – No. 3 contents

Contents of first aid boxes	No. 1	No. 2	No. 3
1. sterilised dressings (unmedicated):			
(a) finger;	3	6	12
(b) medium size;	2	3	6
(c) large size;	1	3	6
2. adhesive wound dressings, assorted size and wrapped separately;	12	12	24
3. triangular bandage 127 × 90 × 90 cm (51 × 36 × 36 in);	1	2	4
4. adhesive plaster 2.5 cm × 5 m (1 in × 5 yd)	5 yd	5 yd	10 yd
5. 15 g (½ oz) packets of absorbent sterilised cottonwool;	1	2	3
6. sterilised eye pads in separate packets;	1	2	4
7. safety pins;	6	6	12
8. rubber bandage (pressure bandage);	—	1	1
9. Leaflet SH W1 (Ministry of Labour).	1	1	1

Useful additions

large piece of clean linen   crêpe bandage
tweezers   scissors
needle in a cork   box of matches
2p's for telephone   a pad and pencil
a good first-aid book   telephone number of local doctor

Exercise 17

Multiple-choice questions

1. Which of the following is the accepted treatment for shock?
(a) wrap patient in blankets to keep him warm;
(b) give patient a hot cup of sweet tea;
(c) give patient a small amount of brandy;
(d) make him tell you what happened;
(e) lie patient down, hold his hand and comfort him.

2. A child comes to school with a swollen ankle. Would you:
(a) put a bandage on it, and tell him 'it's just a sprain';
(b) put a cold compress on it;
(c) take him to the hospital for an X-ray;
(d) leave it alone;
(e) take the child home and advise his mother to take him to hospital.

3. Which of the following is the best treatment for a nose-bleed?
(a) put a cold key down the child's back;
(b) hold child's wrists under a cold-water tap;
(c) sit child, lean his head forward and pinch his nose;
(d) lie child down with his head back;
(e) plug his nose with cotton-wool swabs.

4. A child has swallowed some berries. Which action would you take?
(a) make him vomit by putting your fingers down his throat;
(b) give him milk to sip;
(c) leave him, but watch his condition;
(d) take him to hospital with a sample of the berries and leaves;
(e) give him salt-water to make him sick.

5. Which of the following is the best immediate treatment for a bleeding hand?
(a) hold hand above head and apply pressure over the wound;
(b) apply a tourniquet around the wrist;
(c) cover wound with a pad and dressing;
(d) clean wound with disinfectant and apply a dressing;
(e) place hand under cold running water.

Essay questions and project

6. Why are accidents in the home one of the commonest causes of death in young children? How can these accidents be prevented?

7. How would you treat a child suffering from each of the following accidents?
(a) a wasp-sting on the lip;
(b) a piece of glass in the foot;
(c) a fall from a height, causing a head injury.

8. Imagine you have three children under five years of age. Look around your own home and list the potential hazards, noting how you would make them safe.

Chapter 18
Travelling with children

We believe that children today should grow up as part of the family, and part of the world in which they are going to live. However, the broadening influence of travel is more to the benefit of older children and adults; young children prefer the continuity and comfort of home and, for the under-sevens generally, as far as holidays are concerned, they will be happier on a local beach than in Majorca. However, parents' needs must be considered too, and often desperation for sunshine or a complete change is felt by the mother or father and must take precedence over small children's requirements. The child need not suffer. In fact he may have a wonderful time, and the whole family benefits.

Apart from holidays, there will be other circumstances when children have to travel – for instance to accompany a father who is in the armed forces or doing other work abroad.

All travel with children needs to be planned in advance. The longer and more ambitious the journey is, the more thought and preparation will be involved.

Modes of travel will depend on time available, finance, preference of adults, and circumstances. It may happen – for instance, in an emergency or after a sudden change of plan – that a journey must be undertaken at quite short notice. This makes it doubly important for a nursery nurse who intends to become a nanny to know what preparations are advisable before setting out, and the difficulties that could arise. 'Nanny' is often put in sole charge of a child or two; she may even be taken on expressly to look after them while travelling.

We shall deal with specific types of travel and the needs of the different age groups in this chapter. Some general advice applies in every case, however. Try to arrange the journey so that there is the least possible disturbance to the child's routine, and, if possible, so that he has some familiar things around him during the journey, and when he arrives. Try to adopt a calm and confident attitude towards the event yourself. Tension, flustered or fussy behaviour on your part will be sensed by the child and make the journey miserable for both of you. Plan to be self-sufficient; you *may* receive offers of help, but do not count on it!

Travelling with a young baby (up to ten months)

If you are going abroad, you will need to obtain information from your doctor or travel agent about health matters such as immunisation, vaccination and

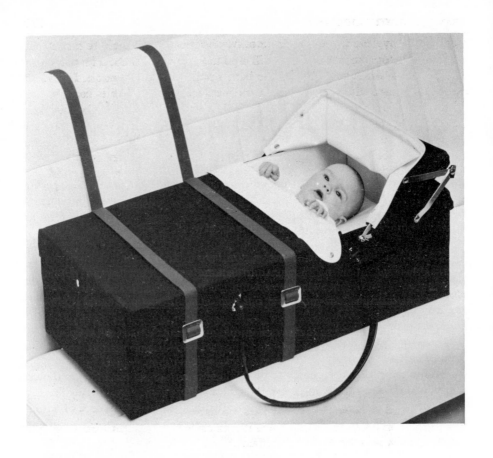

standards of hygiene at your destination. Any immunisation should be carried out some time before the journey. You will need to know whether the milk and water will be safe to drink and whether the baby's milk will be obtainable. It may be necessary to take with you dried milk and sterilising tablets. Babies going to live in tropical countries may need a milk with a lower fat content. Consult your health visitor about this. If the child is on solid food, you need to know if the local food will be suitable; if not, you may have to take stocks of tinned food. The position will be rather different if the purpose of the journey is to take up long-term residence, in which case the baby will gradually have to get accustomed to local food. Whether suitable food and drink is available will also depend on whether the place where you will be staying is to be a hotel or private home.

With a small baby, travelling is fairly simple and straightforward. The only real burden – literally! – is the amount of luggage required, which is out of all proportion to the size of the infant.

As well as minimum disturbance to routine, minimum handling will also benefit the baby. A pram which can be divided into a carrycot and wheels is invaluable here, as the baby can 'stay put' whenever and however he is being moved about.

When planning for his needs, bear in mind that unexpected delays are possible. His food should stay the same, and no changes should be made as the journey draws near. Bottles can either be made up as wanted, or made in advance and refrigerated before being packed in an insulated bag to keep cold. If the baby is being weaned, however, he should become used to tins or jars of baby food *before* the journey. Most babies will accept these foods at room temperature, but the jar can be stood in hot water if preferred. It is safest to feed straight from the jar or tin, and throw away any uneaten remains.

List of baby's requirements

Either:

1. several sterilised bottles with teat and screw-on cap;

2. vacuum flask of hot boiled water;

3. milk powder and scoop.

Or

1. sterilised bottles containing teat and feed made cold in insulated bag;

2. vacuum flask of hot water (for heating bottle to correct temperature when ready);

3. container to stand bottle in;

4. rusks for older baby;

5. bottle containing cool boiled water;

6. jars or tins of food, tin opener, plastic spoon;

7. bag containing baby's toilet requisites (excellent plastic 'duffle' bags, with space for talc, etc., and a separate zipped pocket for soiled nappies, can be bought in baby shops);

8. disposal nappies;

9. plastic pants, if needed;

10. spare set of clothing, including jumper or cardigan;

11. 2 damp flannels or 'wet wipes';

12. tissues;

13. familiar toy;

14. clothing should be in several thin layers so that it can easily be adjusted according to temperature.

Emergency sterilising of a bottle can be carried out by cleaning it and then filling it to overflowing with boiling water – obtainable in cafés and restaurants where tea-making urns are used.

Requirements for stay at destination

These will be dictated by your knowledge of the situation, but you will certainly need sterilising equipment. You will need to find out whether the cows who supply the local milk are tuberculin tested, and whether the milk has been pasteurised. If the quality of the local milk is suspect you should use powdered milk instead. As a general rule, boil all water and milk before use for the under two year old.

Travelling with a child from 10 months to 2 years

This can be the most difficult age, because toddlers dislike change. If they become tired or miserable, they regress in behaviour and need to be treated like babies. When wide awake and in good spirits they want to be active, independent, noisy and self-assertive.

More than ever, the principle of trying to stay within their routine is important. If the child is used to a nap in the morning, afternoon or both, then means must be found for this. A combined pram and carrycot will still be useful at this stage; although a pushchair is easier to manoeuvre, a pram is a comfortable and familiar place for the child to sleep, and at other times, is useful for holding luggage.

Meals should be light and plain – the sort of food he normally has at home. No extra sweets or snacks should be given, but a drink of cool water or unsweetened fruit juice and an apple, might be a good idea from time to time.

If the child is using a potty, then his own familiar one should be taken along. Familiar toys are just as important.

Requirements

1. bottles as for baby, if child still has bottle feeds;

2. toilet articles as for baby;

3. several spare pairs of pants;

4. spare jumper;

5. potty;

6. familiar toys;

7. mackintosh or plastic tablecloth (useful for beds and underneath feeding chairs);

8. apples;

9. drinking water and/or fresh fruit juice;

10. harness with reins.

Travelling with an older child – approximately $2\frac{1}{2}$–7 years

At this age, the child can understand a little of what is in store, if you talk with him beforehand about the journey and together look at suitable children's books about travel. A child of six or seven may well enjoy looking at a simple map or travel brochures.

If possible, the journey should be broken up by stops for stretching legs, going to the toilet and perhaps having picnics, etc. If this is not possible, or even in between stops, the child will need a good deal of amusing if he is not to become restless or bored. Give him his own bag or case containing favourite toys, books and drawing materials. Perhaps a comic or two may be bought specially for this journey, adding to the sense of occasion. The adult in charge should be careful to space out any little treats of this kind to break the tedium.

A damp flannel or 'wet wipes', and spare jumper and pants are still a wise precaution.

At this age the child will enjoy chatting to an interested adult and commenting on all his new and exciting experiences. There are also many simple games which two can play, while just sitting quietly – for instance, 'I spy' and an easy version of 'twenty questions'. If you can see the scenery from the window you can soon think up more 'spotting' games.

Travel by car

A journey by car is probably the commonest and least stressful way to travel with children, because most children are used to car travel. Luggage is easier to manage, timing can be arranged to suit the travellers (during the night can be quite convenient) and you are not dependent on outside factors, except traffic and weather conditions.

A baby can stay in a carrycot on the back seat, anchored by a safety strap.

A toddler should be in his own car seat, safely strapped in the back.

Older children should always sit in the back. If there is more than one child, an adult should sit with them (probably between, to prevent squabbling) and organise a few games. You will not have to worry about annoying strangers, so singing games are ideal, with your own adaptations, if you like. However, children must understand that squealing and horseplay are not allowed, as they can distract the driver and be dangerous. Keeping several children happy on a long journey can be quite demanding. For this reason there should always be in addition to the driver another adult looking after the children. If the two can take turns with the driving, so much the better. The journey should be broken up into spells of approximately two hours, but stopping places will need to be carefully chosen for safety. Adequate ventilation will make conditions more pleasant, and children's car locks should, of course, be present on the doors.

Travel by train

This can be a novelty and quite exciting to a small child. It is better to book in advance to avoid last-minute panics, and also to travel mid-week and avoid the rush hours. If the journey is very long, overnight travel may be a good idea and sleepers can be booked. The corridor lets one stretch one's legs and visit the toilet and will help to break the monotony. A meal or snack on the train can also be exciting for a toddler or older child, and is probably easier than taking a packed meal.

Travel by coach

There will be little chance to get at your luggage, or to move around or go to the toilet during coach journeys. There will not be much space for belongings and toys; activities, too, will be limited. But you will have a good vantage point to watch the passing scenery and there will probably be plenty to interest a young child.

Travel by ship

It is as well to ask in advance exactly what provision there will be for a baby or toddler, especially for meals and washing. On a long journey, a nursery kitchen is available for making up feeds, while any special food or milk can be ordered in advance if sufficient time is allowed. There will be facilities for the adult to do washing, and most probably a laundry with nappy service. This service, and buying disposable nappies on board, will, of course, involve some expense. There is usually a special early evening meal for toddlers, and stewards will act as a baby alarm so that adults can eat together later. On a large liner there will also be a crèche and trained nursery nurses, but such facilities may be crowded, depending on demand. A cot will be provided, but a pram will be useful for going on deck.

Travel by air

This has the advantage of getting you to your destination quickly, and many airlines are extremely helpful to adults with babies and children, provided they are informed in advance. For airline purposes, all children under two years of age are called babies, and are allowed to travel at 10 per cent of the adult fare. No seat is provided, but on request the accompanying adult(s) will be given a bulkhead seat, which allows plenty of leg room as there are no passengers in front. A 'skycot' is also provided. This is a small cot suspended from the bulkhead. The baby has no luggage allowance, but all his travel needs are free of charge, and usually this is generously interpreted.

A baby under one year will travel happily under these conditions, but if the child is a lively, active toddler between one and two it could well be worth considering whether to pay the child's fare of 50 per cent so that he may have a seat of his own, and a normal luggage allowance and normal meals.

If you let the airline know beforehand they will probably allow an adult who is travelling with young children to board the plane first, and they will provide help to settle the children in their seats. On take-off some children may be frightened at the extra noise and strange sensation. They should be told about this before the actual flight, if they are of an age to understand. The ears tend to pop because of changing pressure. This can be eased by swallowing, or, for a baby a drink of fruit juice in a bottle will help.

Many airports have nurseries where changing and feeding can be done conveniently and in privacy.

Visits with children

Nursery nurses working in private families and in day care and nursery education will appreciate the stimulation that comes from visits – outings undertaken for their own sake. Apart from the obvious benefits of fresh air and exercise, and a welcome break from normal routine, a visit offers valuable opportunities to broaden children's horizons. A city child, for instance, can see life on a farm; another child may perhaps travel on a train for the first time. Excellent incidental teaching can easily arise from such topics as road safety, conservation of the countryside, kindness to animals, dealing sensibly with litter, respecting property, and showing appreciation. There are bound to be many talking points which will later lead on to follow-up activities and books.

Sometimes a visit like this just happens spontaneously, inspired by a lovely day, or perhaps the arrival of an interesting ship at a nearby dock, or workmen at a local building site. At other times, a visit will be organised well in advance, needing arrangements about transport, packed meals, etc. As a general rule, the younger the children, the shorter and less ambitious should be the outing, particularly the travelling time.

In every case, the permission of the head of the establishment is required, and also, of course, the permission of the parents. Care must be taken that domestic and other arrangements at the nursery or in the family are not disturbed, and that all the staff concerned with the children is kept informed about the plans.

Adequate adult supervision must be provided – preferably not more than four children to one adult and fewer than this if the children are very young. If a large group is going, mothers can often be invited too; they will need to be reliable people who will understand what the staff hope the children will gain from the outing and co-operate with them. Badges with names of children and school are a good idea, and each child must be clear about whose group he is in.

The children can be told a little of what is to happen. For example, if they are going to the zoo, a few animal songs or poems can be introduced. However, one of the benefits of an outing is the freshness and directness of impact that the experience will make on the children, so do not overdo the preparatory talk.

Where an outing involves travel, take along spare clothes, damp flannels, plastic bags, first aid kit and other 'accident' provision. If a coach is being hired, it is best to make enquiries from several firms about prices, as these can vary considerably, and cost should be kept as low as possible, so as not to embarrass any parents. It is also wise to find out about parking facilities at your destination, picnic sites, and alternative arrangements in case of wet weather. Admission charges to public places are usually reduced for parties of children, and sometimes waived altogether.

During the visit, the children must be closely supervised, and number of children studying any one aspect of the place you are visiting should be kept very small. In this way there will be enough viewing space, opportunities to answer questions and take up comments, and there will be less chance of children getting over-excited. Provide for regular visits to the toilet, and a comfortable break for a meal, if you are having one. Keep a careful eye on the picnics that individual children have brought, as these can vary from a huge feast to almost nothing. For this reason, many nurseries and schools like their kitchen to provide a standardised picnic for everyone. You should, in any case, have previously discouraged the bringing of sweets and sticky foodstuffs, and also glass bottles and tumblers. Arrangements about spending money should also have been made clear in advance. If children are bringing money it is wise to stipulate a small maximum sum, and allow only one fixed time for spending it. Money easily gets lost, causes jealousy, and encourages children to dart off in the direction of an ice-cream van, or disappear into a shop, causing delays to one's schedule, worry to the adults, and possibly breaking up the group.

The adult should see that periods of walking are alternated with resting and periods of concentration and listening alternated with periods of vigorous exercise. Otherwise the children will become overtired, fractious or bored.

If the visit is a success, and visits usually are, most children will want to talk eagerly about it to others when they return, or during the next few days. While enthusiasm lasts, this is a good time to make a display of their mementos on a related subject – for instance castles – while sometimes a group or class 'book' is made. Each child should be encouraged – but not forced – to contribute. A display of this nature frequently attracts much interest from parents and affords a valuable opportunity for friendly contacts and conversation. This is a way of showing appreciation for parents' co-operation over outings, and probably ensures it also for next time.

Exercise 18

Multiple-choice questions

1. Which would be the most suitable choice of an outing for nursery school age children?
(a) an all-day trip to the seaside;
(b) a coach-tour to a stately home;
(c) a guided tour of a factory;
(d) an afternoon at the local park;
(e) a day at a museum.

2. The most suitable breakfast for a child before starting a journey would be:
(a) bacon, egg, and fried bread;
(b) nothing at all;
(c) whatever he wants;
(d) fresh fruit-juice, cereal with sugar and milk;
(e) dry toast only.

3. After a visit with infant children interest in follow-up work seems totally lacking. Which course of action would you take?
(a) insist that each child draws a picture;
(b) insist that each child contributes to a class book;
(c) talk relentlessly to the children about the visit to arouse interest;
(d) organise an exhibition for parents, hoping this will motivate the children;
(e) drop any ideas of follow-up work altogether.

Essay questions

4. You are required to accompany a six-month-old baby and a three-year-old child on a car journey lasting four hours. Describe how you would plan the journey and entertain the children en route.

5. You are a nanny to a family of two children, John aged two and a half years and Emily aged five years, and have to take them on a two-week farm holiday in Wales. The journey will be by train, taking one and a half hours. Describe the preparations. How would you help to make the holiday an enjoyable experience for both children?

Chapter 19
Social and welfare services

Although, in the past, attempts were made to aid people in distress, especially poor families with young children, the welfare state that exists in Britain today did not come into being until after the Second World War. Before the war many people felt that if a family was destitute it must be its own fault. They argued that if help was too readily available then families on very low incomes would only take advantage of it and would not try to help themselves. However, it was eventually realised that poverty could arise from events beyond a person's control. Therefore help given at the right time and in the right amount could prevent unfortunate families from sinking irrevocably into destitution, and give them the hope and the means to keep on trying.

Much of the assistance available to poor people before the war was given by charitable institutions and by kindly, well-meaning individuals, so the degree of help varied widely from area to area. But in 1942 Sir William Beveridge produced a report recommending a comprehensive national insurance system and a re-organisation of the Health Service. In his report he described the five evils which lay in the path of a better society – want, disease, ignorance, squalor, and idleness. He said that all members of a society should be freed from these evils.

This concept marked the final stage of development of the social and health services which had started at the beginning of the century. The report was followed by several acts of Parliament which laid the foundations of the services we enjoy today:

1944 *The Education Act* (took effect from 5 April 1945)

This provided for free education from a statutory five to fifteen years according to age, ability and aptitude, in a system of public education organised as a continuous process in three stages – primary, secondary and higher (for those who wished to go on beyond fifteen). Until this time free education had been largely elementary and from five to fourteen years only.

1945 *The Family Allowances Act*

This provided an allowance for each child in a family, other than the first child. The allowance is now called child benefit and all the children of a family are now entitled to it.

1946   *The National Health Service Act* (took effect from 5 July 1948)

This provided free medical care for all, whether they paid contributions or not. From 1951 charges were made for dental treatment, prescriptions, spectacles and some appliances, although children and some special categories of patient are exempt.

1946   *The National Insurance Act* (took effect from 5 July 1948)

This scheme paid certain financial benefits in return for fixed weekly contributions from employed persons and their employers – for example, unemployment benefit and sickness benefit.

1948   *The National Assistance Act* (took effect from 5 July 1948)

This provided financial assistance for those whose needs were not met by National Insurance or any other source. It also provided residential accommodation for the aged, infirm and homeless. These arrangements are now known as social security benefits.

1948   *The Children Act*

This Act was designed 'to make further provision for the care and welfare, up to the age of eighteen years and, in certain cases, for further periods, of boys and girls when they are without parents . . .' It has since been amended by the 1963 Children and Young Persons Act.

After 1950 many more Acts of Parliament were passed which modified and changed the provisions of the original acts, in an attempt to make good any deficiencies and to ensure that the various provisions and services continue to meet the changing needs of British society.

Today, the following services are available to everyone who lives in Britain:

1. Health

General practitioner (GP)

Everyone can register with a doctor and receive medical treatment free of charge, apart from prescription charges where applicable.

Area health authorities (who provide *health centres*)

Health centres are premises used by GPs and by the following services:
(a) health visitors – who visit all families (especially those with children under five) to advise on health matters, including the prevention of illness;
(b) midwives – home visitors who care for mothers before, during and after the births of their babies;

(c) home nurses – who nurse sick people in their homes at the request of their GPs;

(d) child health clinics;

(e) immunisation clinics;

(f) ante- and post-natal clinics;

(g) ante-natal classes for mothers;

(h) family planning clinics.

Free drugs and medicine

These are provided for:

(a) children under sixteen years of age;

(b) pregnant women;

(c) mothers of children under one year;

(d) people suffering from certain medical conditions;

(e) people on low incomes;

(f) people receiving family income supplement or supplementary benefit;

(g) people receiving retirement or war-disablement pensions.

All other patients receive drugs at reduced costs.

Dental care

This is free for:

(a) children under seventeen years (except dentures, if a child is working);

(b) children up to eighteen years, in full-time education;

(c) pregnant women;

(d) mothers of children under one year;

(e) people on low incomes, receiving family income supplement or supplementary benefit.

Dental care is provided at reduced cost for all others.

Ophthalmic services

Eye tests are free and spectacles are provided at reduced cost, but are free for people on low incomes.

Free hospital services

These include: general, children's, orthopaedic, eye, maternity, and mental hospitals; the services of consultants, registrars, housemen (doctors), nurses, physiotherapists, radiologists, occupational health therapists and medical social workers; in-patient and out-patient treatment; ambulance service and VD clinics.

School health service

This provides the services of:

(a) school doctor – school medical inspection;

(b) health visitor/school nurse – hygiene inspections, hearing and vision tests, etc.;
(c) dentist – dental inspections;
(d) audiometrician – hearing tests;
(e) ophthalmic services – eye test and provision of spectacles;
(f) nutritionist – advice on diets;
(g) chiropodist – foot clinics;
(h) speech therapist – speech clinics;
(i) family welfare visitors.

2. Social services:

(a) social workers – who visit families in trouble to give advice and support, and can arrange for help if necessary;
(b) residential services for the elderly (old people's homes);
(c) residential services for the handicapped;
(d) residential services for children in need of care;
(e) day centres for the elderly;
(f) day centres for the handicapped;
(g) foster care – registration and supervision of foster parents;
(h) adoption service – registration and supervision of adoption cases;
(i) daily-minders registration;
(j) play groups;
(k) provision of home-helps – for those in need of domestic help for reasons of infirmity, sickness or pregnancy;
(l) provision of meals-on-wheels – hot meals delivered to house-bound, usually elderly, people.

3. Education:

(a) nursery schools;
(b) primary schools;
(c) comprehensive schools;
(d) special schools for handicapped children;
(e) hospital schools;
(f) home teachers;
(g) evening classes;
(h) colleges of further education;
(i) colleges of higher education;
(j) universities.

Staff

Teachers and lecturers; nursery nurses; ancillary helpers; school inspectors; school welfare officers.

Subsidies and grants (at the discretion of the local authority)

(a) free school meals for children of low-income families;
(b) subsidised school meals for all children;
(c) free milk for all children of up to seven years, and for all handicapped children;
(d) uniform grants;
(e) fares paid for primary school children if they live more than 3.2 km (2 miles) from their school;
(f) fares paid for secondary and further education students if they live more than 4.8 km (3 miles) from school or college;
(h) grants for further and higher education;
(i) transport to and from school for handicapped children.

4. Finance

Child benefit   A weekly sum payable to mothers for each child in the family.

Maternity grant   A lump sum to help with the extra expense of having a baby.

Maternity allowance   A woman normally in full-time employment is entitled to a weekly allowance for eighteen weeks, ending six weeks after the birth of her baby.

Sickness benefit   A weekly payment to an employed person who is unable to work because of illness. The payment is increased where there are dependant relatives.

Invalidity benefit   A pension which replaces sickness benefit after 168 days of illness. This allowance depends upon the age of the sick person.

Industrial injuries benefit   A weekly allowance paid to a person whose work caused illness or injury.

Unemployment benefit   A weekly payment, for fifty-two weeks, for an unemployed person, with increased payments for dependants.

Retirement pension   Weekly pension paid to men over sixty-five and to women over sixty years of age.

Widow's benefit
(a) an allowance for twenty-six weeks following her husband's death, if the widow is under sixty years of age.
(b) widowed mother's allowance which commences after the first twenty-six weeks, providing there are dependent children.
(c) widows pension following (a) or (b), if a widow is over forty years of age.

Guardian's allowance   A weekly allowance paid to an adult who undertakes the care of an orphan.

Child's special allowance   A weekly amount paid for each dependent child of a divorced woman on the death of her former husband, if he was helping to support them.

Death grant   A sum of money to offset funeral expenses.

Family income supplement   A weekly allowance paid to a family whose father is in full-term employment but on a low income.

Supplementary benefit   A person of over sixteen, not in full-time employment, who has insufficient money to live on can apply for supplementary benefit.

Mobility, Attendance and Invalid Care allowances   Allowances awarded for helping handicapped people.

5. Housing. Local housing authorities are responsible for:
(a) the provision and maintenance of council houses, to rent, for people who need homes;
(b) the provision of accommodation for homeless families;
(c) encouragement and help to housing associations who provide cost-rent houses and flats, and co-operative or co-ownership housing;
(d) the provision of mortgages to home-buyers who cannot get loans from other sources;
(e) the provision of grants and loans to home-owners to improve and modernise their houses;
(f) Rent rebate scheme for people on low incomes.

6. Environmental health. Environmental health inspectors are responsible for:
(a) provision of clean air, water and food;
(b) noise abatement;
(c) pest control;
(d) removal of rubbish and sewage;
(e) inspection of housing.

7. Other services in the community:

Free library   Provided by local authorities.

Police

Fire brigade

Probation officers

Citizens Advice Bureaux   A general advisory service which helps people, especially those with legal, matrimonial or housing problems.

Law centres   Provide free legal advice.

School crossing patrols   By an Act of Parliament of 1954, a school crossing patrol can stop traffic if the patrol-person is wearing a uniform or emblem approved by the Secretary of State.

8. Voluntary services. There are many of these and they vary from area to area. Some examples are:

Women's Royal Voluntary Service   Branches of this service often help families in need, by providing second-hand items of clothing, etc.

British Red Cross Society   This society operates a loan service of walking-aids, wheelchairs, bed-pans and other nursing equipment.

National Society for the Prevention of Cruelty to Children (NSPCC)   The society's workers are trained in preventive work and help families and children in distress.

Marriage guidance clinics   This is a service for people who need help with their marriage problems.

Gingerbread Club   An organisation which helps one-parent families.

Exercise 19

Multiple-choice questions

1. Family Income Supplement is:
(a) money paid weekly to one-parent families;
(b) a weekly sum of money for all children;
(c) a variable rent allowance;
(d) a weekly tax rebate;
(e) a weekly sum of money paid to families with low incomes.

2. Which of the following officials is responsible for visiting all families with children of under five years of age?
(a) health visitor;
(b) environmental health officer;
(c) housing officer;
(d) social worker;
(e) medical officer of health.

3. A social worker visits:
(a) all families with children under five;
(b) all families with a handicapped member;
(c) all families which have problems and seek help;
(d) all families living on social security;
(e) all one-parent families.

Essay questions

4. Describe briefly the services provided by the state to help prevent the break-up of families which have young children.

5. Who would you approach for help for a one-parent family experiencing difficulties? What statutory services are available to this family?

Project

6. Obtain all the leaflets you can find which deal with the help available to handicapped children and their families. From these leaflets find out:
(a) What cash benefits are available to a handicapped child's family.
(b) What other help, if any, is available.
(c) How to obtain any benefits or help.

7. Find out about the different voluntary societies in your home area.

Suggestions for further reading

Winifred Huntly, *Personal & Community Health*, Baillière, Tindall & Cassell

Phyllis Willmott, *The Consumers' Guide to the British Social Services* (Pelican Original), Penguin Books Ltd

Brian Meredith Davies, *Community Health & Social Services*, English Universities Press Ltd

Leaflets from Social Security Offices

Chapter 20
Looking after other people's children

Provision for the under-sevens

You will find children under seven (and mainly under five) being looked after by a variety of people, including nursery nurses, in many establishments, and for a variety of reasons.

Working mothers

More than half Britain's working women are mothers, and a small but steadily increasing proportion of these are mothers of under-fives. Inflation, an increase in marriage breakdown, greater educational attainments and job opportunities, a desire to improve one's standard of living and a need for companionship are all influencing this trend.

Contrary to many older people's beliefs, there is little evidence to prove a link between working mothers and juvenile delinquency, truancy, vandalism and under-achievement at school.

For *some* women, it is not true that they are the best people to look after their children for these first impressionable years. Moreover, a contented woman is more likely to raise a well-adjusted child than one who is tense, resentful or frustrated. The quality of time spent together is much more important than the quantity.

However, substitute care depends on good organisation, good health, and the unfailing reliability of a number of people. A mother's feelings of fatigue, strain and guilt are never far away, especially when things go wrong.

Britain lags behind many European and other countries in the pre-school provision for children of working mothers.

Only families with pressing social or health needs will be granted a day nursery place. There are not enough registered child-minders. Nursery schools and classes are unevenly distributed (almost non-existent in rural areas), have long waiting lists, and do not pretend to cater for the schedules of working mothers. Full-time nannies are beyond most people's means. Grandmother, if she lives nearby, which is not usual today, may well have a job herself, or else be unwilling to be permanently tied. Playgroup hours are even less compatible with a working mother's timetable than are those of a nursery school.

The mother who needs or chooses to work, and also the stay-at-home mother who seeks peer companionship or wider play opportunities for her child, therefore need to be fully informed about what provision is available to them. In this chapter we outline the various types of pre-school facilities and describe them briefly.

Pilot schemes and new approaches are constantly being tried in an attempt to meet more adequately the needs of today's small children and their families. Facts and figures are valuable pointers, but in the nature of things they soon go out of date.

We have made only passing references to voluntary and community schemes. This is from lack of space only, and in no sense underestimates the immense contribution these make. The personal concern, close relationships, and freedom from red tape and officialdom which characterise voluntary schemes are often exactly what is most needed by the families they are serving.

Nursery nurses (or nursery officers or nursery assistants, as they are known in some jobs) working in the public sector are paid in accordance with the National Joint Council scale. There is no such prescribed scale for nursery nurses working in the private sector; here, it is negotiable by individuals.

Provision for children from birth to seven

Public Sector	Day nurseries Day (family) centres Registered child minders Residential homes Foster parent placement	Authority responsible – local Social Services Department
	Hospitals	Authority responsible – Area Health Authority
	Nursery schools Nursery classes Nursery centres Infant schools Special schools	Authority responsible – Local Education Authority
Private Sector	Private nurseries Crèches Playgroups Playbus Adoption	Approval, liaison and consultation with local Social Services Department necessary
	Mother and toddler clubs Private work (nannies)	

Day nurseries

The expansion of day nurseries was a wartime measure to free women to work in factories and in the service industries. After the war, many were closed, and since then, growth has been confined to socially needy areas.

A day nursery is staffed by a nursery officer-in-charge (N.N.E.B. and/or S.R.N. trained), a deputy, and trained nursery nurses – who are termed 'nursery officers' – on a ratio of one adult to five children, not including the officer-in-charge. Several domestic staff will also be employed, as the children (aged from six weeks to five years) can take breakfast, lunch and tea on the premises, and, of course, there is a good deal of laundry and cleaning involved. The children are divided into 'family groups' of between six and eleven children, covering the total age span and keeping members of real families together. A separate baby room may be provided, but mothers are not encouraged to leave babies under nine months. Some children may stay at a day nursery for several years; others remain there only months or weeks during a temporary domestic crisis.

Day nurseries open from about 7.30 a.m. or 8.0 a.m. until 5.30 p.m. or 6.0 p.m., although few children are likely to be there for the whole day. Nurseries stay open all the year round except for Bank Holidays, and in some cases, one extra day. Some children attend part-time, others attend for a long day, although there is a good deal of flexibility.

A good day nursery offers children first-class physical care, including medical inspections, and the services of various professional people such as audiometrician, speech therapist, etc. It also offers stability, security, and linguistic and intellectual stimulation. Although nurseries commonly accept more children than they were intended to, priority has to be given to working single parents, children with physical or mental handicap, impoverished or severely-strained home environment, ill or handicapped parents. Many of these children might be subjected to concealed parental violence (C.P.V.) if the day nursery did not take away some of the strain. Sometimes the relief offered to, for instance, a very young mother or harassed lone father is sufficient to keep the family together and functioning reasonably well. Parents pay only minimal costs for meals taken – nothing else – and many parents apply and are eligible for free meals. It is therefore an expensive form of local authority care, but can be regarded as a preventive measure, and infinitely less expensive than residential care.

Because many of the children come from troubled backgrounds, disturbed behaviour is inevitable, and, at its worst, this *can* give rise to another unfavourable environment for the child. However, dedicated staff can work wonders in maintaining a homely, happy atmosphere in which the children settle and often blossom.

Contacts with parents are of vital importance, if all the chief influences in the child's life are to be working towards the same ends. But such contacts can be difficult. Feelings of failure and guilt are sometimes masked by feigned indifference or even aggression. Some parents can be involved with nursery activities; others will be happy to leave their children in expert hands. Single and working parents do not find it easy to attend nursery functions.

Day Care centres

Attempts have been made in recent years to extend the services offered by day nurseries, because it is argued that to help a child in isolation is superficial and ineffectual. Rising figures of child abuse have added urgency to the need for more prevention and rehabilitation.

It is almost impossible to generalise about day care centres, as they vary so much. In some areas, this pattern of care is being introduced, and day nurseries will probably be phased out eventually, as deliberate policy on the part of the Social Services Department. Elsewhere, day centres are set up by voluntary agencies in response to local needs – for instance, if there are many families with young children in bed and breakfast accommodation. Several different services will be offered on the same campus, including possibly medical attention, and a meeting place for the handicapped. Some day centres are set up jointly by the Social Services Department and the local health authority.

Family Centres are another attempt to support whole families in difficulties. At the centre in the London borough of Camden, day care for children for up to seven days a week is offered, as well as parent units. The teaching at family centres is aimed at helping the adults to be more adequate and interesting people, as well as parents; help with budgeting, cooking, diet, household chores, appearance and leisure skills might all be included. At Camden there are also home visits by centre staff, to give parents a better insight into their children's needs, for instance in play and language stimulation. Some family centres have an assessment unit.

Child minders

For many thousands of working mothers, using the services of a child minder is the only realistic arrangement. It can also be the best, as hours can be fixed to suit the mother. Moreover, the child minder often lives near the mother's home, and for the child the surroundings are probably familiar and remind him of his own home. Thus it is less demanding and stressful than day nursery for most children under three. There is also the advantage that when the child starts school, he can continue to use the same child minder before and/or after school.

✳ Anyone who looks after an unrelated child for more than two hours a day for money must register as a child minder and conform with regulations laid down in the Nursery and Child Minders Act, which became law in 1948. Its provisions were later amended, and loopholes tightened up in the Health Services and Public Health Act of 1968. The standards set by local authorities for registered minders vary enormously, but few minders are registered to take more than four children. Social workers visit at intervals to supervise the child minder, and the health visitor visits 'her' children and gives advice on home safety, play, language stimulation, menu planning, etc.

It is a hard-working, long day for a child minder, and she will not earn a great deal of money. She will be advised on what to charge her clients by the D.H.S.S., but out of this money she will have to pay for meals, toys, equipment, outings, wear and tear on her home, as well as additional heating and lighting costs. Steps are being taken in various areas by the D.H.S.S. and health visitors to provide more support and in-service training for registered child minders. The B.B.C. ran a very good series of programmes on this subject. Access to playgroups, toy libraries and other resources can also improve the lot of the child minder and her charges. Day fostering/sponsored child minding schemes have been started by a number of authorities, particularly to meet the needs of children who are considered 'at risk'.

We must add a note on unregistered child minders, of whom there are large, unknown numbers. Some slip into child minding, and are ignorant of the laws governing this work. Others evade the law, in order to take more children and earn more money. It is very difficult for social workers and health visitors to track down such practice. Sometimes space and facilities are hopelessly inadequate, but large numbers of babies and children are minded; horror stories are not uncommon. Naturally, in such a cramped situation, emphasis will be laid on quietness, sleep and 'tidy' activities. Children who spend several years in such an atmosphere are likely to grow up with retarded language and stunted intelligence.

Before we condemn such practice, however, we should appreciate that where it is rife, the women concerned are responding to a local need which the state is not meeting.

Residential care

Children whose parents are not able to look after them permanently or, more likely, temporarily, for reasons of physical or mental illness, death, eviction, accident, alcoholism, imprisonment, or who have been parted from their parents by Court Order, because of assault or neglect, are taken into residential care. Such care used to come under the auspices of the Home Office, but is now administered under the social services. All residential work calls for a particular kind of dedication from those who are involved.

The homes used often to be large, soulless places, offering sanctuary to orphans and illegitimate children, who might stay there many years. The care they received was often tainted with a Victorian aftermath of rescuing unfortunates from immoral backgrounds; there was much emphasis on godliness and cleanliness, and children were supposed to appreciate all that was being done for them.

Post-war government studies and generally-accepted research findings about the potentially damaging effects of institutionalisation have led to great changes in the last thirty or so years.

For psychological reasons, and also financial ones – residential care being very expensive for local authorities – social workers try to prevent the break-up of families whenever possible. Where separation is unavoidable, the period of time a child spends in care is kept as short as is compatible with home circumstances, and all staff involved will be working towards the rehabilitation of the family.

Children over five will probably be placed in small family group homes of about six children of varying ages up to sixteen. The house may be council-owned on an estate. There will be a house mother and sometimes a house father, who may or may not have had some kind of formal training for this job.

Alternatively, children in care may be fostered out. The under-fives, particularly if they have been subjected to parental violence, or if they are handicapped, will be placed in residential nurseries. There has been a marked increase in recent years in parental violence to children, usually small children. It is of vital importance that such children are handled with the utmost sensitivity, skill and care. Trained nursery nurses' knowledge of children and observation skills will be invaluable in many different ways, not least of which may be court involvement, and judgements involving a child's wellbeing and future.

Besides local authority homes, several voluntary bodies such as Dr. Barnardo's, National Children's Homes, etc. also fund and administer residential children's homes, but their approach, too, has changed and diversified greatly over the years. Frequently, they now offer preventive and support services such as family (day) centres, playgroups and holiday schemes for handicapped children.

Fostering

Fostering is a form of residential care. It can last for a few days or several years. Since the Children Bill of 1975, foster parents can now apply for the custodianship of a child – a sort of halfway stage between fostering and adopting – which safeguards the child from his natural parents changing their minds. Adoption can follow custodianship.

Babies who are going to be adopted are fostered out to registered foster parents for approximately six weeks.

Long-term fostering with infants is most likely to be successful. The more disrupted and traumatic a life an older child has experienced, the more difficult will be his settling in. Other difficulties he may encounter are the jealousy and resentment felt towards him by the natural children of the family, and unrealistic expectations about his adjusting process by the foster parents. Counselling by social workers can go a considerable way towards avoiding disenchantment and breakdown.

Foster parents, who undergo careful screening, particularly of motives, before they are accepted, need endless patience and selfless love. They will be paid only enough to cover the child's food, clothing and pocket money. This, of course, is to ensure that no unscrupulous couples take it on purely for money. Recently, appropriate monetary recognition has been shown to foster parents who take on older and difficult children (teenage truants, bedwetters, etc.). Local authorities are usually short of registered foster parents.

Where a child is accepted naturally, fully and happily into a foster family, it can make the crucial difference and greatly improve his chances of growing up as a well-adjusted, happy individual.

Adoption

There is a great shortage of normal healthy babies who are free to be adopted. This is because contraception and abortion have reduced the number of unwanted babies born, while the social stigma of keeping an illegitimate baby has diminished. Adopting couples often have to wait a year or two before a baby becomes available.

There are voluntary adoption societies, as well as local authority adoption services. As far as the state is concerned, adoption is easily the cheapest way of looking after children who are not kept by their natural parents. It is, incidentally, illegal to arrange adoption privately for money.

Some 'adoptable' babies are orphans or have been totally rejected because they are handicapped or of mixed (coloured) parentage, but most are illegitimate. Since the Children Bill of 1975 there is a shorter interval of time during which the natural mother can revoke her decision, thus reducing the tensions and heartbreak of hopeful would-be adopters.

Since adopted children are clearly so much wanted, there is every chance that, provided adoption takes place early in their lives, the arrangement will be highly successful.

In the past, adoption agencies tried to 'match' children and parents for colouring, intelligence and background. This was obviously to minimise embarrassment and disappointment, but today it is thought to be a mistake. After all, natural parents cannot predict exactly what their children's hair colour or intelligence quotient will be!

Before an adoption can be approved, the couple's home will be visited by a social worker to see that adequate standards of cleanliness, space, economic security, etc. are assured. But most important will be the couple's own relationship, and attitude towards the forthcoming child. Adopting a child to rescue an ailing marriage would bring happiness to no-one. One enthusiastic and one reluctant partner could also bode trouble.

Some of the issues the couple will have to think and talk over will be their attitudes to illegitimacy, and so-called 'bad blood', their own capabilities as parents, their views on how and when to tell the child he is adopted, their possible reaction if he later wishes to trace his natural parents, which he is now legally able to do.

Hospitals

Many sick children are kept in hospitals today for only very short stays, compared with the practice of a generation ago. The reasons are partly financial and partly psychological, based on what we know about the harm that can be caused when children are separated from their families, and another factor is improved surgery and medication. The exceptions, of course, are seriously ill children, orthopaedic cases, and children requiring specialised treatment. The unrestricted access which allows their families to visit them freely has also greatly changed the lot of children in hospital, and life on the wards. Many hospitals run a playgroup.

More and more area health authorities are employing nursery nurses to work with babies and children in hospital. We can find them in maternity wards, special care wards, ear, nose and throat wards and children's hospitals. With the babies, they will help with feeding, bathing, changing and general duties, as well as supporting and teaching the mothers. With older children, nursery nurses may be employed at night in a general surveillance capacity, or during the day to offer companionship, play, and educational opportunities. Some hospitals employ nursery nurses as play leaders or workers. Nursery nurses in hospitals may have close contact with the children's parents who are often encouraged to remain involved with the physical handling and emotional care of their children.

Nursery schools

Because statutory schooling in Britain begins at five, the position of nursery schools in the education system has always been vulnerable. No child has a *right* to a nursery school place, and long waiting lists are common.

Rachel and Margaret McMillan, working in the slums of Bradford and Deptford in the early twentieth century, pioneered the idea of the nursery school. Their work, beginning as a rescue operation, soon evolved into a source of mental and spiritual stimulation for the parents concerned as well as the children.

Ever since those days, expansion has been sporadic. Nursery schools are usually among the first victims when government spending has to be cut.

In recent years, many headmistresses have seen the role of their nursery schools as forming the heart of a local community – a base for neighbourhood schemes.

Undoubtedly a good nursery school can enormously benefit a child physically, socially, emotionally and intellectually in the opportunities and expertise it offers. It can provide not only a good start for later schooling, but a good start for life.

Nursery schools are administered as part of the state primary school system and are the responsibility of the Department of Education and Science which works through the local education authorities. They are housed in separate buildings from infant and junior schools, and have their own head teacher. They are staffed by qualified teachers and nursery nurses. A nursery school might comprise two or three classes of twenty to twenty-five three to five-year-olds, each class attached to a teacher and nursery nurse team.

Hours of opening will probably be from 8.45 a.m. or 9.0 a.m. to 3.30 p.m. School holidays are the same as for primary schools. A subsidised mid-day meal is available; education/care is free. Some children attend full-time but many more part-time.

Among her many other tasks, the nursery school head must select from her waiting list a balance of boys and girls, a 'spread' of birthdays among her intake. She must weigh the relative needs of, for instance, children with behaviour difficulties or language retardation, with the needs of children who lack safe play space or stimulation in the home. She will receive many referrals from doctors and health visitors. In order to benefit those children with special needs, she must also keep a balance of 'normal' children.

There will be a pattern to the nursery school day, but it will consist mainly of free play and informal group activities. Foundations for later '3R' work will be laid down in many different ways, but formal reading, writing and number work has no place at this stage.

The nursery nurse will carry out the programmes that the class teacher puts in hand, supporting and complementing her all the way.

Nursery classes

These are attached to infant schools, and are administered by the infant head, although the nursery teacher often enjoys a degree of autonomy. Hours, holidays and staffing are the same as for the nursery school.

Most nursery expansion in recent years has been in the form of nursery classes or units built on to existing schools, for obvious reasons of economy.

It is often possible for the nursery children to enjoy P.E. on the exciting infant school apparatus, and to take part in special festivals and occasions, all of which makes for an easy transition for the child at five.

Combined approach to nursery provision

The Plowden Report in 1967, and later the Halsey Report in 1972, both recommended that the two be combined in an as yet unknown form. This was made financially possible in the ensuing Urban Programme, and the nursery centre was the result.

Its aims are to avoid duplication and overlap between what is provided by social services and education departments; to combine the best of both; to create enough flexibility to meet all children's needs; to cut capital and running costs by centralising pre-school resources in each area.

There are now some twenty nursery centres, mostly funded and administered by local authorities, but in some cases by a charitable trust or independent body, as for instance at the Thomas Coram Children's Centre in London. Social services and the local education authority share the external administration, but it is not always shared in the same way. There may be one nursery head (teacher) overall, with a matron (N.N.E.B.) as her deputy, or two such trained people may be heads of their own departments within the centre. Trained nursery teachers and nursery nurses make up the staff, but may be employed by one or both authorities.

The day will be longer, so that early opening or late closing can meet different families' needs. Therefore the staff usually work in shifts. Many children attend part-time for as little as two and a half or three hours, but some others may be there as long as ten hours (extended day provision). The children are usually expected to remain at the centre from their time of admission until reaching five, but some may be there only temporarily during a domestic crisis. In any case, their length of day may change during their period of attendance at nursery centre, depending on their own needs and their family's circumstances. The nursery centre is usually open all the year round except for statutory holidays. The teaching staff mostly enjoy the same number of weeks' holiday as their counterparts in nursery schools, but it may have to be staggered throughout the year and not more than three weeks taken at a time. N.N.E.B. staff usually have five weeks' holiday.

There are usually good links between the nursery centre and health visitors and social workers, which makes for a more effective and comprehensive service to the community. Many nursery centre personnel have made great progress with parental involvement, and offer a parents' room, 'drop-in' centre, or other facilities. Through such contacts, much indirect teaching of child care can be transmitted to parents.

All the nursery centres built so far are close to housing estates in socially needy areas. This naturally makes for an intensification of problems among the intake. It was found early on that a completely 'free flow' of all ages and kinds of children in the building and grounds did not work well and the under-threes are now segregated to an extent, that is to say they are given a geographical secure home base within the building, although patterns of grouping throughout vary greatly. A child who attends a centre for a long day may meet up to one hundred children and be expected to relate closely to several different adults, all in the course of a day. This fact, and also the open-plan design and noise level of some centres, can make great demands on the child.

Other experimental avenues in joint approach are extended hours at the nursery school, and introducing teachers into day nurseries.

Infant schools

Depending on prevailing educational policies and population trends, the 'rising fives' will sometimes be found in infant schools. Generally speaking, children at school will be in the five to seven age range.

The delight and relief many mothers experience when their children reach the statutory school age, and they feel free to earn some money, is often short-lived. Five-year-olds are easy prey to the many new infections they meet. Child minding arrangements are still necessary at times. Moreover, even if the child remains completely fit, he will badly need love, support and attentive care from his mother at the time of taking this big new step in his life.

Infant schools are part of the state primary school system. They may be separate from junior schools, and have their own head teachers, or they may be part of a junior mixed infant (J.M.I.) school.

Most children attend the school in whose catchment area they live. Sometimes the nearness of several schools makes choice possible, provided there are vacancies. Children pay for optional mid-day meals; some will be eligible for free dinners.

Grouping of children within infant schools may be based on either age bands, or family grouping. Numbers within a class may vary between about fourteen and nearly forty.

Play and creative activities form a proportion of the day's programme, but in the main will now be structured so that they more obviously lead the children into literacy and numeracy skills.

Teaching of these skills will include some formal approaches and a good many informal ones. Children will be allowed a degree of choice; there will be active learning, movement, and work performed by groups of children. There will also be opportunities for art, music and physical exercise. The day's programme may be loosely timetabled, or all activities may be integrated. Even the most apparently informal approach, if the teacher knows her job, is based on a great deal of organisation, preparation and record-keeping.

For some excellent further reading on the functioning of the modern Infant School, see Cynthia Mitchell's *Time for School*, Penguin Education Press.

Ancillary workers in infant schools may be known as general assistants, general assistant/secretaries, welfare assistants, and nursery assistants. Some will have been trained, either as nursery nurses, or on short in-service courses, others will not.

Sometimes a nursery nurse is employed to help a handicapped child cope at ordinary infant school. If the Warnock Report is implemented, this trend could grow. Generally speaking, the employment of nursery nurses as full-time assistants to teachers is patchy throughout Britain.

Special schools

(See Chapter 16, Children with Special Needs.)

Private nurseries

These are set up in private individuals' houses and offer their services to any parents who can affort to pay for their three- to five-year-olds to attend. Charges made have to cover all overheads, staff wages, children's meals, etc. Private nurseries do good business in areas where there is inadequate state provision, and where there are opportunities for better paid women's jobs. Therefore they are often to be found in pleasant residential districts and country towns.

Premises and facilities must be inspected and approved by social service personnel and a fire prevention officer and environmental health officer must see the kitchen. If the person in charge has neither a N.N.E.B. nor S.R.N.

qualification, one person on her staff must be thus qualified. Sometimes a nursery is registered to take children under three, in which case the ratio of adults to children must be higher than the normally stipulated one to six.

Keeping of records is compulsory, and the nursery will be visited regularly by social service staff and the health visitor to see 'her own' children, to safeguard against any negligence or exploitation of children and parents.

Crèches

This French word meaning cradle is still used to describe a private nursery in factory, shop or other business premises which offer child minding facilities to children of employees (or in the case of shops, customers). It is interesting to note that Robert Owen, the social reformer, saw the usefulness of this idea and put it into practice at his New Lanark mills as long ago as the early nineteenth century.

In this century and in Britain it has been an idea which has been slow to evolve, but it has been adopted by employers of large numbers of women, for example, those who work in hospitals. In some areas workers, students and teachers have pressurised employers into providing facilities for their children. But some trades unionists have resisted the idea, fearing that the existence of a crèche will act as an unfair hold on the employees.

At best, a crèche can offer care superior to that of many child minders. It can mean a shorter day for the child than if he were being taken to child minder or day nursery, and mother is at hand in case of emergency.

At worst, it can be merely child minding by unqualified staff. The children may also miss the neighbourhood atmosphere and neighbourhood friends.

Playgroups

Playgroups first appeared on the British scene in the early 1960's. Mrs. Belle Tutaev, who had started a voluntary group in London, was overwhelmed by the response which her letter to a national newspaper on the subject brought forth. The resulting loose association of playgroups evolved into the Pre-school Playgroups Association. By 1975, there were one third of a million children in such groups.

Eventually the movement gained government recognition and now receives financial aid. This is paid to P.P.A. nationally, some of the money going to each of the eleven regions in England and Wales.

Although there is no overall pattern of funding playgroups, most receive local authority help. It may be in the form of rent-free premises (schools, halls, etc.) or the means to bulk-buy play equipment. Some social service departments pay for socially needy children to attend playgroups.

Some playgroups are run by charities like N.S.P.C.C. and Save the Children, but most are run by groups of mothers.

Groups vary tremendously. They may be home-based or community based.

They may consist of six or twenty-four children. The children are aged three (very occasionally two) to five. There is a paid supervisor. If she is not an ex-teacher or nursery nurse, she will be expected to attend recognised playgroup courses. The supervisor will involve other mother helpers, sometimes one or two 'regulars', sometimes several on a rota basis.

Some groups are essentially informal. Some are highly organised, and own a mass of bought and improvised equipment which all has to be stored away at the end of each session, and the premises left in a suitable condition for the Brownies or Karate Club who may be using it that evening. Although a group may function every morning, the same children will be encouraged to attend only two or three times a week, as there is often great demand for places.

Playgroups operate on a low budget. Fees for each session – usually paid termly – in 1981 were between 30p and £1.00, depending on area and overheads. Equipment, breakages, rent, electricity, edible snacks (one-third of a pint of milk per child can be obtained free) and the supervisor's pay must all be met out of playgroup funds. Social events to raise money are frequently occasions for neighbourhood co-operation and fun. Fathers can contribute a great deal to the success of a playgroup.

The original aim of P.P.A. was to provide stop-gap pre-school provision, and to continue to support and press for nursery schools for all. Since then, its aims have widened considerably, but parent involvement has always been of paramount importance.

Despite some professional jealousy from nursery education personnel, and the accusation that governments have encouraged the playgroup movement *at the expense of* nursery school expansion, playgroups have undoubtedly brought much benefit to children, and much satisfaction, growth in understanding and self-confidence to mothers. Lonely, or new-to-the-area mothers can find friends and a useful role, without taking on too onerous a commitment, or being frightened off by a school-like atmosphere.

P.P.A. have taken playgroups into remote rural areas. Save the Children have taken playgroups into travellers' sites. Local needs are catered for. In Hammersmith, for example, there is a playgroup that specialises in preparing non-English-speaking children for school at five.

Standards of play are variable, but all playgroups prepare children for the break with mother, and all offer children the chance to mix with their peers.

Opportunity Playgroups are for handicapped young children. These may be organised by P.P.A. or voluntary agencies.

Playbus

In Britain in 1979 there were one hundred playbuses. These specially equipped buses often result from the efforts of community-conscious individuals – students or volunteer workers with other organisations. There is no overall pattern of funding, but once started, Playbus schemes usually attract finance and practical help from local authorities, P.P.A., and associations such as Adventure Playgrounds and Fair Play for Children.

Buses are bought from bus companies or commercial vehicle dealers. They cost between £500 and £1000, and considerable further expense is involved in renovating them and adapting them to their future use. The outer appearance of the bus is important, and the colourful and imaginative manner in which it is decorated helps to give it a sort of 'Pied Piper' appeal to children whenever they see it.

This novel and lively first impression, combined with a Playbus's mobility and flexibility, has produced an effective community resource. The original idea of a Playbus was to take playgroups to areas where pre-school provision was inadequate. By working with parents, Playbus staff – drivers/social worker and assistant(s) – would then gradually wean the groups away to permanent premises and a self-sufficient organisation. There have been great successes here, and mothers who probably would not have been confident enough to initiate a playgroup of their own have become happy and capable playgroup leaders.

The functions of Playbuses have widened considerably over the years, and now many are to be found involved in work for the community with a variety of different groups and age bands. The Bristol Playbus, for instance, takes part in holiday play schemes for primary age children, gives puppet shows, provides accommodation for Asian mothers learning English, and is constantly seen around the city on Saturdays, providing attractions at fêtes, carnivals, and so on. This trend towards community, rather than exclusively pre-school, work is likely to develop in the future.

There is a National Playbus Association, and each Playbus has its own committee, unless run solely by a local authority, as happens in Wandsworth and Edinburgh.

A few large manufacturing companies have shown interest in financing and equipping Playbuses. The firms gain from good advertising and the community benefits from extra facilities.

Mother and toddler clubs

These are sometimes offshoots of playgroups, although they can also be set up by health visitors at health centres, by teachers at secondary schools, or can arise independently. In some areas, they can receive a grant under Urban Aid, but they are not at the moment statutorily controlled; as the mother is present, she is responsible for her child, therefore registration is not necessary.

They form part of the support network for mothers of pre-school children who often experience social isolation.

Private work (nannies)

During the nineteenth century, and later, English nannies became a byword for propriety, hygiene, discretion, and firm handling tempered by love. A nanny might stay with 'her' middle or upper-class children for many years, and was often closer to them than their parents, maybe even remaining with the family after the children had grown up.

Changed social conditions today have meant that nannies are more commonly employed by mothers who are also professional or show business people, or public figures. Few houses today can offer 'staff quarters' which the nanny of old would have enjoyed, and so some nannies may lack privacy or time off. Living as one of the family is quite common, and so are nannies employed on a day-time basis. A nanny may be required for a year or so only, or else she may choose to move on. She may be offered chances of travel abroad. A good nanny gives her charges above all companionship, stability, stimulation and affection.

Exercise 20

Multiple-choice questions

1. You are told that a child at nursery has just come out of care. This means:
(a) he is not now being looked after by anyone;
(b) he has just come out of hospital;
(c) his mother deserted him;
(d) he had been battered at some time;
(e) he has spent a period in a residential home.

2. People accepting payment for minding other people's children should be registered as child-minders because:
(a) they will get more money;
(b) they can claim free meals for their children;
(c) it will make them more caring people;
(d) they can take more children;
(e) they are required by law to do so.

3. CPV usually stands for:
(a) a plastic material, resembling leather, useful in collage work;
(b) a strong white glue used in junk modelling;
(c) Committee of Parent Voters;
(d) Council for Pre-School Vaccination;
(e) concealed parental violence.

4. The most senior person in a day nursery should have the title:
(a) nursery officer-in-charge;
(b) sister;
(c) matron;
(d) headmistress;
(e) supervisor.

5. A crèche is:
(a) a sore place on the skin;
(b) the French name for nursery school;
(c) another name for a state day nursery;
(d) a private nursery in shop, factory or other work premises;
(e) a person who does baby-minding.

6. Margaret McMillan was:
(a) late wife of the former Conservative Prime Minister;
(b) proprietress of a firm which publishes children's books;
(c) founder of the Playgroup Movement;
(d) matron of a famous day nursery in the London slums;
(e) one of the founders of nursery education.

7. Only one of the following statements about the Playgroup Movement is true:
(a) Playgroups are funded solely by Social Services.

(b) Playgroups are funded solely by local education authorities.
(c) Playgroups arose voluntarily because of lack of nursery provision.
(d) Playgroup leaders must be trained teachers or nursery nurses.
(e) Playgroups are handy for working mothers.

8. The main aim of the Playbus Movement was to:
(a) make playgroups seem more fun;
(b) bring about cheaper playgroups;
(c) create jobs for the unemployed;
(d) take playgroups into areas where there were none;
(e) prevent people getting stale.

Essay questions

9. What are the essential differences between a day nursery and a nursery school?

10. How does the Playgroup Movement serve the community?

11. What qualities do you think are most needed by nursery nurses taking up residential work?

12. A friend comes to tell you that she is thinking of starting child-minding. What advice would you give her?

Project

13. Find out what facilities exist in your home locality for your child of three. Imagine that you are a single mother. Where do you think you would place your child?

Discussion topic

14. All mothers of under-fives should stay at home to make the most of these first impressionable years.

Suggestions for further reading

Elizabeth Bradburn, *Margaret McMillan*, Denholm House Press
Marion Dowling, *The Modern Nursery*, Longman Group Ltd
Ivonny Lindquist, *Therapy through Play*, Arlington Books
Lesley Webb, *Purpose and Practice in Nursery Education*, Basil Blackwell Ltd
Joan Cass, *The Role of the Teacher in the Nursery School*, Pergamon Press Ltd
Marianne Parry and Hilda Archer, *Pre-School Education*, Macmillan Education Ltd
Lesley Webb, *Making a Start on Child Study*, Blackwell's Practical Guides, Basil Blackwell Ltd

Chapter 21
Child observations

Learning about babies and children through first-hand observation satisfactorily combines theory and practice.

Through observing, we can learn how children look, move, behave, express themselves, react to people and events, feel, understand, develop and progress. We can learn about play, relationships and children's interaction with their environment.

Sharpening our skills of observation alerts us to a child who is ill or miserable, in trouble, left out, frustrated, elated or overwhelmed. Gradually we learn to interpret what we see. We also learn how to anticipate situations of potential difficulty, and gain from watching more experienced adults' techniques of handling children.

How to record   By committing to paper what you have seen, heard and noticed about the children with whom you work, you help to fix these impressions in your memory for future reference. This written record also enables tutors to evaluate your progress.

Approaches to written work vary from one course and tutor to another. The following few short extracts from written observations by nursery nurse students indicate their growing powers of perception. There is an additional benefit in the students' evident enjoyment of the children.

Examples
Observation of early attempts at communication

Simon: 11 months   Simon's mother sat down on the sofa and I sat opposite. Simon remained on her lap, sitting quite still while his mother and I talked. However, after about two minutes, Simon became restless and started to play with his mother's hair and features, feeling each one in turn with his finger tips. While exploring his mother's face, Simon started to babble away to himself, using various sounds at different pitches. The sound he used most often was a 'coo-ing' sound like a wood pigeon, which he used at different pitches, as if he was experimenting with his voice.

Observation of developing movement

Jeremy: 14 months   Jeremy had been walking for about six weeks. When I visited his home, he was apprehensive of me at first, dropped the things he was holding and stumbled over to his mother for a hug. After this, and a very suspicious look at me, he waddled off, with straight firm legs, towards the enormous toy box in the corner. Out came 'Tommy Turtle' and Jeremy crouched down by putting his hands on the carpet and bending his legs. Still crouching rather than sitting, he turned the turtle the right way up, took hold of the string round the neck and prepared to rise to play with the toy. He put his hands back down on the carpet, pushed himself forward on to his straightened arms, straightened his legs, and slowly stood up.

Observation of young child eating

Andrew: 23 months   Andrew picked up the spoon in his right hand, the fork in his left, and began to tackle his meal of cheese flan, peas and boiled potatoes. He handled his spoon and fork rather well, and found no difficulty in getting the peas on to his spoon, using the fork to push the peas on to it. When he came to the flan, he attempted to make the pieces smaller by raising his spoon and banging at the flan until the pieces were eventually broken down.

Observation of children with books

Lorelle, Rebecca and Joanne, all 4 years: Lorelle settled herself on the chair in the Book Corner, adjusting her skirt and undoing the zip of her cardigan. She crossed her legs and picked up a book from the table in front of her. She balanced it on top of her knees, flicked through it and put it back. Then her attention was diverted to Rebecca, who had just entered the Book Corner and sat down close to Lorelle with a friendly, conspiratorial smile. Lorelle said to Rebecca, 'I'm gonna read you a story. You'd better sit carefully'.

She snatched another, large-looking book from the bookcase and carelessly flung it open. She picked up all the pages of the book and let them drift slowly through her fingers. Every now and then she would slam her hand hard down on the pages to stop one when she saw a colourful interesting picture.

Later, when another child came into the Book Corner and took the same book which Lorelle had just been 'reading', her smile vanished. She stared angrily at Joanne. Without a word she marched over and pulled fiercely at the book until Joanne gave in. Lorelle smiled boldly at everyone in triumph. She sat down again and held the book to her face, rubbing it along her lips and round her cheeks with slow, smooth movements.

Observation of contrasting use of large outdoor equipment by older and younger children

Paul: 2 years   Paul had been playing in the garden and had walked over to the climbing apparatus and stood and looked at the children playing and climbing. Very slowly, Paul walked over to the ladder, and then knelt down on the first rail, and then with his hands resting on the next rail began to climb gingerly up the ladder, first moving his right knee and left arm, with his foot dragging behind, and then his left knee and right arm. So he proceeded until he got to the top, where he began to pull himself up by gripping hold of the rail and heaving himself up, grunting as he did so.

Neil: 5 years   His hands released the rung, and he caught hold of the side of the slide. Confidently he pushed himself down the slide, using his hands for acceleration and braking. He reached the bottom, and expertly did a head roll on the foam mat. This action was repeated twice more in complete silence.

Observation of a new child's period of adjustment to nursery school

Gary: 3 years   Gary was drinking his milk. He sat alone. He had still not spoken to any adult or child. His picture of a barrel dangled around the bottle neck. Gary sucked the straw, his prominent eyes staring into space. He tilted the bottle and some of the milk spilled over the top, down Gary's jumper, dripped onto the floor and formed a puddle. Gary froze, the straw still in his mouth, but now he had stopped sucking. He looked absolutely terrified; his big eyes grew bigger, his lips puckered, and as the teacher drew near he reminded me of a trapped animal.

Observation of nursery children on a visit

Ages 3—5 years   The children poured in through the door, eyes bright and alert with anticipation. Most children were dressed in best clothes, usually kept well away from nursery, and the atmosphere was very explosive and happy . . .

. . . At last we were all securely seated on the coach. I noticed how tiny the children looked, with their legs stiffly protruding straight out, their heads only barely reaching the middle of the seat back.

The children energetically waved goodbye to their mothers out of the windows.

'Are we nearly there?' asked five-year-old Diane as we rounded the first bend.

Observation of children engaged in domestic play

Emma and Kerry: 4 years   Emma quickly finishes rubbing the doll's skirt, finds the pegs and runs over to the washing line. She has difficulty snapping the pegs open, but eventually manages it.

At this point Kerry shouts to her,' Where's the soap? I haven't got any soap.' The bubbles in the water are beginning to spill over the top of the bowl as Kerry gropes around in them for the soap. Kerry finds it and lathers her hands with great concentration. Emma helps Kerry to wash her doll's face. They squeeze the doll's face and neck into contortions, first frowning aggressively, then laughing delightedly.

An idea occurs to Emma.

'She's our naughty girl an' we're cross with her.'

'Yeah, an' when she's clean, we've got to hang her up on the washing line . . . She's got to have pegs in her hair.'

They both giggle, and continue happily rubbing, squeezing and soaping.

Observation of mental processes evidenced in play

Robert: 6 years   'Well, now, this is a sort of gun,' he explained, pointing to a piece of wooden construction. 'You see, when I bang this down, those smaller bricks will go shooting into the air to hit the other ship.'

He demonstrated by banging his hand down vigorously on a piece of wood on which were balanced five bricks. Some went backwards and some went forwards – a little way.

'Yes, well, I need to adjust that as it's not quite right,' Robert admitted.

Conclusion

The qualified nursery nurse has a responsibility to go on learning and enhancing her professional skills and expertise.

There are in-service training courses, and evening classes, which she can attend. She should also read newspapers, books and book reviews, and keep abreast of what is happening in both her local community and the wider world outside. Only in this way can she remain reasonably well-informed on all the many issues which affect families and children today, and so make the greatest contribution to those in her care.

Answers to Exercises

Exercise 1 (page 13)
1(b), 2(e).
Exercise 2 (page 25)
1(b), 2(d), 3(a).
Exercise 3 (page 39)
1(d), 2(e), 3(b), 4(b), 5(b).
Exercise 4 (page 47)
1(c), 2(d), 3(e).
Exercise 5 (page 64)
1(b), 2(d), 3(b), 4(d), 5(c).
Exercise 6 (page 88)
1(c), 2(b), 3(d), 4(c), 5(a).
Exercise 7 (page 107)
1(d), 2(a), 3(d), 4(c), 5(d).
Exercise 8 (page 121)
1(d), 2(c), 3(c), 4(a), 5(c).
Exercise 9 (page 136)
1(d), 2(e), 3(e), 4(a), 5(c).
Exercise 10 (page 150)
1(b), 2(e), 3(c).

Exercise 11 (page 159)
1(e), 2(d), 3(d).
Exercise 12 (page 177)
1(d), 2(a), 3(a), 7(d), 8(a), 9(e).
Exercise 13 (page 190)
1(b), 2(d), 3(d).
Exercise 14 (page 203)
1(e), 2(b), 3(c).
Exercise 15 (page 225)
1(e), 2(a), 3(a), 4(e), 5(e), 6(c), 7(a).
Exercise 16 (page 256)
1(a), 2(b), 3(d), 4(a), 5(c).
Exercise 17 (page 270)
1(e), 2(e), 3(c), 4(d), 5(a).
Exercise 18 (page 280)
1(d), 2(d), 3(e).
Exercise 19 (page 288)
1(e), 2(a), 3(c).
Exercise 20 (page 305)
1(e), 2(e), 3(e), 4(a), 5(d), 6(e), 7(c), 8(d).

Index

312

1144 Random, Interesting & Fun Facts You Need To Know

The Knowledge Encyclopedia To Win Trivia

Scott Matthews

The more that you read, the more things you will know. The more you learn, the more places you'll go.

- Dr. Seuss

7 BENEFITS OF READING FACTS

1. Knowledge
2. Stress Reduction
3. Mental Stimulation
4. Better Writing Skills
5. Vocabulary Expansion
6. Memory Improvement
7. Stronger Analytical Thinking Skills

ABOUT THE AUTHOR

Scott Matthews is a geologist, world traveller and author of the "Amazing World Facts" series! He was born in Brooklyn, New York, by immigrant parents from Ukraine but grew up in North Carolina. Scott studied at Duke University where he graduated with a degree in Geology and History.

His studies allowed him to travel the globe where he saw and learned amazing trivial knowledge with his many encounters. With the vast amount of interesting information he accumulated, he created his best selling books "Random, Interesting & Fun Facts You Need To Know."

BONUS!

Thanks for supporting me and purchasing this book! I'd like to send you some freebies. They include:

- The audiobook for this book
- My other best seller: 101 Idioms and Phrases
- 500 World War I & II Facts

Go to the last page of the book and scan the QR code. Enter your email and I'll send you all the files. Happy reading!

Table of Contents

Airplanes & Airports

1. Turbulence on an airplane cannot be predicted. It can occur even on a cloudless, clear day.

2. Airports had to standardize their names in the 1930's with airport codes, so those with two letter names simply added an "x", hence names such as LAX.

3. During an emergency landing, a plane has the ability to dump its fuel from the wings to prevent it from exploding if it crashes.

4. You're not allowed to take mercury onto a commercial passenger plane as it can damage the aluminum the plane is made out of.

5. The first commercial flight only lasted twenty three minutes and cost $8,500 in today's money. It was between St. Petersburg, Florida, and Tampa, Florida.

6. It's possible to see a rainbow as a complete circle from an airplane.

7. The filtration technology used in airplanes is the same technology they use to filter air in hospitals.

8. The rules of most airlines require that the pilot and co-pilot of a plane eat different meals. This is just in case one of the meals causes food poisoning.

9. For less than the cost of a Ferrari you can buy a renovated Boeing 737.

10. The average Boeing 747 plane has 160 miles (260 kilometers) of wiring inside of it.

11. The Antonov An-225 is the largest aircraft ever made and was initially created for the task of transporting spaceplanes. It weighs 285 tons, has a wingspan of 288 feet (eighty-

eight meters), and cost $250 million.

12.   In 2014, a man in China bought a first class ticket on China Eastern Airlines, went to the airport, and ate free food for almost an entire year in the VIP lounge. Astoundingly, he cancelled and re-booked his flight an incredible 300 times over the course of the year and then cancelled his ticket for a full refund once the airline became wise of his scam.

13.   Most airplane crashes happen either three minutes after taking off or eight minutes before landing.

14.   MI-5 once planned to use gerbils to detect terrorists and spies at airports, given that their great sense of smell could acutely detect increased adrenaline in people. However, the project was abandoned when they noticed that the gerbils were not able to tell the difference between terrorists and those who were just afraid of flying.

Amazing

15.   In 1993, a Chinese man named Hu Songwen was diagnosed with kidney failure. In 1999, after no longer being able to afford the hospital bills, he built his own dialysis machine which kept him alive for another thirteen years.

16.   The longest possible uninterrupted train ride in the world is over 10,000 miles (17,000 kilometers) long which goes from Vietnam to Portugal.

17.   The Solvay Hut is the world's most dangerously placed mountain hut, located 13,000 feet (3,962 meters) above ground level in Switzerland.

18.   At the 1912 Olympics, a Japanese marathon runner named Shizo Kanakuri quit and went home without telling officials and he was considered a missing person in Sweden for fifty years. In 1966, he was invited to complete the marathon, finishing with a total time of fifty four years, eight months, six days, and five hours.

19.   Carmen Dell'Orefice is the world's oldest working model. She started modelling at the age of fifteen and is still an active model to this day at the age of eighty three.

20.   In 2005, a Nepalese couple climbed Everest and got married on its peak.

21.   In 1955, a six hundred year old plaster Buddhist statue was dropped when it was being moved locations only to reveal that the plaster was covering another Buddhist statue made of solid gold inside.

22.   In 2011, archaeologists discovered the skeletal remains of a Roman couple who had been holding hands for over 1,500 years.

23.   The Shangri-La Hotel in China captured a record for the largest ball pit ever created

measuring eighty two by forty one feet (twenty five by thirteen meters) and contained over a million balls.

24.   The average led pencil can draw a line that will be thirty five miles (fifty six kilometers) long.

25.   Keikyu Aburatsubo Marine Park is an aquarium located in Japan where you can shake hands with otters.

26.   In 2011, archaeologists at the ground zero 9/11 terrorist attack site in New York City uncovered half of an 18th century ship; it's believed to have once been used by merchants.

27.   In Finland, there is a giant rock named Kummakivi that is sitting perfectly on a seemingly curved mound. The name translates to "strange rock" since nobody knows how it got there.

28.   When Jadav Payeng was sixteen, he began planting trees since he was concerned for the disappearing habit for the local animals. He continued doing this for over thirty five years. Today he has single handedly restored more than 1,360 acres of forest.

29.   The youngest person to ever climb Everest was young Jordan Romero at the age of thirteen.

30.   Philani Dladla is a homeless man from Johannesburg, South Africa, who's known as the pavement bookworm. He survives by reviewing books for people passing on the street and sells them the book if they like it.

31.   The human brain cell, the universe, and the Internet all have similar structures.

32.   Jose Mujica, a former president of Uruguay, was the poorest president in the world at the time as he gave away most of his income to charity.

33.   Stephen Hawking was diagnosed with ALS at twenty one and was expected to die at twenty five. He lived till seventy.

34.   The oldest living person on earth, whose age has been verified, is Japanese Misao Okawa, who is 116 years old.

35.   The most powerful organism is the Gonorrhea bacteria which can pull up to 100,000 times their size.

36.   Sixty three year old former math professor Joan Ginther, who has a PhD in statistics from Stanford University, has won the scratch and lottery four separate times for a grand total of $20.4 million. She never revealed how she did it, but the odds of accomplishing what she did is one in eighteen septillion.

37.   A Californian couple named Helen and Les Brown were both born on December 31,

1918, were married for seventy five years, and then died one day apart at the age of ninety four in 2013.

38.   A woman from Michigan named Barbara Soper gave birth on 8/8/8, 9/9/9, and 10/10/10, the odds of which are fifty million to one.

39.   In 1860, Valentine Tapley, a pike County farmer and loyal democrat, promised to never trim his beard again if Abraham Lincoln was elected president. He kept his word and his beard grew to 12.5 feet (3.8 meters) long.

40.   If we somehow discovered a way to extract gold from the core of Earth, we would be able to cover all the land in gold up to our knees.

41.   When he was a freshman in 1987, a man named Mike Hayes got a friend, who worked at the Chicago Tribune, to write him an article asking the millions who read it to donate one penny each towards his tuition. Immediately, pennies, nickels, and even larger donations came pouring in from all over the world. After accumulating the equivalent of 2.9 million pennies, he graduated and paid for his degree in Food Science.

42.   There is a metal called "gallium" that melts in your hand.

43.   In 2010, a black Nigerian couple living in the UK gave birth to a blond white baby with blue eyes that they called "the miracle baby."

44.   In the 1980's, a man known only as George, who had severe OCD, shot himself in the head in an attempt to commit suicide. Instead of the bullet killing him, it destroyed the part of the brain that was causing the OCD and he went on to get straight A's in college five years later.

45.   Real diamonds don't show up in x-rays.

46.   Adam Rainer, an Australian man, is the only person in medical history to have been classified as both a dwarf and a giant in his lifetime. He stood at 3.8 feet (1.17 meters) on his twenty first birthday and he was classified as a dwarf; but by the time he died at the age of fifty one, he stood at seven feet and six inches (2.34 meters) tall due to a growth spurt.

47.   In 1983, a sixty one year old potato farmer named Cliff Young, who was not an athlete, won the 544 mile (875 kilometer) Sydney to Melbourne Ultra Marathon. This was simply because he ran while the other runners slept.

48.   By the time Donald Trump was twenty seven, he owned 14,000 apartments.

49.   In the 1960's, the US did an experiment where two people without nuclear training

had to design a nuke with only access to publicly available documents. They succeeded.

50.   Stamatis Moraitis was diagnosed by doctors with cancer and was told he only had a couple of months to live. He was still alive ten years later and went back to tell the doctors that he was still alive only to find out that the doctors who diagnosed him had passed away. Stamatis lived until he was one hundred and two.

51.   In 2013, a man named Harrison Okene survived for three days at the bottom of the ocean in a sunken ship by finding a pocket of air.

52.   Over a hundred people drew for the second prize of the Powerball Lotto in 2005. It was suspected that cheating was going on, however, later it was discovered that the winners had simply used the same numbers they'd received in a fortune cookie.

53.   There are more than 150 people cryofrozen right now in the hopes that one day the technology will be invented to revive them, with over 1,000 people registered to do the same upon their death.

54.   In 1978, a US Navy ship known as the USS Stein was found to have traces of an unknown species of giant squid attack. Almost all cuts on the sonar dome contained remains of a sharp, curved claw that were found on the rims of the suction cups of some squid tentacles, but some of the claw marks were much bigger than that of any discovered squid species.

55.   Situated on Sark Island in Guernsey, an island between England and France, Sark Prison is the world's smallest prison which only fits two people.

56.   In 2010, a man got lost in the woods of northern Saskatchewan and chopped down power lines just to draw attention to himself, in hopes that someone would rescue him. It worked.

57.   The longest that anyone has ever survived in a shipwrecked raft was 133 days by a Chinese man named Poon Lim in 1942. He survived by fishing, drinking bird blood, and even killing a shark with a jug of water. He lived to the age of seventy two, dying in 1991.

58.   In Tunisia, you can book an overnight stay at Luke Skywalker's boyhood home, which is a real hotel called "Hotel Sidi Driss," for only $10.

59.   In 2011, the Coble family lost their three children, two girls and a boy, in an unfortunate car accident. A year later the mother gave birth to triplets, two girls and one boy.

Animals

60.   In 2013, it was discovered that some bears in Russia have become addicted to sniffing jet fuel out of discarded barrels. They even go to the lengths of stalking helicopters for the drops of fuel that they leave behind.

61.   Humans are not appropriate prey for great white sharks because their digestion is too slow to cope with the ratio of bone to muscle and fat.

62.   The Savannah is the largest domestic breed of cats which resembles a small leopard but behaves like a dog. They can grow up to forty pounds (eighteen kilograms), have an eight foot (2.4 meter) vertical jump, and be trained to walk on a leash and play fetch.

63.   Flamingos are born grey but change to the pink color we see because of the shrimp they eat which dyes their feathers.

64.   The only bird that can fly backwards is the hummingbird.

65.   In real life, a roadrunner can only reach speeds of about twenty miles (thirty two kilometers) per hour while a coyote can reach speeds of up to forty three miles (sixty nine kilometers) per hour.

66.   The "Orca," also known as the killer whale, actually belongs to the dolphin family.

67.   It's possible for a cat to be its own fraternal twin. These cats, known as "Chimera cats," are an oddity that occur when two fertilized eggs fuse together.

68.   One third of the world's polar bear population lives in Canada.

69.   Hippos sweat the color red because it contains a pigment that acts as a natural sunscreen.

70.   Raccoons are extremely intelligent creatures. They can open complex locks in under ten tries and even repeat the process if the locks are rearranged or turned upside down. They can also remember solutions to problems for up to three years.

71. Cows' methane creates just as much pollution as cars do.

72. Dolphins only fall asleep with half their brain at a time so they're only half conscious, which helps them from accidentally drowning.

73. Snails can sleep for up to three years.

74. The average shark has fifteen rows of teeth in each jaw. They can replace a tooth in a single day and lose over 30,000 teeth in their lifetime.

75. There are completely black chickens in Indonesia known as Ayam Cemani. They have black plumage, legs, nails, beak, tongue, comb, wattle, and even black meat, bones and organs.

76.   Christmas Island is a small Australian island located in the Indian Ocean that every year sees fifty million adult crabs migrate from the forest to breed. It's known as the annual red crab migration.

77.   A flamingo can only eat when its head is upside down.

78.   Starbuck is a famous Canadian bull whose genome is so desirable that his sperm has sold for over twenty five million dollars over his lifetime. In this time he has sired over 200,000 daughters.

79.   Giraffes can last longer without water than camels can.

80.   Elephants are constantly tip toeing around. This is because the back of their foot has no bone and is all fat.

81.   An octopus has nine brains, blue blood, and three hearts.

82.   Polar bears' hair is actually clear and it's the light they reflect that makes them appear to look white.

83.   A chameleon can move its eyes two different directions at the same time.

84.   In one night, a mole can dig a tunnel 300 feet (one kilometer) long in soil.

85.   The age of fish can be determined in a similar way to trees. Fish scales have one growth ring for each year of age.

86.   Fully grown giraffes only have seven vertebrae in their necks, the same number as humans.

87.   When bats are born, they come out feet first, and in many cases, the mother bat hangs

upside down so she can catch the baby in her wings as it exits the womb.

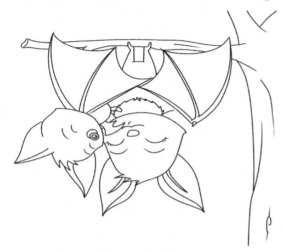

88. In 2007, in Louisiana, a pink albino bottlenose dolphin was discovered and photographed by a man named Eric Rue.

89. When the elephant whisperer Lawrence Anthony died in March of 2012, an entire herd of elephants arrived at his home to mourn him.

90. Ostriches have eyes bigger than their heads.

91. If gorillas take human birth control pills, it will have the same effects on them.

92. Koalas can sleep up to eighteen to twenty two hours a day, whereas a giraffe only needs about two.

93. Fleas can jump over eighty times their own height.

94. Rhinoceros beetles can carry 850 times their weight, which is the equivalent of an average human carrying sixty five tons.

95. The black mamba is regarded as one of the deadliest snakes in the world. It can move up to speeds of eighteen feet (5.5 meters) per second and its bite can kill a human in less than an hour.

96. Woodpeckers are able to peck twenty times per second or around 8,000 to 12,000 pecks per day without ever getting a headache.

97. Sea otters hold hands when they sleep so they don't drift away from each other.

98. Most cats don't like to drink water if it's too close to their food source. Always keep your cat's water and food supply separate so they don't get dehydrated.

99. Jellyfish and lobsters are biologically immortal.

100. Cows have best friends and can be stressed when separated from them.

101. Cats don't meow to each other, they meow to get the attention of humans.

102. Snails have the ability to regrow an eye if it's cut off.

103. A penguin has the ability to jump six feet (1.8 meters) out of the water with no aid.

104. Honey badgers have been known to eat porcupines and poisonous snakes, raid bee hives for honey, kidnap baby cheetahs, and steal food from hungry lions.

105. Beaver eyelids are transparent so they can see through them as they swim underwater.

106. Adult cats don't have enough lactase enzyme to digest the lactose from milk making them lactose intolerant.

107. Koi fish can live for centuries. The oldest Koi to have ever lived was one named Hanako that lived for 225 years before it died.

108. A blue whale can consume 480 million calories of food in a single dive.

109. Ants go to war just like humans and they can, in fact, strategize by doing things like sending out the weaker ants to fight first.

110. A giraffe's tongue is eight inches (twenty one centimeters) long.

111. It would take 1.2 million mosquitoes sucking once each to completely drain the blood in a human adult.

112. Lions have the loudest roar of any animal reaching 114 decibels at a distance of about 3.2 feet (one meter). It can be heard from over two miles (three kilometers) away.

113. Sloths can live up to thirty years and spend fifteen to eighteen hours a day sleeping.

114. When the silk of a spider is stored in its body, it's actually liquid; it only hardens and becomes solid when it leaves the spider's glands and comes into contact with the air.

115. Mosquitoes don't just bite you and suck your blood, they urinate on you before flying off.

116. The largest living beings ever to have lived on Earth are blue whales. Their tongues alone can weigh as much as an elephant and their hearts as much as a car.

117. Humans have the largest brain in terms of brain to body ratio. The animal with the biggest brain overall is a sperm whale weighing in at seventeen pounds (seven kilograms).

118. Besides the crocodile's belly and top of its head, the rest of the skin is bulletproof.

119. In 2001, a lion cub, bear cub, and tiger cub were found abandoned in a drug dealer's basement. They were soon adopted by a sanctuary and have lived together ever since.

120. There's a chimpanzee in a Russian zoo named Zhora that became addicted to booze and smoking after too many visitors began giving him alcoholic treats and cigarettes. In 2001, the chimp actually had to be sent to rehab to be treated for his addictions.

121. In 2006, a rare grizzly and polar bear hybrid species was confirmed in Canada called "pizzly bears" or "grolar bears." Global warming is causing polar bears habitats to melt so they find shelter elsewhere and end up mating with grizzlies.

122. Crocodiles cannot stick out their tongues or chew.

123. In order to drink, giraffes have to spread their almost 6.5 feet (two meter) long legs apart just to get close enough to the water.

124. Bed bugs survive longer in beds that are made, so scientists actually suggest that you leave your bed unmade once in a while as it ends up being healthier for you.

125. Pandas are the national animals of China. They are also only found in this country, and if you happen to see one in another country, they're on loan there.

126. A grizzly bear's jaw strength is so powerful that it could crush a bowling bowl with it.

127. A leopon is a hybrid animal cross between a male leopard and a lioness.

128. Sand tiger shark embryos fight each other to the death within the mother's womb until there's one survivor, which is the one that gets to be born.

129. There is an insect called the "assassin bug" which wears its victim's corpse as armor.

130. There was a golden haired Tibetan Mastiff puppy which sold for twelve million yuan, or two million dollars, making it the most expensive dog in the world.

131. Unlike many other members of the cat family, tigers actually enjoy water and can swim well. They often soak in streams or pools of water to cool off.

132. The skin of a honey badger is so thick that it can withstand machete blows, arrows, and spears. The only sure way to kill one is by using a club or a gun.

133. Dolphins don't drink seawater as it makes them ill or could even potentially kill them. Instead they get all their liquids from the food that they eat.

134. There are giant hornets in Japan with venom so strong that it can melt human skin.

135. Rabbits are able to sleep with their eyes open. They go into a trance-like state, which makes them only half asleep. The advantage of this is that, in the wild, it allows them to be more alert and get away from predators in a hurry.

136. It takes twelve bees a lifetime of work to create a teaspoon of honey.

137. There used to be horse sized ducks called "dromornithidae" roaming around present day Australia 50,000 years ago.

138. Camels have three eyelids that protects them from the rough winds in deserts.

139. Due to the placement of a donkey's eyes, it can see all four of its feet at all times.

140. Slugs have tentacles, blowholes, and thousands of teeth.

141. In praying mantises, 25% of all sexual encounters result in the death of the male as the female begins by ripping the male's head off.

142. The loneliest animal in the world is a male whale in the North Pacific which can't find a mate due to the way it communicates. The whale's frequency is on another level and can't be heard by other whales.

143. Depending on the species of sharks, they can either give birth to live young or lay eggs.

144. A cockroach can live up to several weeks without its head. It only dies due to hunger.

145. A man in Wisconsin took a photo containing three albino deer in the woods. The chances of this happening is one in seventy nine billion.

146. An elephant drinks thirty four gallons (130 liters) of water a day.

147. Skunks have muscles next to their scent glands that allow them to spray their fluids accurately up to ten feet (three meters) away.

148. There are fifty different types of kangaroos.

149. Between the 1600's and 1800's, lobsters were known as the cockroaches of the sea. They were fed to prisoners and servants and were used as fish bait.

150. There is a super tiny species of antelope called the "Dick-Dick," named after the sound they make when alarmed.

151. Termites are currently being researched by scientists at UConn and Caltech as possible renewable energy sources. They can produce up to half a gallon (two liters) of hydrogen by ingesting a single sheet of paper, making them one of the planet's most efficient bio-reactors.

152. In Japan, there are owl cafes where you can play with live owls while enjoying a drink or meal.

153. Cats are one of the only animals that domesticate themselves and approach humans on their own terms.

154. When ants die, they secrete a chemical that tells other ants to move the body to a sort of burial ground. If this chemical is sprayed on a live ant, other ants will treat it as a dead ant, regardless of what it does.

155. Australia is home to the golden silk orb weave spiders, arachnids that are so big that they can eat entire foot and a half (half meter) long snakes.

156. There was a goat in Utah named Freckles that was implanted with spider genes as an embryo and it's now known as the Spider Goat. She produces spider silk proteins in her milk, which is used to make bio-steel, a material stronger than Kevlar.

157. There is an insect called "the tree lobster" which is almost the size of a human hand. They can only be found in one place, on the huge mountainous remains of an old volcano called "Ball's Island" off the coast of Australia.

158. Naked mole rats are one of the only animals to not get cancer.

159. Crocodiles don't have sweat glands. In order to cool themselves down, they keep their jaws open.

160. Crows have the ability to recognize human faces and even hold grudges against the ones they don't like.

161. Jaguars in the wild are known for frequently getting high by eating hallucinogenic roots, which also increase their senses for hunting.

162. Prairie dogs say hello with kisses.

163. The smallest poisonous frog is only ten millimeters in length and it secretes a toxic poison from its skin as a defense mechanism.

164. A scorpion can hold its breath underwater for up to six days.

165. There's a fish called the black dragon fish that looks very similar to the creature from the Alien movies.

166. The reason birds fly in a "V" formation is to save energy due to wind resistance. The birds take turns being in the front and fall to the back when they're tired.

167. The African driver ant can produce three to four million eggs every twenty five days.

168. Polar bears evolved from brown bears somewhere in the vicinity of Britain and Ireland 150,000 years ago.

169. The fastest land animal is the cheetah which has a recorded speed of seventy five miles (120 kilometers) per hour.

170. A jellyfish has no ears, eyes, nose, brain, or heart.

171. If two rats were left alone in an enclosed area with enough room, they can multiply to a million within eighteen months.

172. Crabs are able to regenerate their legs and claws to 95% of their original size.

173. A camel can drink fifty three gallons (200 liters) of water in three minutes.

174. Male puppies will let female puppies win when they play, even though they are physically more powerful, to encourage them to play more.

175. An Indiana state prison allows murderers to adopt cats in their cells to help teach them love and compassion for other living things.

176. The infinite monkey theorem states that a monkey hitting keys at random on a typewriter for an infinite amount of time will eventually type out any given text, including the complete works of William Shakespeare.

177. Cockroaches were here 120 million years before the dinosaurs.

178. The most popular animal for a pet is freshwater fish. Next comes the cat followed by the dog.

179. Baboons in the wild have been known to kidnap puppies and raise them as pets.

180. The smallest known reptile in the world is the Brookesia micra, which is so small it can stand on the head of a match.

181. In Moscow, stray dogs have learned to commute from the suburbs to the city, scavenge for food, then catch the train home in the evening.

182. There was an orangutan named Fu Manchu who was repeatedly able to escape from his cage at the Henry Doorly Zoo in Nebraska. It was found that he was using a key that he fashioned out of a piece of wire. The reason he was able to do it so many times and kept getting away with it was because every time the zookeeper's inspected him, he would hide the key in his mouth.

183. Pigs are physically incapable to look up into the sky.

184. There are over 1,200 different species of bats in the world, and contrary to popular belief, none of them are blind. Bats can hunt in the dark using echolocation, which means they use echoes of self-produced sounds bouncing off objects to help them navigate.

185. In 2006, a study done by Alex Thornton and Katherine McAuliffe at Cambridge University showed how adult meerkats teach their youngest pups how not to be stung by scorpions, one of their main sources of prey. First, they bring dead scorpions to the pups; then they bring ones that are alive but injured; and, eventually, they work their way up to live prey.

186. Most of the camels in Saudi Arabia are imported from Australia.

187. China is home to half of the pig population on earth.

188. There are 1.2 million species documented in existence today, however, scientists estimate the number to be somewhere around 8.7 million. Due to extinction, however, we may never know the exact number.

189. Grasshoppers have ears in the sides of their abdomen.

190. There are miniature wolves in the Middle East that only reach about thirty pounds (six kilograms). In comparison, the largest wolves in the world found in Canada, Russia, and Alaska can reach up to 175 pounds (eighty kilograms).

191. There's a dog named Faith that was born with no front legs but learned to walk on its hind legs. The dog and its owner both travel to military hospitals to demonstrate that even a dog with a severe disability can live a full life.

192. There's a thirty four year old chimpanzee named Kanzi that not only knows how to start a fire and cook food, but knows how to make omelets for himself.

193. There is a lake in the country of Palau called "Jellyfish Lake" where jellyfish have evolved without stingers. These golden jellyfish are completely harmless to humans and you can even swim with them.

194. In 1997, a seventeen year old Merino sheep named Shrek, in New Zealand, ran away and hid in a cave for seven years. When he was finally found in 2004, he had gone unsheared for so long that he had accumulated sixty pounds (twenty seven kilograms) of wool on his body, the equivalent to make twenty suits.

195. Mike, the Headless Chicken, was a famous chicken from 1945 that was beheaded by a farmer for his dinner but continued to live for another eighteen full months.

196. Lobsters taste with their feet. The tiny bristles inside a lobster's little pincers are their equivalent to human taste buds.

197. ManhattAnts are an ant species unique to New York City. Biologists found them in a specific 14-block strip of the city.

198. All dogs are banned from Antarctica since April 1994. This ban was made because of the concern that dogs might spread diseases to seals.

Art & Artists

199. A Dutch artist discovered a way to create clouds in the middle of a room by carefully balancing humidity, lighting, and temperature. He uses this regularly in his artwork.

200. Xylography is the art of engraving on wood.

201. The well-known Leonardo da Vinci was a huge lover of animals. In fact, he was a vegetarian and was also known to buy birds from markets only to set them free.

202. A Mexican artist created an underwater sculpture series that double as art and an artificial reef.

203. There is a method of art called "tree shaping" where living trees are manipulated to create forms of art.

204. The singing tree is a wind powered sound sculpture located in Burnley, England, and was designed by architects Mike Tonkin and Anna Liu. Each time you sit under it, you'll hear a melody played depending on the wind for that day.

205. The Mona Lisa has no eyelashes or eyebrows.

206. In 1961, Italian artist Piero Manzoni filled ninety tin cans of his own feces, called them "Artist's sh*t," and sold them according to their equivalent weight in gold.

207. In China, there is a 233 foot (seventy one meter) tall stone statue built of Buddha that was constructed over 1,200 years ago.

208. The famous painter Salvador Dali would avoid paying the bill at restaurants by drawing on the back of his checks. He knew the owner wouldn't want to cash the checks as the drawings would be too valuable.

209. There's an artist named Scott Wade who is famous for creating dust art on dirty cars using only his fingers and a brush.

210. In the Curve Gallery at the Barbican Center in London, there's something called "the rain room" where through the use of sensors, rain falls everywhere in the room except for where you're walking.

211. Instead of using spray cans, some artists create semi-permanent images on walls or other places by removing dirt from a surface. It's known as reverse graffiti or clean tagging.

212. There's a Turkish artist named Esref Armagan who is blind, yet taught himself to write and paint and has been doing so on his own for the last thirty five years.

213. In Mexico, artists like painters, sculptors, and graphic artists can pay their taxes by donating pieces of artwork that they create to the government.

214. In 2006, artist Kim Graham and a group of twenty five volunteers spent fifteen days using entirely non-toxic recycled paper products to create a twelve foot (3.7 meter) tall paper mache tree doll.

215. There's an artist named Brian Lai that has the unique ability to draw in negatives.

216. The Terracotta Army is a collection of more than 8,000 clay soldiers, chariots, and horses that took around thirty seven years to make. They were buried with the Emperor in 210 B.C. with the purpose of protecting him in his afterlife.

217. Michelangelo wrote a poem about how much he hated painting the Sistine Chapel.

218. Eight of the ten largest statues in the world are of Buddhas.

219. The three wise monkeys actually have names. The see no evil monkey is named Mizaru, the hear no evil monkey is named Mikazaru, and the speak no evil monkey is named Mazaru.

Bizare

220. In London, there's a public toilet encased in a glass cube that's made entirely of one-way glass where you can see passersby, but they can't see you.

221. It's possible to hire an evil clown to terrorize your son or daughter for an entire week before their birthday. For a fee, artist Dominic Deville will increasingly pursue your child and leave scary notes, texts, and phone calls, and ultimately attack your child on their birthday by smashing a cake in their face.

222. In response to China's worsening air pollution, a Chinese millionaire started selling cans of fresh air for the price of eighty cents a can. Incredibly, he made over six million dollars.

223. The longest someone has stayed awake continuously is 265 hours, which was in 1964 by a high school student.

224. There are now snuggery services where you can hire someone to snuggle with you for $60 per hour.

225. In Switzerland, if you fail your practical driver's license three times, you are required to consult an official psychologist to assess the reason for your previous failures before you're allowed to retake the exam.

226. There is a Japanese practice known

as "forest bathing" where you just hang out around trees. It's proven to lower blood pressure, heart rate, reduce stress, boost your immune system, and increase your overall well being.

227. You are not allowed to flush the toilet after 10 p.m. in Switzerland. Other bizarre things you can't do in this country are: using a high-pressure power hose on your car, hiking naked, hanging out laundry, cutting your grass, or recycling on Sundays. Some random things you must do in this country are paying tax on your dog if you have one and having a buddy for pets such as guinea pigs, gold fish, and budgies so they have company.

228. Outside of Watson Lake, Yukon, there's a Sign Post Forest. It was started back in 1942 when a soldier named Carl K. Lindley was injured while working on the Alcan Highway. He was taken to the Army air station in Watson Lake to recover, and while he was there, he was homesick, so he decided to place a sign of Danville, Illinois, his hometown. Tourists continued the practice and there are currently about 72,000 signs from around the world.

Books, Comic Books & Writers

229. The creator of Sherlock Holmes, Sir Arthur Conan Doyle, helped to get two falsely accused men out of prison after solving their already closed cases.

230. There are Wizard of Oz-inspired shoes that get you home when clicking your heels together using a GPS system. Side note: the author of the novel created part of the name of the book when he was looking at a filing cabinet and saw the letters o-z.

231. There are three books in the Harvard University that are bound in human skin.

232. Yale has a rare book and manuscript library that has no windows, but instead it has walls made entirely of translucent marble that prevents the books from being exposed to direct sunlight.

233. Author J. K. Rowling wrote the final chapter of the last Harry Potter book in 1990, seven years before the release of the first book.

234. The children's book "Where the Wild Things Are" was originally titled "Where the Wild Horses Are," however, the author and illustrator Maurice Sendak ended up changing the name of it after he realized he had no idea how to draw horses.

235. The best selling book in history is the Bible with five billion copies in sales.

236. DC Comics published an alternate universe where Bruce Wayne dies instead of his parents. In it, Thomas Wayne becomes Batman and Martha Wayne goes crazy and becomes the Joker.

237. The first ever occurrence of the name "Wendy" was in Peter Pan. This name had never been registered before the book's publication.

238. There is an ancient book called "The Voynich" from the Italian Renaissance that no one can read.

239. In 1994, Leonardo da Vinci's Codex Leicester notebook was bought by Bill Gates for $30.8 million. Besides adding the item to his personal collection, he used it to also help promote Windows Vista's launch, by using a program called Turning the Pages 2.0 that would let people browse through virtual versions of the notebook.

240. In 1983, Marvel published a comic called "Your Friendly Neighborhood Spider Ham." The character was a spider pig named Peter Porker.

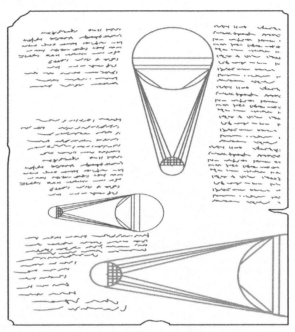

241. There's a book that exists called "Everything Men know about Woman" that has 100 pages all of which are blank.

242. In 1975, Professor Jack Hetherington from Michigan State University added his cat as a co-author to a theoretical paper that he had been working on. He did this because he mistakenly used words like "we" and "our" in the paper and didn't feel like revising it.

243. There is a Russian published novel called the "Last

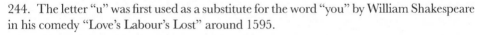

Ringbearer" which retells the Lord of the Rings from the perspective of Sauron.

244. The letter "u" was first used as a substitute for the word "you" by William Shakespeare in his comedy "Love's Labour's Lost" around 1595.

245. In 1996, DC and Marvel Comics published a crossover series where Wolverine and Batman were made into one character called "Dark Claw" or "Logan Wayne."

246. Although the Holy Bible is available for free at many places of worship, it is the most stolen book in the world.

247. In the original version of "The Little Mermaid" by Hans Christian Anderson, Ariel doesn't marry the prince. She actually marries someone else and she dies.

248. In the early versions of the "Little Red Riding Hood," the girl cannibalizes her own grandmother and then gets eaten by the wolf after getting into bed with him.

249. The original script of Lord of the Rings was one long saga, but it was split into three books for the publishers to make more money.

250. The code of Hammurabi is a well preserved Babylonian law that dates all the way back to 1772 B.C. which had progressive laws in it such as minimum wage and the right to be a free man. It was written well before the Bible.

251. Adult coloring books are becoming a huge trend and publishers actually struggle to

keep up with demand. The books seem to be a way to successfully reduce stress and relieve anxiety. They are even used as rehabilitation aids for patients who are recovering from strokes.

252. In the novel Forrest Gump that the movie was based upon, Forrest goes into space with NASA but upon returning, he crash lands on an island full of cannibals and only manages to survive by beating the head cannibal every day at chess.

253. Journalist Sara Bongiorni and her family attempted to live without Chinese-made goods for an entire year and found it almost impossible. They documented their experience in a book called "A year without 'made in China'."

254. Richard Klinkhamer, a Dutch crime writer, wrote a suspicious book on seven ways to kill your spouse, one year after his wife disappeared. He became a celebrity and spent the next decade hinting that he murdered her, and in 2000, it turned out that he really had after her skeleton was discovered at his former residence.

255. The reason Harry Potter and the Goblet of Fire is longer than the first three books is because author J.K. Rowling made a plot hole half way through and had to go back and fix it.

256. The Old Testament was written over the course of 1,000 years whereas the New Testament was written within seventy five years.

257. Before the renaissance era, three quarters of all books in the world were in Chinese.

258. J.K. Rowling is the first author to reach billionaire status. She also holds the status of losing her billionaire status due to giving away most of her money.

Buildings & Massive Monuments

259. It took over twenty two centuries to complete the Great Wall of China. It was built, rebuilt, and extended by many imperial dynasties and kingdoms. The wall exceeds 12,000 miles (20,000 kilometers).

260. There's a building in London called the "Walkie Talkie Building" that's shaped in such a way that it reflects sunlight like a giant magnifying glass, literally melting cars on the street below.

261. The Lego-Brucke is a concrete bridge in Germany that has become famous for being painted to look like a giant bridge made of Lego blocks.

262. The world's largest tree house is located in Tennessee and is ten stories, 10,000 square feet (900 square meters), took eleven years to make, but it cost only $12,000 since it was made of mostly recycled materials.

263. The Pyramid of Giza was built from two million stone bricks with stones weighing more than two tons each. It was built over the course of eighty five years.

264. There is a sixteen story office building in Osaka, Japan, called "The Gate Tower Building" that has an entire highway that passes through the fifth, sixth, and seventh floors of the structure.

265. In 2014, Budapest broke the world record for the tallest Lego tower ever built. Made of 450,000 colorful bricks, topped with a large Hungarian Rubik's cube, the structure stands at 114 feet (thirty four meters) tall in front of Saint Stephen's Basilica.

266. In 2013, Vietnam unveiled a steel bridge that's shaped like a dragon that literally shoots fire out of its mouth; it's called the "Dragon Bridge."

267. The world's largest privately constructed nuclear fallout shelter is the "Ark Two." It began being built in the 1980's by Bruce Beach just north of Toronto. It's ten thousand square feet (929 square meters) and is composed of forty two school buses mixed with concrete, runs on internal generators, and has its own chapel, decontamination room, and radio station.

268. Some buildings in the US, such as the White House, the Empire State Building, the Sears Building, and the Dodger Stadium, are so large that they have their own zip codes.

269. Even though the Eiffel Tower is stable on its four legs, it is known to move. The 900 foot (320 meter) structure can sway if the wind is strong enough or expand seven inches (17.7 centimeters) if the sun is hot enough.

270. The Burj Khalifa is the tallest building in the world standing at 2,700 feet (830 meters). Construction started in 2004 and took four years to complete.

271. Until its demolition in 2012, 1% of Greenland's entire population lived in one apartment building called "Blok P."

272. The most expensive thing ever created is the International Space Station at a cost of $160 billion and rising as new sections are added.

273. There is a skywalk on Tianmen Mountain, in China, which is a 200 feet (sixty one meters) long with 8.2 feet (2.5 meter) thick glass. The bridge is so high up that it allows visitors to look down on the peaks of smaller mountains below.

274. The "Intempo" skyscraper in Spain has forty seven floors but no elevators.

275. The first building to have more than 100 floors was the Empire State Building.

Cool

276. Thailand celebrates a festival each year named Loy Krathong where they release thousands upon thousands of sky lanterns filling up the night sky as tradition.

277. When Stephen Hawking was asked what his IQ was, he responded: "I have no idea, but people who boast about their IQ are losers."

278. There is a cruise ship named "The World" where residents permanently live as it travels around the globe. An apartment on board costs $2 million while you fork out $270,000 a year for maintenance costs.

279. China is building a car free city called "The Great City" that will house 80,000 people. It'll use 48% less energy, 58% less water, produce 89% less landfill waste, and 60% less carbon dioxide than a conventional city of the same size.

280. Harris Rosen was a self-made millionaire that decided to fund a small neighborhood named "Tangelo Park." Harris helped reduce the crime rate by over 50% and increased graduation for high school from 20% to 100% by giving everyone free child care and scholarships.

281. The Burj Al Arab Hotel in Dubai offers their guests a twenty four karat gold iPad for the duration of their stay.

282. There's a vending machine in Singapore that dispenses a Coke to anybody that hugs it.

283. Newman's Own Food has donated 100% of its post-tax profits to charity since 1982, totaling over $400 million.

284. There's a resort in Japan called the "Tomamu Resort" that's located on top of a mountain peak that allows patrons to view a sea of fluffy white clouds beneath them.

285. In the UK, people that reach their 100th birthday or their 60th wedding anniversary are sent a personalized card from the Queen.

286. The oldest hotel in the world is the "Nishiyama Onsen Keiunkan" in Japan. It was founded in 705 A.D. and has had fifty two generations of the same family operating it since it was founded.

287. In Australia, there is a bookstore where books are wrapped in paper with short descriptions. This way they are buying a book without judging it by its cover.

288. There is man named Tim Harris with Down syndrome who owns and runs a restaurant in Albuquerque, New Mexico, called "Tim's Place," where they serve breakfast, lunch, and hugs. It's the only known restaurant owned by a person with Down syndrome and it's known as the world's friendliest restaurant.

289. Dalhousie University in Halifax, Nova Scotia, has opened a puppy room where students can go play with puppies to relieve stress.

290. Former billionaire Chuck Feeney has given away over 99% of his $6.3 billion to help underprivileged kids go to college resulting in him having $2 million left.

291. Every factory employee at Ben and Jerry's gets to take home three pints of ice cream every day.

292. A 102 year old man named Alan Swift, from Connecticut, drove the same 1928 Rolls Royce Phantom 1 for close to seventy seven years before he died in 2005.

293. In 2005, Johan Eliasch, a Swedish millionaire, bought a plot of land almost half a million acres big in the Amazon rainforest just so he could preserve it.

294. The largest indoor water park in the world is the Seagaia Ocean Dome in Japan at 900 feet (300 meters) long and 328 feet (100 meters) wide.

295. In 2011, Barack Obama became the first president to have ever brewed beer in the White House; the beer was named "White House Honey Ale."

296. In Finland, when you earn your PhD, you're given a doctoral hat that looks like a top hat as well as a doctoral sword.

297. There's a school called "Ordinary Miracle" in Yoshkar-Ola, Russia, that looks like a fairy-tale castle. A man named Sergey Mamaev had built it for his wife who wanted to teach at a school that children would actually want to go to.

298. The small pocket in your large pocket of your jeans was originally meant for your

pocket watch.

299. In March 2013, a man got a tattoo of the word Netflix on his side for which, after tweeting a picture of it to the company, gave him a free year of service.

300. At the Crocosaurus Cove Aquarium in Australia, there's a popular tourist attraction called the "Cage of Death" which allows you to get up close and personal with giant crocodiles.

301. There is a luxury hotel in Fiji called "Poseidon Resort" where, for $15,000 a week, you can sleep on the ocean floor and even get a button to feed the fish right outside your window.

302. Photographer Andrew Suryono was under heavy rain when he noticed an orangutan using a leaf for shelter. He quickly took the shot that made him earn an honorable mention in the 2015 National Geographic photo contest.

303. There's a Canadian toy company called "Child's Own Studios" that turns children's drawings into stuffed animals.

304. There's an alarm clock named Clocky that has wheels and runs away and hides if you don't get out of bed on time.

305. Norway allows any student from anywhere in the world to study at their public universities completely free of charge.

306. Tourists throw over a million euros into the Trevi Fountain in Rome each year. The city uses this money to fund a supermarket for the poor.

307. Henry Ford was the first industrial giant to give his workers both Saturday and Sunday off in hopes that it would encourage more leisure use of vehicles, hence popularizing the concept of the weekend.

308. Lamborghinis, Bentleys, Aston Martins are all used as police cars in Dubai.

309. The "Santa Rita do Sapucai" prison in Brazil allows its inmates to pedal exercise bikes to power lights in a nearby town in exchange for reduced sentences. For every sixteen hours that they pedal, one day is reduced from their sentence.

310. In 2012, a man in China named Zao Phen had 9,999 red roses sewn into a dress for his girlfriend before asking for her hand in marriage.

311. There is a house sized shoe box in Amsterdam that is an Adidas store.

312. Sweden recycles so well that it actually has to import garbage from Norway in order to fuel its waste to power energy plants.

313. There is a swing at the edge of a cliff in Ecuador that has no safety measures. It hangs from a tree house overlooking an active volcano called the "Swing at the End of the World."

314. In the University of Victoria in British Columbia, Canada, you can take a course in the science of Batman. It uses the caped crusader to explain the human condition and the limitations of the human mind and body.

315. In Chongqing, China, there is a zoo called the "Lehe Ledu Wildlife Zoo" where visitors are placed in cages instead of the animals. The cages are stalked by lions and tigers, so the guests are warned to keep their fingers and hands inside the cage at all times.

316. On the first day of school, children in Germany, Austria, and the Czech Republic are given a cardboard cone filled with toys and sweets known as a Schultute.

317. The deepest indoor pool is located in Brussels, Belgium, named "Nemo 33" at 108 feet (thirty two meters) deep.

318. The WWOOF, or the Worldwide Opportunities on Organic Farms, is an international program that allows you to travel the world with free food and accommodation in exchange for volunteer work.

319. In 2007, a twin was born thirty four minutes after her brother, but because of a daylight savings time adjustment, she was actually born twenty six minutes before her brother.

320. George Barbe, a billionaire from Alabama, had several life sized dinosaurs built and placed over his ten thousand acre home in 1991.

321. In 2013, a company called "Limite Zero" created a 2,300 foot (720 meter) international zip-line between Spain and Portugal.

322. It's estimated that there are approximately three million shipwrecks on the ocean floor worth billions of dollars in value and treasure.

323. Mark Zuckerberg has signed the "Giving Pledge," a campaign created by Warren Buffet and Bill Gates which encourages wealthy people to contribute the majority of their wealth to

philanthropic causes.

324. In 1993, Dave Thomas, the founder of Wendy's, went back to high school to earn his GED decades after dropping out because he was worried kids may see his success as an excuse to also drop out of school.

325. The Technical University of Munich built slides four stories high to help their students get to class quickly instead of them having to take the stairs.

326. The Canadian post office has assigned a postal code of H, O, H, O, H, O, to the North Pole where anyone can send a letter to Santa Claus. Every year more than one million letters are addressed to Santa Claus, each of which are answered in the same language they were written in.

327. Tap water in Canada is regulated to a higher standard than bottled water.

328. In Siberia, there's a toilet located 8,500 feet (2,591 meters) above sea level at the top of the Altai Mountains. It serves the workers of an isolated weather station and is known as the world's loneliest toilet.

329. On Marajo Island, Brazilian police ride water buffalos when they patrol the streets instead of horses.

Countries & Cities

330. In Cuba, it's legally mandated that government vehicles must pick up any hitchhikers that they see.

331. The heaviest drinkers in the world are in Belarus with 17.5 liters consumed per capita every year.

332. The distance between Africa and Europe is only fourteen miles (twenty three kilometers.) There are talks of constructing a bridge between the two continents called the "Strait of Gibraltar Crossing."

333. The country with the most millionaires is the US. The country with the most billionaires is China.

334. There's a village in the Netherlands named Giethoorn that has no roads and can only be accessed by boats, having the nickname "Venice of the Netherlands."

335. Poveglia Island, in Italy, is considered one of the most haunted places in the world as it was the site of wars, a dumping ground for plague victims, and an insane asylum. In fact, it's so haunted that the Italian government has forbidden public access to it.

336. France is the only country in Europe to be completely self-sufficient in basic food production.

337. In the country of Turkilometersenistan, water, gas, and electricity have all been free from the government since 1993.

338. The whole country of England is smaller than the state of Florida by over 10,000 square miles (26,000 square kilometers).

339. In an effort to fight obesity, the government from Mexico City offers a free subway ticket to each person who does ten squats. Currently, 70% of the adult population is overweight.

340. It has only snowed in Cuba once, back in March 12, 1857.

341. There are 158 verses in the national anthem of Greece making it the longest in the world. In comparison, the Canadian anthem only has four verses.

342. In Iceland, if you want to give your baby a name that's never been used before, you must go to the Icelandic Naming Committee.

343. In the city of Mackinac Island, Michigan, all motor vehicles including cars have been banned since 1898.

344. Geographically, China covers five different times zones, however, only one standard time zone within the country is used.

345. Citizens of Norway only pay half their taxes in November so they can have more money for Christmas.

346. The state of Illinois has banned exfoliating face washes because the microbeads in them are so small that they actually slip through the water treatment facilities and end up back in the water supply.

347. The Indonesian Ministry of Marine Affairs and Fisheries determined that a single manta ray, if caught and killed, is worth anywhere from $40-$500. They also determined, however, that if kept alive, they're worth up to a million dollars in tourism revenue. They created the largest manta ray sanctuary in the world.

348. The longest street in the world is Yonge Street in Canada which is 1,178 miles (1,896 kilometers) long.

349. There is no explanation why there are no mosquitoes in Iceland.

350. Cuba has the highest doctor to patient ratio in the world.

351. The highest divorce rate in the world by country is Luxembourg at 87%. The lowest is India with 1%.

352. 99.8% of Cubans can read and write making it one of the most literate countries in the world.

353. Indonesia has more than 17,000 islands.

354. There are more vegetarians in India than in any other country.

355. If you left Tokyo by plane at 7 a.m., you would arrive at Honolulu at approximately 8 p.m. the previous day due to the nineteen hour difference in time zone.

356. The country with the longest coastline on Earth is Canada.

357. Since 1979, no one has been reported to die from a confirmed spider bite in Australia.

Deaths by spiders actually occur more when you are surprised by them, e.g. when you are driving.

358. The first country where a woman was allowed to vote was New Zealand in 1893.

359. In 2013, Google sent a lone employee to an abandoned Japanese island called "Gunkjima" to map it for Google Street View. The island was once the most densely populated island in the world, but it's now completely abandoned.

360. Switzerland has enough nuclear shelters to accommodate 114% of its population. It's a legal requirement for the Swiss to have a protected place that can be reached quickly from their place of residence.

361. Iceland has no army and has been recognized as the most peaceful country in the world for the last six years. In comparison, the UK is forty four, and the US sits at 100.

362. There are zero rivers in Saudi Arabia.

363. There is a city called "Rome" in each continent.

364. In Egypt, actors were once not allowed to testify in court as they were seen as professional liars.

365. Over 90% of the Australian population live within fifty kilometers of its coastline.

366. In the state of Nevada, public intoxication is not only explicitly legal, but it's illegal for any city or town to pass a law making it illegal.

367. In Churchill Manitoba, Canada, it's illegal to lock your car in case someone needs to hide from one of the 900 polar bears in the area.

368. The Okinawa Island in Japan has over four hundred people living above the age of 100 and it's known as the healthiest place on earth.

369. Germany was the first country to realize the link between smoking and lung cancer. Hitler was even one of the first ones to lead the anti-smoking campaign.

370. The Philippine island of Luzon contains a lake that contains an island that contains a lake that contains another island.

371. License plates in the Canadian Northwest territories are shaped like polar bears.

372. The largest cemetery in the world is the Wadi Al-Salaam Cemetery located in Iraq. It's two miles (six kilometers) squared and it's so big that it's unknown how many bodies are in there. It's estimated to be in the millions and half a million more get added each year.

373. There's a natural gas vent in Iraq known as the Eternal Fire that's been burning for over 4,000 years.

374. There is a city being created in the Arab Emirates right now that will be entirely reliant on renewable energy sources with a zero waste ecology.

375. Ethiopia is currently in the year 2006 because there are thirteen months in its year.

376. The City of New York paid $5 million in 1853 for the land that is Central Park, which is now worth $530 billion.

377. For years, an Indian man named Rajesh Kumar Sharma has been teaching slum children who live under a local metro bridge. Five days a week for two hours a day, he leaves his job at the general store to teach over 140 kids who would otherwise not be able to learn.

378. The pollution in Beijing is so bad they have come up with a term called the "Beijing Cough."

379. Almost a tenth of all Chinese have the last name "Wang" which translates to king.

380. If New York City was its own country and the NYPD was its army, it would be the 20th best funded army in the world just behind Greece and ahead of North Korea.

381. In North Korea, it is currently the year 109 because their calendar is based on the birth of Kim Il-Sung, the founder of North Korea.

382. There are still thirty million people living in caves in China.

383. The Vatican City is home to the world's only ATM that gives instructions in Latin.

384. France was the first country to introduce the registration plate on August 14, 1893.

385. The biggest island in the world is Greenland as Australia is a continent.

386. China produces the most pollution in the world contributing 30% of all the countries total. These come from coal, oil, and natural gases.

387. The most visited city in the world is Bangkok, with twenty million people in 2018, followed by London and Paris.

388. The smallest country in the world is the Vatican which only has 0.22 square miles (0.44 square kilometers).

389. As of 2019, the country with the highest homicide rates is El Salvador with 82.84 homicides per 100,000 inhabitants per year, with a population of approximately six million people that equates to 5,000 people per year. The extremely high homicide rate in this country is marked by significant occurrence of gang-related crimes and juvenile delinquency.

390. "Fancy riding" on bikes is illegal in Illinois. That includes riding without hands or taking your feet off the pedals when you're on the street.

391. There are five countries in the world that don't have airports: Vatican City, San Marino, Monaco, Liechtenstein, and Andorra.

392. Nebraska's official state slogan is "Nebraska: Honestly, it's not for everyone."

393. The entire European Union is smaller than Canada alone. In fact, Canada is thirty three times bigger than Italy and fifteen times bigger than France.

Crimes, Drugs & Prison

394. In 1988, a woman named Jean Terese Keating disappeared while awaiting trial for drunkenly killing a woman in a car crash. She was arrested fifteen years later after bragging at a bar about having gotten away with the crime.

395. In the 1960's, Alcatraz was the only federal prison at the time to offer hot water showers for its inmates. The logic behind it was that prisoners who were acclimated to hot water would not be able to withstand the freezing waters of the San Francisco Bay during an escape attempt.

396. In the 1980's, the infamous kingpin Pablo Escobar was making so much money off of his drug cartel that he was spending $2,500 ($7,200 in today's money) every single month on rubber bands just to hold all of the cash.

397. During the early 1900's, French gangsters used a weapon called "Apache Revolver" that functioned as a revolver, a knife, and brass knuckles.

398. Colombia's underground drug cartel trades as much as $10 billion each year, more than the country's legal exports.

399. A psychologist named Timothy Leary was sent to jail in 1970 and given a series of tests to determine which jail he should be placed in. Since he designed many of the tests himself, he manipulated his answers so that he would be placed in a low security prison as a gardener and ended up escaping only eight months later.

400. The crime rate in Iceland is so low that the police there don't carry guns.

401. A quarter of the world's prisoners are locked up in the US.

402. In 2013, the Netherlands closed eight prisons due to the lack of criminals.

403. A French woman named Nadine Vaujour was so determined to get her husband out of jail that she learned how to fly a helicopter to get him out. She succeeded in picking him up off the roof, however, she was arrested shortly after.

404. Brazil's prisons offer their prisoners the chance to reduce their prison sentence by up to forty eight days a year for every book they read and write a report on.

405. In Italy, the richest business is the mafia that turns over $178 billion a year, which is 7% of the country's GDP.

406. In 2011, a man named Richard James Verone robbed a bank for $1 so that he could be sent to jail to receive free medical health care.

407. In 2008, it was discovered that a fifty six year old crime reporter named Vlado Taneski, who was reporting on gruesome murders, was the serial killer himself.

408. In 2006, the FBI planted a spy in a southern California mosque and disguised him as a radical Muslim in order to root out potential threats. The plan backfired when Muslims in the mosque ended up reporting him to the FBI for being a potentially dangerous extremist.

409. Many murder cases in Japan are declared suicides in order for police officers to save face and to keep crime statistics low.

410. In 1991, there was uncontrolled flooding that caused The Oceanos, a cruise ship, to start to sink. The captain and crew abandoned the ship first, leaving passengers on board without sounding the alarm. Moss Hills, an entertainer aboard the ship, used the radio to call mayday, and everyone was saved. The crew were charged with negligence.

Entertainment Industry

411. Walt Disney holds the record for the most Oscars won by any one person with a total of twenty two.

412. Steven Spielberg waited over ten years after being given the story of the Schindler's List to make the film, as he felt he wasn't mature enough to take on the subject.

413. The mother of Matt Groening, the creator of "The Simpsons," was named Marge Wiggum.

414. The song "Happy Birthday" is 120 years old and has a copyright to it. It's owned by Warner Chappell Music who insists that no one uses it; this is the reason you rarely hear it on TV shows or movies.

415. Bob Marley's last words to his son were: "Money can't buy you life."

416. Nemo makes an appearance in the movie "Monsters Inc." as a toy that Boo gives to Sully a full two years before the movie "Finding Nemo" came out. Pixar movies are infamous for being full of Easter eggs like this.

417. Justin Timberlake's mother was Ryan Gosling's legal guardian when he was a child.

418. Macklemore once worked at a juvenile detention center to help detainees express themselves by writing and creating rap lyrics.

419. Johnny Depp has a passion for playing guitar, playing with artists such as Marilyn Manson, Oasis, Aerosmith, and Eddie Vedder.

420. Lady Gaga stars in the Guinness World Records twelve times. One of them is for including the most product placements in a video.

421. Only a third of the snakes you see in the movie "Snakes on a Plane" were real.

422. In 2007, Joshua Bell, an award winning violinist and conductor, conducted an experiment where he pretended to be a street violinist and had over a thousand people pass him without stopping. He only collected $31 that day yet two days previously sold out to a theater where each seat cost $100. The violin he was playing with on the street was worth $3.5 million.

423. The Lion King was considered a small B movie during productions as all the top Disney animators were working on Pocahontas, which they considered an A movie.

424. Brad Pitt was banned from China for twenty years after his role in the film "Seven Years in Tibet."

425. Reed Hastings, the founder of Netflix, got the idea to start the site when he received a late fine of $40 on a VHS copy of Apollo 13. Reed also approached Blockbuster in 2005 offering to sell the company for $50 million which was turned down at the time. Today the company is worth over $9 billion.

426. Animal Planet aired a fake documentary about the existence of mermaids that convinced thousands of viewers twice, once in 2012 and once in 2013.

427. The American singer and songwriter Dolly Parton once entered a Dolly Parton lookalike contest for fun and ended up losing to a drag queen.

428. The Cookie Monster revealed in 2004 during a song that before he started eating cookies and became known as the "Cookie Monster," he was called "Sid."

429. Lotso, the bear from Toy Story 3, was originally supposed to be in the first movie, but the technology needed to create his fur wasn't available at the time so he got pushed back to the third film.

430. Insurance companies have blacklisted Jackie Chan and anyone else who works on his stunt team. This means that if anyone gets injured while on the set of a Jackie Chan movie, he has to pay for their recovery treatment.

431. National Geographic star Casey Anderson has a pet grizzly bear named Brutus. The bear was adopted in 2002 when he was a newborn cub, and in 2008, served as Casey's best man at his wedding.

432. Before Will Smith starred in the Fresh Prince of Bel-Air, he was on the verge of bankruptcy owing the government $2.8 million. For the first three seasons of the show, he had to pay 70% of his income.

433. Dressed up Disneyland characters never ever break character. They're even given special autograph training sessions so that they can always sign autographs in the style of the cartoon character they're playing.

434. Jim Cummings, the voice of Winnie the Pooh, would call up children's hospitals and talk to them in his Winnie voice to make them feel better.

435. Walt Disney was fired from Kansas City Star in 1919 because his editor said that he lacked imagination and had no good ideas.

436. The person who did the voice of Minnie Mouse, Russi Taylor, was married to Wayne Allowing, the voice of Mickey Mouse.

437. Snoop Dogg has a book published named Rolling Words that has lyrics of all his

songs that you can later rip out and use as rolling papers.

438. There's a restaurant in New Jersey owned by Bon Jovi where there are no fixed prices. Instead customers donate money or volunteer to pay for their meals.

439. Comedian Charlie Chaplan was given an honorary Oscar for his contribution to film in 1972, during the Forty-Fourth annual Academy Awards. During the event, he showed up in the United States after staying away for twenty years because he was labeled a communist. As he went to stage, he was welcomed with a twelve minute standing ovation from the audience and celebrities. This still stands as the longest Oscar in history.

440. In 1961, Mel Blanc, the voice of Bugs Bunny, was in a serious car accident that put him in a coma that he could not wake up from. Doctors began speaking directly to the characters that he voiced from which he would actually respond in their voices, and three weeks later he actually woke up.

441. "Sperm Race" was a show that aired in Germany in 2005 where twelve men donated their sperm to a lab. The doctors then observed the sperm race towards the egg and the winner received a new Porsche.

442. In the early 1990's, Michael Jackson tried to buy Marvel Comics so that he could play Spider Man in his own self-produced movie.

443. In 1939, the New York Times predicted that the television would fail because the average American family wouldn't have enough time to sit around and watch it.

444. If you could actually go to Hogwarts, it would cost approximately $40,000 a year.

445. In the Despicable Me movies, the gibberish that the minions speak is actually a functioning language written by the directors called "Minionese."

446. The original founders and owners of Macy's, Isidor and Ida Straus, both died on the Titanic. They were the old couple in the movie who went to sleep as the ship went down, which is what actually happened.

447. The creator of Peter Pan, J. M. Barrie, gave away the rights of the franchise to the Great Ormond Street Children's Hospital so that they could always collect royalties and fund the hospital.

448. The Prince Charles Cinema in London has volunteer ninjas that sneak up and hush anyone in the theater that's making noise or throwing things.

449. Cameron Diaz and Snoop Dogg both went to school together. Cameron even bought some weed off of Snoop once.

450. An employee at Pixar accidentally deleted a sequence of Toy Story 2 during

production. It would've taken a year to remake what was gone but, luckily, another employee had the whole thing backed up on a personal computer.

451. Space Jam is the highest grossing basketball movie of all time.

452. The Beast from Beauty and the Beast is a creature called a "Chimera" which has features from seven different animals.

453. The entire Pixar staff had to take a graduate class in fish biology before making Finding Nemo.

454. Arnold Schwarzenegger was paid $15 million in the second Terminator film where he only said 700 words of dialogue. At a cost by word basis, his famous line "Hasta la vista baby" cost over $85,000.

455. Twilight was rejected fourteen times before it was accepted.

456. Jackie Chan is an actor as well as a pop star in Asia; he has released twenty albums since 1984. He also sings the theme songs to his own movies.

457. All the characters in Toy Story only blink one eye at a time.

458. It would take over fifty million balloons to lift the average house off the ground like in the movie "Up."

459. In 1938, Walt Disney was awarded an honorary Oscar for Snow White. The statuette that he received came with seven mini-statuettes on a stepped base.

460. Before he was Iron Man, actor Robert Downey Junior was a notorious drug addict. He credits his sobriety to the fast food chain Burger King. In an interview with Empire magazine, he revealed that in 2003 he was driving a car full of drugs when he ordered a burger from Burger King that was so disgusting that he felt compelled to pull over, get out, and dump all of his drugs into the ocean.

461. If you rearrange the first letters of the main character's names in the movie Inception: Dom, Robert, Eames, Arthur, Mal, Saito, they spell "dreams."

462. Verne Troyer, the actor who plays Mini-me in the Austin Powers movies, had to do all his own stunts because at 2.7 feet (eighty one centimeters) tall, there was no stunt double his size that could fill in for him.

463. Bruce Lee's reflexes were so fast that he could snatch a quarter off of a person's open palm and replace it with a penny before the person could close their fist.

464. In the late 1990's, there was a Russian TV show called "The Intercept," where contestants had to steal a car. If they didn't get caught by the police in thirty five minutes, they got to keep the car, otherwise they were arrested.

465. Ryan Gosling was casted for the role of Noah in the movie "The Notebook" because the director wanted someone "not handsome."

466. The actor who plays Mr. Bean, Rowan Atkinson, once saved a plane from crashing after the pilot passed out, despite never having piloted a plane before.

467. There's a movie from 2010 called "Rubber" about a murderous car tire named Robert that rolls around killing people and blowing things up.

468. The average Game of Thrones episode costs $2 to $3 million to produce. That's two to three times what a typical network or cable show costs per episode.

469. Jackie Chan's son will receive none of his $130 million fortune as he's quoted saying: "If he's capable, he can make his own money. If he's not, then he'll just be wasting my money."

470. The monkey in "Hangover 2" is the same one seen in "Night at the Museum." His name is Crystal and he's featured in twenty five other movies as well. He was awarded the Poscar in 2015, which is an Oscar for animals.

471. In 2010, Johnny Depp responded to a letter from a nine year old girl named Beatrice Delap by actually showing up at her school in costume as Captain Jack Sparrow. She wrote asking that pirates help her stage a mutiny against her teachers.

472. Bob Marley was buried with his red Bison guitar, a Bible opened to Psalm 23, and a bud of marijuana.

473. The set used in the 2009 Sherlock Holmes film was reused as the house of Sirius Black in Harry Potter and the Order of the Phoenix.

474. The first ever ticket purchase to the first ever Comic Con in New York was by George R.R. Martin in 1964. He was the first of only thirty people there that day.

475. When Shakira was in the second grade, she was rejected from the school choir because her music teacher didn't think she could sing, and thought she sounded like a goat.

476. Before Scar got the scar on his face in "The Lion King," his name was Taka which means garbage in Swahili.

477. Before Sylvester Stallone sold the script for "Rocky," he was broke and had to sell his dog for $50. A week later he sold the script and bought his dog back for $3,000.

478. Jackie Chan's mother was a drug smuggler while his father was a spy. This is in fact how they met, when his father arrested his mother for smuggling opium.

479. George Lucas wanted the role of Mace Windu to originally go to Tupac, however, he died before he could give an audition and the role went to Samuel L. Jackson instead.

480. Kim Peek, the inspiration for the movie Rain Man, was born with significant brain damage. He's read over 12,000 books and remembers every single one of them. He's even able to read two pages at once, one with each eye.

481. In 2005, a documentary called "Reversal of Fortune" was filmed where film makers gave a homeless man named Ted Rodrigue $100,000 in cash and followed him around to see what he would do with the money. Less than six months later he was completely broke and back in the same place he was before it all started.

482. Oona Chaplin, the actress who plays Talisa in the Game of Thrones, is actually

Charlie Chaplin's granddaughter.

483. Zach Galifianakis was approached by Nike to be in their advertising after the success of The Hangover. During the conference call he broke the ice by asking: "So do you still have seven year olds making your stuff?"

484. When Jackie Chan was eighteen, he got into a street fight with bikers; shortly after he noticed a piece of bone sticking out of his knuckle. He spent an entire day trying to push it back in until he realized that it wasn't his bone but the other guy's tooth.

485. Five hundred stormtroopers were placed on the Great Wall of China by Disney to promote "Star Wars: The Force Awakens."

486. After the movie "Princess and the Frog" came out, more than fifty people were hospitalized with salmonella poisoning from kissing frogs.

487. Irmelin Indenbirken was pregnant and felt her baby kick when she was looking at a Leonardo da Vinci painting in Italy. She ended up naming her son "Leonardo" after the painter, and that's how Leonard DiCaprio got his name.

488. After being eliminated from the show Hell's Kitchen, the contestants are immediately taken to get psychiatric evaluations and then to a house where they are pampered with back rubs, haircuts, and manicures. This is because the experience on the show is so draining that the producers don't want the eliminated contestants to kill themselves or someone else.

489. The first film with a $100 million budget was True Lies, which was made in 1994.

Food & Drinks

490. Colonel Sanders disliked what the KFC Franchise had done to the food so much that he described it as the worst fried chicken he had ever had and that the gravy was like wall paper paste.

491. In 2009, Burger King launched a campaign that if you unfriended ten of your Facebook friends, you would receive a free Whopper. Using the Whopper Sacrifice application, your friend would receive a message telling them that their friendship was less valuable than a Whopper.

492. Potatoes have more chromosomes than a human.

493. Ruth Wakefield, who invented the chocolate chip cookie around 1938, sold the idea to Nestle Toll House in exchange for a lifetime supply of chocolate.

494. Butter milk contains zero butter.

495. The Coca-Cola made in the Maldives used to be made from ocean water.

496. A quarter of the world's hazelnuts each year go towards making Nutella. That's 100,000 tons of hazelnuts per year.

497. Pineapple isn't a fruit, it's actually a berry.

498. France was the first country that banned supermarkets from throwing out or destroying food that wasn't sold.

499. McDonald's has more than 37,000 stores around the world making it the largest fast food chain globally.

500. The pizza Louis XIII is the most expensive pizza in the world costing $12,000. Created by Chef Renato Viola, he prepares the entire dish at your house. The toppings include three types of caviar, Mediterranean lobster, and red prawns. The size of the pizza is only eight inches (twenty centimeters) in diameter.

501. There's a mushroom in the wild called "Laetiporus" that tastes like fried chicken.

502. Black tomatoes can be grown without any genetic engineering. They are full of beneficial anthocyanins which are believed to help with obesity, cancer, and diabetes.

503. In Cambodia, they sell "Happy Pizza" which is a cheese pizza garnished with weed on top.

504. Apples, peaches, and raspberries are all members of the rose family.

505. The average strawberry has 200 seeds on the outside. It's also not considered a fruit.

506. Most of the vitamins you get from eating a potato are in the skin.

507. In 1996, McDonald's opened their first ski-through fast food restaurant in Sweden. People can actually ski up to the counter, order food, and ski off. It is called McSki.

508. Burger King in Japan has released two black hamburgers called the "Kure Diamond" and the "Kuro Pearl" with everything including the bun, the sauce, and the cheese colored black with squid ink.

509. People have been eating potatoes since 7,000 years ago.

510. Coca-Cola was invented by an American pharmacist named John Pemberton who advertised it as a nerve tonic that could cure headaches and fatigue.

511. Half of the DNA in a banana is identical to what makes up you.

512. Roughly a third of all food produced in the world for human consumption every year goes to waste. This is approximately 1.3 billion tons equating to roughly a billion dollars down the drain.

513. In 2014, a competitive eater named Molly Schuyler, who weighs only 126 pounds (fifty seven kilograms), won four eating contests in only three days. She ate a total of 363 chicken wings, fifty nine pancakes, five pounds (2.2 kilograms) of bacon, and five pounds of barbecued meat.

514. In the US, April 2 is National Peanut Butter and Jelly Day.

515. Watermelons contain an ingredient called "citrulline" that can trigger the production of a compound that helps relax the body's blood vessels, just like Viagra.

516. Turophobia is the fear of cheese.

517. Doritos can be made without the powder and taste exactly the same, but the company intentionally adds it because they believe it adds to the Doritos experience.

518. You can make your own Gatorade at home by simply adding salt to some Kool-Aid. It's not the exact recipe, but it's got just as many electrolytes.

519. A tablespoon of cake frosting has less fat, calories, and sugar than a tablespoon of Nutella.

520. "Oriole O's" are a type of cereal that's exclusively available in South Korea.

521. There is a secret McDonald's menu item that you can order which is a McChicken in the middle of a double cheeseburger.

522. Ben and Jerry's has a cemetery where they bury all their discontinued flavors.

523. Skittles and jelly beans contain insect cocoons which are used to coat candies to give them that special shine known as shellac.

524. Coca leaves are still used by Coca-Cola to this day. A company in New Jersey first extracts the cocaine from the leaves giving the spent leaves to Coca-Cola to put in their drinks.

525. In China, it's possible to buy baby pears shaped like Buddha. The farmers actually clamp a mold onto a growing fruit to get the shape. There is also a company called "Fruit Mold" that makes heart-shaped cucumbers, square watermelons, and other more deliciously weird shapes.

526. Before the seventeenth century, carrots were purple until a mutation changed the color to what we know now.

527. Diet soda ruins your tooth enamel just as badly as cocaine and methamphetamines.

528. There is a Pizza Hut perfume that smells like a fresh box of Pizza Hut pizza when you spray it.

529. The creator of Pringles, Fredric Baur, had his ashes stored in a Pringles can after he died.

530. Chewing gum when cutting onions prevents you from tearing up as it forces you to breathe through your mouth.

531. Honey is the only food that doesn't spoil.

532. Coca-Cola only sold twenty five bottles its first year. Today, it sells 1.8 billion bottles a day.

533. There are no genuinely blue foods. Foods that appear blue such as blueberries are often a shade of purple.

534. Marshmallows exist because of sore throats. For centuries, juice from the marshmallow plant has been used for pain relief. In the 1800's, it was mixed with egg whites and sugar for children with sore throats, and the recipe was so tasty that people turned it into a treat

called marshmallow.

535. The stickers that you find on fruit are actually made of edible paper and the glue used to stick them on is actually food grade, so even if you eat one, you'll be completely fine.

536. Cherries contain two compounds inhibiting tumor growth and even cause cancer cells to self-destruct without damaging healthy cells.

537. The artificial sweetener Splenda was discovered when a researcher misheard the command "to test this chemical" as "taste this chemical."

538. Oranges are not even in the top ten list of common foods when it comes to vitamin C levels.

539. The top ten cheese eating countries are all in Europe with France being number one. The average French person consumes fifty seven pounds (twenty five kilograms) of cheese per year.

540. Sugar was first invented in India where extraction and purification techniques were developed in 510 B.C. Before that the most popular sweetener was honey.

541. The typical American spends $1,200 on fast food every year.

542. All of the air in potato chip bags that people complain about isn't air at all. It's actually nitrogen which serves the purpose to keep chips crisp and to provide a cushion during shipping.

543. There's a fruit called "black sapote" or "chocolate pudding fruit" which, at the right ripeness, tastes like chocolate pudding, is low in fat and has about four times as much vitamin C as an orange.

544. One hundred acres of pizza are cut every day in the US alone.

545. In 2013, Scottish scientists created a pizza that has 30% of your daily recommended nutrients.

546. A twenty ounce bottle of Mountain Dew contains the equivalent of twenty two packets of sugar.

547. In France, a bakery by law has to make all its bread that it sells from scratch in order to have the right to be called a bakery.

548. Supermarket apples can be a year old. They're usually picked between August and November, covered in wax, hot-air dried, and sent into cold storage. After six to twelve months, they finally land on the grocery store shelves.

549. In the Philippines, McDonald's includes spaghetti in their menu. The pasta comes with a beef tomato sauce and a piece of "McDo" fried chicken.

550. Cucumber slices can fight bad breath. If you don't have a mint on hand, a slice of cucumber will do the job.

551. More than 1/5 of all the calories consumed by humans worldwide is provided by rice alone.

552. There is a McDonald's in every continent except Antarctica.

553. Even though Froot Loops are different colors, they all have exactly the same flavor.

Funny

554. George Garrett, a nineteen year old man from England, changed his name to "Captain Fantastic Faster Than Superman Batman Wolverine The Hulk And The Flash Combined" in 2008.

555. In 2013, in Belo Horizonte, Brazil, construction workers permanently cemented a truck into a sidewalk after the owner refused to move it.

556. There's a travel agency in Tokyo called "Unagi Travel" that, for a fee, will take your stuffed animal on vacation around the world.

557. There's a museum in Europe called the "Museum of Broken Relationships" that exclusively displays objects that were meaningful to heartbroken exes.

558. The "over 9,000" meme that was popularized from Dragon Ball Z was a translation error. The power level was actually over 8,000.

559. The Curiosity Rover sang Happy Birthday to itself on Mars to commemorate the one year anniversary of landing on the planet in 2013.

560. "Backpfeifengesicht" is a German word that means a face that badly needs a punch.

561. If police in Thailand misbehave, they're punished by being made to wear bright pink Hello Kitty armbands.

562. Due to the aging population in Japan, adult diaper sales are about to surpass baby diaper sales.

563. The Vystavochnaya subway station in Moscow accepts thirty squats as payment for a metro ticket as an incentive to exercise more.

564. In the Victorian era, special tea cups that protected your mustache from getting dunked in your tea were used.

565. Disneyland does not sell any gum. This is because Walt Disney didn't want people stepping in gum as they walked around the park.

566. In 2008, The North Face clothing company sued a clothing company called "The South Butt."

567. The earliest "your momma joke" was written on a tablet 3,500 years ago by a student in Ancient Babylon.

568. Bangkok University in Thailand makes their students wear anti-cheating helmets during exams.

569. There's a lake in Australia called "Lake Disappointment" that was named and found by Frank Hann in 1897, who was hoping to find fresh water but instead found salt water.

570. International "have a bad day" day is November 19th.

571. The traffic in London is as slow as the carriages from a century ago.

572. Before alarm clocks were invented, there was a profession called a "knocker up" which involved going from client to client and tapping on their windows or banging on their doors with long sticks until they were awake. This lasted till the 1920's.

573. There is a town in Alaska called "Talkeetna" that has had a cat named Stubbs as its honorary mayor since 1997.

574. Putting dry tea bags in smelly shoes or gym bags is an easy and quick way to absorb any unpleasant odors.

575. From the poll of 2,500 participants, the average person spends forty two minutes a week or almost ninety two days over a lifetime on the toilet.

576. The founders Bill Hewlett and David Packard flipped a coin to decide whether the company they created would be called "Hewlett-Packard" (HP) or "Packard-Hewlett" (PH).

577. In 1860, Abraham Lincoln grew his famous beard because he got a letter from an eleven year old girl named Grace Bedell who said that all ladies liked the whiskers and they would convince their husbands to vote for him for president.

578. Donald Duck comics were banned from Finland because he isn't wearing any pants.

579. The first ever modern toilet was created by Thomas Crapper, hence the phrase "to take a crap."

580. According to an analysis conducted by Swift Key, Canada uses the poop emoji more than any other country in the world. In France hearts are number one, while Australia leads the world in alcohol and drug related emojis.

581. There are gold glitter pills you can buy for $400 online that promise to turn your poop gold.

582. On Valentine's Day 2014, a group of single men in Shanghai bought every odd-numbered seat for a theater showing of Beijing Love Story. They did this to prevent couples from sitting together as a show of support for single people.

583. In 2014, the Department of Transportation in Colorado was forced to change their mile marker from 420 to 419.99 just to get people to stop stealing their sign.

584. In North Korea, citizens are forced to choose from one of the twenty eight government approved haircuts.

585. In 2005, a man named Ronald McDonald robbed a Wendy's in Manchester, England.

586. In 2013, a fifty nine year old man named Alan Markovitz was upset at his ex-wife for cheating on him, bought a house next to hers, and installed a giant $7,000 statue of a hand giving the finger aimed at her house.

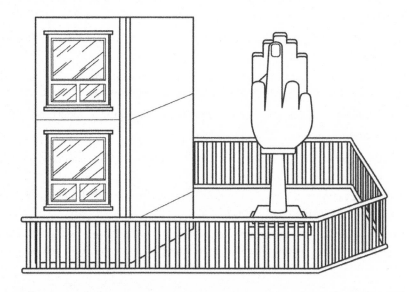

History & Culture

587. The modern handshake dates all the way back to the 5th century B.C., where swordsmen would greet each other with their weapon hand free, showing no sign of a fight.

588. The unbroken seal on Tutankhamun's tomb went untouched for 3,245 years until 1942.

589. An ancient Persian poet recorded the fable of a king that challenged wise men to make him a ring that made him happy when he was sad and sad when he was happy. They succeeded by giving him a ring etched with the phrase: "This too shall pass."

590. Ancient Roman charioteers earned more money than what international sports stars get paid today.

591. One of the clauses in the 1781 US Articles of Confederation states that if Canada wants to be admitted into the US, it'll be automatically accepted.

592. Ancient Rome was eight times more densely populated than modern New York.

593. In Victorian London, mail used to be delivered twelve times per day.

594. The Appian Way in Rome is a road that was built in 312 B.C. that is still used to this day.

595. The largest empire the world has ever seen was the British Empire which covered almost a quarter of the planet in its peak in 1920.

596. In ancient Athens, the world's first democracy, they had a process called "ostracism" where, once a year, the people could vote on the politician that they felt was the most destructive to the democratic process and that person was banished from Athens for ten

years.

597. The Vikings used to find new lands by releasing ravens from their boats and following where they went. They became their favorite symbol and resulted in them using the bird on their flag.

598. Cats used to be sacred in Egypt; if you killed one, you could be sentenced to death. The Egyptians would even shave off their eyebrows to show grief from the death of their cat.

599. The richest man in history was Emperor Mansa Musa's whose wealth is believed to have been around $400 billion when taking into account inflation.

600. In the ancient Persian Empire, men used to debate ideas twice, once sober and once drunk, as they believed an idea had to sound good in both states in order to be considered a good idea.

601. There is a tribe in India called the "War Khasi" that has been passing down for generations the art of manipulating tree roots to create a system of living bridges.

602. Woman have been using pregnancy tests since 1350 B.C. They used to pee on wheat and barley seeds to determine if they were pregnant or not. If wheat grew, it predicted a female baby; and if barley grew, it predicted a male. The woman was not pregnant if nothing grew. This theory was tested and proved accurate 70% of the time.

603. Democracy was invented in Greece 2,500 years ago.

604. Romans used urine to clean and whiten their teeth. They were actually onto something as urine contains ammonia which has a cleaning substance that results into clearing out everything.

605. During the 1600's, there was "Tulip Mania" in Holland where tulips were more valuable than gold. This is the first reported economic bubble. When people came to their senses, the bubble burst and caused the market to crash.

606. In the early 1930's, a social movement became popular although it eventually died out, which proposed replacing politicians and business people with scientists and engineers that could manage the economy.

607. There are still several unexplored hidden passages in the pyramids of Giza.

608. Teddy Roosevelt was shot in 1912 right before giving a speech. Noticing that it missed his lungs, since he wasn't coughing up blood, he proceeded to give the full ninety minute speech.

609. Socialist Karl Marx's final words before he died in 1883 were: "Go away, last words are for fools who haven't said enough."

610. The popular saying "bless you" after a sneeze originated from the 14th century, when Pope Gregory the VII asked for it to be said after every time he sneezed so he could be

protected against the plague.

611. The shortest presidency in the history of the world was by President Pedro Paredes of Mexico, who ruled for less than one hour on February 19, 1913.

612. Ancient Egyptians used headrests made of stone instead of pillows.

613. There are 350 pyramids that were built by the rulers of the ancient Kushite kingdoms now known as Sudan.

614. In 2013, a lost Egyptian city named Heracleion was discovered underwater after being lost for 1,200 years in the Mediterranean Sea.

615. In 1770, the British Parliament passed a law condemning lipstick, stating that any woman found guilty of seducing a man into matrimony by a cosmetic means would be tried for witchcraft.

616. A "butt" was a medieval unit of measurement for wine. Technically, a butt-load of wine is 125 gallons (475 liters).

617. The first ever diamonds were found in India in the 4th century B.C. The next country it was discovered in was Brazil in 1725.

618. In Japanese myth, there's a creature called "Asiarai Yashiki." It's a giant unwashed foot that appears before you and demands to be washed. If you don't wash it, it rampages through your house.

619. The oldest instruments date back 43,000 years ago, which were flutes made out of bones from birds and mammoths.

Human Body & Human Behavior

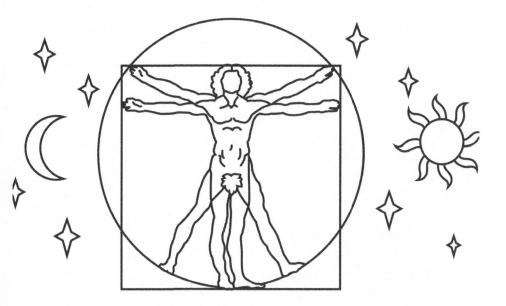

620. If an astronaut got out of his space suit on the moon, he would explode before he suffocated.

621. There are tiny eight legged creatures that are closely related to spiders living in the pores of your facial skin; they are called "demodex."

622. Contrary to popular belief, white spots on fingernails are not a sign of a deficiency of calcium, zinc, or other vitamins in the diet. They're actually called "leukonychia," are completely harmless, and are most commonly caused by minor injuries that occur while the nail is growing.

623. Mobile phones emit electro-magnetic frequencies that heat body tissue and can affect over a hundred proteins in the brain.

624. Ischaemic heart disease and stroke are the world's biggest killers. Ischaemic means an inadequate blood supply to an organ.

625. The average person will fall asleep in just seven minutes.

626. You would be a few centimeters taller in space due to the lack of gravity there.

627. If you were to take out someone's lung and flatten it out, it would have the same surface area as one half of a tennis court.

628. There is enough carbon in your body to make over 9,000 pencils.

629. The hippocampus, which is responsible for memory, is larger in women's brains than in men's.

630. Humans have twenty three pairs of chromosomes while great apes have twenty four.

631. As a person dies, his or her hearing is the last sense to go.

632. The human brain can compute over a thousand processes per second, making it quicker than any computer.

633. The sound you hear when you put a seashell next to your ear isn't the sea but your blood running through your veins.

634. The information travelling inside your brain is moving at 268 miles per hour (430 kilometers per hour).

635. There are only two parts on the human body that never stop growing, the ears and the nose.

636. There's a phobia called the "Jonah complex" which causes a person to fear their own success, preventing them from reaching their full potential.

637. There is a condition called "hyperthymesia" that causes the person to remember every single detail of their lives. Only twelve people on earth have this condition.

638. Although the brain is physically developed by the age of five, the rational part of a brain isn't fully developed and won't be until age twenty five.

639. The average adult has eight pounds (3.6 kilograms) or about twenty two square feet (two square meters) of skin.

640. Humans are capable of feeling the effects of a broken heart. This is known as "stress cardiomyopathy" in medical terms. If you're suffering from a broken heart, your blood can have three times the amount of adrenaline than someone suffering from a heart attack.

641. Even after six hours of being dead, a person's muscles continue to spasm periodically.

642. We miss 10% of everything we see due to blinking.

643. There are 1,000 gigabytes in a terabyte and most neuroscientists estimate that the human brain can hold between ten and 100 terabytes of information.

644. There is a side effect of sleep deprivation called "microsleep" in which a person will fall asleep for a few seconds or even a few minutes without realizing it. It's extremely dangerous and is one of the largest contributors to accidents on the road.

645. There's a syndrome called "Tetris Effect" that occurs when people dedicate so much time and attention to an activity that it starts to pattern their thoughts, mental images, and dreams.

646. A study conducted by Loma Linda University in 2010 concluded that laughter not only reduces stress, but it increases the production of antibodies and kills the activity of tumor cells.

647. Crying is actually very healthy for you. It helps you emotionally, lubricates your eyes, removes toxins and irritants, and reduces stress.

648. According to a study done by Mekuin University in Canada, playing video games before bedtime actually gives a person the ability to control their dreams. It also suggests that gamers are more likely to have lucid dreams as opposed to non-gamers.

649. The offspring of two identical sets of twins are legally cousins but genetically siblings.

650. Atelophobia is the fear of not being good enough or having imperfections.

651. All humans have lines on our bodies called "Blaschko's lines" which can only be seen under certain conditions such as UV light.

652. Dyslexic people actually see numbers and letters backwards. It's basically a reading disorder, not a vision or seeing disorder. This means that Braille readers can also be dyslexic.

653. The human hearing range is from twenty to 20,000 hertz. If it was any lower than twenty, we'd be able to hear our muscles move.

654. Contrary to popular belief, washing your hands in warm water doesn't kill any more bacteria than washing them in cold water. This is because bacteria only die when water is boiling.

655. The nose is connected to the memory center of your brain, hence why smell triggers some of the most powerful memories.

656. Climonia is the excessive desire to stay in bed all day.

657. Blind people who have never seen before will still smile despite never having seen anyone else do it before because it's a natural human reaction.

658. Veronica Seider holds the Guinness World Record for the best sight in the world. She can see twenty times better than the average person, being able to identify someone's face from one mile (1.6 kilometers) away.

659. If your eye were a digital camera, it would have 576 megapixels in them.

660. Contrary to popular belief, cracking your bones doesn't hurt your bones or cause you arthritis. It's simply the gas bubbles bursting that you hear; however, doing it too much does cause tissue damage.

661. When a person lies, they experience an increase in temperature around the nose known as the Pinocchio effect.

662. There are actually seven different types of twins. They are: identical, fraternal, half-identical, mirror image, mixed chromosome, superfetation, and superfecundation.

663. Adding sugar to a wound will greatly reduce the pain and speed up the healing process.

664. Only 1 to 2% of the total world population are redheads.

665. Like fingerprints, our tongues all have unique prints.

666. You are born with 270 bones which form into 206 by the time you're an adult. A quarter of these are in your hands and wrists.

667. During the lifespan of a human, enough saliva can be created to fill up two swimming pools.

668. Humans can only live without oxygen for three minutes, water for three days, and food for three weeks.

669. The length of human vessels in the body equate to 60,000 miles (96,000 kilometers) if you lay them out from beginning to end.

670. Smokers are four times more likely to get grey hair in their lives than non-smokers.

671. All humans have the ability to see ultraviolet light, however, it's passively filtered through our lens. People who get surgery done to remove the lens are then able to see ultraviolet light.

672. Farting helps to reduce blood pressure and is good for overall health.

673. Studies have been shown that people with creative minds find it harder to fall asleep at night and prefer to stay up later.

674. It was discovered that people are most likely to have a good idea when they're doing a monotonous task such as showering, driving, or exercising. This is due to the fact that the body is in a more relaxed and less distracted state, allowing dopamine to flow through the body, triggering thoughts.

675. Patients in an insane mental asylum in the 1950's have the same stress as the average high school student nowadays.

676. Humans take in eleven million bits of information every second, however, we're only aware of about forty of these things.

677. 95% of the decisions you make have already been made up by your subconscious mind.

678. By the time you are two, your brain is already 80% the size of an adult's.

679. The average person has 10,000 taste buds which are replaced every two weeks.

680. Humans can have anywhere from twelve to sixty thousand thoughts per day with 80% of these thoughts being negative.

681. The human brain has 100 billion brain cells.

682. Each sperm contains about three billion bases of genetic information, representing 750 megabytes of digital information.

683. It's impossible to taste food without saliva. This is because chemicals from the food must first dissolve in saliva. Once dissolved, chemicals can be detected by receptors on taste buds.

684. Astronauts would weigh one sixth of their weight if they were in space compared to

on Earth.

685. You cannot invent faces in your dreams, which means you've encountered every face you've seen in real life.

686. The human eye can see a candle flickering up to thirty miles (forty eight kilometers) away on a dark night.

687. Due to a genetic mutation, the first blue eyed humans only began to appear six to ten thousand years ago.

688. The act of "fubbing" or "phone snubbing" is becoming a very real epidemic among Americans according to new research published in the Journal of Computers and Human Behavior. Fubbing is the act of snubbing someone in a social situation by looking down at the phone instead of paying attention to them; this behavior can affect and damage relationships, even leading to severe depression and lower rates of life satisfaction.

689. If you don't identify yourself as an extrovert or introvert, you may be an ambivert, which is a person moderately comfortable with groups and social interactions, but who also relishes time alone away from crowds.

690. We're technically living about eighty milliseconds in the past because that's how long it takes our brain to process information.

691. The human brain has a negativity bias causing us to continually look for bad news. It's an evolutionary trait that stem from early humans as a survival mechanism.

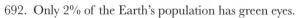

692. Only 2% of the Earth's population has green eyes.

693. Being hungry causes serotonin levels to drop, causing a whirlwind of uncontrollable emotions including anxiety, stress, and anger.

694. When you're buried six feet down in soil and without a coffin, an average adult body normally takes eight to twelve years to decompose to a skeleton.

695. The largest organ on the body is the skin.

696. The human brain uses 20% of the body's energy even though it's only 2% of the body's total weight.

697. The Neanderthal's brain was 10% bigger than ours, the homosapiens, but they were not as intellectual as us. This is because their brains were more devoted to vision while ours is devoted to reasoning, decision making, and social interaction.

698. The human body contains trillions of microorganisms like bacteria, outnumbering human cells by ten to one.

699. People can have a psychological disorder called boanthropy that makes them believe that they are a cow. They try to live their life as a cow.

Interesting

700. Barcode scanners actually read the spaces between the black bars, not the black bars themselves.

701. There's a religion called "Christian Atheism" where practitioners believe in essentially the same things as traditional Christians, except that the Bible is completely metaphorical and that God is an allegory for human morality rather than a real being.

702. A can of regular coke will sink to the bottom of water while a can of diet coke will float.

703. In 1976, an underachieving Princeton student named John Aristotle Phillips wrote a term paper describing how to build a nuclear bomb. He received an "A," but never got his paper back as it was seized by the FBI.

704. Coal power stations put out 100 times more radiation into the air than nuclear power plants producing the same amount of energy.

705. Percussive maintenance is the technical term for hitting something until it works.

706. There are no clocks in the casinos of Las Vegas so customers lose track of time and stay in the premises longer.

707. When you get blackout drunk, you don't actually forget anything because your brain wasn't recording in the first place.

708. Labeorphilist is the collection and study of beer bottle labels.

709. Popes can't be organ donors because their entire body has to be buried intact as it belongs to the universal Catholic Church.

710. There used to be sheep that grazed in Central Park up until 1934. They were moved during the Great Depression as it was feared they'd be eaten.

711. Halieutics is the study of fishing.

712. The Titanic used to have its own newspaper called "The Atlantic Daily Bulletin." It was printed daily on board and it had news, ads, stock prices, horse racing results, gossip, and the day's menu.

713. It is estimated that only 8% of the world's total money is real. The rest exists electronically on computer hard drives and bank accounts.

714. Over 50% of all lottery tickets sold are bought by only 5% of people who buy lottery tickets.

715. A study conducted by the University of Oxford found that for every person that you fall in love with and accommodate into your life, you lose two close friends.

ATLANTIC DAILY BULLETIN
Number 2 1912 ISSN 0965-6391

THE ROYAL MAIL TRIPLE-SCREW STEAMER
TITANIC
will be despatched from
SOUTHAMPTON TO NEW YORK
on her maiden voyage
Wednesday, April 10th, 1912 at noon
REGULAR PASSENGER AND FREIGHT SERVICES

716. If you open your eyes in a pitch-black room, the color you'll see is called "eigengrau."

717. The Pentagon spends over $250,000 each year to study the body language of world leaders like Vladimir Putin.

718. Studies have shown that smoking hookah is no safer than smoking cigarettes and, in fact, may cause the smoker to absorb more toxic substances than cigarettes.

719. The youngest pope to ever be elected was Pope Benedict IX, born in 1012, who was only twelve years old.

720. In 2000, the KKK adopted a stretch of highway near St. Louis so the Missouri government responded by renaming the road Rosa Parks Highway.

721. Triskaidekaphobia is the fear of the number 13.

722. Stalin's guards were so afraid of him that no one called a doctor for over ten hours after he had a stroke resulting in his death. They feared that he might recover and execute anyone who acted outside of his orders.

723. Eccrinology is the study of excretion.

724. There is a condition called "math anxiety" which causes people to perform poorly in mathematics, not because they're ungifted in math, but because the condition causes their brain to enter such a state where they simply cannot perform math.

725. Oikology is the science of housekeeping.

726. A man named Jonathan Lee Riches got in the Guinness Book of World Records for

having filed the highest number of lawsuits in the world with a total of over 2,600.

727. A stock exchange system exists with pirates in Somalia. Locals can invest in a pirate group and, after a successful heist, they will receive a reward. In one instance a woman gave an RPG 7 to a pirate group and ended up receiving $75,000.

728. Papaphobia is the fear of the pope.

729. A false awakening is the term used for a vivid or convincing dream about awakening from sleep when in reality you're still sleeping.

730. One lightning bolt has enough energy to toast one hundred thousand slices of bread.

731. Reciprocal liking is a psychological term used to describe when you start liking someone after you find out that they like you. It's a phenomenon that reflects the way people feel better about themselves and enjoy the company of those that provide them with positive feelings.

732. Sternutaphobia is the fear of sneezing.

733. The chances of an American being killed by lightning is the same chance a person in Japan has being shot and killed by a gun.

734. A study done in 1915 by the Chicago University concluded that the easiest color to see from a distance was the color yellow, hence the most popular taxi color.

735. Chaology is the study of chaos or chaos theory.

736. Getting hit by lightning heats up your skin to 50,000 degrees Fahrenheit (27,000 degrees Celsius), which is hotter than the surface of the Sun.

737. There is term known as "friend paradox" where the average person has less friends than his friend.

738. The Bingham Canyon Copper Mine in Utah is the largest man made hole at half a mile (one kilometer) deep and two miles (four kilometers) wide; it covers 770 hectares.

739. Deltiology is the collection and study of picture postcards.

740. Cherophobia is the fear of being happy or joyful with the expectation that something bad will happen.

741. The reason a whip creates a whipping sound is because it's moving quicker than the speed of sound creating a small sonic boom.

742. It is estimated that about 100 billion people have died since Homo sapiens appeared over 200,000 years ago.

743. The world's largest gold bar is 551 pounds (250 kilograms).

744. In 1979, debris from NASA's Space Station Skylab crash landed in the town of Esperance, Western Australia, for which the town fined NASA $400 for littering. They actually paid it.

745. Many animal shelters will not allow black cats to be adopted around Halloween time because most people just buy them as impulse purchases.

746. The fear of clowns is called "coulrophobia."

747. In 2011, Lego produced 381 million tires, making them the world's largest rubber tire manufacturer by number of units produced.

748. If you went through seventeen tons of gold ore and one ton of personal computers, you'd find more gold from the personal computers.

749. Two thousand five hundred and twenty is the smallest number that can be divided by all numbers between one and ten.

750. Back in the day, when rabbit ears were put behind a man's head, it meant that his wife was cheating on him. The two fingers held up symbolized the horns of a stag, which had apparently lost its mate to a rival stag.

751. More than half of the world's population is under the age of thirty.

752. According to a study conducted by Brock University in Ontario, Canada, racism and homophobia are linked to having lower IQ, as those with lower intelligence tend to gravitate toward socially conservative ideologies.

753. Anuptaphobia is the fear of either remaining unmarried or marrying the wrong person.

754. The Kuwaiti Dinar is the strongest currency in the world with one Dinar equating to $3.29 USD.

755. Pirates used to wear eye patches on one eye during the day so they could see better at night with that same eye.

756. Big Ben in London is not the tower but the bell inside.

757. A bus can replace forty cars if people made the switch.

758. Diamonds are actually not that rare. A company called "De Beers" owns 95% of the market and suppresses supply to keep the prices high.

759. Campanology is the art of bell ringing.

760. The clothing store H&M stands for Hennes & Mauritz.

761. The pinky swear came from Japan and indicated that if someone broke the promise, they must cut off their pinky.

762. Trypophobia is the fear of holes.

763. The reason people traditionally put wedding rings on the left ring finger is because before medical science figured out how the circulatory system functioned, people believed that there was a vein that ran directly from the fourth finger of the left hand to the heart.

764. Anything that melts can be made into glass, however, there will be molten residue stuck to it.

765. The nicotine from one puff of a cigarette reaches your brain in seven seconds. Alcohol take approximately six minutes.

766. Antibiotics are actually ineffective against fighting viruses. They are only effective against bacterial infections.

767. Oil expands with the rise of temperature, hence if you're filling your car up, it's best in the morning or late at night when it's not hot to get the most bang for your buck.

768. The World Health Organization states that from the one billion smokers in the world more than 600,000 people die every year from secondhand smoke.

769. Until the 1930's, the letter "E" was used to represent a failing grade in the US, however, that was changed to "F" as professors began to worry that their students would mistake "E" for excellent.

770. The term for forgetting something after walking through a doorway is called an "event boundary."

771. Using a paper towel after washing your hands decrease bacteria by 40% while using an air dryer increases the bacteria by up to 220%, as bacteria grow quickly in warm and moist environments.

772. The word font only refers to things like italics, size, and boldness. The style of the lettering is called a "typeface."

773. If the 1st of January on a leap year falls on a Sunday, the months of January, April, and July will each have a Friday 13th. In the 20th century, this happened in 1928, 1956, and 1984. In the 21st century, this will happen four times in 2012, 2040, 2068, and 2096.

774. The average IQ rate has been declining over recent decades. This is because smarter people are having less children.

775. Brass door knobs automatically disinfect themselves in eight hours, which is known as the "oligodynamic effect."

776. Schools that ditch schoolyard rules are actually seeing a decrease in bullying, serious injuries, and vandalism, while concentration levels in class are increasing. This is because fewer rules requires critical thinking whereas simply obeying instructions requires very little critical thinking.

777. A study conducted in 2011 by Angela Duckworth proved that IQ tests can be affected by motivation. By promising subjects monetary rewards, she found that the higher the reward, the higher they scored on the IQ test.

778. There's only one Shell gas station shaped like a shell. Eight were built in the 1930's, but the only one left is in North Carolina.

779. You can see four states from the top of Chicago's Willis Tower on a clear day; it's about forty to fifty miles away, beyond Illinois and out to Indiana, Michigan, and Wisconsin.

780. The collars on men's dress shirts used to be detachable. This was to save on laundry costs as the collar was the part that needed cleaning the most frequently.

781. The first roller coaster was used to transport coal down a hill. After people found that it could reach speeds of up to fifty miles per hour, tourists asked to ride on it for a few cents.

Inventions & Inventors

782. The Gatling gun was invented by Doctor Richard Gatling, who noticed that the majority of soldiers during the Civil War who died were due to disease, not gunshot wounds. By inventing a machine that could replace hundreds of soldiers, the need for large armies would be reduced thus diminishing exposure to battle and disease.

783. The first hard drive was invented in 1956 and weighed over a ton.

784. Thomas Edison taught his second wife, Mina Miller, Morse code so that they could communicate in secret by tapping each other's hands when their families were around.

785. Inventor Nikola Tesla and author Mark Twain were best friends and were mutual fans of each other's work.

786. The man who designed Saddam Hussein's secret bunker was the grandson of the woman who designed Adolf Hitler's.

787. Manel Torres, a Spanish fashion designer, invented the world's first spray on clothing which can be worn, washed, and worn again.

788. In 1949, the Prince motor company in Japan developed an electric car that could travel 124 miles (200 kilometers) on a single charge.

789. The "Pythagorean cup," also known as a "Greedy cup," is a cup designed to spill its content if too much wine is poured in, encouraging moderation.

790. When dying in 1955, Einstein refused surgery saying: "I want to go when I want, it's tasteless to prolong life artificially, I've done my share, it's time to go, I will do it elegantly."

791. As of 2019, the largest yacht in the world named Azzam is 590 feet long (the length of two football fields) and cost $600 million to build. It was created in 2013, taking four years to construct and beat the previous world record by a full fifty seven feet. It has 94,000 horsepower and can go up to thirty seven miles (sixty kilometers) per hour, the fastest speed for a yacht longer than 300 feet (ninety one meters).

792. The electric chair to execute people was created by a dentist.

793. Bluetooth got its name from Ericsson's Viking Heritage, the Swedish communication company. It's named after Danish Viking King Harold Blatand. Blatand translates to Bluetooth in English and incredibly the Bluetooth symbol is actually Blatand's initials inscribed in runic symbols.

794. In 2004, Volvo introduced a concept car called "YYC" that was built specifically for women without a hood and dent resistant bumpers.

795. Created in Germany, ESSLack is the world's first edible spray paint that comes in gold, silver, red, and blue.

796. There is a device known as "ventricular assist" device or VAD that can permanently replace the function of your heart. The only side effect is you have no pulse.

797. There are now digital pens that can record everything you write, draw or sketch on any surface.

798. Scientists from ATR Computational Neuroscience Laboratories in Tokyo, Japan, have successfully developed a technology that can put thoughts on a computer screen.

799. When tractor owner Ferruccio Lamborghini voiced his frustration over his clutch in the Ferrari to car's founder Enzo Ferrari, Enzo insulted him telling him that the problem was with the driver, not the car. Ferruccio decided to start his own car company and thus the Lamborghini was born.

800. In 1936, the Russians created a computer that ran on water.

801. Bubble wrap was originally invented in 1957 to be sold as wallpaper.

802. The Kevlar bulletproof vest was invented by a pizza delivery guy after being shot twice on the job.

803. The tin can was invented in 1810. The can opener was invented forty eight years later. People used hammers and chisels between this time.

804. The Centennial Light Bulb in Livermore, California, has been burning since 1901 and is the world's longest lasting light bulb according to the Guinness Book of World Records. The bulb is at least 113 years old and has only been turned off a handful of times.

805. It took a whole month for Erno Rubik, the inventor of the Rubik's cube, to solve his own creation.

806. In the summer of 1932, while sitting in a restaurant, Adolf Hitler designed the prototype for what would become the first Volkswagen Beetle.

807. Volvo invented the three point seat belt, but opened up the patent to any car manufacturer who wanted to use it, as they felt it had more value as a lifesaving tool than something to profit from.

808. There's a company called "True Mirror" that makes non reversing mirrors that show you how you actually appear to other people.

809. There's a company named Neurowear that sells a headphone that can read your brainwaves and selects music based on your state of mind.

810. In 2007, a man named Mike Warren-Madden designed a device called the "Aquatic Pram" that allows you to take your fish for a walk.

811. The lighter was invented before the matchstick.

812. Otto Fredrick Rohwedder was the first person to sell sliced bread, and he did it in America in 1928, in Davenport, Iowa. In 1912, Otto invented the single loaf bread slicing machine, which was the first in the world. He marketed his invention as the single greatest advancement in the baking industry, since they started wrapping bread, and he was right, because we term great ideas these days as "the greatest thing since sliced bread."

Kids

813. Some estimates report that one in eight babies is given to the wrong parents at some point during their hospital stay.

814. In Armenia, all children age six and up are taught chess in school as a mandatory part of their curriculum.

815. In Iceland, it's forbidden to give your child a name that hasn't been approved by the Icelandic naming committee.

816. In 2013, France banned child beauty pageants because they promote the hypersexualization of minors. Anyone who organizes such a pageant could face jail time for up to two years and a fine of up to 30,000 euros.

817. A seven year old second grader was suspended for biting a pop tart into the shape of a mountain which school officials mistook for a gun.

818. The reason Lego heads have holes in them is so air can pass through them if a child ever swallows one.

819. In Quebec, Sweden, and Norway, it's illegal to advertise directly to children. This is to prevent companies from encouraging children to beg their parents to buy them stuff.

820. A study done by the Bureau of Economic Research concluded that first born children have higher IQs than their younger siblings.

821. In a study to improve hospital design for children, researchers from the University of Sheffield polled 250 children regarding their opinions of clowns. Every single one reported disliking or fearing them.

Languages

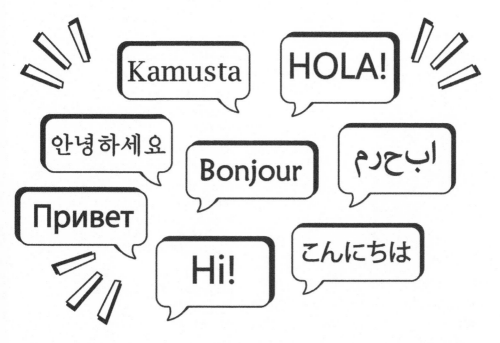

822. Coffee was so influential in early Turkish culture that the word for "breakfast" literally translates to "before coffee," and the word "brown translates" to "the color of coffee."

823. German used to be the second most widely spoken language in the United States before it was forcibly repressed during World War One.

824. "Almost" is the longest English word in alphabetical order.

825. The Hawaiian alphabet only has twelve letters. They are a, e, i, o, u, h, k, l, m, n, p, and w.

826. The English word orange was the name of the fruit for a few hundred years before the color was later named after the fruit. Before that what we now know as orange was known as yee-o-ler-eed.

827. Since the beginning of communication, it has been estimated that 31,000 languages have existed.

828. The word "muggle" was added to the English dictionary and is defined as a person lacking a particular skill.

829. Noah Webster, the creator of the first ever American dictionary, learned twenty six languages so that he could understand and research the origins of his own country's tongue in order to write it.

830. The word "jay" used to be used as slang for a dull or stupid person, so when anyone ignored traffic regulations and crossed roads illegally, the person would be called a "jay walker."

831. Overmorrow is a word that means the day after tomorrow.

832. "Uncopyrightable" is the longest normal word you can use that doesn't contain repeat letters. "Subdermatoglyphic" is longer, however, it's only used by dermatologists.

833. "Sir, I demand, I am a maid named Iris" is the longest palindrome, that is, it makes the same sentence if you say it backwards.

834. The scientific word for picking your nose is rhinotillexomania. Rhino means nose, tillex means habitual picking, while mania means rage or fury.

835. Mandarin is the most spoken language in the world with 1.1 billion speakers.

836. The words Tokyo, Beijing, and Seoul all translate to "capital" in English.

837. The French-language Scrabble World Champion doesn't actually speak French. Nigel Richards memorized the whole French Scrabble dictionary, which contains 386,000 words, in nine weeks.

838. The term "googol" is actually a mathematical term for a very large number which is one followed by one hundred zeroes.

839. The word "checkmate" in chess comes from the Arabic "Shah Mat," which means the king is dead.

840. Vodka in Russian translates to "little water" in English.

841. Written language was invented by the Mayans, Egyptians, Chinese, and Sumerians independently.

842. Experts believe that New York is home to as many as 800 languages, making it the most linguistically-diverse city in the world.

843. Ioannis Ikonomou, the Chief Translator in the European Commission, can speak thirty two different languages. His native language is Greek, and he's the only in-house translator in the European Commission who's trusted to translate classified Chinese documents.

844. Just like all languages, sign language has different accents based on country, age, ethnicity, and whether the person is deaf or not.

845. There are approximately 6,500 languages spoken in the world today, however, 2,000 of those languages only have 1,000 speakers or less.

846. Grammatical Pedantry Syndrome is a form of OCD in which sufferers feel the need to correct every grammatical error they see.

847. The dot over the "j" or "i" is called a "tittle."

848. "I am" is the shortest English sentence.

Nature, Earth & The Universe

849. If you removed all the empty space from the atoms that make every human on Earth, all humans could fit into an apple.

850. The surface area in South America is greater than that of Pluto's.

851. The largest living creature on Earth is the Great Barrier Reef, which measures 1,200 miles (2,000 kilometers) long.

852. The Sun and the Moon appear to be the same size in our sky because of the amazing coincidence that the Moon is 400 times smaller, but also 400 times closer.

853. Graphene is pure carbon in the form of a very thin, nearly transparent sheet, only one atom thick, and it's the world's strongest material. It's one million times thinner than paper, but 200 times stronger than steel.

854. Earth is the only planet not named after a god.

855. There are more living organisms in a teaspoon of soil than there are humans in the world.

856. The largest volcano in our Solar System is also the largest mountain in the Solar System. It is Olympus Mons on Mars which is three times the height of Mt. Everest.

857. More than 20% of the world oxygen is produced in the Amazon rainforest.

858. Since Venus is not tilted on an axis like the Earth, it experiences no seasons.

859. The largest cave in the world is in Vietnam and it's called the "Son Doong Cave." It's just under six miles (nine kilometers) long, and its interior is so big that it has its own clouds

and forests. In fact, its ceiling is so high that you can fit an entire forty-story skyscraper inside.

860. There's a lake in Western Australia called "Lake Hillier" that has water that's naturally pink.

861. One-third of the Earth's surface is partially or total desert.

862. The oldest living system ever recorded is the cyanobacterias, a type of bacteria that originated 2.8 billion years ago.

863. The word "Sahara" in Arabic means desert, so "Desert Desert" in Arabic. It also once snowed in the Sahara back in 1979.

864. Fifty nine days on Earth is the equivalent of one on Mercury.

865. There is a hole in the ozone layer sitting right above Antarctica that is twice the size of Europe.

866. Saturn's largest moon named Titan has an atmosphere so thick and gravity so low that you can actually fly through it by flapping any sort of wings attached to your arms.

867. Around 350 to 420 million years ago, before trees were common, the Earth was covered in giant mushroom stalks.

868. The scent that lingers after it rains is called "petrichor."

869. It's estimated that the world's helium supply will run out within the next twenty to thirty years.

870. The Witwatersrand Basin was the densest area containing gold in the world. More than 40% of all the gold ever mined has come out of the Basin.

871. You would lose a third of your body weight on Mars due to lower gravity.

872. The biggest moon in our solar system is called "Ganymede" which is bigger than the planet Mercury.

873. Antarctica is considered a desert as it only receives two inches (fifty millimeters) of precipitation a year.

874. Astatine is the rarest element in the world with only thirty grams total in the Earth's crust.

875. Angel Falls is a waterfall in Venezuela that is the world's highest uninterrupted waterfall at a height of 3,200 feet (979 meters).

876. Portuguese navigator Ferdinand Magellan named the Pacific Ocean due to the calmness of the ocean. Pacific translates to peaceful.

877. Zenography is the study of the planet Jupiter.

878. Astronauts aboard the International Space Station see fifteen sunrises and fifteen sunsets a day averaging one every forty five minutes due to the station's proximity to the Earth and the speed of its orbit.

879. Over 50% of the oxygen supply we breathe comes from the Amazon rainforest.

880. The largest ocean on Earth is the Pacific Ocean covering 30% of the globe.

881. 90% of the Earth's ice is in Antarctica.

882. It rains diamonds on the planets Uranus and Neptune.

883. We know more about the surface of the Moon than we do about our own oceans.

884. The most polluted place on Earth is Lake Karachay, in Russia. It was used as a nuclear dumping site in the past by the Soviet Union. The radiation levels are so high that just one hour of exposure represents a lethal dose of radiation.

885. There's a phenomenon that occurs in the Mekong River in Thailand where red fireballs called "Naga Fireballs" randomly shoot into the air and nobody knows why it happens.

886. Only 30% of the Earth is covered by land.

887. The largest natural bridge in the world is the Ferry Bridge in China; it was virtually unknown to the rest of the world until it was observed on Google Maps.

888. Fire whirls, also known as fire tornadoes, are whirlwinds of flame that occur in countries where it's sufficiently hot enough such as Australia.

889. Scientists have discovered a planet using the Hubble telescope, a deep azure blue planet sixty three light years away that rains glass sideways.

890. If the Sun was scaled down to the size of a cell, the Milky Way would be the size of the United States.

891. Pluto is smaller than Russia.

892. Hudson Bar, in Canada, has less gravity than the rest of the Earth. It's unsure exactly why, but scientists hypothesize that it has something to do with the convection occurring in the Earth's mantle.

893. On the planet Venus it snows metal.

894. There are 100 to 400 billion stars in the Milky Way and more than 100 billion galaxies in the Universe.

895. Astronomers have found what appears to be one of the oldest known stars in the Universe which is located about 6,000 light-years away from Earth. The ancient star formed not long after the Big Bang, 13.8 billion years ago.

896. According to scientists, the weight of the average cloud is the same as 100 elephants.

897. The highest temperature ever recorded on Earth was in El Azizia on September 13, 1922, at 136 degrees Fahrenheit (fifty eight degrees Celsius).

898. The largest earthquake recorded was in Chile in 1960. It was placed at 9.4-9.6 on the magnitude scale and lasted for ten minutes.

899. The amount of water on Earth is constant, however, a billion years from now, the Sun will be 10% brighter, increasing the heat and causing the Earth to lose all its water.

900. The Challenger Deep in the Mariana Trench is the deepest point in Earth's oceans that we know about at 36,060 feet (10,994 meters).

901. Sand from the Sahara is blown by the wind all the way to the Amazon, recharging its minerals. The desert literally fertilizes the rainforest.

902. Over 99% of all species, equating to five billion species in total, that have ever been on Earth have died out.

903. Lightning strikes are not as rare as you think. Approximately 100 strikes hit the Earth per second. Each bolt can have up to a billion volts of electricity.

904. According to records, the last time that all the planets in the Solar System were aligned was 561 BC. The next alignment will take place in 2854.

905. The Moon is capable of having "moonquakes." They are less frequent and intense as the ones on Earth however.

906. In 1977, we received a radio signal from space that lasted seventy two seconds and was dubbed "the wow signal." To this day we still don't know where it came from.

907. On Monday March 23, 2178, Pluto will complete its full orbit since its original discovery in 1930.

908. It takes 40,000 years for a photon of light to travel from the core of the Sun to its surface. For the same photon to travel from the Sun to Earth it only takes eight minutes.

909. Occasionally, in the arctic, the sun can appear square when it's on the horizon.

910. The Sahara is only in a dry period and is expected to be green again in 15,000 years.

911. Sunsets on Mars are blue.

Plants, Flowers & Trees

912. In Australia, there are trees that grow several different types of fruits known as fruit salad trees.

913. The average tree is made up of about 1% of living cells at any given time.

914. Bamboo can grow up to thirty five inches (ninety one centimeters) in a single day.

915. The Maldive coconut is the largest growing seed in the world.

916. In 2012, a Russian scientist regenerated an arctic flower known as "Silene stenophylla" that has been extinct for over 32,000 years from a seed that was buried by an ice-age squirrel.

917. The Eucalyptus deglupta, or more commonly known as the rainbow tree, is a tree that sheds its outer bark to reveal a bright green inner bark that turns blue, purple, orange, and maroon as it matures.

918. The average lifespan of a redwood tree is 500-700 years old while some coast redwoods have been known to live to over 2,000 years. They can grow to over 360 feet in height (109 meters).

919. There are more artificial Christmas trees sold in the world than real ones.

920. The world's biggest flower garden sits in the middle of a desert in Dubai, which has over 500,000 fresh flowers.

921. The country Brazil is named after a tree.

922. Only 15% of all plants are on land.

923. You can create 170 thousand pencils from the average tree.

924. There is a species of orchid that looks pretty much like a monkey. It only grows at high elevations, in certain mountainous areas of Ecuador, Colombia, and Peru.

925. The Baobab tree native to Madagascar can hold up to 31,000 gallons (120,000 liters) of water.

926. There is a flower called the "chocolate cosmos" that smells like chocolate but isn't edible.

927. There are roses that exist that are all black, but they can only be found in Halfeti, Turkey.

928. Sunflowers can be used to clean up radioactive waste. Their stems and leaves absorb and store pollutants. It's also why the sunflower is the international symbol for nuclear disarmament.

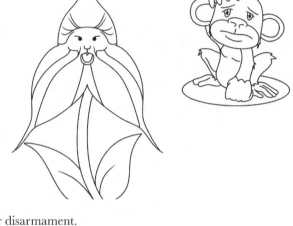

929. The largest organism in the known world today is a fungus that lives in the mountains of Oregon. It spans across 2.4 miles (3.8 kilometers).

930. The oldest recorded tree in the world is reported to be 9,550 years old located in Dalarna, Sweden.

931. In 2009, a new species of pitcher plant was found by scientists in the Philippines jungle, becoming the largest carnivorous plant ever discovered. It's called the Nepenthes attenboroughii, named after Sir David Attenborough. Carnivorous plants usually eat things like insects and spiders, but this one is so big that it actually eats rats.

932. Elephant grass can grow up to ten feet (three meters) tall that even elephants can hide in.

Really?

933. When Charles Darwin first discovered the huge tortoises on the Galapagos Islands, he tried to ride them.

934. In 2008, a businessman from Abu Dhabi spent $14.3 million at an auction to buy a license plate labeled "1," making it the world's most expensive license plate.

935. Yu Youhzen, a fifty three year old Chinese millionaire, works as a street cleaner for $228 per month to set a good example for her children.

936. In 2013, a man named Rogelio Andaverde was abducted from his home right in front of his wife by two masked men with guns. Luckily he returned two days later, unharmed. It was later discovered that he staged his own kidnapping just so he could go out and party with his friends.

937. A study by the University of Westminster in the UK determined that watching horror movies can burn up to almost 200 calories, the same as a half hour walk.

938. One of the iTunes user agreement policies explicitly states that you're not allowed to use the program to build nuclear, chemical, or biological weapons.

939. If you inhale a pea, it is possible to sprout and grow in your lungs.

940. The cheapest gas prices in the world belong to Venezuela at just over a penny a liter.

941. When you see an advertisement of a watch, it's almost always ten past ten.

942. Most of the dust you'll find in your house will be your dead skin.

943. The majority of lipsticks contain fish scales.

944. North Korea is the biggest counterfeiter of US currency.

945. In Russia, wealthy citizens often hire fake ambulances that beat the city traffic which are known as ambulance taxis. They can cost as much as $200/hour, have luxurious interiors, refreshments, and include caviar and champagne.

946. In 1985, a New Orleans man named Jerome Moody drowned at a party attended by 100 life guards who were celebrating having made it through the summer without a single drowning at a city pool.

947. The country of Niue, an island north of New Zealand, put various Pokémon on its one dollar coins in 2001. They included Pikachu, Squirtle, Meowth, Bulbasaur, and Charmander.

948. In the early years of the twentieth century, horses were causing so much pollution with their poop that automobiles were seen as the green alternative.

949. It was known that after examining the animals, Charles Darwin used to eat them too.

950. Walt Disney used to visit his parks in disguise and test ride operators to make sure that they weren't rushing guests.

951. All US presidents pay for their own food while staying at the White House.

952. The companies Audi, Bentley, Bugadi, Ducati, Lamborghini, and Porsche are all owned by Volkswagen.

953. At the University of Oaksterdam, you can graduate with a degree in Cannabis Cultivation.

954. There is currently 147 million ounces of gold in Fort Knox. At the price of about $1,776 per ounce, that's worth $261.6 billion.

955. More people die from attempting selfies than from shark attacks.

956. In 2012, a woman from New York named Deborah Stevens donated a kidney to her boss and was fired almost immediately after.

957. Jesse James, a notorious outlaw from the 1800's, once gave a widow who housed him enough money to pay off her debt collector, and then robbed the debt collector as the man left the widow's home.

958. Martin Luther King Jr. got a C in public speaking.

959. You're more likely to die on the way to buying a lottery ticket than you are to winning the lottery.

960. If you're taller than six foot two (two meters), you can't become an astronaut.

961. Both companies Louis Vuitton and Chanel burn their products at the end of the year preventing them to being sold at a discount.

962. A man named Sogen Kato was thought to be the oldest man in Tokyo until 2010 when officials arrived at his home to wish him a happy 111th birthday only to find his mummified remains. It turns out he had been dead for thirty years and his family had been collecting his pension money.

963. Falling in love produces the same high as taking cocaine.

964. At the end of the 1990's, BMW actually had to recall their GPS systems because male German drivers didn't want to take directions from a female driver.

965. On Good Friday in 1930, the BBC announced there was no news, followed by piano music.

966. In 2012, a sixty-three year old man named Wallace Weatherhold from Florida had his hand bitten off by an alligator and he was charged with illegally feeding the animal.

967. The average commuter wastes around forty two hours waiting in traffic each year.

968. The Romans considered women with unibrows attractive and desirable from 753 to 476 AD. Lots of women who didn't naturally have unibrows used paint to join their eyebrows to look prettier.

969. If you wear headphones for an hour, it will increase the amount of bacteria you have in your ear by 700 times.

970. Today there are more people suffering from obesity than there are suffering from hunger.

971. Despite having billions of dollars and being one of the wealthiest businessmen in the world, Ikea founder Ingvar Kamprad is notoriously cheap. He lives in a small home, eats at Ikea, takes the bus, and only flies economy class.

972. Bill Gates, Steve Jobs, Albert Einstein, Walt Disney, and Mark Zuckerberg all dropped out of school.

973. Benjamin Franklin wasn't trusted to write the US Declaration of Independence because it was feared he would conceal a joke in it.

974. President JFK purchased over a thousand Cuban cigars just hours before he ordered the Cuban trade embargo in 1962.

975. Carl Gugasian is serving seventeen years in jail after robbing fifty banks over a thirty year period, stealing $2 million.

976. A single factory in Ireland makes more than 90% of the world's botox.

977. Paul Getty was a billionaire who refused to pay the ransom of sixteen million dollars when his grandson was kidnapped. The group who kidnapped him later sent Paul the boy's severed ear and he finally accepted and said he'd pay three million dollars. He actually only gave a little over two million because that's all he could claim on tax.

978. In 2011, a ninety nine year old Italian named Antonio C. divorced his ninety six year old wife Rosa C. after finding secret love letters revealing that she had an affair in the 1940's.

979. Under extremely powerful pressure, peanut butter can be turned into diamonds.

980. In 2018, four billion people have access to the Internet yet 844 million people still don't have access to clean water.

981. In 1859, English settler Thomas Austin released twenty four rabbits onto his property in Australia; he thought that the introduction of a few rabbits could provide a touch of home in addition to a spot of hunting. By 1920, the rabbit population had reached ten billion.

982. On average, brunettes have less hairs on their head compared to red-haired and blondes.

983. Hitler was Time's "Man of the Year" in 1938.

984. Saddam Hussein, the late President of Iraq, wrote several novels and a number of poems which were published anonymously.

985. In 2017, 19% of brides said they met their spouse online. This industry now brings in $3 billion a year.

986. In order to be a London Black Cab driver, one is expected to know 25,000 roads and 50,000 points of interest to pass the test called "The Knowledge." Applicants usually need twelve appearances and thirty four months of preparation to pass it.

987. Deceased North Korean leader Kim Jong II's official biography lists among his achievements a thirty eight-shot round of golf, the ability to control weather, the need to never have to poop, and being the creator of the hamburger.

988. It costs 1.5 cents to make a penny and the US Mint issued $46 million worth of these coins in 2018.

989. In China, the extremely wealthy can avoid prison terms by hiring body doubles.

990. Before toilet paper was invented, Americans used to use corn cobs.

Royalty

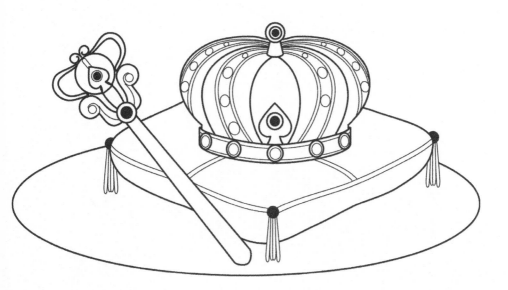

991. Queen Elizabeth the second has someone to wear the shoes she gets before she wears them to make sure they're comfortable.

992. The Queen of England legally owns one third of the Earth's surface.

993. In the United Kingdom, the queen cannot be arrested no matter what crime she commits. This is because the Crown itself is the prosecuting force in the UK and hence the Crown cannot verse the Crown itself. The other members of the Royal Family do not share the same immunity.

994. Bhumibol Adulyadej, the King of Thailand, was actually born in Cambridge, Massachusetts, in the United States, in 1927. When he was born, the hospital room that he was delivered in was briefly declared Thai territory so he could be born on Thai soil.

995. A prince in Abu Dhabi spent $2.5 million to create a Mercedes Benz with a V10 engine with 1,600 horsepower that goes 0 to 100 in less than two seconds running on biofuel.

996. Queen Elizabeth does not have a passport. Since the British passport is issued in her name, she does not need to possess one, however, the other members of the Royal Family do.

997. Royal tradition states that Prince Charles and Prince William cannot board the same plane together in case there is a crash and the monarch loses two heirs at once. Technically the same rule applies for Prince William and his five-year-old son, Prince George.

Science

998. Sound can travel quicker through solids. This is because molecules in a solid medium are much closer together than those in a liquid or gas, allowing sound waves to travel more quickly through it.

999. It is false that you can bite through a finger as easily as a carrot. It takes 200 newtons to bite through a raw carrot and 1,485 newtons just to cause a fracture to a finger.

1000. A solid glass ball can bounce higher than a rubber ball when dropped from the same height. A solid steel ball can bounce even higher than a solid glass ball.

1001. Hot water freezes quicker than cold water. This is called the "Mpemba effect," named after a Tanzanian student who discovered it.

1002. Light doesn't actually move at the speed of light. The full quote is actually: "the speed of light in a vacuum" which is 186,282 miles (299,792 kilometers) per second. If you were able to move at this speed, you could go around Earth seven and a half times in a second.

1003. You would weigh more at the poles than you would weigh at the equator, however, the difference would only be 0.5% approximately. You would weigh slightly more at sea level than at the top of a mountain. This is due to oblateness and gravitational pull.

1004. Aerogel, also known as frozen smoke, is one of the world's lowest density solids being made up of anywhere from 95-99% air. It's almost impossible to see or feel, but it can support 4,000 times its own weight.

1005. The first man made element was technetium created in 1937. It is used for medical diagnostic studies and as a corrosion inhibitor for steel.

1006.   The scientific term for pins and needles is paresthesia.

1007.   Only 0.1% of an atom is matter. The rest is air.

1008.   If you put an apple in the sea, it will float because it's less dense than seawater.

1009.   Sterling silver is not completely made out of silver. A little copper is added as pure silver is too soft and would bend otherwise.

1010.   In 1951, a woman named Henrietta Lacks died of cervical cancer, but her tumor cells were removed and later discovered to be the first ever human cells that could thrive in a lab. Her cells have been the subject of more than 74,000 studies, many of which have yielded profound insights into cell biology, cancer, vaccine, and cloning.

1011.   LSD has been known to cure Post Traumatic Stress Disorder, such as in the case of Yehiel De-Nur, a Holocaust survivor who, after taking the drug, was able to sleep for the first time in thirty years without nightmares.

1012.   Two neuroscientists were successful in implanting a fake memory in a mouse's brain in 2012. The mouse was aghast as it remembered something that never really happened to it.

1013.   A flame is round and blue when in zero gravity.

1014.   Scientists from Georgia State University have found that monkeys are susceptible to optical illusions, just like humans. To test this, capuchin and rhesus monkeys looked at a visual illusion where two dots were surrounded by rings, but were actually the same size, and they were tricked much like many people were.

Shocking

1015.   In 2011, a forty six year old man named Mark Bradford hunted down and choked a thirteen year old boy who killed him several times in the game "Call of Duty."

1016.   In 1967, the Prime Minister of Australia went missing. It was only four decades after he went missing that it was confirmed that he had accidentally drowned.

1017.   In 1971, a man named Jean-Claude Romand lied about passing important medical exams and he continued crafting elaborate lies until everyone he knew thought he was an actual medical doctor. He got away for it for eighteen years until he eventually killed his entire family to avoid being revealed.

1018.   Doctors with messy handwriting kill more than 7,000 people and injure over a million people each year due to receiving the wrong medication.

1019.   In 1954, a man named John Thomas Doyle committed suicide by jumping off the Golden Gate Bridge. His suicide note read absolutely no reason other than "I have a toothache."

1020.   The first recorded human flight with artificial wings in history was in the 6th century in China. Emperor Kao Yang would strap prisoners to kites and throw them off a building to see if they could fly.

1021.   The longest someone has been in a coma and come out of it is thirty seven years. A six year old went to the hospital for a routine appendectomy, went under general anesthesia, and didn't come out for reasons doctors can't explain.

1022.   In 1567, Hans Steininger, who once had the longest beard in the world at 4.5 feet (1.4 meters) long, died when he broke his neck after accidentally stepping on it.

1023.   Luis Garavito, one of the world's most dangerous serial killers with 140 victims, had his sentence reduced to only twenty two years and could be out as early as 2021.

1024.   In 2006, an extremely old clam was found by a group of researchers in Iceland. In order to find out its age, researchers didn't count the rings on the outside of the clam, but instead they opened it and counted the rings on the inside, causing the clam to die. The clam turned out to be 507 years old, the world's oldest animal.

1025.   Lake Chagan is the only lake artificially created by a nuclear test. Even though the nuclear test was fired in 1965, it's still unsafe for swimming due to radiation.

1026.   In 2008, a Japanese man noticed that food in his home was disappearing so he set up a webcam and discovered that a fifty eight year old homeless woman was living in his closet for an entire year.

1027.   Ramon Artagaveytia once survived a sinking ship in 1871. He was so scared from this experience he didn't get on another ship till forty one years later. Unfortunately for him that ship was Titanic.

1028.   In 2011, a New Zealand trucker named Steven McCormack fell on a high-pressure valve which lodged in his butt and inflated him to twice his size nearly killing him. He did survive, but it took a full three days to burp and fart out the excess air.

1029.   Vending machines kill about thirteen people a year.

1030.   The biggest family in the world is from Baktawng, India, where father Ziona Chana has ninety four children by thirty nine different wives.

1031.   The pollution in China is so bad in some parts that just being in that area for one day is the equivalent of smoking twenty one cigarettes.

1032.   Some Japanese companies such as Sony, Toshiba, and Panasonic have banishment rooms where they transfer surplus employees and give them useless tasks or even nothing to do until they become disheartened or depressed enough to quit on their own, thus avoiding paying them full benefits.

1033.   In 1886, a man named H.H. Holmes built a three-story hotel in Chicago specifically to kill people in it. Its design included stairways to nowhere and a maze of over 100 windowless rooms which he used to kill over 200 people.

1034.   There has only been 240 years of peace in the last 3,000 years.

1035.   An Indonesian boy named Aldi Rizal began chain smoking when he was just eighteen months old and continued smoking over forty cigarettes a day until he was five years old when he was sent to rehab.

1036.   The strongest beer in the world is called "Snake Venom" containing 67.5% alcohol.

1037.   It is estimated that malaria has been responsible for half of the deaths of everyone who has ever lived.

1038.   The world record for the most bones broken in a lifetime is held by Evel Knievel, the pioneer of motorcycle long jumping exhibitions, who has suffered 433 fractured bones.

1039.   Approximately one in every six Jewish people killed in the Holocaust died at Auschwitz.

1040.   Sharks kill about twelve people a year. People kill about eleven thousand sharks an hour.

1041.   Four American presidents have been killed by gunshot.

1042.   In 1967, a magazine called "Berkeley Barb" published a fake story about extracting hallucinogenic chemical from bananas to raise moral questions about banning drugs. Unfortunately people didn't realize it was a hoax and began smoking banana peels to try to get high.

1043.   You are 14% more likely to die on your birthday than any other day.

1044.   In Bern, Switzerland, there's a 500 year old statue of a man eating a sack of babies and nobody is sure why.

1045.   The "China National Highway 110" traffic jam was considered the longest traffic jam in history. It was sixty two miles (100 kilometers) long and lasted eleven days.

1046.   The brothers Adolf Dassler and Rudolf Dassler, who started Puma and Adidas, were part of the Nazi party.

1047.   The youngest mother in medical history was Lina Medina from Peru who gave birth when she was five.

1048.   Your mobile phone carries ten times more bacteria than your toilet seat.

1049.   As of 2016, about 280 climbers have died on Everest. Their bodies are so well preserved that they are used as markers.

Sports

1050.   The temperature of tennis balls affects how a ball can bounce. Wimbledon go through over fifty thousand tennis balls a year that are kept at sixty eight degrees Fahrenheit (twenty degrees Celsius) to make sure only the best are used.

1051.   In 2022, the World Cup will be played in Lusail, Qatar, a city that doesn't even exist yet.

1052.   The longest human jump is further than the longest horse jump. In the 1968 Olympics, the world record was set at 8.9 meters while the record for a horse is twenty eight feet (8.4 meters).

1053.   Jousting is the official sport in the state of Maryland.

1054.   Today's gold medals are only 1.3% gold. The last time a pure gold medal was given out was in the 1912 Stockholm Olympics.

1055.   A tribe in West Africa, known as "The Matami Tribe," play a version of football which consists of using a human skull as the ball.

1056.   In 2013, Sean Conway became the first man ever to swim the entire length of Great Britain. The 900 miles (1,400 kilometers) trek took him 135 days to complete. Ninety were spent in water while the rest were spent avoiding bad weather and resting.

1057.   There is a real sport called "Banzai Skydiving" which involves throwing your parachute out of the plane and then jumping out after it.

1058.   Quebec only finished paying off its 1976 Summer Olympics debt thirty years later, in 2006.

1059.   The most popular sport in the world is football. Second place goes to cricket followed by field hockey.

1060.   As a child, Muhammad Ali was refused an autograph from his boxing idol Sugar Ray Robinson. When Ali became a prized fighter, he vowed to never deny an autograph request, which he honored throughout his entire career.

1061.   In 1984, when the Air Jordans were introduced, they were banned by the NBA. Michael Jordan wore them anyways as Nike was willing to pay the $5,000 fine each time he stepped onto the court.

1062.   In 1947, Sugar Ray Robinson, one of the greatest boxers of all time, backed out of a fight because he had a dream that he was going to kill his opponent. After being convinced to fight, he went into the ring and actually killed his opponent.

1063.   The highest scoring soccer game in history recognized by the Guinness Book of World Records was 149 to zero between two teams in Madagascar in 2002. It happened because one of the teams began scoring on themselves in protest of a bad call by one of the referees.

1064.   There's a sport called "squirrel fishing," in which participants try to catch squirrels and lift them into the air by using a nut on a fishing pole.

1065.   Wales holds a world mountain bike bog snorkeling championship. Contenders have to ride a mountain bike as fast as they can along the bottom of a bog, which has a 6.5 feet (two meter) deep, water-filled trench. To make it more difficult, the bikes that they use have led-filled frames, the tires are filled with water, and the competitors wear led weight belts so that they don't float off of their bikes.

Technology, Internet & Videogames

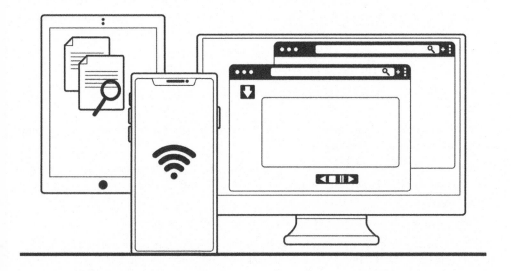

1066.   Workers of Amazon's distribution centers can be expected to walk up to eleven miles (seventeen kilometers) per shift picking up an order once every thirty three seconds.

1067.   When they made "Breakout" for Atari, Steve Jobs and Steve Wozniak agreed to split the pay 50/50. Atari gave Jobs $5,000 for it, but Jobs only told Wozniak he got $700, only giving him $350.

1068.   Intel employs a futuris named Brian David Johnson whose job is to determine what life would be like to live ten to fifteen years in the future.

1069.   Yang Yuanqing, Lenovo's CEO, received a $3 million bonus as a reward due to record profits in 2012, which he redistributed to 10,000 of Lenovo's employees. He did the exact same thing in 2013.

1070.   Shigeru Miyamoto, the creator of the famous games Mario, Zelda, and Donkey Kong, was banned from riding a bicycle. This is because he became so valuable to Nintendo that they didn't want to risk anything happening to him, forcing him to drive a car instead.

1071.   A hacker group named UGNazi once took down Papa John's website because the company was two hours later than expected in delivering their food.

1072.   There are at least seven apps on the app store that are priced $999.99, which is the maximum price you can charge on the app store.

1073.   If a Google employee dies, their spouse gets half their salary for the next ten years, stock benefits, and their children get $1,000/month until they're nineteen.

1074.   Facebook tracks and records your IP address as well as the URL of every website that you visit that uses any of its social plugins such as the like button.

1075.   There are fewer than fifty of the original Apple 1 computers in existence with some of them selling for over $50,000.

1076.   In 1998, Larry Page and Sergey Brin, the founders of Google, offered to sell their little startup to AltaVista for $1 million so they could resume their studies at Stanford. They were rejected, and have now grown the empire to $101 billion as of 2019.

1077.   There was a third Apple founder named Ronald Wayne who once owned 10% of the whole company. He decided to sell that 10% stake for $800 in 1976.

1078.   In 2009, Wikipedia permanently banned the church of Scientology from editing any articles.

1079.   The one click option was invented by Amazon, who have a patent on it, and Apple pays them a licensing fee to use it.

1080.   In 2013, over 200 strangers responded to a Facebook invitation to attend a funeral for British veteran James McConnel, who had no friends or family members to attend otherwise.

1081.   Nomophobia is the fear of being without mobile phone coverage.

1082.   Michael Birch, the founder of the social networking site Bebo, sold it to AOL for $850 million in 2008, only to later buy it back for a million dollars in 2013.

1083.   Futureme.org is a website where you can send e-letters to yourself at any time in the future.

1084.   Jeff Bezos net worth is so high that it wouldn't be worth him picking up a $100 bill if he dropped it. In fact, he has to spend $28 million a day just to stop getting richer.

1085.   The average iPhone only costs $200 to make.

1086.   Watson, IBM's artificially intelligent computer, learned how to swear from the urban dictionary. Because of that, it began talking sassy so scientists had to remove the entire urban dictionary database from its memory.

1087.   Internet addiction disorder, also known as "IAD," is a real mental disorder in which somebody engages in addictive, compulsive, or pathological Internet use.

1088.   There are over four million apps available for download on both the Android and Apple app store.

1089.   300 hours of video are uploaded to YouTube every minute and almost five billion videos are watched on YouTube every single day.

1090.   Amazon is the first company to ever hit a trillion dollars.

1091.   The first web page went live on August 6, 1991, and was dedicated to information.

1092.   Over 90% of mobile phone sales in Japan are for waterproof devices because the Japanese are so fond of their mobile phones they even use them in the shower.

1093.   Google, Amazon, Microsoft, and Facebook alone have 1.2 million terabytes of information stored on the Internet.

1094.   If you Google "Zerg rush," Google will begin to eat the search page.

1095.   The first email was sent in 1971. The email was sent to the computer right next to it as a test.

1096.   Theringfinders.com is an online site where you can find metal-detecting experts you can hire for a fixed fee to search for and find items of jewelry that you may have lost. They've successfully recovered 3,000 items worth over $5.2 million.

1097.   1,000 selfies are posted to Instagram every ten seconds. This is ninety three million selfies a day.

1098.   97% of all emails sent are spam.

1099.   Digital storage doesn't go up in measurements of thousands. 1024 bits make a byte, 1024 bytes makes up a kilobyte followed by megabyte, gigabyte, terabyte, and petabyte.

1100.   In April of 2014, the Danish government built an exact replica of their country in the online game Minecraft using four trillion Minecraft building blocks. It was intended for educational purposes, but within weeks, American players had invaded the game planting American flags everywhere and blowing things up.

1101.   Half the world has never made or received a phone call.

1102.   The red mushrooms featured in Nintendo's Mario games are based on a real species of a fungi called "Amanita muscaria." They're known for their hallucinogenic properties and can distort the size of perceived objects. This is also the same mushroom that is referenced in Alice in Wonderland.

1103.   A software company called "PC Pitstop" once hid a $1,000 prize in their terms of service just to see if anyone would read it. After five months and three thousand sales later, someone finally did.

1104.   The four ghosts in Pacman are all programmed to do certain things. Blinky, the red ghost, chases you; Pinky, the pink ghost, simply tries to position herself in front of Pacman; Inky, the blue ghost, tries to position himself in the same way; and Clyve, the orange ghost, moves randomly.

1105.   The UN has deemed access to the Internet a human right.

1106.   The famous torrent site Pirate Bay once tried to buy its own island to make their own country with no copyright laws.

1107.   The app Candy Crush was making $956,000 a day in its prime.

1108.   There are 2.32 billion monthly active users on Facebook as of 31st December, 2018.

1109.   There are approximately 250,000 active patents applicable to the smartphone.

1110.   In a study conducted by the Bay State Medical Center in Springfield, approximately 68% of people experience phantom vibrations syndrome, a sensory hallucination where you mistakenly think your phone is buzzing in your pocket.

1111.   Jeff Bezos, the owner of Amazon.com, is also the owner of the Washington Post.

1112.   Google rents goats to replace lawn mowers at their Mountain View headquarters.

1113.   Zoe Pemberton, a ten year old girl from the UK, attempted to sell her grandma on eBay because she found her annoying and wanted her to disappear.

1114.   It took approximately seventy five years for the telephone to reach fifty million users, the radio thirty eight years, thirteen years for the television, four for the Internet, two for Facebook, and only nineteen days for Pokémon Go.

1115.   There are currently 1.6 billion live websites on the web right now. However, 99% of these sites you cannot access through Google and it's known as the Deep Web.

1116.   In the year 2020, there will be approximately forty billion gadgets connected to the Internet.

1117.   Google actually hires camels to carry its trekker camera in order to get street views of deserts.

War & Military World

1118.   Russia trained and deployed 40,000 anti-tank dogs in World War Two. The dogs were loaded with explosives and trained to run under tanks where they would be detonated, except many of the dogs became scared and ran back to their owner's trenches where they killed their own people.

1119.   There were at least forty two known assassination plots against Hitler.

1120.   Chiune Sugihara was a famous Japanese diplomat that operated in Lithuania during World War Two. He helped more than 6,000 Jewish refugees escape to Japanese territory by issuing them transit visas risking his life and his family's life in the process.

1121.   In World War Two, Jacklyn Lucas lied his way into the military and became the youngest marine ever to earn a medal of honor. When he was seventeen, he threw himself on two live grenades to protect his squad members and survived.

1122.   144 successful prisoners escaped Auschwitz.

1123.   There are now twenty two countries worldwide that have no army, navy, or air force.

1124.   During the Cold War, the US's passcode to nuclear missiles was eight zeroes so they could fire them as quick as possible.

1125.   Hitler planned on invading Switzerland but gave in as it was too difficult with the surrounding mountains.

1126.   Russia and Japan have still not signed a peace treaty to end World War Two.

1127.   During World War Two, prisoners in Canadian war camps were so well treated that they were given games and entertainment like soccer tournaments and musical groups. When the war ended, many of them didn't want to leave Canada.

1128.   There was a bear named Wojtek that fought in the Polish army during World War II. His name meant "he who enjoys war." He carried shells to the front line and was taught to salute; he became a mascot for the soldiers and even developed a habit for drinking beer and smoking cigarettes. He survived the war and lived the rest of his life in the Edinburgh Zoo.

1129. In 1945, a man named Tsutomu Yamaguchi survived the atomic blast at Hiroshima only to catch the morning train so that he could arrive at his job on time in Nagasaki where he survived another atomic blast.

1130. Since 1945, all British tanks have come equipped with tea making facilities.

1131. The most successful interrogator of World War Two was Hanns Scharff who, instead of using torture, would befriend the prisoner. He would gain their trust by taking them to a cinema on camp and sharing a coffee or tea with them.

1132.   Being clean-shaven became popular in the US after the troops returned home as heroes from World War I. Soldiers had been required to shave so that gas masks could securely fit on their face.

1133.   The British submarine HMS Trident had a fully grown reindeer onboard as a pet for six weeks during WWII.

1134.   Before Nazis used the salute we now know as Hitler's salute, it was called the "Bellamy salute," and it was used by Americans to salute the flag until it was replaced in 1942 by the hand over heart salute.

1135.   Every year the Netherlands sends 20,000 tulip bulbs to Canada to thank them for their help in the Second World War.

1136.   During World War Two, two Japanese officers named Tokiashi Mukai and Tsuyoshi Noda had a contest or race to

see who could kill 100 people first using only a sword. Disturbingly, it was covered like a sporting event in Japanese newspapers with regular updates on the score.

1137.   The Filipino flag is flown with its red stripe up in times of war and blue side up in times of peace.

1138.   The US Navy owns over thirty killer dolphins. They are trained to hunt, and carry guns with toxic darts in them that are lethal enough to kill someone in one shot.

1139.   Chinese soldiers stick needles in their shirt collars in order to keep a straight posture during military parades.

1140.   Hitler collected Jewish artifacts for a museum of what he hoped to be an extinct race after the Second World War.

1141.   Ambrose Burnside was a general in the American Civil War known for his unusual facial hairstyle, and is where the term "sideburns" come from.

1142.   The largest detonated bomb in the world was the Tsar Bomb on October 30, 1961, by the Soviet Union. The blast was 3,000 times stronger than the bomb used on Hiroshima. The impact was strong enough to break windows 560 miles (900 kilometer) away.

1143.   The wars between Romans and Persians lasted about 721 years, the longest conflict in human history.

1144.   David B. Leak was an American soldier from the Korean War who was given the Medal of Honor after killing five soldiers, four with his bare hands, while giving medical attention to one of his comrades after being shot.

If you enjoyed this book and learned anything, it would mean the world to me if you could please leave a review so others can easily find this book and itch their curiosity!

BONUS!

Thanks for supporting me and purchasing this book! I'd like to send you some freebies. They include:

- The audiobook for this book
- My other best seller: 101 Idioms and Phrases
- 500 World War I & II Facts

Scan the QR code below, enter your email and I'll send you all the files. Happy reading!

Made in the USA
Coppell, TX
21 October 2022